The Foreign Exchange Handbook

THE FOREIGN EXCHANGE HANDBOOK

A User's Guide

JULIAN WALMSLEY

A Wiley-Interscience Publication

JOHN WILEY & SONS

New York   Chichester   Brisbane   Toronto   Singapore

Copyright © 1983 by Julian Walmsley

Published by John Wiley & Sons, Inc.
All rights reserved. Published simultaneously in Canada.

Reproduction or translation of any part of this work
beyond that permitted by Section 107 or 108 of the
1976 United States Copyright Act without the permission
of the copyright owner is unlawful. Requests for
permission or further information should be addressed to
the Permissions Department, John Wiley & Sons, Inc.

This publication is designed to provide accurate and
authoritative information in regard to the subject
matter covered. It is sold with the understanding that
the publisher is not engaged in rendering legal, accounting,
or other professional service. If legal advice or other
expert assistance is required, the services of a competent
professional person should be sought. *From a Declaration
of Principles jointly adopted by a Committee of the
American Bar Association and a Committee of Publishers.*

Library of Congress Cataloging in Publication Data:
Walmsley, Julian.
  The foreign exchange handbook.

  "A Wiley-Interscience publication."
  Includes index.
  1. Foreign exchange—Handbooks, manuals, etc.
2. Money market—Handbooks, manuals, etc.   I. Title.

HG3851.W387   1983   332.4′5′0202   82-21804
ISBN 0-471-86388-2

Printed in the United States of America

10 9 8 7 6 5 4 3 2

PREFACE

Foreign exchange is becoming more important to banks and corporations as their business becomes more international and as the markets become more volatile. This book aims to help those who are professional traders in these markets. It concentrates on the detail that a trader needs rather than the broad philosophy, which is covered in a number of good books already. The first section, on the background to the markets, goes into the major currencies' markets—the United States, the United Kingdom, Germany, Japan, France, Switzerland—in some depth. It also sets out, as simply and clearly as possible, some of the economic and technical influences on currency and money markets. The second section sets out the calculations involved. It explains the standard foreign exchange and money market formulae. It also shows how to handle short-date deals before spot; adjustments for holidays in cross rate calculations; forward forward swap and deposit calculations; SDR and ECU deposits; broken date deposit and forward rates; withholding tax adjustments; and numerous other calculations. The third section ties in financial futures and gold markets, payments systems, and exposure measurement and control. In addition there are appendices giving key dates, currency basket calculations, Islamic value date calculations, and other special topics.

A great many people have helped me in writing this book. In particular I must thank Roy Brinsden, Chris Bennett, and Chris Pavlou for allowing me the run of the dealing rooms under their control. I must also thank Trevor Cass, Nick Donnelly, Frank Dunphy, Tony Hall, Brian Higgins, Albert Holmes, Brian Kay, Phil Savarese, and Martin Warmsley, to name only a few from the various trading rooms at Barclays around the world who have helped me, as well as all the other people in the market in London, New York, and elsewhere who have patiently explained to me the hows and whys of their work. I would also like to thank Alan Davies, Darrell Barnes, and Nick Selbie of Barclays, Guy Field at Derby & Co. (and now Morgan), Raymond Nessim at Phibro Corp., Kurt Dew of the IMM (and now an independent consultant), Patricia Revey of the Federal Reserve Bank of New York (and now Lehman Brothers), Ian Giddy of Columbia University, and Christine Hekman of Duke University for their help and comments on various parts of the manuscript. Any remaining errors, of course, are my own responsibility. I must also thank Heather Marchant, Jacqui Kriescher, Jean Barella, and Mary Sarandrea for their

v

help in typing various parts of the manuscript. Finally and most especially I must thank Jane, my wife, without whose help and forbearance this book would never have been finished.

JULIAN WALMSLEY

New York, New York
March 1983

CONTENTS

LIST OF FIGURES

LIST OF TABLES

CURRENCY ABBREVIATIONS

The following abbreviations are used throughout the book for the sake of internal consistency. Alternatives will in some cases be found in the International Standards Organization list in Appendix 6.

AAD	Arab Accounting Dinar
AUS$	Australian dollar
CAN$	Canadian dollar
CR	Brazilian cruzeiro
DKR	Danish krona
DMK	Deutsche mark
FBC	Belgian franc (convertible)
FFR	French franc
HFL	Dutch guilder (Holland florin)
HK$	Hong Kong dollar
IEP	Irish pound
LIT	Italian lira
LUXFR	Luxembourg franc
NKR	Norwegian krone
RAN	South African rand
SAR	Saudi Arabian riyal
SFR	Swiss franc
SKR	Swedish krona
£STG	Pound sterling
	(or £ alone where the context makes it clear)
TT$	Trinidad and Tobago dollar
US$	United States dollar
	(or $ alone where the context makes it clear)
¥	Japanese yen

PART **1**

THE BACKGROUND

1

THE MARKETS

This chapter explains the key markets which we will be looking at in this book. It describes who is involved, what instruments are dealt in, and how the central banks are involved.

SECTION 1.   INTRODUCTION

1.1.1.   This book is concerned with two closely related sets of markets: that for foreign exchange and that for the borrowing and lending of money internationally. The latter has many links with domestic money markets, and some reference will be made to these. The main emphasis, however, will be on the international aspects of the money markets.

1.1.2.   This chapter is designed to provide a brief description of some of the major markets in different countries. It begins with a "global" view and then touches on individual countries. It mentions briefly a number of concepts which are explained later. Some of these are outlined in Figure 1.1.

SECTION 2.   THE WORLD MARKET FOR FOREIGN EXCHANGE

1.2.1.   Nobody knows how big the world market for foreign exchange really is. What we do know is that it has grown fast. Some idea can be got from the growth of world exports and foreign exchange reserves. The level of world exports in 1950—according to the International Monetary Fund's *International Financial Statistics*—was $57.2 billion. By 1979 it had risen to $1,508.2 billion. World foreign exchange reserves, according to the same source, grew from US$ 13.3 billion in 1950 to US$ 324.2 billion in 1979. But these figures only give us an idea of the magnitude of the growth. The present size is unknown. An estimate of the 1977 volume of trading put the daily turnover in London at $29 billion, compared with $24 billion in Germany, $18 billion in Switzerland, $9 billion in Amsterdam, $8 billion in New York, and $5 billion in Paris.[1] The annual turnover on that basis in the world market was on the order of $26,000 billion, which compares with an estimate of $30,000 billion for the year made by a Federal Reserve official.[2] Another estimate, based on Clearing House Interbank Payment System (CHIPS) transfers, suggested $20,000 billion,[3] while Citibank is reported to have estimated $50,000 billion.

1.2.2.   The differences among these figures show that nobody knows. But even according to the smallest estimate, the daily volume of trading was about

1. A foreign exchange deal (see Chapters 8, 9, and 10)

   A purchase of one currency against a sale of another.

2. Intervention by a central bank (see Chapter 5 for details)

In foreign exchange	In the money market
Buying and selling the domestic currency against foreign currencies to push the rate up or down.	Lending or borrowing money (or buying/selling securities) in the money market to push interest rates up or down. Buying or selling securities is often referred to as "open market operations."

3. Foreign exchange deal types (see Chapters 8, 9, and 10)

Spot:	Deal done for settlement in two working days.
Outright forward:	Deal done for settlement at some future date.
Swap:	Deal involving a purchase for one date and a sale for another date.

4. Exchange controls (see Chapter 4)

   A system of regulations that limits the freedom of banks and corporations to deal in the foreign exchange or Eurocurrency market. Used to protect a currency from speculation.

5. Euromarket (see Chapter 1, Section 2)

   An international money market, generally free from central bank controls and free from reserve requirements.

6. Reserve requirement (see Chapter 5)

   A rule requiring banks to deposit reserves with the central bank. This tends to reduce what they will pay for deposits, and raise what they will charge to lend, to offset the cost of holding reserves.

7. Repurchase agreement (see Chapter 11 and Chapter 1, Sections 3 and 4)

   A sale of a security, coupled with a commitment to buy it back at a later date. Used by banks in some markets to borrow from each other or from corporations, and by some central banks to intervene in the money market.

FIGURE 1.1. Some Basic Ideas.

$80 billion, compared with total world reserves for 1977 of $318 billion and total industrial–country reserves of $180 billion.[4] In other words, in three days more money moves through the world market than all the reserves of the industrial nations put together. That shows the extent of the pressure which can be exerted on an individual central bank by the world market.

1.2.3. The next question is, who takes part in the market? Central banks, commercial banks, other financial institutions (such as merchant banks, investment banks, pension funds), corporations, and—to a small extent—wealthy individuals all trade. Then, too, there are the brokers who bring banks together to deal (see 1.2.6). The interbank market (direct or through brokers) is dominant. It accounts for at least 95% of transactions. Of the rest, one estimate[5] has suggested that no less than 45% was accounted for by commodity dealers, particularly in the metals markets, who are continually involved in arbitrage and position taking. (This figure is consistent with the author's personal experience.) Oil companies account for another 10%, nonbank financial institutions (pension funds, securities dealers, etc.) for 10% also, and the rest of world industry's foreign exchange for 30%. Putting it another way, multinational corporations (excluding oil) probably account for 1½% of total world foreign exchange activity. The same source reports a study of U.S. Treasury statistics finding that 55% of reporting corporations *never* reported any forward contracts in any currency. The experience of the last few years' rate volatility, though, has meant that more and more large corporations are setting up their own dealing rooms, so the role of corporation in the market is increasing.

1.2.4. Three kinds of business are done in the market: spot, swap, and outright. (A spot deal is for settlement after two working days. An outright forward deal is for settlement at some future date. A swap is a combination of a spot deal with a reverse deal at some future date. These are discussed in depth in Chapters 8 through 10). Again, there are no world figures. An indication for New York can be had from the Federal Reserve survey of March 1980 (discussed in Section 3 below). This showed that 64% of trading was in the spot market. About 6% was outright forward, and 30% was in the swap market. These figures are probably not wildly out of line with the world total, although Zurich's and London's proportions in the swap markets will be higher because of the better arbitrage markets there (and the absence of outright forward business with the International Monetary Market financial futures market which accounted for fully 35% of New York's outright forward business).[6]

1.2.5. The major currencies traded in the market are the U.S. dollar, the deutsche mark, the pound sterling, the Japanese yen, the Canadian dollar, the Swiss franc, and the French franc. Once again, hard statistics are difficult to come by, but the New York survey showed that in 1980 the main currencies in order of importance—apart of course from the U.S. dollar against which all currencies were traded—were the deutsche mark (32%), pound sterling (23%),

Canadian dollar (12%), and Japanese yen (10.2%). The yen had overtaken the Swiss franc, French and Belgian francs, and the Dutch guilder between 1977 and 1980. These statistics reflect the pattern of New York's business, certainly for the relative importance of the Canadian dollar. In Continental Europe or London, the Swiss and French francs would be more important.

1.2.6. The way of doing business again varies from center to center. More and more, though, a worldwide pattern is emerging. It only varies according to the regulations of the center involved. The major participants are central banks, commercial banks, corporations, and foreign exchange brokers. The job of the broker is to bring two banks together to make a deal, for which he receives a brokerage fee (of a specified percentage). Banks typically trade directly with other banks on the international markets, although in certain cases they will trade through a broker if this is more convenient. In domestic markets they will often also trade directly with one another, but tend (perhaps more than internationally) also to use the services of a broker. Each of the two methods has its own advantages. In dealing directly, a bank can normally be sure of getting a price at which it can deal. The convention is that a bank which receives a call from another bank asking for a quotation will quote a "two-way" price at which it is prepared to buy or sell the currency. But this price may not be the best available in the market at the time, or it may only be good for a limited amount. It is the job of the broker to find his customer the best possible price in the market, by using a large communications network with many other banks in the market. Accordingly, on some occasions, a better price may be obtained through the broker: this, however, incurs a brokerage fee. At the same time, a bank contacted by a broker need not necessarily make a "two-way" price, so that the broker may not always be able to find the right side of the deal.

1.2.7. In some centers brokers are allowed to service corporations in the foreign exchange market. It is quite common to see this in domestic money markets, but still unusual in the foreign exchange market. Banks dislike the practice, generally, because of the possible credit risk problem and the possible jeopardy to customer relationships. In other centers the practice is forbidden. Another restriction can be a ban on dealing with banks outside the country. When operating tight exchange controls, a central bank will usually require all commercial deals to be done with an authorized bank in that country (since otherwise the controls are very hard to police). This happens, for instance, in France, Ireland, and Italy.

1.2.8. Exchange controls are the earthworks that prevent the foreign exchange tide from flowing freely round the world. But the world's communication networks are now so good, and so many countries have fairly unrestricted markets, that we can talk of a single world market. It starts in a small way in New Zealand around 9:00 A.M., just in time to catch the tail end of the previous night's New York market. Two or three hours later, Tokyo opens, followed an hour later by Hong Kong and Manila and then half an hour later by Singapore. By now, with the Far East market in full swing, the focus moves to the Near and Middle East. Bombay opens two hours after Singapore, followed after an hour and a half by Abu Dhabi, with Jeddah an hour behind, and Athens and Beirut an hour behind still. By this stage trading in the Far and Middle East is usually thin and perhaps nervous as dealers wait to see how Europe will trade. Paris and Frankfurt open an hour ahead of London, and by this time Tokyo is starting to close down, so the European market can judge how the Japanese market has been trading by the way they deal to close out positions. By lunch-time in London, New York is starting to open up, and as Europe closes down, so positions can be passed westward. During the afternoon in New York, trading tends to be quiet. The problem is that there is nowhere to pass a position to. The San Francisco market, three hours behind, is effectively a satellite of the New York market. Very small positions can be passed on to New Zealand banks, but the market there is extremely limited. In theory a late shift could hold on to 7:00 or 8:00 P.M. and bridge the 14-hour gap till Tokyo opens: but that market is almost entirely in US$/¥, and positions of any size in other currencies are difficult to shift there.

1.2.9.   So at the moment "the buck stops at the Big Apple." In time, as Tokyo and the Far East become bigger markets and as the U.S. domestic market becomes more international, the market will be truly 24 hours. But for now there is still something of a gap west of New York. The same applies, of course, to the international deposit market, to which we now turn.

SECTION 3.   THE INTERNATIONAL MONEY MARKET (EUROMARKET)

1.3.1.   During the early 1950s a market in foreign currency deposits existed in the United Kingdom, France, and Italy, but the volume of deposits for these centers was rather small. The total volume outstanding in the mid-1950s is estimated to have been not more than $1.5 billion.[7] The takeoff point seems to have been the end of 1958, with the restoration of general convertibility (freedom to buy and sell foreign exchange) in Western Europe. This boosted the market by allowing access to foreign exchange and less strict balancing of trade flows. Deposits in the London currency deposit market are estimated to have more than doubled in the first six months of 1959 to $715 million.[8] An important part in this early expansion was played by certain Socialist banks, notably the Moscow Narodny Bank and the Banque Commerciale pour L'Europe du Nord. This was because of some reluctance by Eastern European monetary authorities to place deposits in the United States, for fear of a freezing of assets.

1.3.2.   The later growth of the market was largely stimulated by two U.S. regulations. The first of these, Regulation Q, laid down maximum rates on do-

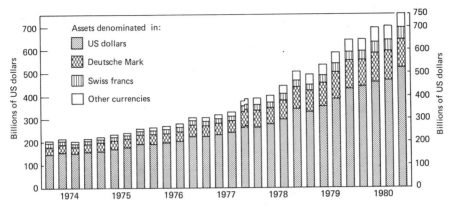

FIGURE 1.2. Currency Structure of the Euromarket: External Assets in Foreign Currencies of Reporting European Banks (Quarterly Figures, Amounts Outstanding). Reproduced from Bank for International Settlements' *51st Annual Report,* June 1981, p. 112.

mestic dollar time deposits. It severely restricted domestic time deposit rates compared with those quoted on external currency markets at times when U.S. rates were high. The second was the ʼInterest Equalization Tax. This was imposed by President Kennedy in 1963, to discourage foreigners' use of the domestic U.S. bond market. The I.E.T. made it attractive for U.S. corporations and other borrowers of dollars to arrange their dollar borrowings outside the United States. Finally, the fact that the Euromarket was exempt from the Federal Reserve's reserve requirement regulations meant that it could operate on a narrower spread between borrowing and lending rates than was possible within the United States.

1.3.3.   These factors made for rapid growth in the market during the 1960s. From 1965 to 1980, the net size of the market grew from $17 to $735 billion, while the gross size grew from $24 to $1,470 billion. The net size of the market is defined as the market size after subtracting total interbank transactions. The figures quoted here are based on those compiled by the Morgan Guaranty Trust Co. of New York, which are generally regarded as authoritative. The other authoritative source of statistics is the Bank for International Settlements (BIS). Their basis differs slightly, producing a generally smaller estimate.[9]

1.3.4.   The figures from the BIS, however, are more detailed as regards the currency breakdown of the market. In 1980, for example, the shares were: US$, 69.0%; DMK, 16.4%; SFR, 6.6%; £STG, 1.7%; HFL, 1.0%; FFR, 1.5%; and other currencies, 3.8%. (Most notable of the other currencies will be the Japanese yen; in Japan the external market has expanded quite rapidly in recent years.) The BIS also produces figures showing the extent to which the Euromarkets serve as the repository for countries' official reserves (insofar as they are held in bank deposits). (See Figure 1.2 and Table 1.1.)

TABLE 1.1. Identified Official Deposits with Commercial Banks Outside the United States.

Items	Amounts Outstanding in Billions of U.S. Dollars				
	End-1977	End-1978	End-1979	Mid-1980	End-1980
A. Deposits with banks in European countries,[1] Canada and Japan					
I. In national markets	7.6	9.3	8.8	15.9	17.6
Deutsche Mark	2.2	3.1	3.4	4.7	4.8
Swiss francs	1.3	0.6	0.6	1.2	1.6
Yen	0.9	2.7	0.9	3.8	4.6
Pounds sterling	1.6	1.2	1.9	2.9	3.0
Other currencies	1.6	1.7	2.0	3.3	3.6
II. In Euro-markets	71.0	80.1	115.0	119.1	122.4
Dollars	53.0	52.8	73.3	75.3	79.4
Deutsche Mark	12.0	16.8	24.1	24.7	24.2
Swiss francs	3.2	4.6	6.0	7.3	8.0
Yen	0.9[2]	2.2[2]	4.2[2]	2.7[2]	2.2[2]
Pounds sterling	0.3	0.7	1.5	2.3	2.2
Other currencies	1.6	3.0	5.9	6.8	6.4
Total I & II	78.6	89.4	123.8	135.0	140.0
of which in non-dollar currencies	25.6	36.6	50.5	59.7	60.6

TABLE 1.1. (Continued)

B. Deposits with offshore branches of US banks	4.4	5.7	6.4	6.2	5.6
Total A + B	83.0	95.1	130.2	141.2	145.6
Memorandum items:					
Total OPEC deposits with reporting banks outside the United States	68.2	73.4	106.2	129.5	146.2
US liabilities to foreign official institutions	126.1	156.8	143.1	142.6	156.9

NOTE: The figures in the table include exchange rate-induced changes in the dollar value of reserves held in currencies other than the dollar.

[1] Austria, Belgium-Luxembourg, Denmark. France, Germany, Ireland, Italy, the Netherlands, Sweden, Switzerland and the United Kingdom.

[2] Excluding deposits with banks in Switzerland.

SOURCE: Reproduced from Bank for International Settlements *51st Annual Report*, June 1981.

1.3.5. The development of the Eurocurrency market has had a large impact on the international banking system. The Eurocredit has proved an innovative form of financing. For example, the U.S. technique used in the bond market for the underwriting of new issues by means of a syndicate was transferred to the Eurobond market, and from there developed into the syndicated medium-term credit. Under this system, a borrowing which is too large for a single bank to handle is "syndicated" among a number of banks. For example, a credit for US$ 1 billion might be syndicated among 10 banks, each of which is only lending $100 million.

1.3.6. A second important innovative feature of the Eurocredit was the roll-over concept. By this means, a five-year borrowing can be financed by the means of six-month deposits. To illustrate, suppose that the credit is for seven years. Then the normal technique would be that each bank would raise $100 million for six months, at an agreed interest rate, and on-lend the funds to the borrower for a six-month period at a margin or "spread" over the cost of funds. At the end of the six-month period, the exercise is repeated, at a new rate of interest. That is, the banks are committed to lend funds for seven years, but at rates of interest which will vary over the time of the loan. The rates will reflect the cost to them at different times of raising funds to finance the loan. This technique has given rise to the concept of the London InterBank Offered Rate (LIBOR), the rate at which the banks in London can fund themselves for such an operation. (For a more detailed discussion, scc 11.1.8–9.)

1.3.7. All of these innovations, together with the very rapid growth of the market, have been very largely due to the fact that the market has been almost entirely free from direct official regulations. There is no single body which is responsible for the control and supervision of the Euromarket. As a result of this, no reserve requirements are applied to banks operating in the Euromarkets. The effect is that each bank can (in theory) potentially create an unlimited amount of credit. The reasons for this are explained in Chapter 5. In fact, of course, in the real world there are a number of "leakages" which act to reduce the size of the multiplier.

1.3.8. Another consequence of the banks' freedom from regulation in the Euromarket is the lack of limit on "maturity transformation," or "maturity mismatch." This is the process whereby a bank transforms a short-term liability, that is, a deposit with a short maturity, into a longer term asset: namely, a medium-term loan. This entails the risk that the bank will be unable to replace the deposit when it matures, leaving it with no money with which to fund the lending. From time to time, concern is expressed that mismatch in the market is getting out of hand. But in fact, mismatch in the Euromarket (at least in London) has remained fairly stable over time, as may be seen from Table 1.2. Also, mismatch is monitored by certain central banks for banks whose headquarters are located in their jurisdiction (see 1.3.14).[10]

TABLE 1.2.   Maturity Mismatching by Banks in the United Kingdom.

Remaining maturity	Less than 1 month	1–3 months	3–6 months	6–12 months	1–3 years	3 years and over
Mid-February						
1975	− 6.8	− 4.3	− 2.7	− 0.7	3.7	13.2
1976	− 6.2	− 4.8	− 3.5	− 0.3	4.2	12.9
1977	− 7.5	− 4.9	− 2.9	− 0.3	5.0	12.3
1978	− 7.6	− 4.5	− 2.8	− 0.3	4.9	11.8
1979	− 7.8	− 3.6	− 3.7	− 0.5	4.3	12.5
1980	− 7.4	− 5.3	− 2.7	− 0.4	3.5	12.8
1981	− 7.0	− 5.3	− 2.8	− 0.3	3.4	11.7
Mean of twenty-seven quarters	− 6.9	− 4.8	− 3.0	− 0.3	4.2	12.3

NOTE: Net foreign currency liabilities (−)/claims (+) as percentage of total foreign currency liabilities.
SOURCE: Reproduced from *Bank of England Quarterly Bulletin*, September 1981.

1.3.9.   In addition to the question of maturity transformation risk, which is dealt with more fully later (see Chapter 17, Section 4), other risks arise from Euromarket operations. Of these, the most notable is "country risk." This is the risk that the bank's loan to an individual country may not be repaid, either because the country itself falls into economic difficulties, or because of political factors. This risk is in addition to that incurred by lending to companies; it applies even if the borrower is a sovereign government. A notable case of country risk in recent years has been seen with Iran. Other countries where special problems have arisen include Poland, Zaire, and Turkey.

1.3.10.   Much of the concern over the country risk aspect of the Euromarkets comes from the fact that Euromarket lending is concentrated on relatively few countries. Most prominent of these is Brazil, with an external debt standing at $90 billion, closely followed by Mexico, with an external debt of $80 billion.*

1.3.11   This country exposure has grown from the part the Euromarkets played in financing the balance of payments deficits of developing countries after the "oil shocks" of the 1970s. The Euromarkets took funds from the Arab oil producers and lent them out to finance the deficits of developing countries. But this meant the banks started to incur heavy exposure to only a few countries.

1.3.12.   All of these developments began to worry banking supervisory authorities in various countries during the 1970s. The crisis point was the collapse of the Herstatt Bank in 1974. In the words of one authority, "Looking back, it is now clear that at the beginning of the 1970s . . . neither the supervisors nor the banks themselves had fully appreciated the degree to which the banking environment was changing in character and the new increased risks involved in international business."[11]

1.3.13.　After the collapse of the Herstatt Bank, the central bank governors agreed to set up a committee of supervisors, the so-called Basle Committee. This meets at the Bank for International Settlements, normally three times a year. Its members include representatives from the central banks of the Group of Ten major industrialized countries, and Switzerland. The first step forward was a general statement of the committee's views made in December 1975, which has generally become known as the Concordat.

1.3.14.　The second major step forward taken by the Basle Committee has been the establishment of the policy that banks with international business should be monitored on a consolidated basis. In this way central banks can assess a bank's capital adequacy and interest exposure on the basis of its worldwide business. For some years, banks in Canada, the Netherlands, and the United States have been required to consolidate their foreign branches as well as significant wholly-owned subsidiaries. Japanese banks have been required to consolidate the accounts of their foreign branches for several years, and, since 1978, those of significant wholly-owned and majority owned subsidiaries. In the United Kingdom, new reporting arrangements were introduced during 1979 to cover the international risk exposure of all U.K. incorporated banks on a fully consolidated basis. In West Germany, under a recent voluntary agreement, the major commercial banks are reporting to the Bundesbank on a basis which includes consolidation of their major overseas subsidiaries. (See Chapter 3 on individual country arrangements.)

1.3.15.　As well as problems of supervision and control, the Euromarkets raise the specific problem that there is no definite "lender of last resort." This makes the question of adequate liquidity extremely complex. Many currencies are involved, and there is no formalized "lender of last resort" responsibility (see Chapter 17, Section 7). It seems likely that supervisory authorities will in time begin to require liquidity reserves to be held against worldwide Euromarket operations by banks who have headquarters in their countries. This step is some way off, however.

1.3.16.　In addition to the normal liquid asset holdings required by prudential management, commercial banks have developed a technique to protect themselves against liquidity problems in the Euromarkets. This is the standby credit. Let's look at a standby arrangement between a U.S. bank and a British bank. The two banks will agree that the U.S. bank will provide the British bank with a dollar line of credit. The British bank will provide the U.S. bank with a sterling line of credit. Thus, if for any reason the British bank's U.S. branch should run into difficulties, it will be assured of a dollar facility, while the U.S. bank's British branch is assured of a sterling facility should the need arise.

1.3.17. Finally, I should mention the important role of the BIS. The BIS has been involved in informal monitoring of the Euromarkets since the start; it has provided the secretariat of the Committee of Supervisors and also of the Standing Committee on the Euromarkets set up by Central Bank Governors of the Group of Ten in April 1980.[12] Its *Annual Report*, recently supplemented by *Quarterly Statistics*, has for many years been the classical source of information on the markets. The BIS is an important participant in the markets, both in its own right and as a channel for the placement of central bank funds (see 3.3.1).

SECTION 4.   THE U.S. FOREIGN EXCHANGE AND MONEY MARKETS

1.4.1. We turn now to specific markets, beginning with the United States. The U.S. foreign exchange and money markets are among the most diverse and sophisticated in the world. For the foreign exchange market, the main difficulties are the lack of domestic interest in Eurocurrencies, which limits the forward markets' scope, and the time zone problem referred to earlier. Although there are about 14,000 banks in the United States, only about 1% of these are active in foreign exchange markets. Of these, perhaps at most 50[13] can be considered true "market-makers" in the sense that they are continuously willing to trade at least one currency with other banks. A growing feature of the market is the involvement of traders from financial futures markets (see Chapter 15). The latest (1980) survey by the New York Federal Reserve indicated that as much as 15% of banks' customer deals were with traders on the International Monetary Market.[14] Other corporate activity had been relatively low because of the traditionally small share of American GNP held by international trade, and the widespread use of the dollar as invoicing currency. But international trade has been growing in importance, and the volatility of the dollar has meant that corporations have paid more attention to exchange risk. Also, the requirements of the Financial Accounting Standards Board on Statement No. 8 (and now the FASB Statement No. 52—see Chapter 19) on the translation of foreign currency assets have made U.S. multinationals very aware of the need to cover foreign currency exposures.

1.4.2. These exposures can be freely hedged because the United States has no exchange controls (unlike, say, Italy, where such balance sheet hedging is not allowed). In theory, the absence of exchange controls means that the market for foreign exchange in the United States is unregulated, since private individuals are free to trade currency among themselves. In practice, foreign currency business is usually done through banks or the financial futures markets. Banks' foreign exchange activities are not controlled, but they are supervised by bank examiners from the Federal Reserve or from state banking departments (see 3.7.8).

1.4.3. The main currencies traded in New York are set out in Table 1.3. It will be seen that the fastest growth was in the yen market and in sterling, the latter recovering from a previous decline. The proportion of interbank versus customer spot and forward trades is set out in Table 1.4.

1.4.4. Official intervention in the foreign exchange market is handled by the Federal Reserve Bank of New York. It acts on behalf of the Board of Governors of the Federal Reserve Bank, and of the U.S. Treasury Exchange Equalization Account. Information on official intervention in the market is published by the Federal Reserve Bank of New York in quarterly reports, in quite some detail. These are contained both in the *Quarterly Bulletin of the Federal Reserve Bank of New York* and in the *Bulletin of the Board of Governors of the Federal Reserve System.* Intervention by the Federal Reserve can be either directly in its own name, or covertly through the medium of a commercial bank. Typically, the Federal Reserve operates by approaching the brokers' market indirectly through commercial bank agents. However, the Federal Reserve's trading desk also intervenes by dealing directly with commercial banks. Sometimes this includes quoting two-way prices during intervention operations. Intervention in the forward market appears insignificant. Federal Reserve intervention has taken place in New York, Europe, and occasionally in the Far East.

1.4.5. Another aspect of the Federal Reserve's international activity, because of the pivotal role of the U.S. dollar in international markets, is its services for foreign central banks and international institutions. The Federal Reserve Bank of New York services about 150 foreign central banks and international institutions. As of January 1982, the New York "Fed" held for these accounts more than $100 billion in marketable and nonmarketable United States Treasury securities—primarily bills—and other dollar-denominated assets. It also held 350 million troy ounces of gold, valued at about $123 billion at the then free market price of $350 per ounce. The Federal Reserve also invests funds and maintains custody services under instructions from correspondents. In 1981, the dollar volume of investment activity for correspondents exceeded $1,500 billion.[15] Additionally, the Fed buys and sells foreign exchange for correspondent central banks. Such operations are often done at the same time as operations by central banks in their own home market, in order to help their intervention.

1.4.6. Euromarket activity in the United States has always been extremely small (partly, it is reported, because of official discouragement). However, a

TABLE 1.3. Growth in Monthly Foreign Exchange Turnover among U.S. Banks, April 1977 to March 1980.

Currency	Institutions Represented on Both Surveys			All Institutions Represented on Each Survey		
	April 1977 ($ Billions)	March 1980 ($ Billions)	Change (%)	April 1977 ($ Billions)	March 1980 ($ Billions)	Change ($)
German mark (DM)	28.7	92.6	+ 222.6	29.0	155.9	+ 437.6
British pound (£)	17.4	77.4	+ 344.8	18.1	112.1	+ 519.3
Canadian dollar (C$)	18.1	39.1	+ 116.0	20.4	60.5	+ 196.6
Japanese yen (¥)	5.6	30.5	+ 444.6	5.7	50.1	+ 778.9
Swiss franc (SF)	14.6	43.0	+ 194.5	14.6	49.7	+ 240.4
French franc (FF)	6.6	21.4	+ 224.2	6.7	33.6	+ 401.5
Dutch guilder (NG)	6.0	9.0	+ 50.0	6.0	9.3	+ 55.0
Belgian franc (BF)	1.5	4.3	+ 186.7	1.6	5.1	+ 218.8
Italian lira (LIT)	1.2	3.1	+ 158.3	1.2	4.2	+ 250.0
All other	3.0	5.5	+ 83.3	3.1	10.8	+ 248.4
All currencies	102.7	325.8	+ 217.2	106.4	491.3	+ 361.7
Sample size	41	41	—	44	90	—

SOURCE: Federal Reserve Bank of New York, Exchange Market Survey, March 1980.

TABLE 1.4. March, 1980 Foreign Exchange Turnover Survey of Ninety Banks in the United States.

Aggregate Results
(In Millions of U.S. Dollars Equivalent)

Type of Transaction	German Mark	British Pound	Swiss Franc	Japanese Yen	Canadian Dollar	French Franc	Dutch Guilder	Belgian Franc	Italian Lira	All Other	All Currencies
I. Outright Spot Transactions											
A. Interbank											
1. Through brokers	55,520	39,135	16,367	16,810	12,858	13,246	4,142	1,278	1,127	2,007	162,490
2. Direct, with:											
a. Banks in the U.S.	28,091	11,765	6,347	4,827	5,360	3,874	640	488	241	759	62,392
b. Banks abroad	21,553	13,274	10,591	5,059	15,204	3,472	1,610	1,080	839	2,793	75,475
B. Customer											
1. Nonfinancial institutions	2,431	2,827	859	544	2,518	776	130	142	135	450	10,812
2. Financial institutions	1,011	1,386	509	202	803	226	95	8	10	46	4,296
II. Swap Transactions											
A. Interbank											
1. Short-dated (1 week or less)	22,296	17,591	8,099	11,838	11,132	6,066	1,743	1,399	990	1,756	82,910
2. Long-dated	16,168	15,226	3,539	7,137	6,096	4,044	484	336	402	1,421	54,853
B. Customer											
1. Nonfinancial institutions											

a. Short-dated	481	1,439	215	57	732	101	12	36	11	20	3,104
b. Long-dated	697	1,555	261	164	636	104	21	21	26	87	3,572
2. Financial institutions											
a. Short-dated	152	225	44	188	227	1	3	—	—	46	886
b. Long-dated	117	315	108	159	237	52	21	20	—	106	1,135

III. Outright Forward Transactions

A. Interbank	3,852	2,744	869	1,118	746	887	182	203	224	729	11,554
B. Customer											
1. Nonfinancial institutions	2,036	2,553	614	1,165	2,341	751	229	90	190	514	10,483
2. Financial institutions	134	244	91	68	440	34	13	12	8	55	1,099
3. Arbitrage members of currency futures exchange	1,333	1,785	1,176	750	1,211	2	—	—	—	5	6,262
Total outright spot transactions	108,606	68,387	34,673	27,442	36,743	21,594	6,617	2,996	2,352	6,055	315,465
Total swap transactions	39,911	36,351	12,266	19,543	19,060	10,368	2,284	1,812	1,429	3,436	146,460
Total outright forward transactions	7,355	7,326	2,750	3,101	4,738	1,674	424	305	422	1,303	29,398
Total interbank	147,480	99,735	45,812	46,789	51,396	31,589	8,801	4,784	3,823	9,465	449,674
Total customer	8,392	12,329	3,877	3,297	9,145	2,047	524	329	380	1,329	41,649
Total turnover	155,872	112,064	49,689	50,086	60,541	33,636	9,325	5,113	4,203	10,794	491,323

SOURCE: Federal Reserve Bank of New York, Foreign Exchange Market Survey, March 1980.

great deal of activity has been channeled through "nameplate" centers—mainly the Bahamas and the Cayman Islands. This is because dollar deposits in New York have always been reservable (until the advent of the International Banking Facility—see 1.4.8). Deposits in other currencies have also been reservable, and in any event there has been relatively little demand for placements or lendings in Eurocurrencies other than dollars.

1.4.7.   Eurodollar deposits through the Caribbean have been an important activity for New York banks, because of the convenience of a similar time zone. As a result, total U.S. banks' liabilities to the Bahamas and British West Indies combined, in September 1981, were US$ 37.7 billion, compared with US$ 26.2 billion owed to the United Kingdom. The other main sources of funds for U.S. banks from overseas were: the Middle East oil exporters (US$ 13.3 billion); Switzerland (US$ 17.0 billion); Germany (US$ 4.4 billion); France (US$ 7.6 billion); and Japan (US$ 20.7 billion).[16]

1.4.8.   On December 3, 1981, however, U.S. banks were allowed to open International Banking Facilities, which can transact international business free from most Federal Reserve regulations, and which benefit from certain state and local tax concessions. Briefly, an IBF is a set of segregated asset and liability accounts maintained on the books of a banking organization. (It follows from this definition that the IBF is not a separate legal entity: it is a subunit of the organization which created it.) The Federal Reserve had initially opposed the creation of IBFs. The Fed's reluctance stemmed from a fear that the IBFs would lead to its losing control of the domestic money supply, and so it laid down a number of restrictions on the operations of an IBF. An IBF can only take deposits unrestricted as to amount and maturity from (1) another IBF; (2) a U.S. or overseas office of the IBF's parent; (3) an overseas office of a U.S. bank or Edge Act or agreement corporation; (4) a foreign bank; or (5) certain institutions exempt from Regulation Q (on U.S. interest rate levels.) It can take deposits of over $100,000 and a minimum maturity of two days from (1) non-U.S. residents, or (2) foreign branches, offices, subsidiaries, or affiliates of U.S. corporations provided that the funds are used to support operations overseas.

1.4.9.   The lendings permitted to an IBF are to (1) another IBF, (2) a foreign bank, (3) a U.S. or overseas office of the parent; (4) an overseas office of a U.S. depository institution or an Edge Act or agreement corporation; (5) certain institutions exempt from Regulation Q; (6) an overseas resident or an overseas branch, office, subsidiary, or affiliate of a U.S. corporation provided that the funds are for use overseas.

1.4.10.   Despite all these restrictions, the IBFs got off to a reasonably good start. By May 1982, total IBF assets outstanding were $90 billion, compared with $1,470 billion for the Euromarkets as a whole in December 1980. However, the breakdown of figures given by the Fed shows that—as of the time of this writing—IBFs depended overwhelmingly on associated offices overseas for their funding, and secondly on other overseas banks; that is, the volume of natural deposits (particularly from foreign governments, who it had been thought would be attracted by the "sovereign risk" benefits of keeping their funds in New York rather than, say, the Bahamas or the Cayman Islands) was not in fact that large. Clearly, though, the IBFs represent a major challenge by New York to London's traditional dominance of international banking, and I think it's fair to expect that over the next decade they will start to play a very important part in the international money market. However, the Fed restrictions—notably the refusal to allow IBFs to issue negotiable instruments such as CDs and to do business with U.S. residents—means that their growth will be slow.

1.4.11. The Eurodollar deposit market and the domestic U.S. deposit market have always been closely linked, since there is no exchange control. Eurodollars are often dealt from the same room as a bank's domestic money operations. The domestic market which is most relevant to the Euromarket is the Federal funds market. Fed funds, or Feds, as they are often called, can be defined as funds held in a bank's reserve account at its local Federal Reserve Bank. By virtue of the Federal Reserve wire transfer system, such funds can be transferred around the United States with same-day value. They are therefore sometimes spoken of as "immediately available" funds. Dealings in the Fed funds market are normally overnight: the domestic interbank market for "clean" term money is not well developed, as it is in the United Kingdom. A limited market exists in "term Federal funds" but it is small in comparison with the overnight market.

1.4.12. The basic feature of Fed funds is that they satisfy the system's reserve requirements. These required reserves are calculated on the basis of the daily average of deposits held over a seven-day period two weeks earlier. (From May, 1983 the Federal Reserve will require reserves to be based on current figures rather than two weeks previously.) The current level of reserve requirements[17] is shown in Table 1.5. From these requirements, plus the average levels of deposits held during the seven-day period concerned, a bank and the Fed know the level of required reserves that the bank must hold during the current statement week. This begins on a Thursday and ends on a Wednesday. The level of reserves held need not be exactly correct each day. It must, though, average out correctly. This means that Wednesday is the day when banks must get their reserves exactly right so as to balance out the week's average.

1.4.13. Only Fed funds will satisfy the system's reserve requirements. In the United Kingdom, for instance, deposits with the discount market as well as deposits at the Bank of England qualify toward the reserve requirement, but in

TABLE 1.5. U.S. Reserve Requirements.

Account type	Percentage
Net transactions accounts[a]	
$0–25 million[b]	3
$25 million +	12
Nonpersonal time deposits[c]	
Less than four years original maturity	3
Over four years original maturity	0
Eurocurrency liability: all types	3

[a] Transaction accounts are deposits on which the account holder is permitted to make withdrawals to pay third parties.

[b] The 3% applies to the first $25 million of a bank's transaction accounts; the rest is subject to the 12% requirement.

[c] Time deposits that are not transaction accounts and are not owned by individuals.

the United States Fed funds are the only reserve asset. This means that the rate payable on Fed funds is an important indicator of the availability of reserves and hence the current ease or tightness of monetary policy. However, since October 1979 the level of total reserves and nonborrowed reserves has assumed greater importance as a policy variable. (See 1.4.23.)

1.4.14. As we said earlier, the Fed funds market is mainly an overnight market. Banks or securities dealers needing funds for a slightly longer period will normally turn to the repurchase market. A repurchase deal (or "repo") is the sale of a security under an agreement to repurchase. In effect, it is a borrowing which uses the security as collateral. It is normally free of reserve requirements.[18] The deal is very similar to the French *"pension"* (see 1.7.7) and the Japanese *"gen-saki"* markets (see 1.8.8). The mechanics are discussed in Chapter 11, Section 9.

1.4.15. The importance of the repo market lies in providing a large and flexible money market for any desired term (though the bulk of repos are overnight or "continuing contract," i.e., until the lender calls in his funds), and in its frequent use by the Federal Reserve for open market operations (see 1.4.21). The size of the market is difficult to estimate, but is at least $70 billion[19] compared with about $50 billion for the Federal funds market.[20]

1.4.16. The next important source of funds for U.S. banks along the maturity scale after repurchases is certificates of deposit (CDs). These are more precisely defined in Chapter 11. For our purposes, the prime fact is that a CD is a negotiable certificate stating that a deposit has been placed with a bank. The CD can be resold (because it is negotiable) if the investor finds that he needs his deposit back. An ordinary deposit, of course, cannot be "taken back" in this way, so a CD is an inherently more liquid investment. Hence the yield on a CD is usually below that on a deposit of comparable maturity. CDs are a useful marginal source of funds for banks, and the volume outstanding has expanded from US\$ 10 billion in the early 1960s to US\$ 100 billion in the early 1980s, although the volume fluctuates with the level of loan demand. Banks "write" more CDs when they need extra funds to finance rising loan demand.

1.4.17. Commercial paper is another source of funds for banks, although less important than the other three sources. In August 1970, the Federal Reserve ruled that reserve requirements applied to funds raised by sale of commercial paper by a bank holding company and passed on to that holding company's banking subsidiary.[21] This restricted banks' use of CP. However, bank holding companies can use the CP market to fund nonbanking activities such as credit cards and leasing. The amount of CP outstanding from bank holding companies was \$32 billion in September 1981 compared with \$51.2 billion for nonfinancial companies and \$80.9 billion for finance companies, who dominate this market.[22]

1.4.18. The U.S. money market is diverse and sophisticated, and the above is a sketchy outline of the part of the market which concerns us. A number of excellent books on the market are available and are listed in the bibliography. We look now at the authorities' behavior in the market. Intervention takes three forms: the "discount window," outright purchases/sales of securities, and repurchases/reverse repurchases of securities.

1.4.19. Historically the term "discount window" arose from the Fed's practice of discounting bills or securities presented to it by member banks requiring funds.[23] In 1971, discounting ceased, to be replaced by loans using the bills as collateral. At present the following are "eligible" collateral: Treasury securities, federal agency securities, municipal securities with less than six months to run, and commercial and industrial loans with 90 days or less to run.[24] The discount window is designed for very-short-term loans to cover anticipated funds requirements. The Federal Reserve has laid down purposes for which use of the discount window is not approved. They include borrowing to profit from interest rate differentials, to substitute Federal Reserve credit for normal sources of short-term interest-sensitive funds, and to support increases in loan or investment portfolios.[25] The Monetary Control Act of 1980 extended the privilege of discount window access, previously confined to banks that were members of the Federal Reserve System. All nonmember banks, savings and loan associations, savings banks, and credit unions holding transaction accounts or nonpersonal time deposits were allowed access.[26] In September 1980 the Federal Reserve revised its Regulation A, which governs discount window activity, to allow this wider access, and also to allow the Fed to impose a surcharge on the discount rate. In this way the Fed can prevent too-frequent use of the discount window by banks looking for cheap funds. Such a surcharge (of

3%) had been already imposed between March and May 1980 on banks with over $500 million in deposits which borrowed in two successive weeks, or in more than four weeks per calendar quarter.[27]

1.4.20. The second major money market intervention technique is outright purchases or sales of securities. If the Fed buys securities from a bank, the bank's account at the Fed is credited with the proceeds. This automatically increases the bank's reserves at the Fed. Conversely, if the Fed sells securities to a bank, the bank's account is debited with the cost, reducing its reserves at the Fed. The total scale of the system's Open Market Account operation is huge, as Table 1.6 shows.

1.4.21. Outright purchases or sales of securities have a permanent effect on reserves of the banking system. Very often the Fed wants to add or drain reserves for only a few days. In this case a more flexible instrument is repurchase or reverse repurchase agreements. Suppose the Fed has to supply reserves for three days. Then it will buy securities from a bank, while agreeing that the bank will repurchase the securities from the Fed in three days' time. If we

TABLE 1.6.   Federal Reserve Open Market Transactions (in Millions of US$).

U.S. Government Securities— All Maturities	1978	1979	1980	1981
Outright				
Gross purchases	24591	22325	12232	16690
Gross sales	13725	6855	7331	6769
Redemptions	2033	5500	3389	1816
Matched Transactions				
Gross sales	511126	627350	674000	589312
Gross purchases	510854	624192	675496	589647
Repurchase Agreement				
Gross purchases	151618	107051	113902	79920
Gross sales	152436	106968	113040	78733
Federal Agency Obligations and Bankers' Acceptances				
Outright transactions, net	−107	+320	+523	+494
Repurchase agreements, net	−684	+477	+105	−838
Total net change in System Open Market Account	6,951	7,693	4,497	9,175

SOURCE: *Federal Reserve Bulletin*, December 1981 and March 1982, Table 1.17, p. A10.
NOTE: Sales, redemptions and negative figures reduce open market account holdings.

TABLE 1.7.   Mechanics of a Repurchase Agreement.

Day 1—The Initial Position				
Federal Reserve			Bank	
Assets		Liabilities	Assets	Liabilities
Cash	100	100 Bank Reserves	Securities 100	100 Deposits
Day 2—The Fed Buys Securities on Repo				
Federal Reserve			Bank	
Securities 100		100 Reserves	Cash 100	100 Deposits
Day 2—Bank Deposits Cash at Fed				
Securities 100		200 Reserves	Reserves 100	100 Deposits
Cash	100			
Day 3—Repurchase Takes Place				
Cash	100	100 Reserves	Securities 100	100 Deposits

imagine that the deal is done with cash we get the sequence of Table 1.7. In the same way, if the Federal Reserve wishes to drain reserves, it will sell securities to the banks, while agreeing to repurchase them from the banks at a specified date. These are known as "reverse repurchases" or "matched sales."

1.4.22.   As we said in 1.4.5, the Fed is active on behalf of correspondent central banks and other foreign official bodies. Hence, it may enter the market to buy securities, or make a repurchase agreement, on behalf of another central bank wishing to invest. So a Fed repurchase agreement may be announced as a "system repo" or a "customer repo" depending upon whether the Fed is acting on its own account or for one of its "customers." A system repo has greater direct significance as a reflection of a deliberate Federal Reserve decision to supply reserves, although the fact that the Fed chooses to show a customer repo to the market can mean it is showing the market its intentions.

1.4.23.   The way in which the Fed uses its basic tools—the discount window, outright purchases/sales, and repurchases (RPs) or reverse RPs—changes over time. The last major change was in October 1979 when the system changed its operating target from the Federal funds rate to the total level of reserves held by banks. That is, instead of trying to achieve its money supply targets by fixing the interest rate on Federal funds, it aimed to achieve them by controlling the growth of reserves. This resulted in the following procedure. At each Federal Open Market Committee (FOMC) meeting (see Chapter 3, Section 7) a short-term target is set for growth in the monetary aggregates. The Fed then estimates the growth path for total reserves and nonborrowed reserves that will be consistent with those targets. (Nonborrowed reserves are defined as total reserves held by banks, less borrowings at the discount window.) First, the likely growth of currency in circulation and the breakdown of the deposits level contained in the FOMC targets are estimated. These estimates give a forecast of the level of required reserves. To these are added estimates of excess reserves. This process yields a forecast of total reserves. A level of borrowing from the Fed is assumed, in line with recent trends. The forecast of nonborrowed reserves is estimated by subtracting the assumed borrowing from forecast total reserves.[28]

1.4.24. Having derived a target path for nonborrowed reserves, the trading desk at the Federal Reserve Bank of New York will compare the target path with the projected path of nonborrowed reserves if no action is taken. This projection takes account of operating factors such as currency in circulation, Treasury balances, and Federal Reserve float. (The latter arises from transfers over the Federal wire, which are often credited to the payee before the payor's account is debited. An unexpected hitch in the transportation of checks—because of a fog-bound airport, for instance—can sharply increase float as debits are held up. The extra float injects reserves into the system.) If the projected growth of reserves exceeds the target, the desk will move to drain reserves, and vice versa.

1.4.25. The manager of the system's open market account takes part in a daily telephone conference call with a designated Reserve Bank president who is currently sitting on the FOMC and senior staff of the Board of Governors of the Federal Reserve System in Washington. The call is usually made around 11:15 A.M. The manager proposes a plan for the day, amending it in the light of comments from the president. From around 11:30, the trading desk will enter the market to act on the plan. If reserves are to be supplied, the desk will do repos: if excess reserves are to be drained, it will do reverse repurchases. The intervention is done by a "go-around." That is, the desk contacts all of the primary dealers in government securities and asks them for quotations for its planned transaction; the best quotes are dealt on.

1.4.26. The switch to the new operating system produced extraordinarily rapid swings in interest rates, with consequent pressures on financial institutions who ran mismatched funding positions. One or two were almost forced into bankruptcy. A second major problem was rapid financial innovation which made it difficult to assess the meaning of the money supply targets the Fed was trying to hit.[29] These problems are discussed in Chapter 6. They meant that during 1982 the Fed tended to shift away from rigid adherence to its new policy.

SECTION 5. U.K. FOREIGN EXCHANGE AND MONEY MARKET

1.5.1. Traditionally, London has been the largest foreign exchange market in the world. No figures for turnover in London are published, and therefore this claim is difficult to prove. Until the removal of U.K. exchange controls, the U.S. foreign exchange market was probably growing much faster than London, but the removal of exchange controls has undoubtedly given the London market a large boost. The very wide range of participants in the London market and its natural time zone advantages mean that it is probably still the largest market in the world. But because of the increasing internationalization of the New York market, New York is probably continuing to gain on London in terms of total turnover.

1.5.2. The range of participants in the London market is the same as for New York, although the financial futures markets are not so large. On the other hand, pressure from successive governments to finance exports and "merchanting" trade in foreign currency has meant that familiarity with foreign currency financing, invoicing, and hedging is probably much wider spread than in companies of comparable size in the United States.

1.5.3. Exchange controls until recently held the market back in certain areas. The relatively liberal attitude of the Bank of England toward genuine trading transactions meant that even under the previous regime, major corporations had a very wide range of options open to them. The chief impact of the removal of exchange controls has been in financial transactions—foreign currency securities and the like—and in the gradual buildup of foreign currency trading for its own sake, for example by firms originally engaged in commodity trading. Balance sheet hedging is at present rather rare, although the introduction of the accountancy Exposure Draft 27 (ED27) (see Chapter 18) may have an impact.

1.5.4. The monetary sector in the United Kingdom consists of 663 institutions.[30] Its members are divided into banks and licensed deposit takers (LDTs): there are about 400 recognized banks. Of these about 300 are foreign. Not all of these are active in the market on their own account, but they all offer a service in foreign exchange, because that is one of the services needed to qualify for recognition as a bank. And a good number do deal actively in their own currency, helping to give the market depth and flexibility. Also, there is a large and well-developed broking system. There are 12 firms of brokers, mostly members of international groups with a worldwide network.

1.5.5. Official activity in the market is handled by the Bank of England which manages the Exchange Equalisation Account for the Treasury of the United Kingdom. The EEA holds the United Kingdom's foreign exchange reserves. The Bank also deals on behalf of its customers—government departments, central banks, and other monetary institutions abroad. In addition, the Bank intervenes to stabilize the rate for sterling from time to time. The amount of intervention varies. During the fixed rate period—especially before 1967—it was large, and was also carried out in the forward market. (See Chapter 5, Section 3.) Since then it has generally been less, although during 1976 as sterling fell and 1977 as it rose, the Bank intervened heavily. Because of the effects of intervention on the money supply (see Chapter 5, Section 5) the adoption of "monetarist" policies after 1979 meant that the Bank's dealing has usually been confined to smoothing abrupt changes in the rate.

1.5.6.   The Bank of England normally intervenes in the foreign exchange market through a commercial bank, to ensure that its presence is not widely known. (Money market procedures are discussed below.) If it needs to advertise its presence, the Bank will usually give the brokers rates at which it will deal at stated amounts. As this tends to mean that the Bank ends up on the other side of a number of deals, its presence is quickly known. Intervention in the forward market is very limited, though swaps are occasionally done to stabilize the domestic market (see Chapter 5, Section 3). Finally, in some circumstances, the Bank will do commercial transactions if they are judged in the national interest: large long-dated forward contracts arising from export projects, for instance.

1.5.7.   Exchange control regulations were entirely removed in October 1979. Hence supervision of the foreign exchange market is only through general supervision of banking operations. This is conducted by the Bank of England in a generally flexible way. During 1980, however, the Bank of England produced a paper on foreign exchange positions of the banks, which proposed limits on total exposure in relation to the banks' outstanding capital. Details are in Chapter 3. A paper on the control of banking liquidity was also produced, which permitted in principle the imposition of reserve requirements on Eurocurrency activities.

1.5.8.   At present, however, this is relatively unlikely: freedom to operate in the Euromarket has been a major help to London's role as an international financial center. Indeed, London's role as the center of the Euromarkets was the main factor in the establishment of a very large number of foreign banks in London. The total number of foreign banks having offices in London (directly, or indirectly through consortium banks) rose from 114 in 1967 to 420 in 1981.[31] London's telecommunications facilities, trained banking personnel, and widely respected legal system all combined to encourage the development first of a short-term market in foreign currency deposits, and then later a market for the on-lending of these deposits in the form of medium-term credits. The bulk of the London market, as elsewhere, is in U.S. dollars: these account for probably 75% of transactions, with the balance being in deutsche marks, Swiss francs, Dutch guilders, Japanese yen, and a number of other currencies in relatively minor amounts.[32] Eurodollars and Euro-deutsche marks can easily be dealt for periods of up to five years, for reasonable amounts providing that market conditions are normal, and in certain cases possibly for longer. Longer-term business in the other currencies can sometimes be undertaken but is dependent on market conditions. The absence of exchange controls means that the domestic money market is now intimately linked with developments in the Euromarket. In particular, because of the very broad and deep nature of the dollar/sterling market, investors have the ability to switch among deposits with banks of comparable standing in the two currencies, certificates of deposit, and Treasury bills, to name but a few of the shorter-term instruments. Given the ability of the forward market to absorb very substantial sums of money for periods up to 12 months, there is a close link between the domestic U.K. money markets and the U.S. markets. And the removal of exchange controls, coupled with technical changes (see 1.5.12), has made the sterling banker's acceptance market a significant international market. For example, in 1981 PEMEX raised a five-year £365-million acceptance credit facility.

1.5.9. The domestic U.K. money markets cover a number of areas, including those for local authorities (municipalities), commercial bills (acceptances), and finance houses; for our purposes, the chief interest lies in the discount market and the sterling interbank market. The discount market is a uniquely British tradition, although counterparts to it have been established elsewhere (e.g., South Africa, Singapore). Its importance lies in the fact that the Bank of England—unlike the Federal Reserve—does not normally lend directly to commercial banks in the money markets. It is to the 12 discount houses that the Bank of England will lend (as "lender of last resort") when money is tight in the market. Essentially the discount houses are traders in Treasury bills, short-dated government bonds, commercial bills, and CDs. They finance themselves by borrowing "at call" (loans which are repayable on demand—when they are "called").[33]

1.5.10. Traditionally, when the money market was tight, the U.K. clearing banks—who were the main lenders at call to the discount houses—would call funds in from the discount houses. The latter would then borrow from the Bank of England, or sell bills to it. The terms on which the Bank of England provided assistance set the level of short-term interest rates. In 1980 and 1981, however, the Bank of England began to modify its intervention techniques. In August 1980 it changed its dealing rates in Treasury bills to encourage the houses to sell bills to it rather than to borrow against them. Later, the Bank abandoned step by step the fixing of dealing rates for bills. It left the discount houses to quote prices at which they will sell to the Bank. The aim was to give market forces a larger role in setting the interest rate structure. During this period the Bank of England also increased the proportion of eligible bank bills it bought in relation to its purchases of Treasury bills. Its aim was to widen the sphere of its operations when Treasury bills were in short supply.[34]

1.5.11. In August 1981, the Bank abolished the reserve asset ratio, under which banks had to hold a fixed percentage of their "eligible liabilities" in certain reserve assets. These consisted chiefly of money at call with the discount houses, Treasury bills, and government bonds. The ratio was replaced by a requirement that banks hold 6% of eligible liabilities with the discount market (and certain other specialist firms). They were also required to hold ½% of eligible liabilities in interest-free accounts at the Bank of England.[35]

TABLE 1.8. The Bank's Money Market Operations.

The daily arithmetic	£ millions	What is published
		The Bank releases information in the course of the day to the main press agencies and by daily input to the Reuter Monitor service.
1 Morning estimate of the day's position (before taking account of any official operations that may be in prospect during the day):		1 The following announcement is made at about 9:45 am:
Clearing banks' operational balances at Bank, above (+) or below (−) assumed target last night.	+ 30	Not usually disclosed
Exchequer receipts (−) net of disbursements (+)	− 210 ⎫	A shortage of around £300 million is expected today. Among the main factors are:
Proceeds of net official sales (−) of gilt-edged stocks	− 20 ⎬	Exchequer transactions − 220
Net receipts (−) of sterling on Exchange qualisation Account (EEA)	+ 10 ⎭	
Increase (−) or decrease (+) in note issue	+ 30.	Decrease in note issue + 30
Take-up (−) of Treasury bills by market, less maturities in market hands	− 20 ⎫	Bills maturing and take-up of Treasury bills − 140
Local authority and commercial bills maturing in the Bank's hands	− 120 ⎬	*The overall figure is rounded to the nearest 50.*
Bills being resold by the Bank to the market	— ⎭	*The position of bankers' balances is only exceptionally disclosed, while that of other customers is never revealed. 'Exchequer transactions' include in this context the effect of gilt-edged and EEA settlements. Bills being resold to the market would usually be disclosed if significant, as would the repayment of any published lending.*
Repayment (−) to Bank of earlier lending by it	—	
Other, including other Bank customers	− 10	Not disclosed
	− 310	
2 At about noon the Exchequer figure is revised to − 190, and that for the note issue tp + 40. The revised total is	− 280	2 The revision is not large enough to warrant publication.

3 Details of these operations are published. Thus, when the operations are complete the following announcement is made:

'The Bank has undertaken operations, making the following purchases totalling £260 million:
Band 1 Bank bills, £75 million at 13¼%
Band 2 Treasury bills, £12 million at 13³/₁₆%
Band 2 Local authority bills, £18 million at 13³/₁₆–⅜%
Band 2 Bank bills, £155 million at 13⁵/₁₆–⁷/₁₆%.'

The rates shown for bill purchases are rates of discount.

4 The revision is now large enough to justify publication, so the following announcement is made:

'The shortage of around £300 million published this morning has been revised to one of around £250 million, before taking account of today's operations.'

5 The following announcement is made, at approximately 2:30 pm:

'The Bank has not operated in the money market this afternoon.'

6 No further announcements are made.

---

3 Soon after midday the Bank purchases bills from the market (see opposite) totalling   + 260

4 At about 2 pm the Exchequer figure has again been revised, to − 160; and the figure for 'other' items has been revised to + 10. The revised total, before taking account of the operations in (3), is now   − 230

5 If the estimate of − 230 is correct, the bill purchases of 260 will leave the market with a net surplus of 30 on the day. The Bank decides to undertake no further operations.

6 When the town clearing has been settled it becomes apparent that the actual Exchequer figure was − 170. Thus the true position for the day was:

Total market shortage   − 240
Bank's operations   + 260
        + 20

The clearing banks' operational balances will be 20 above the assumed target overnight.

SOURCE: Reproduced from *Bank of England Quarterly Bulletin*, March 1982.
NOTE: The figures are illustrative of a typical day on which, prior to any operation by the bank, there is a market shortage.

1.5.12. These changes had two purposes. The first was to widen the network of monetary control and spread the cost of holding interest-free reserves at the Bank. Until then, this was largely paid by the clearing banks. In compensation, the August 1981 measures allowed many foreign and other banks to qualify as banks whose bills were eligible for discount at the Bank of England, helping them to compete for short-term domestic business. (Between June and October 1981, sterling acceptances at U.S. banks in London rose 77%.) The second aim was to widen the role of market forces in setting U.K. interest rates. The Bank of England announced that henceforth it would operate within an unpublished band of interest rates for short-term money. These rates would mainly be set by the rates at which it bought bills in the open market. To help the discount houses in judging the rates at which to offer bills, the Bank also announced that it would publish daily forecasts of the money market surplus or shortage on pages RTCA, RTCB and RTCC of the Reuters Monitor computer system (perhaps the first case of a central bank's using an electronic medium to convey its official intervention policy) together with the rates at which it had intervened in the market. It has set up four "maturity bands" for the bills in which it deals. Band 1 is for 1 to 14 days, Band 2 for 15 to 33 days, Band 3 for 34 to 63 days, and Band 4 for 64 to 91 days. The clearest signal of the desired level of rates is normally Band 1.

1.5.13. This change of policy brings us back to the situation in October 1972. Then Minimum Lending Rate (MLR) replaced Bank Rate. MLR was set by a formula linked to Treasury bill rates. The Bank of England hoped to escape political responsibility for setting interest rates, which would be "determined by market forces." But responsibility was still pinned on the Bank, and in May 1978 MLR reverted to being fixed by the Bank. The new system does not remove that responsibility: it too will probably be abandoned in time.

SECTION 6.   GERMANY

1.6.1. In foreign exchange terms, Germany probably ranks second after London in importance and ahead of Switzerland, because of the country's industrial strength; but in Euromarket terms Frankfurt is a less important center, largely because German reserve requirements operate not by currency (as in the United Kingdom or France) but by residence status. Hence a Frankfurt bank taking a Eurodollar deposit has to pay minimum reserves (subject to some exceptions). This has meant that the German banks' Eurodealings have mainly been done out of Luxembourg or London.[36]

1.6.2. The foreign exchange market in Germany has two parts: the daily official "fixing" and the normal market. The daily fixing takes place at Frankfurt at 12:45 P.M. with an officially designated broker in the chair. The broker in charge in Frankfurt establishes the rates on the basis of the orders communicated to him orally or over the telephone by the brokers operating in the Frankfurt Bourse, and the other bourses in Berlin, Düsseldorf, Hamburg, and Munich. If the orders do not balance out, the exchange rate is changed until they do, or until the Bundesbank intervenes to absorb or supply the balance.[37]

1.6.3.   The bulk of German foreign exchange activity, though, as in other countries, is carried out by telephone and telex. The German banking system has about 6,000 banks, but of these 5,000 are small cooperatives. Of the rest perhaps 100 trade actively in the foreign exchange market. They are headed by the three big universal banks—Deutsche, Dresdner and Commerz—the two large Bavarian regional banks, and other regional banks, notably various *Landesbanks* and *Girozentrale.* (The *Landesbanks* are central banks for a province, or *Land; Girozentrale* are central banks for groups of savings banks. In many cases—such as the Westdeutsche Landesbank Girozentral—the two have merged together.)

1.6.4.   There are no measures of the size of the market (cf. Section 2), but the Bundesbank does give statistics on its own activity. In its annual report for 1981 it stated that its turnover in foreign exchange (spot deals for foreign currency against DMK) was DMK 63.4 billion in 1980 (compared with DMK 60.5 billion in 1979) and that it had done 6,178 deals; in addition it did 620 cross deals (foreign currency against foreign currency) totaling DMK 4.5 billion equivalent. Forward deals done to manage domestic liquidity (see Chapter 5) totaled DMK 31.2 billion.[38] Much of the Bundesbank's intervention is carried out against the U.S. dollar but its European Monetary System (EMS) intervention (see Chapter 4) is also important, as Table 1.9 shows. In this context it is worth noting that it is not entirely straightforward to assess the Bundesbank's day-to-day intervention from the weekly movement in its reserves. This is not just because reserve movements are the net balance of many factors. It is also because since January 1982 the Bundesbank has valued its reserves of foreign currency at "the lower of cost or market value." Since some US$ reserves were in the past acquired at DMK 1.73 per US$, this is the rate currently applied. Hence if the Bundesbank sells or buys $100 million, its reserves will be shown as changing by DMK 173 million rather than, say, the DMK 220 million actually involved if the deal were done at DMK 2.20.[39] The Bundesbank's overall attitude to intervention can perhaps best be gleaned from a comment in its 1981 *Annual Report:* "The experience gained in 1980 demonstrates that in the final analysis interventions in the foreign exchange market are just as powerless against interest-rate induced capital movements . . . as against one-sided market expectations, such as were evident for years in the case of the DMK . . ." (p. 60)

1.6.5.   Often in the past the Bundesbank has imposed various controls designed to prevent the inflow of foreign currency. They have included reserve requirements on nonresidents' deposits, bans on foreigners' purchases of Ger-

TABLE 1.9.   Changes in the Net External Position of the Bundesbank Due to Interventions in the Foreign Exchange Market and Other Foreign Exchange Movements.[a]

DM billion

| | | Caused by | | |
| | | Interventions | | |
Period	Changes in the net external position, total	in the Deutsche Mark/ dollar market 1	in the European narrower margins arrangement or EMS 2	other foreign exchange movements 3
1979, total	− 5.1	+ 7.3	+ 8.2	− 20.6
1980				
January–April 8 Strong rise in the U.S. dollar	− 14.4	− 15.4	− 3.9	+ 4.9
April 9–July 9 World-wide fall in the U.S. dollar	+ 0.5	+ 6.6	+ 0.1	− 6.2
July 10–November 7 Renewed rise in the U.S. dollar	− 10.6	− 5.9	− 6.6	+ 1.9
November 10–end-December Recovery of the Deutsche Mark in the EMS after lowering of interest rates in France	− 2.6	− 3.6	− 0.1	+ 1.1
1980, total	− 27.1	− 18.3	− 10.5	+ 1.7
1981				
January–February 11 Further strengthening of the U.S. dollar	− 3.3	− 3.0	− 1.2	+ 0.9
February 12–end-March Decline in the U.S. dollar	+ 6.5	− 2.1	+ 5.8	+ 2.8

[a] Excluding changes due to valuation adjustments. Recorded according to the date on which the transaction was concluded and not according to the value date or the date of the accounting entry; these figures therefore do not correspond to those of the balance of payments.—1 Interventions in U.S. dollars by the Bundesbank for its own and U.S. accounts and in Deutsche Mark by the Federal Reserve Bank of New York.—2 Including intramarginal interventions.—3 Including conversions of foreign Deutsche Mark bonds and certain other external loans through the Bundesbank; also including net liquidity swaps with domestic banks that were not settled within the periods selected.

SOURCE: Reproduced from *Deutsche Bundesbank Annual Report,* 1980, p. 59.

man securities, and so forth. But in general the foreign exchange market has not been hindered by exchange controls (except the prudential and liquidity controls described in Chapter 3). Banks have been free to trade as they wish in foreign currency and precious metals. As the comment from its 1981 *Annual Report* quoted above suggests, the Bundesbank has learned from bitter experience that it is hard to control market forces.

1.6.6. It is time to turn to the German money market, which is large and relatively sophisticated. It does not have quite the range of paper available in the United States or the United Kingdom. Certificates of deposit have been forbidden by the Bundesbank, and the Treasury bill market is hampered by the fact that bills are usually held to maturity. Hence "secondary" market trading (i.e., in outstanding rather than newly issued bills) is very limited. But the market deals extensively in "clean" term deposits (i.e., unsecured placements). In this it resembles U.K. or Euromarket practice rather than that of the U.S. or French domestic markets which is to emphasize secured term lending.

1.6.7. Various kinds of deposit are dealt. *Tagesgeld* is money lent overnight and repaid automatically the next day. It is the equivalent of Fed funds or overnight money. *Tägliches Geld* is money lent out and repayable at one day's notice. It can be thought of as one-day call money. The main market in short-date money, though, is *Tagesgeld bis auf weiteres.* This is money which is to be repaid on the same day that it is called. (Normally the call is made by, say, 11:00 A.M. for same-day repayment.)[40] It can be thought of as the equivalent of call money in the U.K. discount market. Occasionally banks deal in *Terminierte Tagesgeld*, which is fixed-term money for less than a month (usually five or 10 days) or *Terminiertes Tägliches Geld* which is the equivalent of *Tägliches Geld* but with longer notice.[41] But these are rather unusual. It is *Tagesgeld bis auf weiteres* that counts in the short-date market.

1.6.8. Term money (*Termingeld*) is dealt in the normal monthly periods. Over the one-year period, a lender is quite likely to be funding himself from the proceeds of bond issues, so a taker of one-year money would probably be charged the one-year bond rate plus a margin. It is worth noting that the German money market, like other domestic European markets, deals on the basis of a 360/360-day year, whereas the United States generally uses 365/360 and the United Kingdom a 365/365-day year (see Chapter 11 for details).

1.6.9. Money market paper is normally traded with the Bundesbank rather than among banks, so there is hardly any secondary market. It can be split into "intervention" paper, public paper, and private paper. "Intervention" paper consists of Treasury bills or Treasury discount bonds (bonds issued at a discount rather than bearing interest). It is issued by the government to the Bundesbank on request, for use in open market policy. The reason for its use is that the government rarely issues Treasury bills for its own account: it has not done

TABLE 1.10.   German Public Sector Debt and Its Characteristics: September 1981 (in DMK).

Debt	Amount
Loans from Bundesbank	529
Discount treasury bonds (*Unverzinsliche Schatzanweisungen*)[a]	10,312
Medium-term notes (*Kassenobligationen*)[b]	13,619
Federal bonds (*Bundesobligationen*)[c]	17,418
Federal savings bonds (*Bundesschatzbrief*)[d]	14,529
Federal loans (*Bundesanleihen*)[e]	55,665
Loans from banks[f]	359,207
Loans from social security funds	10,785
Other	39,901
Total	521,965

[a] *Unverzinsliche Schatzanweisungen* (*U-Schätze*) are issued for 6, 12, 18, or 24 months at a discount. Issued in amounts of DMK 110,000 and upward in steps of DMK 10,000.

[b] *Kassenobligationen* are issued in amounts of DMK 5,000 and upward (usually larger) for three to four years in interest-bearing form, mainly to banks and other large investors.

[c] *Bundesobligationen* are issued in amounts of DMK 100 upward for up to five years, only to private German individuals; sales to foreigners not allowed. Interest bearing.

[d] *Bundesschatzbrief* are issued in amounts of DMK 100 (Type A) or DMK 50 (Type B) and upward for six (Type A) or seven (Type B) years to private German individuals; foreigners excluded. Interest bearing.

[e] *Bundesanleihen* are issued in amounts of DMK 100 and upward for up to 12 years without restrictions. Interest bearing.

[f] Mainly *Schuldscheindarlehen*, interest-bearing loans against borrower's note which can be resold in secondary market, but normally only once or twice. Normal market minimum amount is DMK 500,000. Maturity: 1–5 years. Includes loans from abroad.

SOURCES: *Deutsche Bundesbank Monthly Report*, January 1982, Statistical Section VII, Table 8. Informationsdienst für Bundeswertpapiere, *Handmappe über Bundeswertpapiere*, Frankfurt, March 1981. P. Ganschinietz, "The Attractions of Schuldscheindarlehen," *Euromoney*, November 1978.

so since 1969. Its only outstanding short-term paper, as of September 1981, was DMK 10.3 billion of Treasury discount bonds[42] of which a large amount (the "N" paper) must be held to maturity. (At the end of 1980 the total of discount bonds outstanding was DMK 5.96 billion of which DMK 4.84 billion was "N" paper.)[43]

1.6.10.   The vast bulk of Government borrowing is through medium-term *Schuldscheindarlehen* (see Table 1.10 and 11.9.7) which are not easily tradable on a day-to-day basis as transferability is restricted. This explains the Bundesbank's need for "intervention" paper to be created so that it can carry out open market operations. It is worth noting that by law the federal government is not allowed to spend the cash it receives from issuing intervention paper to the Bundesbank. It must retain the proceeds to redeem the paper at maturity.[44]

1.6.11. There is a limit of DMK 16 billion on the total intervention paper outstanding. But the Bundesbank also deals in private paper. Private paper includes normal bills of exchange and also paper drawn under the scheme operated by the export credit body, AKA. To be used in open market operations, bills must be "eligible": the bill must be backed by three parties known to be solvent; it must mature within three months of the date of purchase; and it must be a good trade bill.

1.6.12. Now that we have looked at what is traded in the German money market, we need to see how the Bundesbank controls the market. We look first at the techniques, then later at how they have evolved. In order of current psychological importance to the market, the Bundesbank's main techniques are the Lombard or Special Lombard credit, repurchase agreements, and discounting of bills. Other important policy instruments are minimum reserve requirements and rediscount quotas.

1.6.13. The Special Lombard facility is a loan by the Bundesbank secured on eligible collateral. The ordinary Lombard facility is a similar loan, granted at the Bundesbank's official Lombard rate, which is usually 1% or 1½% above the official discount rate. From February 1981 to May 1982, the Lombard facility was suspended. The Special Lombard facility which replaced it was identical except that the Bundesbank retained total freedom to decide whether or not to lend and at what rate. While the discount rate was kept at 7½% during 1981, the Special Lombard rate varied between 10½% and 12%. Effectively it was a penal rate: when it was first introduced the shock to the market drove call money up to 20 to 30%. It was withdrawn in May 1982.

1.6.14. The Bundesbank makes repurchase agreements with the banks quite often when it needs to adjust money market conditions, but not nearly as often as the Federal Reserve does and usually for much longer periods. During 1980, repurchase agreements for bonds were made seven times (none were made for bills). They were done for periods of between 25 and 45 days.[45] The Bundesbank does seem to be using the repurchase technique more frequently, though. On occasion in early 1982, two or three repurchase agreements were outstanding at the same time, for overlapping periods.

1.6.15. The classical instrument of monetary policy in Germany (as in other countries) has been the discounting of eligible bills. For various reasons discounting has become less important for day-to-day operations. But it is still the main method of providing for long-term growth in reserves. Unlike most central banks, the Bundesbank sets a limit on the use that banks can make of the discount facility. This is called the rediscount quota. The Bundesbank varies this according to its view of market conditions. Hence in 1980 the quota was lifted three times, by a total of DMK 10 billion, but the expansion in 1981 was much less, DMK 3 billion. By the end of November the total quota for all banks was DMK 46.5 billion; it was nearly 100% utilized.[46] In addition, the

TABLE 1.11.   German Reserve Requirements.

Deposits	Domestic Liabilities	Foreign Liabilities
Sight deposits	11.25%	11.25%
Term deposits	7.95%	7.95%
Savings deposits	5%	5%

NOTE: For banks with deposits over DMK 100,000.

Bundesbank discounts bills indirectly: it buys them from Privatdiskont AG, which has bought bills in the market. The benefit to the banks of dealing indirectly like this is that they don't use up their rediscount quota. In 1980 the Bundesbank bought DMK 10.8 billion of bills from the market in this way.[47]

1.6.16.   The other main instrument used by the Bundesbank is reserve requirements. These are varied much more often than in the United States or the United Kingdom (which does not use them at all as an instrument of policy). They were changed twice in 1980 and once in 1981. Separate reserve requirements are applicable on liabilities to foreigners. (They have been as high as 40%, and 60% on marginal increases, but are now the same as domestic requirements.) See Table 1.11 for the current levels.

1.6.17.   The reserve requirements are governed by the Anweisung der Deutschen Bundesbank über Mindestreserven, often referred to as the AMR.[48] The AMR lays down what reserve ratios are to be applied to the monthly average of reservable liabilities from the 16th of one month to the 15th of the next. But to reduce the work load the Bundesbank allows banks to calculate their liabilities from those outstanding on the 23rd and last day of the preceding month and on the 7th and 15th of the current month. (It has the power to order a bank to calculate the full monthly average if it suspects that the bank has been "window-dressing" the figures.) Reserves held are calculated as the daily average of the current month. So by the 15th of the month a bank will usually know what its reserve requirement is, and will be able to build up or run down its reserves for the rest of the month.[49]

1.6.18.   The use of these instruments by the Bundesbank has changed over time. In 1969, when speculative inflows from abroad started to have a serious impact on monetary policy, the Bundesbank really had only three instruments: interest rates on its discount or Lombard loans, minimum reserve requirements, and rediscount quotas. Since then open market operations, repurchase agreements, currency swaps, and the Special Lombard facility have been introduced. Apart from a limited range of instruments, the Bundesbank's other main problem until 1973 was its commitment to a fixed exchange rate. Massive intervention produced very large increases in the money supply. (See Chapter

TABLE 1.12. Main Changes in Methods of Monetary Policy in Germany.

Date	Change
1958	Introduction of dollar/mark swaps to influence capital movements.
1967	Open market transactions in medium- and long-term securities begun.
1970–1973	Rediscount quotas cut from approximately DMK 20 billion to DMK 6 billion.
1973	June. Repurchase agreements for bills introduced. November Special Lombard credits introduced.
1979	May. Bundesbank announces it is prepared on occasion to buy back "N" paper before maturity. Repurchase agreements introduced for securities (as well as bills—see June 1973). Extensive use of foreign exchange swaps for liquidity management introduced. August. Lombard credit availability restricted by linking it to rediscount quotas.
1981	February. Lombard credit suspended. Special Lombard facility introduced.

5 for a discussion of this problem.) In fact, from 1967 to March 1973 the total growth of M1 can be attributed to inflows from abroad.[50] These showed up in "free liquid reserves" in the banking system which the Bundesbank then had to try to sterilize. Since 1973 this problem has generally been less serious, which has meant that open market operations and other policy changes can be made to bite faster as the banking system is no longer always awash with liquidity. See Table 1.12.

1.6.19. Since 1973 the Bundesbank has been able to maintain a tighter control. The rundown in free liquid reserves has meant that it can control the expansion of the system by controlling minimum reserve requirements and rediscount quotas. Short-term management can be carried out by repurchase agreements, foreign exchange swaps (which have the benefit that large sums can be shifted inconspicuously into or out of deutsche marks), and the Lombard and Special Lombard facility.

SECTION 7. FRANCE

1.7.1. The French government has traditionally wanted to protect the franc while building up Paris' role as an international financial center. Hence, Paris has been almost the exact opposite of Frankfurt. For instance, there is a tight network of exchange controls. But because reserve requirements are applied by currency and not by residence status (as in Germany), Paris is an important Eurocenter. The traditional link between France and the Arab world in the past has brought a good deal of Arab money to Paris.

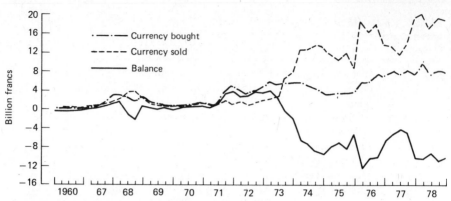

FIGURE 1.3. French Banks' Forward Positions vis-à-vis Residents. Source: J. Mathis, "L'évolution des mouvements de capitaux à court terme ... 1967–78," *Économie et prévision* no. 47, Ministère De L'Économie, Paris, 1981.

1.7.2.   The foreign exchange market consists mainly of 15 or so major banks, with other banks dealing on an occasional basis. There are also a number of domestic and international brokers. As in Germany, there is a daily "fix" at the Paris Bourse, at which prices are set by an auction system (*à la criée*). If necessary, the Banque de France will intervene at the fix to stabilize a rate. Prices are recorded by a representative of the Chambre Syndicale des Agents de Change de Paris. Apart from the fix, the market is the normal telephone and telex market. Because exchange controls only restrict positions against the French franc, French banks can deal in US$/DMK or US$/£STG quite freely. In fact, the volume of such cross business is much larger than the volume against the French franc.

1.7.3.   The exchange control system dominates French franc business. (For example, Figure 1.3 shows that forward exchange business was very small until restrictions were eased in 1973 through 1974). Lending of French francs to nonresidents is forbidden, which cuts the supply of funds to the Eurofranc market and prevents speculators from borrowing francs to sell them off. Residents are not allowed to hold foreign currency or to buy forward for imports more than one or two months ahead (depending on the situation). They must surrender foreign currency receipts within a short time limit. Banks have to balance spot and forward exchange positions against the French franc on a daily basis. All these tight controls do not prevent the French franc from being devalued or revalued: they simply control the speed at which it happens.

1.7.4.   But their effectiveness is shown by the fact that there are two forward markets for French francs, one external and one internal. For example, in the middle of August 1981, when there were fears of a French devaluation, a London bank was quoting 700/900 for the one-month swap—a signifi-

FIGURE 1.4. Banks' Foreign Currency Positions vis-à-vis the Banque de France. Source: Same as for Figure 1.3.

cant dollar premium against the franc—while a French bank in Paris quoted 75/55—a marginal dollar discount.

1.7.5. The Banque de France is an important participant in the market in other ways. For example it is heavily involved in the foreign exchange business arising from oil payments, which probably account for about 40% of total activity,[51] and which the Banque largely handles. Since the third quarter of 1968, as Figure 1.4 shows, it has done swaps with the commercial banks to raise foreign currency from them when the franc is weak (as when these swaps were begun in 1968 and 1969) and to lend them currency when the franc is strong (as in 1975).[52] This hides changes in France's official reserves. More recent figures, unfortunately, have not been published, but the practice probably continues. Also, the Banque keeps a very tight grip on the domestic money market, to which we now turn.

1.7.6. There is an official list of traders in the money market: banks, financial establishments, public or semipublic financial institutions, stockbrokers, unit and investment trusts, insurance companies, and provident and mutual funds. But many of the major industrial groups also own small banks or financial institutions and so have indirect access. There are seven discount houses (*maisons de réescompte*) of which six are owned by banks, operating similarly to the U.K. discount houses. Also there are about 20 money brokers (*courtiers*), of which about a dozen specialize in the domestic money market. The largest single trader in the market, apart from the Banque de France, is the official Caisse des Dépôts et Consignations (CDC). This gathers the funds of the savings banks and various retirement and pension funds, as well as certain other funds. It is the largest single lender in the day-to-day market (*marché au jour le jour*) and in 1979 averaged about 14% of the day-to-day market. It is very closely supervised by the Banque. Its dealings in the day-to-day market rarely differ from the official rate by more than ⅛%. (As a quid pro quo, it benefits by not having to keep reserves at the Banque.)[53] Other major lenders include the Crédit Agricole, which tends to lend more in the term market, and the Caisse Nationale de L'Energie, which in 1979 averaged about 7.7% of day-to-day money market operations.[54] Borrowers include medium- and long-term credit banks, specialized financial institutions, and the Banque Française du Commerce Extérieur (BFCE). Most commercial and investment banks (*banques d'affaires*) are normally two-way traders in the market.

1.7.7.   Most money market business is secured against paper, as it is in the United States, but not in Germany or the United Kingdom. The share of "clean" (*en blanc*) interbank deposits is very small. Business is done on the basis of *pensions*—repurchase agreements. Occasionally outright sales of paper are done, but these together with other unsecured lendings only account for perhaps 10% to 15% of business, compared with 80% done through *pensions*.[55] One reason for this is that the bulk of normal domestic banking involves the discounting of paper, rather than overdraft or other kinds of lending.

1.7.8.   The paper dealt in the money market can be of three types: public, private (first category), and private (second category). Public paper consists of Treasury bills, medium-term paper issued by the Credit Foncier, Credit National, and the BFCE, normally for two to seven years, and certain other paper. First category private paper consists of certain types of foreign trade finance, credits guaranteed by ONIC and CEPME (specialized credit institutions), and certain other credits, providing that the Banque de France has added them to the list of eligible paper. All other paper is second category. This covers normal private commercial bills, paper related to refinancing of installment sales, bills negotiable to order (*billets à ordre négociable*—see 1.7.9), and other private paper.[56] Intervention by the Banque is only conducted against public and first category private paper. Second category private paper is the basis for normal interbank trading; very occasionally, a severe shortage of first-category paper will induce the Banque to use second category paper for its money market lending.

1.7.9.   A feature worth noting is an important new money market instrument, the *billet à ordre négociable* or B.O.N. This is a negotiable instrument, introduced in May 1979. By July 1981 the market had grown to FFR 20 billion[57] (which compares with a total of FFR 80 billion of treasury bills outstanding at the end of 1980).[58] The B.O.N. was invented to overcome certain weaknesses in the French money market system, notably the *pension* or repurchase deal. The U.S. system of repurchase agreements works easily because it depends on electronic transfer of the underlying securities. They go through the CPD (Commission of Public Debt) wire transfer system operated by the Federal Reserve.[59] But in France there is no such system. The custom is for the bank which has sold securities (the borrower) in the repurchase to hold the securities physically, "earmarked" (*sous dossier*) in the name of the lender. This means that the lender finds it difficult to unwind the repurchase before maturity by reselling the securities to borrow on them. They are still in the vaults of the bank it lent to originally.

1.7.10. So a group of banks got together to create the B.O.N. This is effectively the French equivalent of a banker's acceptance, drawn by a bank on itself. The issuing bank draws a bill of the required maturity to the order of the buyer of the bill. Bills drawn payable to bearer are made out at the same time for the amounts of interest due. If the buyer of the bill later decides he needs cash, he simply sells the bill (and the interest-amount bills) in the market, after endorsing it. The paper involved is mainly medium term. A survey in March 1980 showed FFR 0.5 billion of B.O.N. issued for up to one year, FFR 15.0 billion for one to five years, and FFR 4.5 billion for more than five years. The secondary market volume was estimated at only FFR 1 billion, and it remains to be seen whether the market will become a truly liquid one.[60]

1.7.11. The development of the B.O.N. may help improve the flexibility of the market, which suffers from the tight control of the Banque de France (see 1.7.12). It will provide another type of paper to trade in. The market in public paper (mainly Treasury bills) is distorted by the so-called "circuit" system of Treasury financing. The classic example is the Caisse des Dépôts et Consignations. The CDC can (with only slight exaggeration) be thought of as a nationwide banking network owned by the Treasury and funneling a large part of its cash to the Treasury. Two Frenchmen in three have an account with one arm or another of the CDC.[61] It supplied 15% of the Treasury's resources in 1979, compared with 4.4% from the Banque de France and 17.9% from domestic bond issues.[62] Its role in the Treasury bill market is enormous. At the end of 1979, the CDC held 47% of Treasury bills outstanding. On average in that year it took 42% of new issues of Treasury bills.[63] As a result of this "circuit," the market for French public sector debt is smaller, and hence narrower than that in the United States or the United Kingdom or even Germany (See Table 1.13).[64]

1.7.12. The Banque de France has an all-pervasive influence in the money market. For example, during 1978, the banking system had a net financing requirement of an estimated FFR 200 billion, of which the Banque supplied FFR 92 billion.[65] Also, as we saw earlier, the CDC and other state financial institutions are very important traders in the money market. And they trade under the close supervision of the Banque. At a guess, the Banque de France probably controls two-thirds of the market on a daily basis, directly or indirectly.

TABLE 1.13. Public Sector
Debt (as Percentage of GNP).

Country	Percent
United Kingdom	51.6
United States	37.1
Japan	26.5
Germany	13.7
France	7.8

The normal daily pattern is that the market opens around 8:00 A.M., with fairly active trading until about 9:00 A.M., when the Banque announces its day-to-day money market intervention rate. For the remainder of the day, trading will normally take place within ⅛ to ¼% of this rate. The only exception is makeup day, when movements of "as much as 3%," to quote one trader, can be seen.

1.7.13. The Banque also intervenes on a day-to-day basis by means of *pensions* (repurchase agreements) with the discount houses. But the authorities prefer to indicate monetary policy by means of the support given at regular auctions (*appels d'offres*), carried out normally on the 21st of each month, or when the situation requires it. (This gives them the initiative. Pensions against public paper are done at the initiative of the banks.) At these auctions the Banque de France will either make a firm purchase of the paper offered or make repurchase agreements, normally for one month. (The period varies depending on the state of the market.)[66]

1.7.14. The regular operations on the 21st of the month are designed to coincide with the start of a new reserve period. Reserves must be held from the 21st of a month to the 20th of the next, and are calculated from the levels of the last day of the previous month. They must reach an average level over the month, so that large day-to-day changes need not affect a bank's overall reserve targeting.[67] Hence shortfalls or surpluses in the market can easily be absorbed without affecting rates, simply by allowing offsetting movements in reserves. Banks tend to build up reserves when rates are low (since the cost of holding interest-free reserves then is low) and run them down when rates are high. The exception, of course, is the last day of the reserve period, the 20th, when last-minute adjustments have to be made to reach the target. But even on makeup day, the strict control exercised by the Banque means that rates do not move much.

1.7.15. Reserve requirements as of May 21, 1981 were 5.5% on domestic sight deposits, 1% on domestic "quasimoney" (time and savings deposits), and nil on sight and quasimoney from abroad. There is also a 1.75% reserve requirement on lending, plus a system of supplementary penalty reserves on lendings in excess of the "norms." The Banque de France first introduced credit ceilings (*encadrement*) in 1957, for two years, then again from 1963 to 1967, and from 1968 to 1970. The present phase, dating from 1972, is the longest single period of credit ceilings since the period just after the war. According to this system, banks and financial establishments can only grant credits within certain norms (*normes de progression*). Since July 1973 these norms have been announced on a monthly basis, usually for a six-month period, several months ahead of the period to which they apply. Supplementary reserves are levied on banks which exceed the norms. They quickly become penal. But there is a quota system which allows banks that have not used the total of their quota to carry the difference for the next six months. The authorities also tolerate banks which exchange credits among themselves to use their quotas more effectively.[68]

1.7.16. Exemptions include credits financed by banks' own funds and bond issues, and certain priority sectors (notably exports, agriculture, energy); advances in foreign currency are also exempt. This has led to a lot of foreign currency borrowing which has to be switched into French francs. The *encadrement* system is very tightly administered, covering leasing and other finance activities as well as normal credit. It is backed up by an extensive apparatus of control (see Chapter 3).

SECTION 8.   JAPAN

1.8.1. It is a cliché in many industries that "Japan is different." But in our case, the cliché is true. The Japanese foreign exchange and money markets are different from the others talked about in this book. But, more and more, they are growing to look like their counterparts abroad. Let's begin with the differences. They can be summed up as time and culture. The Japanese market is isolated in time; there is no overlap with New York, and only an hour or two at the end of the day with Europe. The cultural differences that matter for our purposes—aside from the whole issue of business and social customs in Japan—show up in the attitude to consensus and sharing of information. The Japanese habit of working together on the basis of a shared consensus, when it spills over to dealing in foreign exchange, tends to show up in bandwagon movements as all of the market goes in one direction. Their attitude toward sharing of information shows up in the lack of confidentiality when dealing through brokers (though the Foreign Exchange Market Practices Committee announced in January 1982 that the principal of confidentiality is being adopted)[69] and in the fact that official statistics are often known to well-informed traders before they are announced.

1.8.2. Other differences in the Japanese market are (until recently) the very tight administrative control, the overwhelming dominance the US$/¥ business which accounts for perhaps 95% of deals, and the role of the trading houses.

Although their influence is perhaps declining, the trading houses play a very important role in Japan's external trade and in the foreign exchange market. The six most important trading companies controlled 50% of Japan's imports in 1974.[70] They have a worldwide network of offices and excellent information and contacts. So they are large, well-informed traders in the foreign exchange market. Large exporters (mainly cars and electronics) tend to bypass the trading houses and handle their own foreign exchange needs, while on the import side the oil companies do the same. On the banking side the market is dominated by the 13 "city" banks who handle about 80% of business with two major banks probably handling 45%.[71] As in Germany and France, there is a daily fix (at 10:00 A.M.), but the fixing is done by the city banks, each taking it in turn to fix the rate; the Bank of Japan is not involved. Foreign banks are active interbank but with a few exceptions lack the natural base of commercial customers.

1.8.3. Exchange control used to be tight in Japan. The old law, which was only replaced in 1980, made exchange control very simple. Everything was forbidden, unless specifically permitted. The new law has reversed this: everything is permitted unless forbidden. But restrictions remain. They are operated by the Ministry of Finance, with delegated powers held by the Bank of Japan and authorized banks. Japanese residents may not (without permission) have a bank account with a bank abroad, or deal in foreign exchange except through an authorized bank (which rules out financial futures markets). Nor may firms trade internationally on open account (i.e., without letters of credit, etc.) without permission.[72] Also, "administrative guidance" will still be elaborate and detailed in certain areas such as foreign exchange swaps by banks and the issue of bonds in Japan by foreigners ("samurai bonds").[73]

1.8.4. In the past, the exchange control system was used to discourage an international role for the yen. Only about 3% of Japanese imports are invoiced in yen compared with 30 to 40% invoiced in domestic currency for major European importers.[74] This has meant reliance on dollar invoicing, and to a great extent dollar financing, of imports. In 1974, as Japan's imports of oil exploded upward in value after the price increase, this caused severe problems to Japanese banks who had to pay a "Japan premium" in the Eurodollar market to raise the necessary funds. This situation, together with pressure from overseas to permit a greater international role for the yen, has led to a gradual liberalization. This has gone hand in hand with liberalization of the domestic markets (see Table 1.14). For instance, the relaxation of restrictions in March 1980 on payment of interest to official holders of "free yen" deposits (i.e., freely convertible into dollars) led to a rise in official yen deposits in Japan from $0.9 billion to $4.6 billion equivalent (though a good part of this was probably switched from the Euromarket).[75] Yen assets probably now are about 3 to 4% of total official holdings of foreign exchange.[76]

TABLE 1.14. Money Market Deregulation in Japan.

Date		Event
1978	June	Dealers in call markets instructed by Bank of Japan to change rates more often. Buyers of bills in the discount market allowed to resell them (after a one-month holding period). Bank of Japan begins open market buying of long-term government bonds on a competitive basis (previously noncompetitive system).
	October	Seven-day call money market with free rates set up.
	November	Agreement to create a one-month bill market with free rates and to liberalize three-month rates.
1979	April	All call money rates freed. Call market for up to seven days created.
	May	Nonresidents allowed access to *gensaki* market. Commercial banks allowed to issue CD's up to 25% of a bank's capital (but only three to six months' maturity allowed; ¥500 million; CD negotiable only with issuer's permission).
	October	Two-month bill rate set free.
1980	March	Interest rates paid to foreign official bodies in free yen market set free. Permission to borrow from Euroyen market.
	April	CD limit for bank issuers raised to 50% of capital.
	December	New foreign exchange law.

1.8.5. Reluctance to liberalize came largely from nervousness about the effects on the yen, which already has moved violently against the dollar in the last four or five years despite exchange controls and heavy intervention. From a rate of ¥292 per US$ at the end of 1976, the yen strengthened to a peak of ¥178.50 per US$ on October 31, 1978; a rise of 63% in under two years. Then in the next 18 months there was a sharp reversal as the US dollar's strength took the yen to 256 by April 1980—a fall of 44%. Most of the pressure came in 1979, when the Bank of Japan spent $12.5 billion defending the yen (having bought $16.7 billion to defend the dollar during 1977 and 1978). As these figures show, the scale of capital movements in and out of the yen can be large, and the Bank of Japan is often involved in heavy intervention—on days of real pressure it has been known to do $500 to $900 million in the market. This is proportionately far heavier than any intervention on the part of the Federal Reserve.

1.8.6. With all these problems, it is not surprising that the Bank of Japan has been cautious about exposing the yen to more internationalization. But it has gradually allowed more freedom. And the volume of yen business overseas has grown very sharply. Since 1977 the yen markets in London and New York have grown fast. The volume of yen business in New York in 1980 was estimated at $30.5 billion per month compared with $5.6 billion in 1977.[77] [Daily

TABLE 1.15.   Scale of Money Market at Year-End (in Trillions of ¥).

Date	Call Money	Bills Discounted	Gen-Saki	CDs	Total	Annual Turnover in Bonds (Outright)
1974	2.2	5.2	1.7	—	9.1	7.2
1975	2.3	4.4	1.8	—	8.5	12.2
1976	2.6	5.1	2.1	—	9.8	14.9
1977	2.6	6.1	3.1	—	11.8	26.0
1978	2.3	6.6	4.2	—	13.1	44.4
1979	3.5	6.3	4.0	1.8	15.6	43.9
1980 (June)	2.5	5.5	4.7	3.0	15.7	59.7 annual rate
(Dec.)	4.1	5.7	4.5	2.4	16.7	

SOURCE: "General Features of the Recent Interest Rate Changes," *Bank of Japan Economic Research Department Special Paper* no. 91, December 1980, and Daiwa Securities Co., *Introduction to Japanese Bonds, 1981,* Tokyo, 1981, p. 40.

turnover figures in Tokyo are reported by the Bank of Tokyo on its Reuters Monitor (Code BTTQ)]. The Euroyen market is estimated to have reached $12 to 13 billion by the end of 1980.[78] Since then it has probably grown faster because of the freedom given by the new exchange control law.

1.8.7.   As Table 1.15 shows, liberalization also helped the newer money markets, which were free of controls [the *gen-saki* market (repurchase market) and the CD market] to grow fast compared with the markets for call money and bills discounted. *Gen-saki* grew from 18.7% to 30% of the market, while CDs came from nil to 19% of the market by June 1980. The market which is of most international interest—apart from Euroyen—is the *gen-saki* market. The call money and discount markets are primarily domestic interbank markets, and CDs are restricted in negotiability and subject to withholding tax.[79]

1.8.8.   A *gen-saki* deal is a securities repurchase deal. The market resembles the repo market in the United States. The main borrowers are the securities houses, who use it to finance their holdings of securities. The main lenders are industrial corporations who have no access to the discount or call money markets, and nonresidents.[80] *Gen-saki* are dealt on a 365-day basis in line with domestic Japanese instruments. (See Chapter 11 for details.)

1.8.9.   So far as the other markets are concerned there are several distinctively Japanese ingredients. First, there is the structural background of the banking system. This was until recently (to Western eyes) horrifyingly overlent.[81] Much of this lending is done by the 13 city banks, traditionally closest to

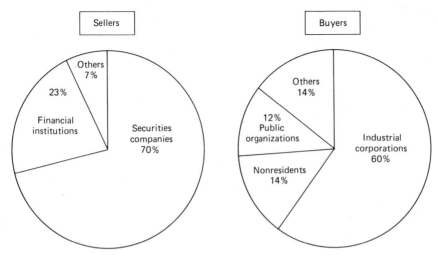

FIGURE 1.5. *Gen-Saki* Market—Major Participants. Source: The Securities Dealers Association of Japan.

the major corporate borrowers. Hence the city banks are almost permanent takers in the money market, while the rural banks, with restricted lending opportunities, are permanent lenders. In 1975, for instance, city banks borrowed 85% of all call money, while regional and trust banks, credit associations and cooperatives, and insurance companies lend 67% of the total.[82] The types of deals done in the call market are: (1) half-day loan, repayable on the same day; (2) overnight loan, repayable next day; and (3) unconditional loan, term call money up to seven days, repayable on one day's notice (minimum maturity two days). Unconditional call money is by far the most important, effectively accounting for 100% of the market. Most deals are done through call loan money brokers.[83] As in France, the call money rate is fixed about 9:00 A.M. by the brokers (after consulting the bank of Japan) and hardly varies during the day.

1.8.10. The bill discount market started in the 1900s at the same time as the call money market, but was unimportant until May 1971 when a market for two- and three-month bills was set up. The Bank of Japan first intervened in the market in June 1972.[84] Eligible bills include (1) prime commercial and industrial bills (including "single-name" bills) and foreign trade bills; and (2) drafts drawn against these bills and acting essentially as depository receipts for the underlying bills. (In practice the latter method is used for convenience.) Bills up to four months are dealt.[85]

1.8.11. The Bank of Japan intervenes in the bill market from time to time, but because of their permanent dependence on the Bank of Japan for funds the

TABLE 1.16. Japanese Government Bond Issue: Amounts Outstanding at Year-End (in Billions of ¥).

Year	Government Bonds
1955	344
1960	311
1965	310
1970	3191
1974	8404
1975	13295
1976	20023
1977	29534
1978	39612
1979	53247
1980	67210

SOURCES: Bank of Japan, *The Japanese Financial System*, Tokyo, 1978, and Daiwa Securities, *Introduction to Japanese Bonds, 1981*, Tokyo, 1981.

city banks are very responsive to official wishes and the volume of intervention does not have to be large. Reserve requirements are not a particularly important policy tool, either. The authorities control developments in other ways, notably the "window guidance" system for controling lending. This has been in operation more or less continuously since 1964, since even when not formally setting guidelines, the Bank of Japan "advises" city banks on their lending policy.[86] The mechanics are roughly this. The Bank of Japan asks the city banks how much they expect to lend in the coming quarter. It fixes an aggregate limit. It distributes the total among the banks, and tells them how much they can lend in the next quarter. Then it applies guidelines to other financial institutions.[87]

1.8.12.   Open market operations may in future become more important. First, "window guidance" tends to freeze the existing banking structure, and hinders competitive banking. Second, the volume of government debt outstanding is growing very fast. Until 1965, the Japanese government obeyed the so-called Dodge Line. (Mr. Dodge was an American banker who decreed, during the reconstruction period after the war, that the government should aim for a balanced budget.) So the government bond market was very thin—trading was actually suspended during 1962 through 1965. Since then outstanding bond issues have grown steadily, and since the 1974 oil crisis, the growth has been explosive. In this respect, as in many others, the Japanese markets are starting to look more like their Western counterparts. (See Table 1.16.)

SECTION 9. SWITZERLAND

1.9.1. Switzerland has a tradition of sophistication in foreign exchange and money market operations going back for generations. The domestic economy is small, but the country serves as a traditional haven for overseas investors and, in recent years, for the treasury operations of many multinational corporations. Because of its unique reputation, Switzerland has attracted huge amounts of overseas funds which are largely invested in fiduciary deposits managed by the Swiss banks. It is quite common for the funds managed by a Swiss bank to be as large as, or larger than, its published balance sheet total. The volume of fiduciary funds continues to grow. In 1978 they totalled SFR 54 billion; by the end of March 1981 they stood at SFR 150 billion (compared with SFR 490 billion for the entire Swiss banking system's published balance sheets). These funds are dealt by the Swiss banks in their own name, to preserve secrecy for the client. It is thought that the five largest Swiss banks handle about one-third of the fiduciary business, with foreign banks in Switzerland handling a further third, and the balance spread over the private and cantonal banks.

1.9.2. Apart from the special case of fiduciary deposits, Switzerland's growth as a banking center has been partly held back by the harsh exchange controls the Swiss National Bank had to impose to prevent the Swiss franc from rising during the 1960s and 1970s. In many ways the Swiss banking environment became quite difficult. The growth of internationalization in London and New York in the 1970s was not paralleled in Switzerland; the total number of branches and subsidiaries of foreign banks in Switzerland was unchanged between 1970 and 1980.

1.9.3. At the time of this writing, Swiss exchange controls are liberal. During 1977 through 1979, though, they were draconian. (As an indication, Table 1.17 shows a summary of the state of exchange control in December, 1977.) Any sustained rise in the Swiss franc would probably cause some of these controls to be reimposed. For the limited scale of the Swiss economy, in relation to the volume of international funds seeking a home in Swiss francs, means that the Swiss National Bank's control of the money supply is swamped by currency inflows. This can be vividly seen in Figure 5.4, which shows the overwhelming effect of currency inflows during 1977 and 1978.

1.9.4. These external currency flows have dominated the Swiss National Bank's operations in recent years. In fact, the bank's domestic open market operations have been negligible. The whole of the growth in the Swiss money supply during the last 30 years is due not to the central bank's supply of reserves (as in the United States or the United Kingdom, for example) but to external flows, as can be seen from Table 1.18. In January 1982, though, the bank announced that it would aim in future to build up its domestic operations. It

TABLE 1.17.   Summary of Swiss Exchange Controls as of December 31, 1977.

1. Borrowing from nonresidents in SFR or foreign currencies subject to permission, rarely granted.
2. Interest payment on SFR deposits banned; compulsory commission ("negative interest") of 10% per quarter on net increases after October 31, 1974 in nonresident-held SFR deposits.
3. Spot or forward deals over $5 million to be reported to Swiss National Bank.
4. Banks required to balance foreign exchange positions daily; short positions in foreign currencies *banned.* Forward positions to be reported monthly. Sales of SFR forward up to one month to nonresidents *banned.* Sales forward over one month limited to 40% of level on October 31, 1974.
5. Internationally active firms in Switzerland to report deals over $5 million, and to report monthly on expected transfers in following month.

SOURCE: IMF's *29th Annual Report on Exchange Restrictions,* 1978.

gave the following reasons: (1) Using foreign currency assets to support growth of the money supply made it dependent on the good will of the overseas central banks involved. (2) It would involve exchange risks unless swaps were used. (3) Swaps were inherently temporary and it would be better to use more permanent means. It said that its money market operations would use Swiss government (confederation) bonds, bonds issued by the cantons and the cantonal banks, and other easily negotiable bonds issued by Swiss banks and communes.[88]

TABLE 1.18.   Growth in Counterparts to Swiss Central Bank Money Stock; Annual Averages (in Millions of SFR).

Year	Gold	Foreign[a] Currency	Swiss Francs			Total
			Loans	Securities	Other[c]	
1950	6,179.4	297.9	123.3	41.2	− 890.1	5,751.7
1960	8,151.0	522.4	78.9	43.6	− 641.2	8,154.7
1970	11,615.5	3,418.7[b]	241.7	167.6	− 96.3	15,347.2
1975	11,892.7	10,005.3	776.5	85.8	1,191.1	23,951.4
1980	11,903.9	20,806.8	1,364.4	1,064.6	− 5,499.4	29,640.3

[a] Including swaps.

[b] Including foreign Treasury bills denominated in SFR.

[c] Government account at the SNB, bank funds that are temporarily sterilized, and other items (net).

SOURCE: *Bulletin mensuel,* Banque nationale suisse, January 1982, pp. 9–10.

NOTES

1. Quoted in I. H. Giddy, "Measuring the World Foreign Exchange Market," *Columbia Journal of World Business,* Winter 1979.

2. Ibid.

3. Ibid.

4. IMF's *IFS Yearbook 1981,* p. 49. Gold is valued at SDR 35 per ounce.

5. Giddy, "Measuring the World Foreign Exchange Market."

6. P. Revey, "Evolution and Growth of the U.S. Foreign Exchange Market," *Federal Reserve Bank of New York Quarterly Review,* Autumn 1981.

7. K.J.H. Robbie, "Socialist Banks and the Origins of the Eurocurrency Markets," *Moscow Narodny Bank Quarterly Review,* Winter 1975/6.

8. Ibid.

9. See I. H. Giddy and G. Dufey, *Measuring the Size of the Eurocurrency Market,* Report no. 7636, Center for Mathematical Studies in Business and Economics, Department of Economics, Graduate School of Business, University of Chicago, October 1976.

10. Of course stability in aggregate mismatch can hide individual problem cases. For a contrary view of mismatch, see P. R. Duncan, "When Mismatching in International Lending May Matter," *The Banker,* London, December 1981.

11. W. P. Cooke, "Developments in Cooperation Among Banking Supervisory Authorities," *Bank of England Quarterly Bulletin,* June 1981, p. 238. The Concordat includes the following principal guidelines and recommendations (Parent country or authority refers to where the parent bank is located; host country or authority refers to the country in which the branch or subsidiary of the parent bank is located.): (1) The supervision of foreign banking establishments should be the joint responsibility of host and parent authorities. (2) No foreign banking establishment should escape supervision. Supervision should be adequate as judged by both host and parent authorities. (3) The supervision of liquidity should be a prime responsibility of host authorities. (4) The supervision of solvency of foreign branches should be essentially a matter for the parent authorities. In the case of subsidiaries, while primary responsibility lies with the host authority, parent authorities should take account of the exposure of the domestic bank's foreign subsidiaries and joint ventures, because of the parent bank's moral commitment.

12. BIS's *51st Annual Report,* June 1981, p. 149.

13. Revey, "Evolution and Growth of the U.S. Foreign Exchange Market."

14. Ibid.

15. Federal Reserve Bank of New York, *Services for Central Banks, FED Points 20.*

16. *Federal Reserve Bulletin,* December 1981, Table 3.16, p. A60. On IBFs, see J. K. Walmsley, "International Banking Facilities," *The Banker,* London, February 1982. Detailed regulations are in the Federal Reserve's Regulation D.

17. *Federal Reserve Bulletin,* December 1981, Table 1.15, p. A8.

18. But RPs were included in the marginal reserve requirements imposed from October 1979 to July 1980; see T. Q. Cook and B. J. Summers (eds.), *Instruments of the Money Market,* Federal Reserve Bank of Richmond, Virginia, 1981.

19. *Federal Reserve Bulletin,* December 1981, Table 1.24, p. A16.

20. Ibid.

21. M. Stigum, *The Money Market: Myth, Reality and Practice,* Dow-Jones Irwin, 1978, p. 485.

22. *Federal Reserve Bulletin,* December 1981, Table 1.32, p. A25. See also T. Q. Cook and B. J. Summers, *Instruments of the Money Market,* pp. 94–114.

23. See T. Q. Cook and B. J. Summers, *Instruments of the Money Market,* pp. 59–72.

24. Federal Reserve Regulation A.

25. T. Q. Cook and B. J. Summers, *Instruments of the Money Market*, p. 62.

26. Ibid., p. 64.

27. Ibid.

28. *Federal Reserve Bank of New York Quarterly Review*, "Monetary Policy and Open Market Operations in 1980," pp. 63–65.

29. For an assessment, see S. H. Axilrod, "New Monetary Control Procedure: Findings and Evaluation from a Federal Reserve Study," *Federal Reserve System Bulletin*, April 1981; and S. H. Axilrod and D. E. Lindsey, "Federal Reserve System Implementation of Monetary Policy: Analytical Foundations of the New Approach," *American Economic Review*, May 1981.

30. "Money and Banking Figures: Forthcoming Changes," *Bank of England Quarterly Bulletin*," December 1981.

31. "Foreign Banks in London," *The Banker*, London, November 1981.

32. Cf. 1.3.4.

33. For a general description, see W. M. Scammell, *The London Discount Market*, Elek Books, London, 1968; M. Craig, *The Sterling Money Markets*, Gower Press, United Kingdom, 1976.

34. *Bank of England Quarterly Bulletin*, March, 1981, pp. 24–5.

35. "Monetary Control-Provisions," *Bank of England Quarterly Bulletin*, September 1981.

36. Organization for Economic Cooperation & Development, *Regulations Affecting International Banking Operations of Banks and Non-Banks in France, Germany, The Netherlands, Switzerland, the United Kingdom*, Paris, 1978, pp. 26–7.

37. See H. Lipfert, *Devisenhandel*, F. Knapp Verlag, Frankfurt, 1968, pp. 66–69.

38. *Deutsche Bundesbank Annual Report*, 1980, pp. 68–69.

39. *Deutsche Bundesbank Monthly Report*, January 1982, "The Foreign Exchange Reserves of the Bundesbank As Shown in the Weekly Statement."

40. H. E. Buschgen, *"Der deutsche Geldmarkt,"* Schriftenreihe der Österreichischen Bankwissenschaftlichen Gesellschaft, Vienna, 1969, pp. 26–7.

41. H. D. Deppe, "Geldmarkt and Geldmarktkonzepte," *Kredit und Kapital*, Duncker and Humblot, Berlin, vol. 3, 1980.

42. *Deutsche Bundesbank Monthly Report*, Statistical Section VII, Table 8, January 1982.

43. *Deutsche Bundesbank Annual Report*, 1980, p. 73.

44. There is a good discussion of German money market operations in S. F. Frowen, A. Courakis, and M. H. Miller (eds.), *Monetary Policy and Economic Activity in West Germany*, John Wiley & Sons, New York, 1977.

45. *Deutsche Bundesbank Annual Report*, 1980, p. 71.

46. *Deutsche Bundesbank Monthly Report*, January 1982, Statistical Section II, Table 1b.

47. *Deutsche Bundesbank Annual Report*, 1980, p. 71.

48. It is published annually in the Bundesbank's annual report but unfortunately only in the German version.

49. AMR paragraphs 7, 8, 9. See also H. Bockelmann, "Die Zinsbildung am Geldmarkt," *Kredit und Kapital*, Duncker and Humblot, Berlin, vol. 3, 1980, pp. 339–347.

50. See H. Schlesinger, "Die Geldpolitik der Deutschen Bundesbank, 1967–77," *Kredit und Kapital*, Duncker and Humblot, Berlin, vol. 1, 1978, pp. 3–27.

51. Private estimate.

52. J. Mathis, "L'évolution des mouvements de capitaux à court terme entre la France et l'extérieur de 1967 à 1978," *Economie et prévision no. 47*, Ministère de l'Economie, Paris, 1981.

53. D. Marteau and E. de la Chaise, *Le marché monétaire et la gestion de trésorerie des banques*, Dunod, Paris 1981, pp. 8–9.
54. Ibid., pp. 10–11, 14.
55. Ibid., p. 73.
56. Ibid., pp. 69–70.
57. "Le B.O.N. ou billet à ordre négociable sur le marché monétaire," *Revue banque*, Paris, July/August 1981, p. 829.
58. Banque de France, *Compte rendu*, March 1981, p. 67.
59. See T. Q. Cook and B. J. Summers, *Instruments of the Money Market, p. 54.*
60. "Le B.O.N.", *Revue banque*, Paris, July/August 1981, pp. 832–4.
61. A. Coutière, *"Le systeme monétaire français,"* Editions Economica, Paris 1981, p. 62.
62. Ibid., p. 30.
63. D. Marteau and E. de La Chaise, *Le marché monétaire*, pp. 8–9.
64. A. Coutière, *"Le systeme monétaire français,"* p. 29.
65. D. Marteau and E. de La Chaise, *Le marché monétaire*, p. 71.
66. Banque de France, *Compte rendu*, March 1981, p. A5.
67. D. Marteau and E. de La Chaise, *Le marché monétaire*, pp. 164–5.
68. Ibid., pp. 49–52.
69. According to a report on the Reuters Monitor.
70. A. Helou, "Sogo Shoshas and Japan's Foreign Economic Relations," *Journal of World Trade Law*, United Kingdom, May/June 1979.
71. M. Borsuk, "The Theory of Myopic Momentum," *Euromoney*, August 1980.
72. H. Fukui, *Commentary on the Amendment of the Foreign Exchange and Foreign Trade Control Law*, Legal Division of the International Finance Bureau of the Ministry of Finance, Tokyo, March 1980.
73. There is a general discussion in "Japanese Exchange Control Liberalization and the Yen," *World Financial Markets*, Morgan Guaranty Trust Co. of New York, March 1981.
74. Ibid. and S. Carse, J. Williamson and G. E. Wood, *The Financing Procedures of British Foreign Trade*, Cambridge University Press, 1980.
75. BIS's *51st Annual Report*, June 1981, p. 147.
76. IMF's *Annual Report*, 1981, p. 67.
77. Federal Reserve Bank of New York Survey, April 1980.
78. "Japanese Exchange Control Liberalization and the Yen," *World Financial Markets*, Morgan Guaranty Trust Co. of New York, 1981, p. 11.
79. Nomura Securities International Inc., *What is Gen-saki?*, New York, February 1980.
80. Nomura Securities Co. Ltd., *Gen-saki: An Alternative Way of Cash Management*, London, September 1981.
81. See for example A. Prindl, *Japanese Finance*, John Wiley, New York, 1981, pp. 28–9, 38–9.
82. Bank of Japan, *The Japanese Financial System*, Tokyo, 1978, p. 119.
83. Ibid., pp. 118–121.
84. Ibid., p. 116.
85. Ibid., p. 122.
86. H. Eguchi and K. Hamadi, "Banking Behavior under Constraints," *Japanese Economic Studies*, M. E. Sharpe Inc., New York, Winter 1977/8.
87. B. Kure, "Window Guidance of the Bank of Japan," *Japanese Economic Studies*, Winter 1977/8.
88. *Bulletin mensuel*, Banque nationale suisse, January 1982, pp. 9–10.

THE SYSTEM

2

This chapter explains how the system that connects the markets we saw in Chapter 1 came into being. It begins by describing some of the key problems with which any international monetary system has to cope. Then it explains how we came to be where we are today.

SECTION 1.   BASIC IDEAS

2.1.1.   Now that we have looked at some of the major markets, it is time to see how they fit together. In this section we look at some of the problems and ideas that have influenced the development of the international monetary system. In the next section we see how the system itself evolved.

2.1.2.   If one had to pick out three strands that weave the story together, they would probably be *international liquidity, adjustment,* and *choice of reserve asset.* We will look at each briefly. The word *liquidity* is a kind of shorthand. Basically, it means having enough cash to meet day-to-day needs. For an individual, that means having enough cash in the bank, or readily saleable assets such as government bonds, to meet the regular monthly bills. For a country, it means having enough foreign currency to pay its monthly bills: the balance of imports and exports, and other cash flows into and out of the country. It has to be in foreign currency because (with certain exceptions, such as U.S. dollars) other countries prefer to be paid in their own currency.

2.1.3. Liquidity and *adjustment* are in a sense opposites. If I do not have enough liquidity to meet my monthly bills, I have to cut my spending (or borrow). In other words, I have to adjust my behavior. It is the same for a country which is continually spending more abroad than it earns from abroad. In the end, it usually has to adjust its policies. The more liquidity it has, the less hurry there is about adjusting. The less liquidity it has, the more rapidly it must act. So liquidity and adjustment are a kind of tradeoff. We shall see in the next section that countries have very often tried to put off adjusting their economies by using up liquidity, or by trying to get liquidity by borrowing. The adjustments they made usually were either to devalue their currency (to make their exports more competitive internationally and help the country earn more abroad) or to cut back spending on imports, often by painful domestic tax increases or interest rate rises. Over and over again the United Kingdom, Italy, France, Belgium, and other countries have had to make the forced choice between adjustment and international liquidity. If they didn't have the latter they had to accept the former. And much of the western world faced the same choice during the two oil shocks of 1973 to 1975 and 1979 to 1980.

2.1.4. The third strand is *choice of reserve asset.* International liquidity consists of reserves of foreign currency, or gold, which is generally saleable for currencies, and certain other items. At the start of our story—1945—international liquidity was held almost entirely in gold, U.S. dollars, and sterling. As confidence weakened in these two currencies, liquidity was switched into other currencies or gold. And the shock waves from these shifts of liquidity were seen in repeated currency crises, which ended in sterling's 1967 devaluation and the 1971–1973 devaluation of the U.S. dollar. Still today, as confidence in a currency fades or grows, international liquidity ebbs away from or flows into that currency, causing big movements in exchange rates (see Table 2.1). And the question of what the best reserve assets are is still unresolved, as we shall see when we trace what has been happening in the markets over the years.

SECTION 2.   HISTORY OF THE INTERNATIONAL MONETARY SYSTEM AFTER THE WAR

2.2.1. The aim of this section is to explain why our present international monetary system works the way it does. It is not the result of rational planning. It was created by emergency decisions when the original framework broke down. To begin our story, we have to go back to 1944 when the Bretton Woods conference was held. This set up the International Monetary Fund and the World Bank. (The latter is mainly involved with development finance. It

TABLE 2.1. Share of National Currencies in SDR Value of Total Official Holdings of Foreign Exchange, End of Selected Quarters, 1973–80 (in Percent).[a]

Currency	1973:I	1975:IV	1976:IV	1977:IV	1978:IV	1979:IV	1980:IV	1979:IV Excluding ECU[bc]	1980:IV Excluding ECU[dc]
U.S. dollar	84.5	85.2	86.7	85.2	82.8	66.1[d]	59.0[e]	78.9	73.1
Pound sterling	5.9	4.1	2.1	1.8	1.6	1.9	2.6	2.0	3.0
Deutsche mark	6.7	6.6	7.3	8.3	10.1	10.3	12.1	11.3	14.0
French franc	1.2	1.3	1.0	0.8	1.0	0.9	1.1	1.0	1.3
Swiss franc	1.4	1.7	1.6	2.2	2.1	2.9	3.5	3.2	4.1
Netherlands guilder	0.4	0.6	0.5	0.5	0.5	0.6	0.8	0.7	0.9
Japanese yen	—	0.6	0.7	1.2	1.9	2.6	3.2	2.8	3.7
ECU	—	—	—	—	—	14.6[d]	17.8[e]	—	—
Total	100.0	100.0	100.0	100.0	100.0	100.0	100.0	100.0	100.0

[a] The detail in each of the columns may not add to 100 because of rounding.

[b] In this alternative calculation, the SDR value of European Currency Units (ECUs) issued against U.S. dollars (SDR 12,784 million at the end of 1979 and SDR 10,176 million at the end of 1980) is added to the SDR value of U.S. dollars, but the SDR value of ECUs issued against gold (SDR 19,725 million at the end of 1979 and SDR 37,354 million at the end of 1980) is excluded from the total distributed here.

[c] The five-currency basket SDR has weights of 42 per cent for the U.S. dollar, 19 per cent for the deutsche mark, and 13 per cent for each of the pound sterling, the French franc, and the Japanese yen.

[d] The share of U.S. dollars would rise by 5.8 percentage points and that of the ECU would fall by the same amount if ECUs issued against U.S. dollars were treated as U.S. dollars in foreign exchange reserves.

[e] The share of U.S. dollars would rise by 3.8 percentage points and that of the ECU would fall by the same amount if ECUs issued against U.S. dollars were treated as U.S. dollars in foreign exchange reserves.

SOURCE: Various Fund publications and Fund staff estimates. In *IMF Annual Report*, 1981, p. 69.

does not concern us here.) The IMF aims to see that its members run their exchange rate and balance of payments policies in an orderly way. If need be, it helps them do so by lending them money. The funds to do this come from members' subscriptions (quotas), the IMF's borrowings, and other sources (see Chapter 3). Under the Articles of Agreement of the IMF laid down at Bretton Woods, members agreed to make their currencies convertible, that is, not to restrict exchange of their currencies for others. They also agreed to fix "par" values for their currencies in terms of gold. This meant fixed exchange rates among currencies. It also meant (in theory) convertibility from currencies into gold. To help members meet these aims, the IMF would lend to them in proportion to their quotas.

2.2.2. But these ideals took time to achieve. Economic conditions after the war, especially in Europe, were very difficult. Most countries were short of foreign exchange. In particular they were short of dollars to pay for U.S. exports. So a series of clearing systems were arranged. These offset surpluses and deficits among member countries (see Chapter 4, Section 4). This saved payments of scarce dollars or gold among members. The first clearing system was the Agreement on Multilateral Monetary Compensation of 1947. It was followed by the Intra-European Payments Agreements of 1948–1949 and the European Payments Union of 1950–1958.[1]

2.2.3. By 1958, most European economies had recovered enough to restore convertibility. But this move exposed problems which, until now, had been concealed by the lack of convertibility. The exchange rates of several countries, notably Germany, were clearly undervalued. Others, such as those of the United Kingdom and the United States, were becoming overvalued. The first sign of trouble came in the autumn of 1960. There was a major gold crisis. Then in March 1961 the deutsche mark was revalued. This triggered pressure on sterling. At the next monthly meeting of central bankers at the Bank for International Settlements (a body which is described in Chapter 3, Section 3), the first Basle Agreement was reached. This was an informal agreement. The French Finance Minister described it as no agreement at all: "il n'y a jamais eu de gentlemen's agreement à Bâle, mais à Bâle il n'y a que des gentlemen."[2]

2.2.4. The agreement's aim was that no party to it "should be forced by speculative movements of funds to deviate from the declared policy."[3] Despite this, pressure on sterling and the dollar continued. It led to further rises in demand for gold. To combat this, the central bankers formed the Gold Pool in the autumn of 1961. This included the United States, the United Kingdom, Germany, France, Italy, Switzerland, Belgium, and the Netherlands. The central banks of these countries agreed informally to centralize their main dealing in gold. The Bank of England managed the pool and sold gold when it judged the dollar or sterling needed support. Pool members agreed to supply the gold needed to do this, in certain agreed quotas. The pool also formed a separate buying syndicate which bought gold from the market when it could.[4]

2.2.5. But the pressure on the two main reserve currencies continued. It became clear that the IMF might find its reserves stretched if the United Kingdom or the United States needed to borrow a large amount from it. Already, by August 1961, the Fund's lendable resources had been largely tied up by (mainly British) borrowings. It was forced to sell $500 million worth of gold.[5] So it was decided to arrange that the major industrialized countries (the Group of Ten) would commit themselves, if need arose, to make extra lendings to the IMF. They would finance an IMF loan to the United States or the United Kingdom (and, since 1968, to other members of the group). These arrangements were made in January 1962. They became known as the General Arrangements to Borrow (GAB). (See 3.2.9.)

2.2.6. The United States developed another line of defense for the dollar during this time. This was the Federal Reserve swap network. In essence these swaps consisted of exchanges of currency between the Federal Reserve and another central bank. The currency acquired could then be used to intervene in the foreign exchange market. At a later date, the exchange of currency was reversed at a fixed rate of exchange. (Chapter 3, Section 6, explains the mechanics.) The reason for the swap network was that between 1945 and 1961 the United States had not intervened in the foreign exchange market. Neither the U.S. Treasury nor the Federal Reserve held balances of foreign currency to enable them to intervene. Consequently, during the March 1961 crisis, the Treasure had no deutsche marks to sell when the deutsche mark was rising against the dollar. It was necessary to get the deutsche marks from the Deutsche Bundesbank in exchange for dollars under an informal agreement. The Federal Reserve then decided to negotiate formal swap arrangements with other central banks. The authorization for this was granted by the Federal Open Market Committee in February 1962. The first formal agreement was with the Banque de France in March 1962. By the end of the year, swap lines had been negotiated with most major central banks and the BIS.[6] An early use of the swap arrangements was made in June 1962. It was in the reverse direction: the Federal Reserve provided a US$ 250 million swap credit to Canada as part of a US$ 1,050 million IMF/central bank credit package. Swap credits were also made available to Italy in March 1964 and repeatedly to the Bank of England.[7]

2.2.7. During 1964 the pound sterling came under pressure again. The Bank of England was forced to arrange a new "Basle Agreement." Under this, US$ 500 million of swap credits were arranged for the Bank. They were followed in December by a further agreement under which the BIS and 11 central banks arranged a US$ 3 billion credit.[8] By 1966 these temporary defenses were put into a new form. The continuing pressure on sterling was seen as partly caused by changes in overseas governments' and individuals' holdings of sterling—the "sterling balances." So the Bank of England made a formal arrangement with the Basle group in June 1966 to protect the United Kingdom from a fall in the sterling balances. The arrangement was renewed in March 1967,[9] and in a revised form in September 1968.[10] In the 1968 renewal, the United Kingdom agreed with individual countries in the Overseas Sterling area that they would hold fixed percentages of their reserves in sterling. In return for this commitment, the United Kingdom guaranteed the exchange rate at which it would repay the sterling balances. These agreements lasted effectively until December 1976, when new arrangements were made (see 2.2.17).

2.2.8. The effect of the 1966 Basle arrangement was only temporary. During 1967, as sterling came under pressure, demand for gold rose. In June 1967, France pulled out of the gold pool. After the Arab-Israeli Six Day War, the flight into gold and out of sterling became more intense. In November 1967 sterling was at last devalued. The effect was simply to switch pressure to other currencies, especially the dollar. The pressure on gold continued, and reached crisis point in March 1968. The gold pool was suspended and a "two-tier" market formed. The effect was that the official gold price (US$ 35 per ounce) was maintained only for transactions between central banks. In practice there were few. The "free market" price for gold was allowed to float freely.[11]

2.2.9. Soon after, the "events of May" in France brought student rioting, strikes, and serious damage to the prestige of General de Gaulle. The French franc came under pressure. The Banque de France was forced to arrange credit lines of $1.4 billion in order to support the currency. During the following year, and especially in the summer of 1969, after the resignation of President de Gaulle, the French franc came under pressure on several occasions. In August 1969 the franc was devalued, and in September the deutsche mark was allowed to float, with a revaluation taking place in October after the German elections.[12]

2.2.10. During the late 1960s there had been discussion of a possible shortage of international liquidity. It was feared that this might slow the growth of world trade. One method of increasing liquidity would have been an increase in the official price of gold. Legally this was tantamount to a devaluation of the dollar. The United States firmly opposed it. An alternative was to create a new form of international reserve asset through the IMF. There was much dispute between the United States and France, which wanted a revaluation of gold and insisted that if a new reserve asset were created restrictions should be placed on it. But in July 1969, the First Amendment to the IMF Articles of Agreement legalized the new instrument. It was called the Special Drawing Right to emphasize that it was a kind of borrowing rather than a new currency. The first allocation of SDRs was made in January 1970 (See Chapter 14 for details). With hindsight, the timing was unfortunate. It coincided with a rapid growth in the U.S. trade deficit. This tended to increase world liquidity anyway. It also put the dollar under pressure.

2.2.11. As a result, in May 1971 the deutsche mark was floated and the weakness of the dollar ended in its formal devaluation on August 15, 1971, when convertibility of the dollar into gold was also suspended. This forced the major countries to agree on a new currency alignment at the Smithsonian Conference of December 1971 (named after the building where the conference was held). But the dollar devaluation did not succeed in curing quickly the U.S. balance of payments problem. The United States was forced to devalue again in March 1973. This second devaluation can be taken as the start of floating exchange rates.

2.2.12. While the dollar was in severe difficulty, the EEC countries had been working on an alternative exchange rate system. Plans had been laid for an economic and monetary union of the EEC, leading (perhaps) eventually to a single currency for Europe. To this end, the "snake" was set up, grouping EEC currencies together in a fixed parity system. (See Chapter 4, Section 2 for further details.) The snake was started on April 24, 1972. The United Kingdom was in the process of joining the EEC and agreed to join the snake on May 1. But a speculative run on sterling forced an ignominious exit after only seven weeks, on June 23. In March 1973, when the dollar was devalued a second time, the EEC decided to let the snake float as a group against the dollar.[13] In June 1973, a further step toward monetary union was taken. The European Monetary Cooperation Fund was set up to finance snake members who needed support (see Chapter 3, Section 4).[14]

2.2.13. The move to general floating in March 1973 had been intended as temporary. But in the autumn of that year the Arab-Israeli war and the subsequent oil crisis radically changed the international climate. Exchange rates became unstable as countries tried to adapt to the economic pressures caused by a huge rise in payment to oil producers.[15] In particular, the French franc was forced to drop out of the EEC snake. Then in June 1974 the Herstatt Bank collapsed with huge foreign exchange losses. This and other banking problems, combined with fears for international stability in the face of the oil problem, made the foreign exchange markets extremely thin and nervous. In response to Herstatt, the central bankers tightened supervision of the markets. A committee on banking regulations and supervisory practices was also created under the auspices of the BIS in Basle.[16]

2.2.14. The oil shock had such widespread effects that we need to break away from chronology for a moment to spell them out. Firstly, major efforts were made during this period to help countries finance trade deficits caused by the oil shock. The IMF set up its "oil facility" in June 1974 to help "recycle" funds from the OPEC surplus countries to Western and less developed countries needing to borrow. In April 1975 it introduced a second oil facility. The two facilities combined totaled SDR 6.9 billion, provided by 17 countries.[17] In February 1975 the EEC took similar action to permit an EEC loan which was floated later on the international capital markets. The proceeds were lent to Italy and Ireland. The borrowings were administered by the BIS on behalf of the European Monetary Cooperation Fund. By March 1981 the total outstanding was approximately US\$ 1.3 billion, of which 85% was lent to Italy.[18]

2.2.15. The oil crisis forced deficit countries to find finance. It also made it clear that floating exchange rates were likely to last for some time. This meant changes in the definition of the SDR, and the European Unit of Account. The IMF introduced a currency basket definition for the SDR in July 1974[19] and in March 1975 the EEC followed suit. (See Chapter 14, Section 2 for the calculations.) Permanently floating exchange rates also meant that the IMF Articles of Agreement had to be changed, because floating was illegal under the original rules. The Jamaica Agreement of January 1976 on the Second Amendment to the IMF Articles legalized floating rates.

2.2.16. This amendment also abolished the official gold price. (This had become increasingly meaningless, especially after the two-tier system had been abandoned in November 1973.) It also prohibited the IMF from managing the gold price, or from establishing a fixed gold price in the future. It laid down that gold will not be the denominator of any future par value system. It required the IMF to dispose of one-third of its gold holdings (4,655 tons). Half— that is, one-sixth of the total—was to be returned to its members, and the rest was to be sold by auction. The profits from the latter were to be used for the benefit of the less developed countries that were members of the fund at the time.[20] These gold auctions took place from 1976 to 1980 and were accompanied in 1978 and 1979 by sales of gold by the U.S. Treasury.[21] Ironically, these official efforts by the United States and the IMF took place while other countries were undertaking a rehabilitation of gold as an international asset. During 1974 Italy had borrowed \$2 billion from Germany, using its large gold reserves as collateral. In December 1974 presidents Giscard d'Estaing of France and Ford of the United States agreed to allow central banks to value gold at market-related prices.[22] In January 1975, France began to revalue its gold in line with market prices and was followed by several other countries. In August 1975, the EEC's finance ministers agreed that central banks should be allowed to trade gold freely among themselves, provided that as a group they did not try to increase their holdings or peg the price.[23] Not long afterward (April 1977),[24] South Africa, like Italy, borrowed on the security of its gold reserves. The mechanics were different: South African gold was swapped for currency provided by certain banks.

2.2.17. The oil crisis therefore contributed to a number of far-reaching changes in the international monetary system. We now return to the sequence of events in the foreign exchange markets. The initial effect of the oil crisis was relatively favorable for sterling and the dollar. OPEC surpluses were mainly invested in these two currencies to start with. But by 1976 it was clear that the United Kingdom was likely to have serious balance of payments problems. The government's determination to solve them was in doubt. Sterling came under very heavy pressure. There was a major crisis in November 1976 when the pound fell to $1.56. The IMF granted a standby credit over two years of up to SDR 3,360 million. This was followed in February 1977 by an arrangement with the BIS in Basle, coordinating support from 11 central banks. Medium-term credits of US$ 3,000 million were arranged to protect the United Kingdom against any withdrawal of sterling balances.[25]

2.2.18.   In the end, these arrangements were not needed. Sterling was firm during 1977 as the market was reassured by the IMF and BIS credits. The dollar was weakening, which also helped, as did the buildup of North Sea oil production. Until October 1977, the Bank of England tried to hold sterling down. But this led to foreign currency inflows which threatened monetary control. (See Chapter 5, Section 5.) At the end of that month the pound was allowed to float upward. Sterling's strength was partly a reflection of dollar weakness. Statements made by Treasury Secretary Blumenthal at the OECD meeting in June 1977 to the effect that surplus countries such as Germany and Japan should allow their currencies to rise were seen as evidence that the United States was happy to see the dollar weaken.[26] Policy was later changed, but not decisively enough. In January 1978, the United States announced that it would intervene to the extent needed to counter disorderly conditions. The resources of the Federal Reserve swap network and the U.S. Treasury's Exchange Stabilization Fund would be used. In March 1978, the United States and Germany jointly announced further steps to counter disorderly conditions. These included an increase in the Federal Reserve/Bundesbank swap line. But the markets were unconvinced: the U.S. trade deficit, the failure to control oil demand, and inflation remained serious problems.

2.2.19.   The summer and autumn of 1978 saw continued dollar selling. There was extreme pressure in September and October. A realignment of the snake exchange rates including a deutsche mark revaluation took place in October 1978, but this did not prevent further pressure on the dollar. So on November 1, 1978, the United States announced a dollar support package. It included a 1% rise in the U.S. discount rate and extensive drawings on the swap network. The U.S. Treasury announced an issue of US$ 10 billion worth of foreign currency denominated bonds in Germany and Switzerland (the so-called Carter bonds). It also sold $2 billion worth of SDRs for deutsche mark, yen, and SFR and borrowed $3 billion from the IMF.[27] The IMF partly financed the operations by borrowing from the Bundesbank and Bank of Japan under the General Arrangements to Borrow.[28]

2.2.20.   Returning for a moment to the wider international monetary issues, 1978 and 1979 saw a number of developments. April 1978 saw the official entry into force of the Second Amendment to the IMF Articles of Agreement. In December 1978 the IMF agreed to make a new issue of SDRs, 4 billion in 1979, 1980, and 1981. This was the first issue since the initial three-year allocation in 1970 and 1972. In February 1979 the IMF's Supplementary Financing Facility (the "Witteveen" facility) was introduced to extend loans to countries already heavily in debt to the IMF (see Chapter 3, Section 2). The other major international initiative at this time was the creation of the European Monetary System. This came into force on March 13, 1979. It was in essence a reorganization of the snake with the Scandinavian currencies excluded. The main difference was the creation of the European Currency Unit (ECU) to serve as the basis for EMS parities. (See Chapter 4, Section 2 on the EMS and Chapter 14, Section 3 on the ECU.)[29]

2.2.21. While these events were taking place, the dollar remained under pressure. In early December 1978, the Shah of Iran's political position began to crumble. Iranian oil production and exports were interrupted, prompting a burst of dollar selling. There was a temporary relief during the early part of 1979 when the dollar recovered strongly. The oil shortage was seen as hurting Germany and Japan more than the United States, and the U.S. current account was improving. But by early summer it seemed that the United States was incapable of responding adequately to the oil crisis. There were shortages of gasoline, and intense political debates over energy policy. Funds flowed into deutsche mark and particularly sterling. The latter had benefited from the election of a Conservative government in May and the 2% increase in the Bank of England's Minimum Lending Rate in June. By July 26 the pound had reached a four-year high of $2.3324.[31]

2.2.22. By the end of July, the appointment of Mr. Volcker as chairman of the Federal Reserve and heavy intervention in the market calmed the position. But pressure flared up in September as the deutsche mark strengthened. On September 23 the deutsche mark was revalued by 5% against the Danish krone and 2% against other EMS currencies. But pressure on the U.S. dollar remained intense until the Federal Reserve acted on October 6, 1979. The discount rate was raised 1% to 12%. An 8% marginal reserve requirement was imposed on "managed liabilities" (CDs, Eurodeposits, etc.) to force banks to cut back their lending by making the costs higher. And the focus of monetary policy was shifted to banks' reserves. Interest rates were to be allowed to rise as high as needed to control reserve growth. The impact was immediate and powerful.[32]

2.2.23. But on November 4 the U.S. Embassy in Iran was seized by militant students. On November 14, in response to an Iranian threat to withdraw US$ assets, President Carter announced the freezing of these assets. Fears for political stability in the region were sharpened by the attack on the Saudi Grand Mosque by Shi'a extremists and above all by the Soviet invasion of Afghanistan on December 27. The price of gold, which in the comparative quiet of September had been around $397, hit $512 on December 31 and rose by $20 and $50 jumps each day to $850 per ounce on January 21, 1980.

2.2.24.   The U.S. dollar benefited somewhat from these uncertainties after an initial fall in January 1980. The instability in the Middle East was seen as posing a greater threat to other countries, notably Germany and Japan. U.S. interest rates remained fairly high, and tightened sharply after the March 14 credit control package announced by President Carter. The Federal Reserve raised its marginal reserve requirement by 2% and imposed a 3% surcharge on persistent borrowers at the discount window. Short-term interest rates in the United States soared to 20% and the dollar rose on a broad front. Gold reacted sharply to the high U.S. interest rates, which made financing expensive, and the calmer Middle East situation. The price fell to $474 in March. But the March package had hit credit demand as it was starting to turn down anyway after the October package. As U.S. credit demand shrank, short-term interest rates collapsed from 20% to 9% between mid-April and early June. The Federal Reserve Board, meanwhile, was dismantling its credit restraints. As U.S. interest rates fell, the dollar weakened, falling 5½% against the deutsche mark between April 8 and 10. During this period the Japanese yen had also been very weak in the face of oil shortages and rising U.S. interest rates.[31] It dropped to 264 per dollar on April 8. But as U.S. interest rates fell, and large shifts of OPEC funds into yen took place, it recovered to 215 by mid-June. Identified official deposits with banks in Japan rose from $0.9 billion to $4.6 billion in 1980, mostly after the lifting in March of restrictions on payment of interest to free yen depositors.[32]

2.2.25.   By late July, U.S. interest rates were firming again. It seemed that the economy had stopped contracting. So the deutsche mark weakened somewhat against the dollar. This trend was reinforced in August by general strikes in Poland and the emergence of Solidarity there. Then during September Iraq invaded Iran. With U.S. interest rates firming again (the discount rate was raised 1% to 11% on September 26), the dollar began to strengthen. The tension in the Middle East and in Poland also pulled the gold price up through $700. The dollar's rise put severe pressure on the deutsche mark, which was weakened by Polish worries and by a heavy current account deficit. There were rumors of a devaluation which were denied. After a temporary reaction, the dollar surged higher again in January. The release of the hostages from Iran and the advent of President Reagan helped confidence. The deutsche mark accordingly remained weak. Polish tension remained and forecasts for the German current account were poor. There were political difficulties within Germany over external and internal policy. So the deutsche mark weakened to DMK 2.13 per US$. In February, the Bundesbank took action to defend the deutsche mark. The Lombard facility was suspended. The Special

Lombard facility replaced it, to be granted as and when the Bundesbank chose. German call money soared to 20 to 30%.

2.2.26. The reaction was the stronger because the Federal Reserve did not intervene except on March 30, after the shooting of President Reagan. The new administration was philosophically opposed to foreign exchange intervention. In mid-April the U.S. Treasury announced that the United States would only intervene to counter disorderly market conditions. Against the French franc the dollar rose particularly fast, following the election of M. Mitterand to the Presidency on May 10. During the next 10 days, to hold the situation for the new administration, the Banque de France lifted its money market intervention rate from 13½% to 22%. Tight exchange controls were introduced, including a separate market for purchases of securities—the *devises-titres*. (See Chapter 4).

2.2.27. Sterling was also under pressure because of the dollar's rise and a weaker oil market. Riots in several cities also led to fears that control over the money supply would be relaxed. By July 31, sterling was at $1.84, over 20% down against the dollar from its January levels. On August 20, in the United Kingdom, the Minimum Lending Rate was abolished under new monetary control arrangements. Henceforth there was no official rate at which the Bank of England would provide funds to the market. An unpublished band was used.

2.2.28. The pressure on the French franc continued. But government policy in France remained firmly committed to an expression of the economy. On October 1, a 35% increase in the planned budget deficit was announced. On October 4, the inevitable EMS realignment took place. The deutsche mark and Dutch guilder were revalued by 5½%, while the French franc and Italian lira were devalued by 3%. On October 6, however, the assassination of President Sadat threw the markets into turmoil. Gold hit US$ 469 per ounce. (During this month, it was later learned, South Africa swapped about $1 billion worth of gold for currency.) The relatively smooth transition of power in Egypt soon calmed the situation. The dollar remained relatively firm, despite rapidly falling interest rates during November. On December 14, the imposition of martial law in Poland led to further shifts of funds into dollars and nervousness over the prospects for the deutsche mark.

2.2.29. By the end of 1981, the foreign exchange markets had experienced a decade of instability since the Smithsonian agreement of December 1971. The move from fixed to floating exchange rates had been legalized. The problems of handling the transfers of funds between OPEC and the West had been accommodated. Gold had been banished but was returning to its former role as an international asset. The SDR had been created and adapted to floating exchange rates. But neither of these had replaced the dollar, which remained the world's major reserve currency despite the relative decline of the U.S. economy. Perhaps the greatest single test ahead for the 1980s would be an orderly transition to a multiple reserve currency world.

NOTES

1. A full description of these systems is given in B. Tew, *International Monetary Cooperation 1945–70*, Hutchinson University Library, London, 1970. See also the annual reports of the Bank for International Settlements, 1945 through 1958 (the BIS managed the successive clearing systems for Western Europe).

2. Quoted in F. Hirsch, *Money International*, Penguin Books, London, 1967.

3. *Bank of England Quarterly Bulletin*, September 1961, p. 10.

4. The gold pool is described in the *Bank of England Quarterly Bulletin*, March 1964.

5. See S. Strong, *International Economic Relations of the Western World, 1959–71, Volume 2: International Monetary Relations*, Oxford University Press for the Royal Institute for International Affairs, 1976, pp. 105–17.

6. See the *Federal Reserve Bulletin*, September 1962, pp. 1138–53, and the chapter provided by the Federal Bank of New York on "The Foreign Exchange Market in the United States" in R. Z. Aliber (ed), *The International Market for Foreign Exchange*, Praeger, United States, 1969.

7. See F. Hirsch, *Money International*, pp. 341–351.

8. B. Tew, *International Monetary Cooperation*, pp. 261–262.

9. B. Tew, *International Monetary Cooperation*, p. 203.

10. S. Strange, *International Economic Relations of the Western World*, pp. 150–166.

11. S. Strange, *International Economic Relations of the Western World*, pp. 278–297.

12. B. Tew, *International Monetary Cooperation*, pp. 268–269.

13. See "The European System of Narrower Exchange Rate Margins," *Deutsche Bundesbank Monthly Report*, January 1976, for a good official description, and also R. Hellman, *Gold, the Dollar and the European Currency Systems: The Seven Year Monetary War*," Praeger, New York, 1979 for a lively discussion of the background.

14. *Deutsche Bundesbank, Monthly Report*, January 1976: "The European System of Narrower Exchange Rate Margins."

15. A good description of the transition is in M. E. Kreinin, "Living with Floating Exchange Rates: A Survey of Developments, 1973–77," *Journal of World Trade Law*, United Kingdom, November/December 1977.

16. W. P. Cooke, "Developments in Cooperation among Banking Supervisory Authorities," *Bank of England Quarterly Bulletin*, June 1981.

17. IMF's 1980 *Annual Report*, p. 82.

18. BIS, *51st Annual Report*, p. 162.

19. See J. J. Polak, "The SDR as a Basket of Currencies," *IMF Staff Papers*, December 1979.

20. The IMF published its revised articles in 1978. See also J. Gold, *The Second Amendment of the Fund's Articles of Agreement*, IMF Pamphlet no. 25, Washington D.C., 1978; and G. N. Halm, *Jamaica and the Par Value System*, Princeton Essays in International Finance no. 120, 1977. In the United Kingdom see HMSO, "The Second Amendment to the Articles of Agreement of the IMF," Cmnd 6705, 1977.

21. Consolidated Gold Fields Ltd., *Gold 1980*, London, 1980, p. 19.

22. D. A. Brodsky and G. P. Sampson, *The Value of Gold as a Reserve Asset*, World Development, Pergamon Press Ltd., United Kingdom, vol. 8, 1980, pp. 175–92.

23. R. Hellman, *Gold, the Dollar, and the European Currency Systems*, p. 143.
24. Consolidated Gold Fields Ltd., *Gold 1978*, London, 1978, p. 13.
25. See *Bank of England Quarterly Bulletin*, March 1977, pp. 7–8 for details.
26. R. Hellman, *Gold, the Dollar, and the European Currency Systems*, p. 180.
27. *Federal Reserve Bulletin*, December 1978, pp. 940–1.
28. IMF's 1980 *Annual Report*, p. 82.
29. See, among others, *Deutsche Bundesbank Monthly Report*, March 1979, "The European Monetary System"; T. de Vries, "On the Meaning and Future of the European Monetary System," *Princeton Essays in International Finance*, September 1980.
30. Federal Reserve Bank of New York, "Treasury and Federal Reserve Foreign Exchange Operations," *Federal Reserve Bank of New York Quarterly Review*, Autumn 1979, pp. 47–64.
31. "Treasury and Federal Reserve Foreign Exchange Operations," *Federal Reserve Bank of New York Quarterly Review*, Autumn 1980, p. 32.
32. BIS, *51st Annual Report*, June 1981, p. 147.

3

THE INSTITUTIONS

This chapter explains the role of the main bodies that influence the way the international markets behave: the International Monetary Fund, the main international lender to countries with payments problems; the Bank for International Settlements, traditionally a key player in international financial crisis management; and the European Monetary Fund, the source of short-term credit for European Monetary System members. It explains what the central bank swap network is, and how the central banks can use it to defend their currencies. Then we look at the central banks themselves: who controls them, how they control monetary policy, how they supervise banks and financial institutions, and how much control they have over their country's gold and foreign exchange reserves.

SECTION 1.   PURPOSE OF CHAPTER

3.1.1.   This chapter describes some of the organizations influencing market activity. It begins with international bodies: the International Monetary Fund and the Bank for International Settlements. It looks next at two regional institutions: the European Monetary Fund and the Arab Monetary Fund. Then it discusses the workings of the central bank swap network. This is not strictly an institution, but it is important to know how it works.

3.1.2.   The rest of the chapter looks at the major central banks. It covers (1) organization, (2) powers and relationship to government and other bodies; (3) the system of controling foreign exchange positions and liquidity, and (4) control of gold and foreign exchange reserves. We have looked at how these central banks intervene in money and foreign exchange markets in Chapter 1. (In Chapter 5 we look at how central bank intervention in the money market and intervention in the foreign exchange markets interrelate.) In Chapter 6 we look at monetary policy in general.

SECTION 2.   THE INTERNATIONAL MONETARY FUND

3.2.1.   The IMF can play a very important part in the foreign exchange markets because its actions can influence confidence in a currency. (See, for instance, 2.2.17–18 for the effect of IMF lending on sterling in 1976 and 1977.) Its decision to lend money to a country is often taken as a "seal of approval." Then, too, the fact that the lending is normally made on stringent conditions gives some kind of guarantee that the country's economic policy will be run in a responsible way. So it is worth knowing a little about what the IMF is, and how it works.

3.2.2.   The IMF was set up in 1944 at the Bretton Woods Conference. (Hence often the system of exchange rates and other arrangements that was set up with the IMF is referred to as the Bretton Woods system.) Its structure is defined in its Articles of Agreement. It has a Board of Governors, which is its highest authority and meets once a year. But its day-to-day running is controlled by an Executive Board and a managing director. There are 21 executive directors. Of these, six are appointed by the countries with the largest subscriptions (or "quotas") to the IMF: the United States, the United Kingdom, Germany, France, Japan, and Saudi Arabia. The others are elected by the remaining members of the Fund. The Executive Board selects the managing director, who is also chairman of the Executive Board.[1]

3.2.3.   The subscription, or quota, of a country depends on its national income, foreign currency reserves, and other factors. Quotas are reviewed at least every five years. The size of the quota decides two important things: how much a country can borrow from the IMF, and how much voting power it has at the Fund.[2] The amount that a country can borrow is up to 100% of its quota, plus certain special facilities. The borrowings are made in a series of slices or tranches. The more a country borrows, the more closely the IMF supervises its policies. For the first borrowing (the first credit tranche) the IMF requires a borrowing country to make "reasonable efforts" to overcome its problems. For second and higher tranches, the Fund usually only lends on a standby basis. This means: (1) there are performance targets that the borrower must meet; and (2) successive installments of the borrowing are only allowed if the targets are met.[3]

3.2.4.   The mechanics of a borrowing (drawing) are that a country uses its own currency to buy the currencies of other countries (or SDRs, which are explained later). So a drawing on the IMF by a country raises the Fund's holdings of the country's currency, but reduces its holdings of the other currency. The makeup of the Fund's resources changes, but not the total. An example is worked through in Table 3.1. The account of the IMF which holds these currencies is called the general account (as distinct from the SDR account—see 3.2.11).

TABLE 3.1. The United Kingdom Borrows DMK from the IMF General Account (£STG 1 = DMK 4.50).

	U.K. Account with IMF (in £STG)	German Account with IMF (in DMK)
I. Before Drawing		
SDR holdings	100	100
Reserve tranche	0	0
Borrowings under		
First credit tranche	0	0
Second credit tranche	0	0
Third credit tranche	0	0
Fourth credit tranche	0	0
General Account holdings	£STG 100	(U.K. original quota)
	DMK 450	(German original quota)
II. U.K. Borrows DMK 450 and Pays in £STG 100		
SDR holdings	100	100
Reserve tranche	0	450
Borrowings under		
First credit tranche	100	0
Second credit tranche	0	0
Third credit tranche	0	0
Fourth credit tranche	0	0
General Account holdings	£STG 200	

3.2.5. Borrowings are made in tranches. The first of these is the reserve tranche: it is equivalent to drawing down a credit balance. For the reserve tranche is the result of a country's lending its currency to the Fund. To see how the reserve tranche works, suppose the United Kingdom needs to borrow deutsche marks. The United Kingdom buys deutsche marks from the Fund and pays sterling. The Fund's deutsche mark holdings are now less than the amount Germany originally paid in: it is as if Germany had lent the Fund deutsche marks to buy the United Kingdom's sterling. The difference between Germany's original quota and the Fund's present deutsche mark holdings is credited to Germany as its reserve tranche. A country has automatic access to the reserve tranche (since, after all, it lent the money to the Fund). After that, it can borrow four subsequent tranches, each equal to 25% of its quota, and, as we saw, subject to tighter and tighter control by the IMF.

3.2.6. In the beginning there were high hopes, at Bretton Woods, that the IMF would lead to a new order in world monetary affairs. And for many years much of its resources were devoted to propping up the fixed exchange rate system, and to financing weaker countries—such as the developing coun-

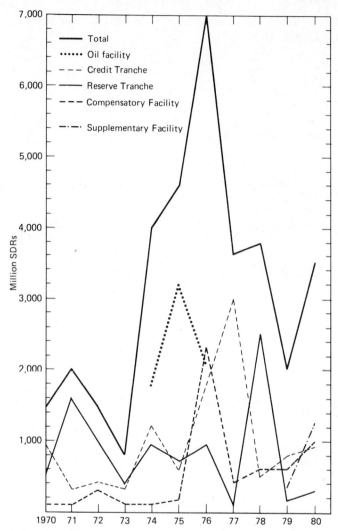

FIGURE 3.1. Balance of Payments Assistance by and Reserve Tranche Drawings on the IMF.

tries—when they got into difficulties. After 1973, with the move to free floating and the oil shock, the IMF's exchange rate role effectively disappeared and
with it the hopes for any great "new order" in the world monetary system. The
IMF became largely an official lender of the last resort to countries in trouble
(although with its creation of the SDR it has also been trying to lay the basis
for a new international monetary system—see 3.2.11). As Figure 3.1. shows,
the IMF's activity has been greatest when the world monetary system has had
to absorb the oil shocks.

3.2.7. The figure also shows borrowings under some of the IMF's special facilities. There are five facilities granted by the IMF, and two administered by

it. The compensatory financing facility is the oldest of these. It was established in 1963 and is the most widely used. By October 1981, 88 countries had borrowed a cumulative total of just under SDR 7 billion (say US$ 8 billion)[4] from the IMF under the compensatory financing facility. The CFF's aim is to help a country adapt to a temporary export shortfall which occurs for reasons beyond the country's control.

3.2.8. The next most popular IMF facility is the oil facility. This was designed to be a temporary facility (it was set up in 1974 and 1975 and finished lending in 1976) to help countries overcome the impact of the oil price rises of 1973 and 1974. It lent SDR 6.9 billion to 55 countries, of which SDR 1.1 billion was still outstanding in October 1981. Other facilities provided by the IMF include the Buffer Stock Facility (used for financing contributions to a commodity buffer stock), the Extended Fund Facility, which is for countries that have structural problems, and the Supplementary Financing Facility which is for countries facing financing problems that are very large in proportion to their quota.[5] The Fund also administers a trust fund and a subsidy account for developing countries.

3.2.9. All this lending has to be financed. The main source of funds is the quotas subscribed to the IMF by member countries. Extra facilities have had to be arranged when the quotas were not enough. The first of these arrangements was known as the General Arrangements to Borrow (GAB). The GAB was set up in January 1962 in case the Fund had to make a large loan to the United States or the United Kingdom, the main reserve currency countries at the time. It was a four-year arrangement with 10 industrialized countries (the Group of Ten). Switzerland later took part as an associate (not directly, because Switzerland is not a member of the IMF). The GAB were later renewed, most recently in 1979 for the period to 1985. As it stands now, the countries involved have agreed to lend their currencies up to a maximum of SDR 6.8 billion in total (say, US$ 7.8 billion).[6] The most recent use of the GAB was to finance the U.S. drawing of SDRs in November 1978: Germany and Japan lent the IMF SDR 583 million and SDR 194 million respectively.[7]

3.2.10. As well as from the GAB, the IMF has borrowed direct from certain countries in two other ways. The Supplementary Financing Facility, referred to earlier, was financed by arranging to borrow a total of SDR 7.8 billion from 13 countries.[8] Then, in March 1981, in the first deal of its kind, the IMF borrowed two annual tranches of SDR 4 billion (with a commitment for further lending in the third year if their position permits it) from the Saudi Arabian Monetary Authority. (An interesting point about this deal is that it was rather "market oriented." SAMA has the option of converting its claim on the IMF into bearer promissory notes which could be sold to other private or official institutions.)[9] Shortly afterward the IMF agreed with central banks of 16 countries that they would lend it SDR 1.3 billion over a two-year commitment period for up to two and a half years. Half of the funds come from loans by the

TABLE 3.2. Borrowing by the IMF in Connection with the Supplementary Financing Facility (in Millions of SDRs).

Lender	Total Agreed	Amount Borrowed up to April 30, 1981
Abu Dhabi	150	31.23
Austrian National Bank	50	15.53
Banque National de Belgique	150	12.34
Canada	200	12.68
Deutsche Bundesbank	1050	290.46[a]
Banco de Guatemala	30	8.00
Japan	900	152.99
Central Bank of Kuwait	400	80.95
De Nederlandsche Bank	100	19.27
Central Bank of Nigeria	220	56.57
Saudi Arabian Monetary Agency	1934	344.62
Swiss National Bank	650	131.42
United States	1450	385.43
Central Bank of Venezuela	500	100.73
Total	7784	1515.45

SOURCE: *IMF's 1981 Annual Report*, p. 128.

[a] Of which SDR 172.01 were transferred to the Saudi Arabian Monetary Authority (SAMA) against US$ on November 13, 1980.

Belgian National Bank, the Bank of England, the Bank of Japan, and the Swiss National Bank. The balance will be channeled through the Bank for International Settlements (see Section 2).[10]

3.2.11. All of the Fund's lending and borrowing activities we have discussed so far are channeled through its General Resources Account. There is another account called the Special Drawing Rights Account. The SDR's history was touched on in 2.2.10., and the SDR is fully explained in Chapter 14, Currency Units. For our purposes, what matters is that it represents an international reserve asset, which can be thought of as a currency issued by the IMF. Members of the IMF can use SDRs to make international payments between themselves just as they could use US$. When it was originally created, the possible uses of the SDR were very restricted. Over the years they have been widened so that central banks can buy or sell SDRs among themselves, use SDRs to make loans or as security for loans, and deal in SDR swaps or forward SDRs. In May 1981 the so-called "reconstitution" restriction (under which countries could not get rid of all their SDRs but had to keep a minimum balance) was lifted. Also, from January 1981 the valuation of the SDR was very much simplified (see Chapter 15).[11] In practical terms, the SDR is now equivalent to any other currency, with one major difference: private individuals cannot own it.

SECTION 3.   THE BANK FOR INTERNATIONAL SETTLEMENTS

3.3.1.   The BIS is the central bankers' central bank. It is very discreet, and very influential. It was founded in 1930 to act as a trustee for the loans associated with the Young Plan for German reparations. The first members of the bank were the central banks of Belgium, France, Germany, Italy, Japan, and the United Kingdom, together with three private U.S. banks.[12] The Federal Reserve Bank subsequently became a member along with all the major European central banks. Current membership consists of 30 central banks, of which 25 are European (including those of the Socialist countries except the U.S.S.R. and the G.D.R.) plus the United States, Canada, Japan, Australia, and South Africa. (The BIS is probably unique in having Albania and South Africa as co-members.) The board of directors is composed of the governors of the central banks of Belgium, France, Germany, Italy, and the United Kingdom, together with coopted directors from among the governors of those member central banks that do not have an ex officio representative on the board. There are also five representatives of finance, industry or commerce appointed by the governors of the permanent member central banks.[13]

3.3.2.   The BIS has three main functions. It acts as a bank, primarily as a central bankers' bank; it acts as a gathering place for central bankers, and a vehicle for international monetary cooperation; and it acts as trustee for various international loans. The BIS's role as an intermediary has a number of advantages to other central banks. The first is anonymity: sometimes it is not convenient for a central bank to be seen to withdraw its funds from the market. The second is risk spreading: a deposit with the BIS is very safe since the bank is highly liquid. (Typically, three-quarters of the BIS's assets have maturities of under three months.) Finally, deposits placed with the BIS can usually be withdrawn at very short notice. The BIS uses the funds received from central banks primarily for lending to other central banks. Its lendings may be swaps against gold, covered credits secured by a pledge of gold or marketable short-term securities, unsecured credits, standby credits, and the like. It places the balance of its funds in short-term deposits with international banks.

3.3.3.   The banking activities of the BIS are probably less vital than its role as a vehicle for international monetary cooperation. The most important part of this role is the least obtrusive: the monthly meetings of the BIS's board in Basle. Before the foundation of the BIS, meetings of governors of central banks were usually attended with a blaze of publicity and speculation concerning a crisis. Routine meetings on a monthly basis have contributed much toward closer international monetary understandings. As a result, the BIS has been closely involved in almost every major international financial crisis since the war. The gold pool from 1961 to 1968 operated on the basis of directives issued in Basle by the governors of the central banks of the Group of Ten. Successive packages launched in defense of sterling were usually arranged at Basle. The network of swap arrangements maintained by the Federal Reserve Bank of New York developed originally from the swap arrangements undertaken at the first Basle agreement.

3.3.4. The BIS also plays a central role in the technical operations of the European Monetary System (see Section 4). In fact, because of its original responsibility as a coordinator for international settlements in Europe, it has been closely involved in European payments arrangements since the war. During its lifetime it has managed the Agreement on Multilateral Monetary Compensation set up in 1947 to handle postwar European clearing arrangements, the 1948 Intra-European Payments Agreement, the European Payments Union of 1950, its successor, the European Monetary Agreement of 1958, and most recently the European Monetary Cooperation Fund (EMCF) established in 1973.

3.3.5. The BIS also acts as agent for the European Monetary Fund, the successor to the EMCF, set up in 1979 (see Section 4). That is, it handles the settlement of balances on behalf of the countries in the European Monetary System. It also runs the EEC's system of short-term monetary support and manages the financial aspects of EEC borrowings from overseas.[14]

3.3.6. Finally, the BIS has an important research and coordination role in the Euromarkets. Its *Annual Report* and *Quarterly Statistics* are widely regarded as the most authoritative sources of information on developments on the Euromarkets. And the BIS also provides the secretariat for the Committee on Banking Regulations and Supervisory Practices set up in December 1974 by the central bank governors to coordinate bank supervision after the Herstatt crisis (see 1.3.12–14).

SECTION 4. THE EUROPEAN MONETARY FUND

3.4.1. The EMF is important because of its short-term lending to EMS central banks when they are intervening in the foreign exchange markets. (It is often referred to as FECOM—Fonds Européen de Coopération Monetaire.) It is a rather shadowy institution, but one day it may take on a more independent life. It runs the settlement and lending operations of the European Monetary System (see Chapter 4, Section 2). But it is itself run by the BIS; it is not like the International Monetary Fund in having a large independent staff. It evolved from the European Monetary Cooperation Fund. The EMCF was set up by the Council of Ministers of the European Economic Community in April 1973. They wanted it to aim at "(1) the progressive narrowing of the margins of fluctuation of the Community currencies against each other; (2) interventions in Community currencies on the exchange markets; (3) settlements between central banks leading to a concerted policy on reserves."[15]

3.4.2. The EMF has helped partially to achieve (1), and also partially (3), through the workings of the European Monetary System (EMS) (see Chapter 4, Section 2). Progress on (2) has been limited, because a great deal of the time intervention has been caused by EEC currencies' movements against the US dollar rather than among themselves. But a good deal of community intervention is now carried on in other EMS currencies, as we can see from the Bundesbank's figures (given in Table 1.9).

3.4.3. The EMF's main job is to run a Very Short Term Financing facility (VSTF) which finances intervention in EMS currencies. The VSTF allows unlimited credit among central banks involved in the EMS. The central bank which borrows from the EMF (say it is the Banca d'Italia) can extend the term of its borrowing by using the Short Term Monetary Support facility (STMS— see 3.4.5). Otherwise it must repay within 45 days of the end of the month when it borrowed the money. (So the maximum the Banca d'Italia can borrow under VSTF is 75 days.)

3.4.4. When it repays, the Banca d'Italia, in our example, must first use its holdings of the lender's currency. If it has borrowed from the Bundesbank it must repay as much as it can in DMK. But usually EMS central banks only hold working balances in other EMS members' currencies, so most of the debt has to be repaid in other currencies. Up to 50% of the remaining debt can be settled in ECUs. (The ECU is the European Currency Unit, a currency basket like the SDR, which is defined fully in Chapter 14. At this point we simply note that a part of the EMS central banks' reserves are held in ECUs.) After that, the Banca d'Italia can only use ECUs for repayment if the Bundesbank agrees. Otherwise, settlement must be made in proportion to the currencies in the borrower's reserves. Say 30% of Italy's reserves were in US dollars: then 30% of its repayment would have to be in US dollars.[16]

3.4.5. If it did not want to repay immediately, the Banca d'Italia would turn to the Short Term Monetary Support facility (STMS). The STMS lends to EMS central banks to finance temporary balance of payments deficits. It has been used only once, by Italy in 1974. The amounts involved are set out in Table 3.3. Each country has a debtor quota, this amount being the maximum it is allowed to borrow, and a creditor quota, the amount it is committed to lend. On top of that there is the *rallonge*, which is a safety margin for the system as a whole. So a country can be asked to lend its creditor quota plus the total of the rallonge. Equally, it can borrow its debtor quota plus half of the rallonge. Take Germany as an example. The total it could borrow is ECU 1,740 million debtor quota plus ECU 4,400 million, half of the rallonge, for a

TABLE 3.3.   European Monetary Fund: Short Term Monetary Support (in Millions of ECUs).

Country	Debtor Quotas	Creditor Quotas
France	1,740	3,480
Germany	1,740	3,480
United Kingdom	1,740	3,480
Italy	1,160	2,320
Belgium-Luxembourg	580	1,160
Netherlands	580	1,160
Denmark	260	520
Ireland	100	200
Subtotal	7,900	15,800
Rallonge	8,800	8,800
Total	16,700	24,600

SOURCE: European Communities Monetary Committee, *Compendium of Community Monetary Texts*, Brussels, 1979, pp. 65–66.

sum of ECU 6,140 million. It must lend, if asked to, ECU 3,480 million, its creditor quota, plus ECU 8,800 million, the rallonge, for a total of ECU 12,280 million. The lending amounts are twice the borrowing amounts. This gives a safety margin for the system as a whole. If a country needs to borrow, and all other countries in the system are also in deficit but one, the larger lending quotas plus the *rallonge* mean that the whole of the burden can be shifted to the country running a surplus.[17]

3.4.6.   The STMS can be used for a total of nine months. A country wanting to borrow for a longer period would apply to the EMF for Medium Term Financial Assistance (MTFA). As a matter of fact, no one ever has, so the MTFA need not concern us much. We should note that lendings, if made, would be for two to five years and subject to economic policy conditions laid down by the EEC Council of Ministers. (This is probably why no one uses it: politically it is easier to be seen obeying the IMF, which is an impartial world body, than obeying other EEC members.)

3.4.7.   As with all lendings, the EMF's credits have to be financed. The resources are provided by member central banks. They have each deposited 20% of their gold and dollar reserves with the EMF. Technically what happens is that they swap the gold and dollars for ECUs issued by the EMF (see Chapter 14, Section 3 on the ECU). The swap is for three months. As each swap matures it is rolled over, but the amount involved is adjusted in line with the market value of gold and the dollar. The EMF's control over these reserves is very limited, though, since the central banks actually retain the dollars and gold involved, and they receive the interest earned on the dollars.[18] However, the arrangement does represent a step toward the pooling of EEC reserves.

SECTION 5. THE ARAB MONETARY FUND

3.5.1. For the record, we should note that there is a regional Arab equivalent to the IMF, the Arab Monetary Fund, although it is not large. The AMF was set up by the Articles of Agreement of the Arab Monetary Fund concluded in April 1976 at Rabat in Morocco. The AMF was modeled closely on the IMF, and includes 20 Arab countries: Algeria, Bahrain, Egypt, Iraq, Jordan, Kuwait, Lebanon, Libya, Mauritania, Morocco, Oman, Qatar, Saudi Arabia, Somalia, Sudan, Syria, Tunisia, U.A.E., Yemen Arab Republic, and People's Democratic Republic of Yemen[19] together with Palestine. Egypt's membership was suspended in April 1979. In the same month the AMF's paid-up capital was increased to 124 million Arab Accounting Dinars (AAD 1=SDR 3).[20]

3.5.2. The major shareholders of the AMF are Saudi Arabia and Algeria. Its headquarters are in Abu Dhabi, and its primary work is to help member states with their balance of payments problems through short-term and medium-term loans (not exceeding seven years). It also gives guarantees designed to ease member borrowings from other sources. The AMF tries, too, to coordinate the monetary policies of member states and to extend technical assistance to their banking and monetary institutions.

3.5.3. Before the creation of the AMF, there were several Arab institutions which provided project finance, but none of them offered balance of payments support. This assistance was usually arranged on an ad hoc, bilateral basis through high-level political discussions with the leadership of the states concerned. The AMF represents an attempt to rationalize and institutionalize this function. On the other hand, with paid-in capital of only approximately US\$ 400 million, it is a rather modest beginning.

SECTION 6. THE CENTRAL BANK SWAP NETWORK

3.6.1. A foreign exchange swap is a spot purchase of a currency coupled with a forward sale. The calculations involved are discussed in Chapter 10. The effects on the timing of a bank's exposure, and how swaps are used by central banks to intervene in foreign exchange and money markets, are discussed in Chapter 5. This section discusses a rather special use of the swap by central banks. Effectively the swap is used to borrow/lend foreign currency in exchange for domestic currency as a secured credit. The purpose is to lend the borrower foreign currency with which to intervene in the market.

TABLE 3.4.   Federal Reserve Swap Agreements as of July
31, 1981 (in Millions of US$).

Bank	Amount
Austrian National Bank	250
National Bank of Belgium	1,000
Bank of Canada	2,000
National Bank of Denmark	250
Bank of England	3,000
Banque de France	2,000
Deutsche Bundesbank	6,000
Banca d'Italia	3,000
Bank of Japan	5,000
Banco de Mexico	700
De Nederlandsche Bank	500
Bank of Norway	250
Bank of Sweden	300
Swiss National Bank	4,000
Bank for International Settlements:	
SFR/US$	600
Other European currencies/US$	1,250
	30,100

SOURCE: *Federal Reserve Bank of New York Quarterly Review*, Autumn
1981, p. 47.

3.6.2.   The technique was first developed systematically by the U.S. Federal
Reserve in the early 1960s. The first agreement was made by the Fed with the
Banque de France in 1962. Between 1962 and 1967 the Fed negotiated agreements with other central banks and the BIS. Table 3.4 shows how the Federal
Reserve swap network looked as of July 31, 1981. Other countries have also
put together swap arrangements, notably the United Kingdom in defense of
sterling;[21] and the Bank of Japan, for example, has a swap arrangement with
the Swiss National Bank for ¥ 200 billion.[22] And as we saw in Section 4, the
European Monetary Fund depends entirely on swaps for its resources.

3.6.3.   We will look at the Federal Reserve network in detail since it is the
most important. It consists of a set of standby credit agreements between the
United States and other countries. The countries, and the maximum limits, are
shown in Table 3.4. Each arrangement provides for an exchange of currencies
between the two countries with a commitment to reverse it in three months.
At first, these swaps gave a full exchange risk guarantee to both central banks.
After July 1973 the exchange risk on drawings by the Federal Reserve was
shared evenly with the foreign central bank from which it was borrowing.
Other central banks borrowing from the Federal Reserve had to take the full
risk. Then in 1981 it was agreed that the earlier system would be restored.[23]

3.6.4. To see how the swap network actually works, let's suppose the Federal Reserve wants to sell deutsche marks to support the U.S. dollar. Suppose it needs DMK 220 million (equivalent, say, to US$ 100 million) from the Bundesbank. What actually happens is that it sells the Bundesbank US$ 100 million in exchange for DMK 220 million, with an agreed reversal in three months' time at a fixed rate. The Bundesbank's reserves of foreign exchange rise by US$ 100 million and those of the Federal Reserve rise by DMK 220 million. In other words, the swap has increased both central banks' reserves. This apparent magic is caused, of course, by the fact that central banks report their reserves as the total of the assets in foreign exchange, without deducting the contingent liability on any forward exchange deals.

3.6.5. Central bank swaps, like any other swaps, can have an effect on the domestic money market. (The mechanics are explained in Chapter 5, Section 3.) But in general the main reason central banks use them is to lay hands on foreign currency with which to defend their own currency. The Federal Reserve for many years did not hold foreign exchange reserves; hence its interest in developing the swap technique in the early 1960s. Once the network was in place, the Bank of England became an active user in the 1960s to defend sterling; the Banque de France around the time of "the events of May" in 1968— and on other occasions—also used the system, as have many other central banks. The main user, though, has been the Federal Reserve itself. It has borrowed mostly from the Bundesbank and the Swiss National Bank. The movement in its borrowings can be seen from Figure 3.2. It shows how drawings rose at times of peak pressure on the dollar. Since April 1981, however, the U.S. policy has been one of nonintervention, so that the swap line has not been used (anyway, during periods of dollar strength the Fed has no need for the network).

		Bundesbank	Swiss National Bank	Bank of Japan	Banque de France
1977	September	215.6	—	—	—
	December	834.6	—	—	—
1978	March	1843.1	69.0	—	—
	June	1078.2	4.8	—	—
	September	724.1	170.5	—	—
	December	4468.7	786.3	106.5	—
1979	March	3040.1	—	—	—

FIGURE 3.2. Federal Reserve Swap Commitments Outstanding; End of Period (In Millions of Dollars). (Source: *Federal Reserve Bank of New York Quarterly Review,* various issues. Outstanding totals do not always match reported changes because of valuation changes.)

	Bundesbank	Swiss National Bank	Bank of Japan	Banque de France
1980 March	—	—	—	—
June	863.7	—	—	—
September	253.2	—	—	100.2
December	—	—	—	107.2
1981 March	—	—	—	—
June	—	—	—	—
September	—	—	—	—
December	—	—	—	—

FIGURE 3.2.
(*Continued*)

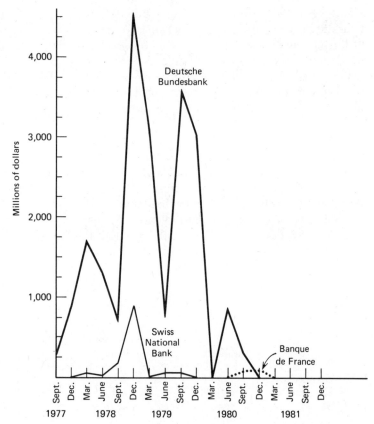

SECTION 7. FEDERAL RESERVE SYSTEM

3.7.1. Of the central banks we shall look at, the Federal Reserve is unique not only because of the central world role of the dollar but also because it is not one bank but 12. It is a system rather than a bank. It was set up by Act of

Congress much later than most other central banks—as late as 1913. The Federal Reserve Act divided the United States into 12 districts. It provided for the creation within each of a District Federal Reserve Bank. The system as a whole is controlled by the Federal Reserve's Board of Governors in Washington. The Board has seven members appointed by the President and confirmed by the Senate. Members of the Board are appointed for 14-year terms, which limits the political control exercised by the President over the Board. The Chairman of the Board, who is named by the President, serves in that capacity for only four years although he can be reappointed. But his term does not start when the President's does, so an incoming President may have to wait until well into his term before appointing a new chairman. Also, the Federal Reserve's independence is bolstered by the fact that it is a legally independent institution. The President and executive arm of the U.S. government can exercise no direct control over it.[24]

3.7.2. The Federal Reserve is, of course, subject to U.S. law, and so in the end comes under the authority of Congress. The relevant law is the Full Employment and Balanced Growth (Humphrey-Hawkins) Act of 1978. The act requires the Federal Reserve to present each year a report on monetary policy to Congress by February 20 and July 20. In the first of these, the Federal Reserve is required to set annual monetary policy targets. These have to be reviewed in the second report which also provisionally sets the next year's.[25]

3.7.3. The way in which the Fed handles monetary policy is as follows. Although it is in principle a group of 12 banks, in practice the Fed works through two major bodies. The New York Fed handles the system's intervention in the money and foreign exchange markets. Policy decisions on intervention are mainly controlled by the Federal Open Market Committee. Members of the FOMC include all seven Governors of the system, together with the president of the New York Federal Reserve Bank, and the presidents of four of the other eleven district banks.[26] Every member of the FOMC has one vote, but the chairman of the Board of Governors has a decisive part in setting policy. He acts as chief spokesman for the system. It would be very unusual for a major policy action to be decided on by the FOMC if the chairman of the Board of Governors had voted against.

3.7.4. The FOMC normally meets about once a month. It reviews economic conditions, its goals, and current policy guidelines. At the end of the meeting, the FOMC issues a directive to the manager of the Open Market Account in New York. (The Open Market Account is the system's portfolio of U.S. Treasury and federal agency securities, and bankers' acceptances, acquired in open market operations.) The directive sets a short-term target for the growth of the money supply which the FOMC thinks is needed to meet its annual targets. And it usually sets a limit on the movement in the federal funds interest rate. For example, the key parts of the November 1981 directive were:

Date of meeting	Specified short-term annualized rates of growth for period mentioned (percent) M-1B*	M-2	Range for Federal funds rate (percent)	Associated initial assumption for borrowed reserves (millions of dollars)	Basic discount rate and surcharge on day of meeting and subsequent changes (percent)	Notes
12/19/80	December to March 4¾	7	15–20	1,500	13 + 3 surcharge	The short-run specifications also included an objective of 4¼ percent growth for M-1A (adjusted for NOW account shifts). The Committee indicated some shortfall in growth would be acceptable if that developed in the context of reduced pressures in the money market.
2/3/81	December to March 5–6	8	15–20	1,300	13 + 3 surcharge	The short-run specifications also included an objective of 5 to 6 percent for growth of M-1A (adjusted for NOW account shifts). In a telephone conference on February 24, the FOMC modified the directive to accept some shortfall on growth of M-1A and M-1B from the rates specified at the February meeting.

	5½	10½ (or somewhat less)	13–18	1,130	13 + 3 surcharge 14 + 4 surcharge on 5/5	decided to focus on M-1B as the measure of transactions balances and to omit any reference to M-1A in its statement of monetary objectives for the short run. In a telephone conference on May 6, the FOMC agreed that the reserve paths should continue to be set on the basis of the short-run money growth objectives set at the March meeting, recognizing that the Federal funds rate might continue to exceed the upper end of the range indicated for consultation at that meeting.
5/18/81	April to June 3	6 (or lower)	16–22	2,100	14 + 4 surcharge	
7/7/81	June to September 7	see notes	15–21	1,500	14 + 4 surcharge	The 7 percent objective for M-1B growth was set provided that growth of M-2 remained around the upper limit of, or moved within, its range for the year.
8/18/81	June to September 7	see notes	15–21	1,400	14 + 4 surcharge 14 + 3 surcharge on 9/22	The short-run specifications for M-1B was again made provisional on M-2 growth remaining around the upper limit of, or moving within, its range for the year.

FIGURE 3.3. Specifications from Directives of the Federal Open Market Committee and Related Information for 1981. Reproduced from *Federal Reserve Bank of New York Quarterly Review*, Spring 1982.

* Abstracting from the effects of deposit shifts connected with the introduction of NOW accounts on a nationwide basis on December 31, 1980.

Date of meeting	Specified short-term annualized rates of growth for period mentioned (percent) M-1B*	M-2	Range for Federal funds rate (percent)	Associated initial assumption for borrowed reserves (millions of dollars)	Basic discount rate and surcharge on day of meeting and subsequent changes (percent)	Notes
10/6/81	September to December 7 (or slightly higher)	10	12–17	850	14 + 3 surcharge 14 + 2 surcharge on 10/13 13 + 2 surcharge on 11/2 13 on 11/17	In setting the objective for growth of M-2, the Committee recognized that its behavior would be affected by recent regulatory and legislative changes, particularly the public's response to the availability of the all savers certificate.
11/18/81	October to December 7	11	11–15	400	13 12 on 12/4	
12/22/81	November to March 4–5 (M-1)	9–10	10–14	300	12	The transaction measure of money was redesignated as M-1 with the same coverage as M-1B. The target no longer reflected the shift adjustment for conversion of outstanding interest-bearing assets into NOW accounts.

FIGURE 3.3 (Continued)

"The Committee . . . seeks behaviour of reserve aggregates consistent with the growth of M1B from October to December at an annual rate of about 7% . . . and with growth of M2 at an annual rate of around 11%. The Chairman may call for Committee consultation if it appears . . . [that this will produce] . . . a federal funds rate persistently outside a range of 11% to 15%."[27] (See Figure 3.3).

3.7.5. As we saw in Chapter 1, the Fed has a number of tools with which to meet these targets. The main one is open market operations. And we saw that in its control of the banking system generally, it has other tools, notably the discount window and reserve requirements. But these also are linked to another task of the Fed: supervision of the banking system. The topics that matter to us are control of banks' liquidity positions, by means of reserve requirements and general supervision, and control of their dealing positions.

3.7.6. Until 1980, the Fed had a problem in setting reserve requirements. It was as if, in umpiring a game, any attempt to penalize players simply led to their walking off the field and joining the next game. For the Federal Reserve could only impose reserve requirements on banks that were members of the Federal Reserve system. But a bank could function perfectly well—at least, at state level—without being a member. The Monetary Control Act of 1980 put a stop to that.[28] All banks had to keep reserves with the Fed, whether or not they were members of the system. So the Fed now has the freedom to set whatever level of reserve requirements it thinks is right, knowing that no bank can escape holding these reserves.

3.7.7. In its other control functions, the Fed shares responsibility with several other agencies. In fact, as Figure 3.4 shows, regulation of banking in the United States is rather complicated. For most banks the bodies that matter are the Fed, the FDIC, and either the Comptroller of the Currency (if the bank is chartered nationally) or the state banking department of its home state (if it is state chartered). The Federal Financial Institutions Examination Council (FFIEC) sets common standards for these bodies, to cut down overlap.

3.7.8. In any event, for our purposes, what matters is that none of these bodies fixes rigid limits for foreign exchange or money market positions. They do, though, regularly inspect the banks and check that position taking is properly controlled. And in June 1980, the FFIEC issued a Uniform Guideline on Internal Control for Foreign Exchange Activities in Commercial Banks.[29] Also, there is a legal lending limit for any one customer. The body setting the limit varies according to who is supervising the bank, but the limit is usually 10% of paid-in capital and reserves. There is also a legal limit on borrowings by a bank. They are defined as the bank's liabilities except for deposits, liabilities on bills of exchange, and so forth. The limit on borrowing is an amount equal to capital plus 50% of reserves.[30] Fed funds are half and half: the comptroller has ruled that for national banks, overnight Feds do not count as borrowings. But

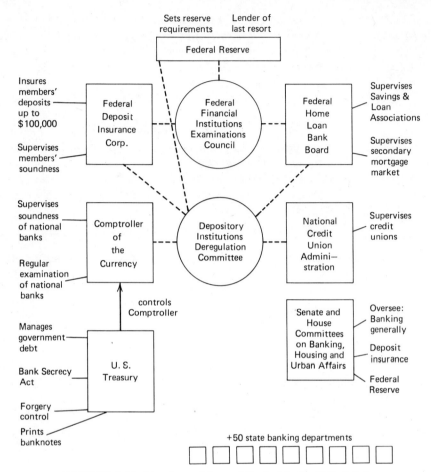

FIGURE 3.4. Banking Supervision and Control in the United States.

in some states overnight Feds count as a borrowing; and for all banks, *term* Fed funds count as a borrowing (or loan, depending on how you look at it).[31] So the legal lending and borrowing limits can be relevant.

3.7.9.   Finally we come to the control of America's gold and foreign exchange reserves. Although it is legally independent of the U.S. Treasury, the Fed cannot really operate independently of the Treasury in the foreign exchange market for long. For the Secretary of the Treasury is legally responsible for stabilizing the exchange value of the dollar, through the Exchange Stabilization Fund which is owned by the Treasury and which controls U.S. gold and foreign exchange reserves. The swap network (see Section 6 above) was a way for the Fed to get hold of foreign exchange to use for intervention. But that is only temporary: it has to be repaid. The Exchange Stabilization Fund owns the U.S. gold reserves and foreign exchange acquired from SDR sales and IMF drawings.[32]

3.7.10. These facts mean that policy is controlled by the Treasury, whether the Fed likes it or not. To an outsider, the policy seems to have been self-contradictory over the years. The United States is the world's largest gold holder. Even though its holdings have fallen over the years (see Chapter 16, Section 3), they still account for a quarter of the world's total. But U.S. official policy has always been that gold should be "demonetized"—that gold reserves should not count as an official reserve asset. If we accept this, then we realize that the dollar has virtually no international assets to back it, since the Treasury traditionally does not hold foreign exchange reserves on any scale. In fact, the ratio of U.S. reserves to annual imports would be 6.2% for 1980, compared with 24.4% for Germany. The logic of the Treasury's policy is that the dollar is to be trusted because it is the dollar, not because it is backed by other assets. Unfortunately, as was seen in 1977 through 1979, this is not always enough. More recently, the policy pendulum has swung back completely, toward a possible gold standard. This seems equally self-contradictory given the time and effort spent on breaking the dollar-gold link.

3.7.11. Intervention policy has also swung back and forth. During the 1960s the Federal Reserve, with Treasury support, became very involved in international efforts to prop up fixed exchange rates. It developed the currency swap network; the Treasury issued Roosa bonds (U.S. Treasury bonds in foreign currency—the ancestors of the more recent Carter bonds). By 1971, the U.S. Treasury had come to an "America-first" view, which led to the dollar devaluation and the breaking of the gold-dollar link. For a few years there was little intervention—"benign neglect" of the dollar was the policy. By 1977 this was leading to unsustainable pressure and the swap network was reactivated (see Figure 3.2). Then in 1981 the pendulum swung back to another kind of benign neglect, based on the idea that intervention was wrong in principle. The price paid was instability in the markets.

SECTION 8. THE BANK OF ENGLAND

3.8.1. The Bank of England is the second oldest central bank (after the Sveriges Riksbank) in the world, and was founded in 1694. Until 1946, when it was nationalized, its shareholders remained private. So its evolution into the role of a central bank has been very gradual, in comparison with that of the Federal Reserve which was born as a full-fledged central bank. The Chancellor of the Exchequer controls the Bank, under the Bank of England Act of 1946. The Treasury has an open-ended power to give directives to the Bank on any subject except the affairs of a particular bank customer. Thus, unlike the Federal Reserve, the Bank of England is legally completely subordinate to the executive arm of the government. However, the Bank has traditionally exercised an independent influence of its own, largely because of its excellent working contacts with the City of London, from which the Treasury has traditionally been rather remote.

3.8.2.   The Bank is controlled by its Court of Directors which consists of the Governor, Deputy Governor, and 16 directors, all appointed by the Crown. The term of office of the Governor and Deputy Governor is five years, that of the directors is four years. Four of the directors retire each year; they are eligible for reappointment. It is the custom that no director is on the board of one of the major banks, and that at least one director is close to the trade unions. The remainder are drawn from industry, commerce, and from the senior officials of the Bank.[33]

3.8.3.   The Bank of England is, with the Department of Trade to a minor degree, solely responsible for controlling what U.K. banks do. This centralization of control, together with the Bank's close working contacts with the banking system, has generally meant that its attitude toward regulation of City activities has been pragmatic and informal, in contrast to the bias toward regulation we saw in the U.S. markets. This flexibility and informality helped the rapid development of the City of London's international financial activities during the 1960s and the 1970s despite the weakness of sterling.

3.8.4.   But during the 1970s various events combined to force the Bank to take a more legalistic approach. The first of these events was the secondary banking crisis of 1973, which was followed by the repercussions of the Herstatt banking failure in Germany. These showed that foreign exchange market dealers' internal controls had become rather lax, although in the United Kingdom strict enforcement of exchange control regulations had prevented any problems. Finally, the United Kingdom's entry into the EEC forced the Bank to harmonize its attitudes with the more legalistic approach of its counterparts in Europe. For example, the Bank had to introduce, for the first time, a legal definition of a bank and banking activity, in the Banking Act of 1979. For the first time, also, this act introduced a requirement that a bank should be recognized as such by the Bank of England in order to operate.

3.8.5.   As a result of these tendencies, the Bank of England brought out various important guidelines during 1980 and 1981. They affected the measurement of a bank's capital, its liquidity management, and its foreign exchange position limits. In each case the pragmatic tradition continues, in that no set ratio is laid down for the whole banking sector. But ratios are agreed upon with individual banks, who are expected to obey them.

3.8.6.   Two capital ratios are used: the gearing ratio, and the risk asset ratio. Crudely, the gearing ratio is the ratio between capital and total liabilities.

(The main items of capital are share capital, loan stocks with more than five years to run, and reserves. The exact definitions are more complex.)[34] The risk asset ratio is the ratio of capital to risk assets. Risk assets are calculated by weighting the value of the asset by a risk factor. Commercial lendings have a risk weight of 1; interbank money market loans have a weight of 0.2; unquoted investments a weight of 1.5. So from the lending bank's point of view a lending to a commercial customer ties up five times as much capital as an interbank lending, but only two-thirds of the capital that an unquoted investment in a company would tie up.

3.8.7. A similar philosophy underlies the liquidity ratios that banks are expected to keep. There are two ratios involved. First, there is the 6% of eligible liabilities that banks are required to keep invested in the discount market (see Chapter 1, Section 5). This is imposed mainly to permit management of the money market. Second, there is the supervision of individual banks' liquidity. As with capital ratios, the Bank of England does not impose across-the-board ratios. "Instead, as part of its regular discussions with senior management, the Bank will require to be fully satisfied that banks have both prudent policies and adequate management systems to ensure that the policies are followed."[35]

3.8.8. Prudential control of foreign exchange positions is similar. But in general, "for banks which are experienced in foreign exchange the Bank will expect to agree the following guidelines:

(i) Net open dealing position in any one currency: not more than 10% of the adjusted capital base . . .
(ii) Net short open dealing positions of all currencies taken together: not more than 15% of the adjusted capital base."

These guidelines apply to U.K. banks' overseas branches, as well as the U.K. operations, and in due course it is intended to include overseas subsidiaries; U.K. branches of foreign banks are treated on a case-by-case basis.[36]

3.8.9. As in the United States, the Treasury controls the gold and foreign exchange reserves. But their day-to-day management is entrusted to the Bank of England, which was responsible for the country's reserves long before the Treasury was. It is interesting that the low gold content of U.K. reserves—U.K. gold holdings in 1980 were half Belgium's—can be traced back to the Bank's private sector origins. During the nineteenth century its attitude was "maximum banking profits consistent with convertibility of sterling"; this meant low holdings of non-interest-bearing gold. More recent gold outflows were caused by the defense of sterling in the 1960s.[37] Since July 1979, 20% of the United Kingdom's reserves are on deposit, in exchange for ECUs, with the European Monetary Fund (see Section 4).

SECTION 9.   THE DEUTSCHE BUNDESBANK

3.9.1.   Unlike the Bank of England, the Bundesbank is legally independent of the government. Unlike the Federal Reserve's, that legal independence is not fettered by any equivalent of the Humphrey-Hawkins Act. Of the world's major central banks, the Bundesbank is probably the strongest: it has benefited from the German people's horror of inflation after their experience of the 1930s. The Deutsche Bundesbank Law of 1957 (Gesetz über die Deutsche Bundesbank—often cited as B Bank G) lays down in Article 12 that the Bundesbank "shall not be subject to instructions from the Federal Government." Of course, the Bundesbank must support government policy as far as it can without compromising its primary duty, the safety of the currency.[38]

3.9.2.   The Bundesbank is controlled by a central bank council, which usually meets every two weeks on a Thursday. (Sometimes these meetings are followed by a press conference, sometimes not. If it is announced that no press conference will be held, the market usually assumes there will be no change in policy.) The council's members are appointed by the President of the Federal Republic, on the government's recommendation (which must follow consultation with the council). The member's terms are usually eight years. The Bundesbank controls 11 provincial central banks (*Landeszentralbanken*) each of which handles official business in its *Land* (province).

3.9.3.   Control of foreign exchange positions and liquidity is carried out jointly by the Bundesbank and the Federal Banking Supervisory Office (Bundesaufsichtsamt für das Kreditwesen) in Berlin which is an independent federal agency under the jurisdiction of the Minister of Economics.[39] The main laws covering this area are the Bundesbank Law (Bundesbankgesetz) of 1957 and the Banking Law (Gesetz über das Kreditwesen, or Kreditwesengesetz—frequently KWG) of 1961. The main principles are laid down in the Principles Governing Capital and Liquidity of Banks (Grundsätze über das Eigenkapital und die Liquidität der Kreditinstitute), amended December 22, 1972, August, 30, 1974, and January 16, 1980. Briefly they may be summarized as follows:

1.   Loans and investments not to exceed 18 times own capital
2.   Net open position in foreign currencies and precious metals in total not to exceed 30% of own capital; net open position in any one-month or six-month period not to exceed 40%
3.   Long-term or illiquid loans and investments not to exceed own capital plus specified percentages of longer-term liabilities
4.   Short-term loans not to exceed specified percentages of short-term funds[40]

It is important to note, for a foreign branch operating in Frankfurt, that the total of "own capital" is defined as being net of any claim on the parent in the form of intercompany account, which restricts flexibility in the branch's lending to the overseas parent.

3.9.4. In line with other central banks, the Bundesbank is working toward supervising German banks on the basis of worldwide balance sheets. The first step was taken in 1978, when German banks with 100%-owned subsidiaries in Luxembourg (through which they had chaneled much business to sidestep German regulations) agreed to provide information to the Bundesbank and the Federal Banking Supervisory Office on what these subsidiaries were lending. Then in September 1981 they began to provide quarterly consolidated balance sheets, as a first step toward the introduction of balance sheet ratios on a consolidated basis.[41]

3.9.5. Unlike the United States, the United Kingdom, or France, but like Switzerland, Germany does not have any equivalent to the Exchange Stabilization Fund. The Bundesbank owns the country's reserves. Every change in the level of reserves alters the size of the Bundesbank's balance sheet and so the level of domestic currency (compare Chapter 5, Section 5).[42] However, this relationship is not so easy to observe since a recent change in the Bundesbank's accounting policy. Its regular press releases on the level of reserves now value foreign currency at "lower of cost or market." Hence since some U.S. dollars were bought at DMK 1.73 = US$ 1, reserves are, at the time of this writing, valued at DMK 1.73. Hence a $100 million outflow would show up as a DMK 173 million change in reserves rather than, say, the DMK 200 million that actually changed hands if the market rate were DMK 2.20. (The difference is posted to an adjustment account.)[43] The Bundesbank also owns Germany's gold reserves, which have remained fairly stable since 1971. Most of the gold holdings were acquired during 1951 through 1961, when the German "miracle" was taking place. In fact, in 1967, under U.S. pressure—exerted in the form of military leverage—Germany made a formal commitment that it would not try to convert its dollars into gold.[44]

SECTION 10. THE BANQUE DE FRANCE

3.10.1 The Banque de France dates back to Napoleon (it was founded in 1800) and, like Napoleon, it is a strong believer in tight central control. More than any of the other central banks we have discussed, its influence is everywhere in its banking system. It has 233 branches around the country, helping it to keep in close contact with credit conditions in each area. Its knowledge reaches down to the most minute details. For example, every bank, when approached to open a new account for a customer, must telex the Banque. It must check whether or not any problems have ever been reported with this customer's account (and must report any problems as they occur). This gives the Banque credit information on every individual and company in the country.

3.10.2.   Until 1946, the Banque de France, like the Bank of England, operated as a private company. Under the nationalization law, a reform of the Banque's statutes was provided for, but it did not in fact take place until 1973. The new statutes gave the Banque a much freer hand and laid down a new structure. Control of the Banque rests with the Governor, two Deputy Governors, and the general council. The Governor and his Deputies are appointed for an unlimited term by the President of the Republic. The council consists of 10 members, of whom one is elected by the staff of the Banque, and the rest are appointed by the government. Councillors serve for six years.[45] The council normally meets once a week.

3.10.3.   As a nationalized bank, the Banque de France does not have the independence of the Bundesbank or the Federal Reserve; but, as with the Bank of England, its prestige gave it authority (especially in the 1950s, when French governments rose and fell like a jack-in-the-box). Its control is shared with two other important bodies, the Commission de Contrôle des Banques and the Conseil National de Crédit. The Commission de Contrôle des Banques (whose secretariat is provided by the Banque de France) consists of the Governor of the Banque, and four or five other members.[46] It is responsible for banking supervision, and also sets—in conjunction with the Banque—certain liquidity and other ratios (see 3.10.4–7). The Conseil National de Crédit is a much larger body, with about 45 members drawn from agriculture, industry, and so forth. It has broad powers of credit control, which are exercised through and by the Banque de France.[47]

3.10.4.   French prudential liquidity and foreign exchange controls are very strict. The Commission de Contrôle des Banques (CCB) lays down minimum capital for banks. It also, with the Banque de France, lays down minimum reserve ratios. The Banque lays down "norms" for credit growth (see Chapter 1, Section 7). The CCB and the Banque lay down four other important ratios. These are the *coefficient de liquidité*, the *coefficient d'opérations à moyen et long terme*, the *coefficient de division des risques*, and the *rapport de couverture des risques*. Foreign exchange limits are agreed with each bank.

3.10.5.   The *coefficient de liquidité* (liquidity ratio) is, very simply stated, the ratio of net eligible liquid assets to liquid liabilities. It must be at least 60%. If more than 10% of a bank's balance sheet is in foreign currency, the ratio has to be calculated separately for both French francs and foreign currencies. The whole exercise then becomes nightmarishly complicated as there are eight possible ratios (and 21 subtotals to calculate) depending on whether the bank is oversold or overbought forward, more liquid or less liquid in foreign currency, and so on.[48]

3.10.6.   The *coefficient d'opérations à moyen et long terme* (medium- and long-term credits ratio) sets a maximum multiple of three times "own resources and savings resources" for the total of banks' lending to other banks for more than two years, long-term lendings, and medium-term credits not eligible for rediscount at the Banque de France.[49] An alternative, more generous ratio is also allowed which sets medium-term lendings against medium-term borrowings.

3.10.7. The *règle de division des risques* requires banks to report all lendings that exceed 25% of their own funds[50] while the *rapport de couverture des risques* is very similar to the Bank of England's weighted-risk-asset measure. Commercial credits are weighted at 1 again; money market lendings are weighted at 0.05 (relatively more favorable than the Bank's 0.2).[51]

3.10.8. France's gold and foreign exchange reserves are owned by the Fonds de Stabilisation des Changes (Exchange Stabilization Fund) which is controlled by the Treasury but managed on a day-to-day basis by the Banque de France. (As we have seen in 1.7.5., the fund's resources are sometimes concealed or exaggerated by swaps done with commercial banks.) The fund's franc resources are kept on current account at the Banque, and its franc requirements are met by interest-free loans from the Banque. Profits and losses of the fund are passed to the account of the Treasury.[52] As we have seen earlier, France for many years favored the role of gold as an international monetary asset; hence the total of gold held at the end of December 1980 was 81.85 million fine troy ounces, worth US$ 50 billion at the official French valuation, compared with foreign exchange reserves of US$ 25 billion: a ratio of two to one compared with almost equality in the case of Germany.[53] Indeed, after the Martinique Agreement between President Ford of the United States and President Giscard d'Estaing of France in 1974, France became the first major country to revalue its gold reserves at a market-related price, in January 1975.[54]

3.10.9. This emphasis on the role of gold flowed primarily from an insistence that the financing of international trade and the source of international liquidity should not depend on any single national currency such as the U.S. dollar. The classic statement of this position was in the press conference of General de Gaulle on February 4, 1965: "We hold as necessary that international exchange be established . . . on an indisputable monetary base that does not carry the mark of any particular country. What base? In truth, one does not see how in this respect it can have any criterion, any standard, other than gold. Eh! Yes, gold, which does not change in nature, which is made indifferently into bars, ingots and coins, which does not have any nationality, which is held eternally and universally. . . ."[55] In the very long run, General de Gaulle's policy has been very profitable, no matter how wrongheaded the original reasoning and no matter how undesirable dependence on gold as a reserve asset might be (see Chapter 16). French diplomacy failed to convince the world that the United States was mistaken in the creation of the SDR as a transnational reserve asset. But it has been financially backed by the rising price of gold in the free market over the subsequent decades.

SECTION 11. THE BANK OF JAPAN

3.11.1. Of the central banks we are looking at, the Bank of Japan and the Swiss National Bank are the only ones with private shareholders. Legally the Bank is a special corporation under the Bank of Japan Law of 1942 (although it traces its origin to 1882) which is held 45% by the public and 55% by the government. In practice, of course, the private shareholders have no say in running it.[56] The Minister of Finance can give general directives to the Bank, and can dismiss its officers. The usual Japanese "consensus" system, though, means that formal instructions almost never have to be given to the Bank.

3.11.2. The Bank is run by the Governor and Deputy Governor, who are appointed by the cabinet for five years, three or more directors appointed by the Minister of Finance for four years, and several advisers, appointed for two years. All these appointments are renewable. Major policy decisions are taken by the Policy Board, which consists of seven members. Two are government representatives and have no voting rights. Then there are the Governor and four representatives of industry, agriculture, country banking, and city banking. These five take decisions by majority vote. The Policy Board's decisions on discount rates and open market operations are independently made. Changes in reserve requirements must be approved by the Minister of Finance.[57]

3.11.3. Supervision of banks is carried out jointly by the Bank of Japan and the Ministry of Finance. The framework is provided by the recent banking law, in effect as of April 1982. Among other items, this confirms the circular issued by the Ministry of Finance in 1974, which limited banks' lending to a single company. The ceiling for ordinary banks was fixed at 20% of capital; for long-term credit banks, 30%, and for the Bank of Tokyo, 40%.[58]

3.11.4. Foreign exchange position limits are individually negotiated between each bank and the Bank of Japan, in coordination with the Ministry of Finance. The limit covers spot and forward positions in all currencies combined. It is set by the authorities on the basis of 'objective indicators' such as the total volume of exchange business with customers and other factors. In addition, since 1968 the Bank of Japan has set limits for foreign banks' net swap position into yen. This is to allow them to fund their domestic yen lending, since typically foreign banks do not have access to a large domestic yen deposit base. Japanese banks have also been allowed to run a net switch into yen since March 1979.

3.11.5. Japan, like the United States, the United Kingdom, and France, has a separate foreign exchange fund. In fact it has a Foreign Exchange Funds

Special Account and a Precious Metals Special Account, for the gold reserves. The Foreign Exchange Funds Special Account raises its yen finance by borrowing from the Bank of Japan, by issuing short-term bills (Foreign Exchange Fund bills), and by selling surplus foreign currency balances to the Bank of Japan. Most of the foreign currency is deposited overseas or invested in foreign currency securities, but at times part is held with Japanese banks on deposit or lent to them via swaps; and it is said that when Japanese reserves are rising unduly fast, this fact is sometimes concealed by means of foreign exchange swaps with commercial banks on a very large scale. (Compare the French case: Section 1.7.5.)[59]

SECTION 12.   THE SWISS NATIONAL BANK

3.12.1.   The SNB, founded in 1905, has two headquarters. The legal and administrative headquarters are at Berne, but the Bank's Directorate is in Zurich. It is a private corporation, but most of its shares have been held since the beginning by the cantons and cantonal banks.[60] The SNB is controlled by a Bank Council consisting of 40 members. Detailed control of the Bank is handled by a Bank Committee chosen by the Council. But for practical purposes the body which matters is the Directorate, which fixes the discount rate and decides on monetary policy. It consists of the Governor and two Deputy Governors, appointed by the federal government for six years. It also has deputy members, also appointed by the government for six years, and section directors, elected by the Bank Committee.[61]

3.12.2.   The SNB's international relationships are different from those of the other central banks we have looked at because Switzerland has a strict policy of international neutrality which has caused it to refuse to join the IMF and the World Bank. But the SNB works in parallel with other central banks, for instance in lending money to the IMF under the General Arrangements to Borrow and other IMF financings (see 3.2.9–10). The SNB is a shareholder in the BIS—not surprising, since the latter's headquarters is in Basle.

3.12.3.   Prudential control is shared by the SNB with the Commission de Contrôle des Banques. Detailed ratios are laid down in Swiss law between "own funds" (basically capital, reserves, and certain longer-term loans) and specified assets. Own funds must total 10% of open foreign exchange positions and 20% of open positions in precious metals.[62] (These last two limits are very generous compared with the Bank of England's although the level of own funds required is high.) Not more than 40% of a bank's own funds can be lent to a customer under guarantee (20% unsecured) without informing the CCB.[63]

3.12.4.   The law also lays down liquidity ratios. Cash and sight assets must meet the following ratios:

6% of total liabilities	up to 15%	of total eligible liabilities
12% of short-term liabilities	over 15% but less than 25%	of total eligible liabilities
24% of short-term liabilities	over 25% but less than 35%	of total eligible liabilities
36% of short-term liabilities	over 35% of the total	

So if a bank with a balance sheet of SFR 100 million were funding itself very short, say, with 30% of its liabilities being short term, it would have to hold cash and sight assets of 6% of the first SFR 15 million, 12% of the next SFR 10 million, and 24% of the last SFR 5 million, making a total of SFR 3.3 million.[64] There is a second ratio, for liquid assets as a percentage of total liabilities. Liquid assets must total:

35% of short-term liabilities	up to 15%	of total eligible liabilities
52½% of short-term liabilities	over 15% but less than 25%	of total eligible liabilities
70% of short-term liabilities	over 25% of the total	

So the same bank would have to hold liquid assets of SFR 14 million against its SFR 30 million short-term liabilities.[65]

3.12.5. Like the Bundesbank, the Swiss National Bank owns the country's reserves, and they form part of its balance sheet. So any currency inflow immediately inflates the SNB's balance sheet. The bulk of the reserves are held in gold: in October 1981 the SNB held 83.28 million ounces of gold worth $35.6 billion at current market price compared with $9.1 billion of foreign exchange. The high level of gold holdings is partly due to the traditional legal requirement that 40% of the Swiss note circulation be backed by gold.[66]

NOTES

1. There is a good general description of the IMF in A. W. Hooke, *The International Monetary Fund: Its Evolution, Organization and Activities*, IMF Pamphlet no. 37, Washington, D.C., 1981.

2. Ibid., p. 10.

3. The issues involved are thoroughly discussed in J. Gold, *The Standby Arrangements of the IMF*, IMF, Washington D.C., 1970; and J. Gold, *Financial Assistance by the International Monetary Fund: Law and Practice*, IMF Pamphlet no. 27, Washington D.C., 1980.

4. International Monetary Fund, *International Financial Statistics*, December 1981, pp. 14–15, column 18.

5. See J. Gold, *Financial Assistance*, and A. W. Hooke, *The International Monetary Fund,*

for details. The amounts borrowed under the Extended Fund Facility were SDR 1.6 billion to October 1981 by 19 countries and under the Supplementary Financing Facility SDR 805 million by 11 countries. The Buffer Stock Facility has been used by 11 countries but only for SDR 104 million.

6. *IMF Survey,* October 15, 1979.

7. IMF, *International Financial Statistics,* December 1981, p. 12.

8. IMF's 1981 *Annual Report,* p. 91.

9. Ibid., see pp. 172–189 also for the full legal details. Technically SAMA lends the Fund Saudi riyals but it agrees to convert the riyals into U.S. dollars request. The loan is denominated in SDRs and the interest rate applied is the combined gross yield to maturity on representative five-year government stocks in the five countries of the SDR (France, Germany, Japan, the United Kingdom, the United States).

10. Ibid., p. 92.

11. Ibid., p. 77. An exhaustive legal discussion of the SDR can be had from a series of pamphlets by Sir Joseph Gold, formerly general counsel of the IMF: *Floating Currencies, Gold and SDRs,* IMF Pamphelt no. 19, 1976; *Floating Currencies, SDRs and Gold,* IMF Pamphlet no. 22, 1977; *SDRs, Gold and Currencies,* IMF Pamphlet no. 26, 1979; *SDRs, Currencies and Gold,* IMF Pamphlet no. 33, 1980; and IMF Pamphlet no. 36, 1981, bearing the same title. The fund has published numerous other pamphlets on the SDR.

12. They were J. P. Morgan & Co., the First National Bank of New York (now Citibank), and the First National Bank of Chicago.

13. BIS Statutes, Article 27.

14. See *BIS's 51st Annual Report,* June 1981, pp. 149–63.

15. Regulation (EEC) no. 907/73 of the Council of April 3, 1973, Article 2. Reprinted in European Communities Monetary Committee, *Compendium of Community Monetary Texts,* Brussels, 1979. See also "The European System of Narrower Exchange Rate Margins," *Deutsche Bundesbank Monthly Report,* January 1976. Good general discussions of the political background can be found in L. Tsoukalis, *The Politics and Economics of European Monetary Integration,* Allen & Unwin, London, 1977, pp. 142–144; and in R. Hellmann, *Gold, the Dollar and the European Currency Systems: The Seven Year Monetary War,* Praeger, New York, 1979, pp. 37–42.

16. "The European Monetary System," *Deutsche Bundesbank Monthly Report,* March 1979.

17. A good discussion is in T. Padoa-Schioppa, "The EMF: Topics for Discussion," *Banca Nazionale del Lavoro Quarterly Review,* September 1980.

18. *Deutsche Bundesbank Monthly Report,* March 1979.

19. J. W. Salacuse, "Arab Capital and Middle Eastern Development Finance," *Journal of World Trade Law,* United Kingdom, July/August 1979, pp. 300–301.

20. *IMF Annual Report on Exchange Arrangements & Exchange Restrictions,* 1980, p. 28.

21. See for example F. Hirsch, *Money International,* Pelican Books, London, 1967, pp. 141–153.

22. Japanese Ministry of Finance, *Monthly Finance Review,* Japan, May 1980, p. 10.

23. *Federal Reserve Bulletin,* March 1981, pp. 211–2.

24. See for a general outline, Board of Governors of the Federal Reserve System, *The Federal Reserve System: Purposes and Functions,"* Washington D.C., 1974, especially pp. 13–19.

25. See "Operating Guides in U.S. Monetary Policy: A Historical Review," *Federal Reserve Bulletin,* 1979, pp. 685–686.

26. Board of Governors of the Federal Reserve, *The Federal Reserve System: Purposes and Functions,* 14–15. An excellent description of Federal Reserve operations is given in M. Stigum, *The Money Market: Myth, Reality and Practice,* Dow-Jones Irwin, United States, 1978.

27. *Federal Reserve Bulletin,* January 1982, p. 43.

28. More pompously, the Depository Institutions Deregulation and Monetary Control Act, 1980.

29. Reprinted in the 1980 *Annual Report of the Foreign Exchange Committee* sponsored by the Federal Reserve Bank of New York.

30. For lending limits for national banks, see United States Code, Title 12, Section 84. The borrowing limit is in USC Title 12, Section 82.

31. See M. Stigum, *The Money Market,* pp. 288, 308.

32. Board of Governors of the Federal Reserve, *The Federal Reserve System: Purposes and Functions,* p. 95; also see *Federal Reserve Bulletin,* March 1979, p. 219.

33. See Bank for International Settlements, *Eight European Central Banks,* Allen and Unwin, London, 1963, and *Bank of England Annual Report,* 1980.

34. "The Measurement of Capital," *Bank of England Quarterly Bulletin,* September 1980.

35. "The Liquidity of Banks," *Bank of England Quarterly Bulletin,* March 1981. See also "The Measurement of Liquidity," *Bank of England Quarterly Bulletin,* September 1982.

36. "Foreign Currency Exposure," *Bank of England Quarterly Bulletin,* June 1981.

37. An interesting, if controversial, article in the *Financial Times* (February 9, 1982) attributed them to secret swap agreements with the BIS.

38. See H. Aufricht, *Central Banking Legislation,* IMF, Washington D.C., 1967, pp. 252–255.

39. Ibid., p. 279; Inter-Bank Research Organisation, *The Regulation of Banks in the Member States of the EEC,* section 4.19, Sijthoff and Noordhoff, The Netherlands, 1978.

40. Published annually in the German version of the *Deutsche Bundesbank Annual Report.*

41. "Banking Supervision on the Basis of Consolidated Returns," *Deutsche Bundesbank Monthly Report,* August 1981.

42. See Bank for International Settlements, *Eight European Central Banks,* London, George Allen & Unwin Ltd., 1963, p. 82.

43. "The Deutsche Bundesbank's Reserves," *Deutsche Bundesbank Monthly Report,* January 1982.

44. S. Strange, *International Economic Relations of the Western World, 1959–71, Volume 2: International Monetary Relations,* Oxford University Press for the Royal Institute of International Affairs, 1976, pp. 270–272.

45. M. Aubert et al., *La Banque de France,* Editions Berger-Levrault, Paris, 1975, pp. 33–5.

46. Ibid. pp. 188–9.

47. Ibid. pp. 185–8.

48. Commission de Contrôle des Banques, Instruction No. 77–02A, Annexe, "Modalités de calcul."

49. CCB, Instruction No. 77–03A.

50. CCB, Instruction No. 79–03A.

51. CCB, Instruction No. 79–02A, Annexe 1, "Eléments de calcul du rapport de couverture des risques."

52. "Le Fonds de Stabilisation des Changes," Note d'Information No. 38, Banque de France, December 1978.

53. IMF, *International Financial Statistics,* March 1981.

54. See for the background R. Hellmann, *Gold, the Dollar and the European Currency Systems: The Seven Year Monetary War,* Praeger, New York, 1979, pp. 139–140.

55. Quoted in F. Hirsch, *Money International,* p. 385. See also for background S. Strange, *International Economic Relations,* R. Hellmann, *Gold, the Dollar and the European Currency Systems;* and E. A. Kolodziej, "French Monetary Diplomacy in the '60's," *World Affairs,* Summer 1972.

56. See L. S. Pressnell (ed.) and Bank of Japan Economic Research Department, *Money and Banking in Japan*, Macmillan, London, 1973, pp. 148–162; and D. E. Fair, "The Independence of Central Banks," *The Banker*, London, October 1979.

57. D. E. Fair, "The Independence of Central Banks."

58. E. Fukao, "A Law for all Seasons," *The Banker*, August 1981.

59. Bank of Japan, *The Japanese Financial System*, Tokyo, 1978, pp. 149–150.

60. BIS, *Eight European Central Banks*, p. 268.

61. Ibid. pp. 270–275.

62. "Loi fédérale sur les banques et caisses d'épargne, du 8 novembre 1934," modification du 1ᶜʳ décembre 1980, article 13.

63. Ibid., article 21, subsection 1.

64. Ibid., subsection 3.

65. Ibid., articles 15–18.

66. Ibid., article 19.

4

EXCHANGE CONTROLS AND CURRENCY GROUPS

This chapter explains how exchange controls affect the markets. It begins with a general outline of how exchange controls work, with a specific example (France). Then it explains two currency groups: the European Monetary System, and the French franc zone. Then it looks at specialized exchange control systems: clearing accounts, blocked currency, and two-tier systems.

SECTION 1.   TYPES OF EXCHANGE CONTROL

4.1.1.   A trader's life in the foreign exchange and money markets is often made harder by exchange controls. It's not his job to understand all the fine points. But it helps to know the kinds of controls there are, what effects they have, and why they are used. It's also helpful to know about currency groups. The two most important currency groups are the European Monetary System and the French franc zone. We look at them in Sections 2 and 3. Exchange controls can create special markets: clearing systems, blocked balances, and two-tier systems. They are covered in Sections 4, 5, and 6. But we start with exchange controls in general.

4.1.2. We can split them into three categories: controls on current account transactions, controls on capital accounts, and controls on interbank dealing. We'll look at the first category first. The most common control on current account transactions is that which tries to prevent residents from holding foreign currency. Typically these controls would include: (1) Compulsory sale of foreign currency receipts to the authorities or authorized banks within a certain time. This prevents exporters from building up foreign currency holdings from overseas earnings. (2) Restrictions on timing and amount of spot or forward purchases of foreign currency. This stops residents from shifting cash into foreign currency. It also stops importers from protecting themselves against devaluation. (3) Control of terms of credit given, or taken, in international trade. A common limit for credit given to foreign purchasers of a country's exports is 180 days, unless special permission is given. Advance payments for imports are often forbidden. These controls prevent people from changing the time of receipts or payments. Otherwise an exporter could delay being paid in foreign currency if he expects it to be worth more after a devaluation. For imports, it would work the opposite way. (4) Control on trading in gold or other internationally transferable commodities. Otherwise, people could buy gold, ship it overseas, and sell it for foreign currency. (5) Compulsory bringing home of dividends and so on from overseas investments. Otherwise foreign currency could be allowed to pile up overseas. (6) Restrictions on spending on overseas travel. Otherwise people might take cash with them and use it to open foreign bank accounts. Another type of control on current account transactions is that designed to restrict inflows of foreign currency. These controls will normally be the reverse of the above—for example, forward purchases of foreign currency will be freely permitted, but not forward sales.

4.1.3. Controls on capital account outflows could include controls of purchases of securities denominated in foreign currency and other overseas assets. Sometimes such purchases are routed through an "investment currency" or "financial currency" market to make them more expensive. (This is a special case of the two-tier system, discussed in Section 6). A country may also ban lending of domestic currency to nonresidents. This prevents them from borrowing the currency and selling it off as a speculation. Or it may require that overseas investments (or trading between two other countries—"merchanting") be financed by foreign currency borrowings. Among controls on inflows is the reserve requirement on banks' liabilities to nonresidents (and perhaps companies' borrowings from nonresidents). This will reduce the amount of interest they can afford to pay on such borrowings (see Chapter 13, Section 5).

There may be a restriction on nonresidents' purchases of domestic assets, or a ban on payment of interest on bank deposits to nonresidents (or a compulsory commission—"negative interest").

4.1.4. Controls on banks' dealing could include: (1) Limit on a bank's total open position against domestic currency. This stops straight speculative selling of a currency. (2) Limit on the total "spot against forward" position. Otherwise a bank could be oversold forward and long spot (see Chapter 17, Section 2). (3) Limit on the permitted maturity of forward deals. (4) Requirement that the underlying commercial details be produced to justify individual deals. (5) Restrictions on foreign banks' "nostro" accounts (working balances), for example, the banning of overdrafts or limits on the maximum balance.

4.1.5. As the above shows, the possible controls are many and varied. The primary source of information about the controls operating in any given country must always be the central bank or monetary authority in that country. Commercial banks, brokers, or lawyers may also be able to give current information. Published information cannot always be relied on because of the frequency with which some countries change their regulations. But some useful background sources are: (1) IMF: *Annual Report on Exchange Arrangements and Exchange Restrictions;* (2) *OECD: Financial Market Trends* (for recent changes); (3) *A Guide to International Exchange and Trade Regulations,* by A. Parker, the looseleaf updating service published by Jordans Ltd., Bristol, United Kingdom.

4.1.6. To give an examle of how controls work, we look at France. Detailed regulations change frequently (there are four thick volumes setting out the French system), so the specific information given here is purely illustrative. The idea is to show how a country needs a whole network of controls as soon as it has any. As soon as one hole in the dike is filled, funds flow out of another. The French system is that receipts of foreign currency (including dividends, etc.) have to be sold normally within one month of the date on which the payment falls due. Forward purchase of foreign currency for imports cannot be made more than two months ahead of the payment date (six months or one year in the case of certain foodstuffs, etc.). Forward cover of interest payable/receivable on foreign currency borrowings is forbidden. Credit terms on exports are normally restricted to 180 days unless authorization is given. Advance payments for imports are permitted but only up to 10% of the contract value (30% for capital goods) unless authorization is given. There is a free gold market in Paris, but it is insulated from the world market: imports and exports of monetary gold are restricted.

4.1.7. The effect of these controls is to restrict the freedom of exporters and importers to speculate against the franc. The restriction on credit terms on exports reduces the scope for delaying foreign currency receipts in the hope that a franc devaluation will make them worth more. Equally, the restrictions on advance payments for imports and on forward purchases of foreign currency reduce the scope for selling French francs to protect oneself against devaluation. But capital controls are also needed. Otherwise it would be possible for foreigners to speculate against the franc by borrowing French francs from domestic banks and selling them for foreign currency. Hence the Banque de France bans loans of domestic francs to nonresidents. And purchase of foreign securities and so forth have to go through a *devises-titres* market, whereby French residents have to pay a premium to acquire foreign currency. Also, overseas investments must normally be financed by foreign currency borrowings.

4.1.8. To complete the network, the Banque de France operates controls on banks' total open positions against French francs and on foreign banks' French franc accounts, on which overdrafts require official approval. But banks are not necessarily required to provide commercial details underlying every forward transaction. This gives some flexibility to the forward French franc market (in comparison to that, say, for Irish pounds or Danish kroner).

4.1.9. The point of this description is that to succeed in controling a currency market, you must apply controls on the entire range of transactions. If there were no capital account controls, controls on forward sales of French francs for import payments could be avoided by, say, purchasing foreign currency bonds and selling them when the payment came due. Hence current account controls have to be matched by capital account controls. The ban on nonresident borrowings of French francs, too, operates to restrict speculation in the forward market by cutting down the supply of Euro-French francs, which makes the forward market outside France thinner and more dangerous to speculate in. (See Chapter 5 for how the Euro- and forward markets relate.)

4.1.10. The *devise-titres* system in operation is the same as that during 1969–1971; it was set up in July 1981 at a time of heavy pressure on the franc. Experience of the earlier period showed two main problems with this type of system. First, while the premium on the *devise-titres* acted as a barometer of pressure on the franc, this in itself could lead to speculation against the currency. Second, the resulting discount on French securities held abroad, compared with the price in the domestic market, could damage the reputation of the issuer of the security through no fault of its own. Finally, it is worth adding that in general, to quote the OECD, "controls on international portfolio operations, even when accompanied by complementary measures, appear to have been largely ineffective in preventing reserve changes or exchange rate adjustments."[1] Indeed, the French foreign exchange market is one of the most tightly controlled of the major currencies in the West, yet this has not prevented the franc from being forced to leave the EEC snake in 1974 and again in 1976, nor from having to devalue on several occasions, most recently in the autumn of 1981. An exchange control system is only a tool for controlling the speed of a currency's adjustment to reality, not a substitute for that adjustment.

SECTION 2.   THE EUROPEAN MONETARY SYSTEM

4.2.1.   The European Monetary System is the successor to the European System of Narrower Exchange Rate Margins (which was generally referred to as the snake). The EMS was set up in March 1979. It consists of two main elements: an agreement about a community exchange rate regime, and a decision to create a European Monetary Fund (see Chapter 3, Section 4). Its development is part of an effort by the members of the EEC to create the conditions for "convergence" of their economies into an economic and monetary union.

4.2.2.   The history of the EMS is briefly as follows. At the Hague conference of the heads of state and government of the EEC in December 1969, a decision was reached on the principle of achieving European monetary union step by step. In October 1970, the methods of achieving this union were outlined in a paper prepared by a group of experts headed by Pierre Werner of Luxembourg, often called the Werner Plan.[2] This program called for completion of monetary integration by 1980. It also called for smaller margins of movement among European currencies and intervention in the foreign exchange market using currencies of the community, rather than the U.S. dollar. This plan was overtaken by the Nixon devaluation of August 1971, but by a resolution of March 1972 the EEC Council decided to reduce the margin of movement among the European currencies to plus or minus 2.25%. This meant that any individual currency in the snake (as it came to be called) could fluctuate against an outside currency such as the U.S. dollar by up to 4.5%, in line with the margin then prevailing internationally, but by only half that amount against another snake currency. In March 1973, following the decision to let the U.S. dollar float, the EEC countries decided to maintain a joint float of their currencies (with the exception of the pound sterling and the Italian lira) independent of the dollar.[3] The European Monetary Cooperation Fund (see Chapter 3, Section 4) was established in June 1973, making it possible to carry out intervention and settlement operations among several countries at once. During 1973 and 1974 the EEC Commission proposed on several occasions the pooling of reserves within the community.[4] And in July 1978 the Bremen meeting of heads of state and government of the community decided to establish a "scheme for the creation of closer monetary cooperation leading to a zone of monetary stability in Europe." (See Appendix 4.)[5]

4.2.3.   So the basic objective of the EMS is ambitious, yet simple. It aims to create a zone of monetary stability in Europe. It should be stressed that this concept does not mean a kind of regional Bretton Woods (see Chapter 2). The EMS has a number of new features. They include wider margins than those permitted under Bretton Woods, the scope and flexibility of the different credit mechanisms, and in particular the creation of the ECU and its central role in the system. At the same time, though, there is no strong evidence that the EMS is likely to progress further toward economic and monetary union in Europe. That would call for a major change of political will among the member nations. They would have to give up their economic sovereignty to some central power. Against this, however, should be set the practical successes of the EMS and its predecessor, the snake. They have achieved relatively stable exchange rates within the currency group during 1972–1980, a period when movements in currencies outside the EEC were particularly sharp and volatile.

4.2.4.   The operational guidelines for the EMS revolve around three key concepts: the *parity grid*, the *European Currency Unit*, and the *divergence indicator*. Each currency participating in the EMS has a central rate—comparable to the parity which prevailed under the Bretton Woods arrangements—which is determined in terms of ECUs. The ECU is fully defined in Chapter 14. For our purposes here we note only that it consists of a "basket" made up of the nine EEC currencies (the Greek drachma will be included later). We will treat it here as if it were a currency like the dollar. Hence the central rate for the deutsche mark, for example, would be ECU 1 = DMK 2.54502. From these central rates a "grid" of bilateral central rates between pairs of EMS currencies is calculated.

4.2.5.   Thus, for example, in the EMS as of March 23, 1981, the central rate for the Belgian franc against the ECU was 40.7985. The central rate for the deutsche mark was 2.54502. As a result, the central rate for the Belgian franc against the deutsche mark can be seen to be 16.0307. Around these central rates margins of plus or minus 2.25% are established. (In the actual calculation of the grid, the margins used are not exactly 2.25%, for mathematical reasons: see Appendix 3 on the currency basket concept). This results in a grid of upper and lower limits for each currency against any other member currency (see Table 4.1). These intervention limits set the levels at which the central banks involved intervene in the market. The parity grid levels are the key limits for the EMS. In principle, intervention takes place in the currencies of the members involved. (Often, however, the movement toward an intervention limit is triggered by a movement against a third currency, particularly the U.S. dollar, so that intervention against the U.S. dollar is required).

4.2.6.   The second operational concept governing intervention activity in the EMS is the divergence indicator. This is intended to serve as a guideline, prompting the relevant central bank to activity. *In practice, however, the par-*

TABLE 4.1. Central Rates and Intervention Points between the European Countries Participating in the European Monetary System (EMS) as at 6/14/82.

	Belgium	Denmark	France	Italy	Netherlands	Ireland	West-Germany
100 FB	—	17.9030	14.3800	2828.00	5.60900	1.50241	5.07400
Belgium		18.3098	14.7072	3002.58	5.73646	1.53659	5.18961
		18.7260	15.0420	3188.00	5.86700	1.57155	5.30800
100 Dkr.	534.000	—	78.5350	15444.00	30.6325	8.20550	27.7150
Denmark	546.154		80.3239	16398.70	31.3300	8.39216	28.3433
	558.600		82.1500	17412.00	32.0425	8.58300	28.9900
100 FF	664.800	121.730	—	19227.00	38.1375	10.2155	34.5000
France	679.941	124.496		20415.70	39.0045	10.4479	35.2863
	695.400	127.330		21677.00	39.8925	10.6855	36.0900
100 Lire	3.13650	0,574300	0.461300	—	0.179925	0.0481970	0.162800
Italy	3.33047	0.609804	0.489818		0.191051	0.0511758	0.172839
	3.53600	0.647500	0.520100		0.202850	0.0543380	0.183500
100 Hfl.	1704.45	312.080	250.67	49296.00	—	26.1915	88.4550
Netherlands	1743.23	319.183	256.38	52341.90		26.7864	90.4673
	1782.85	326.450	262.21	55577.00		27.3975	92.5250
1£	63.6315	11.6509	9.35850	1840.32	3.65000	—	3.30200
Ireland	65.0792	11.9159	9.57129	1954.05	3.73324		3.37736
	66.5600	12.1870	9.78900	2074.80	3.81800		3.45400
100 DM	1884.00	344.970	277.090	54490.00	108.0775	28.9520	—
West-Germany	1926.93	352.817	283.396	57857.40	110.5370	29.6090	
	1970.85	360.830	289.850	61433.00	113.0500	30.2845	
ECU1=	44.9704	8.2340	6.61387	1350.27	2.57971	0.691011	2.33379

ity grid of intervention limits has remained the dominating factor. The divergence indicator has had a rather limited role. To be frank, this is because the grid concept is much more easily understood (and measured). However, the divergence indicator concept could perhaps assume greater importance in future. The intention behind the divergence indicator was to pin "responsibility" on a particular currency for causing a problem of intervention. This was needed because the parity grid requirement is always bilateral. If a currency is at its floor against a second currency, then the second currency is by definition at its ceiling against the first. There is no immediate means of telling which currency is "responsible" for this situation. Is it the strong currency pushing up, or the weak moving down? The divergence indicator tries to provide a broader measure of "responsibility" by measuring a currency's movement against its central rate in terms of the ECU. As we saw in 4.2.5, the maximum permitted movement from the central rate is 2.25%. For the divergence indicator, a threshold of divergence is set at 75% of the maximum divergence allowed for each currency. See Appendix 3 for details.

4.2.7.   When a currency crosses its divergence threshold, in the words of the resolution of the European council on the establishment of the EMS (see Appendix 4 for full text), "this results in a presumption that the authorities concerned will correct this situation by adequate measures, namely:

(a)   diversified intervention;
(b)   measures of domestic monetary policy;
(c)   changes in central rates;
(d)   other measures of economic policy."

The emphasis on diversified intervention is to allow a better spread of the burden of intervention among currencies of the EMS. Intervention should not always be restricted to the currency which is furthest away from the currency of the intervening country. For example, suppose the deutsche mark rises above its divergence threshold, at a time when the Danish krona is the weakest currency in the EMS. If all of the Bundesbank's intervention were concentrated in the Danish krona, this might have undesirable effects in Denmark. However, it should be emphasised that in speaking of intervention in relation to the divergence indicator, we are talking of a "presumption" which in practical terms frequently seems to be ignored. It is the parity grid which is critical.

SECTION 3.   THE FRENCH FRANC ZONE

4.3.1.   Present French legislation no longer makes direct reference to the French franc area. From an official exchange control viewpoint, the concept was abolished with effect from January 31, 1967. But in the context of coun-

tries' overall relationships with France the concept survives. In this sense the
French franc area is a zone allowing free movement of funds among certain
countries in Africa (and certain Pacific islands). It consists of France and
the following countries: (1) the countries of the West African Monetary
Union (Benin, Ivory Cost, Niger, Senegal, Togo, and Upper Volta); (2) the
countries of the Central African Customs and Economic Union (Cameroon,
Central African Empire, People's Republic of the Congo, and Gabon) and
Chad; (3) three North African countries (Algeria, Morocco, and Tunisia);
(4) two former operations account countries (Madagascar and Mauritania);
and (5) two other countries (Comoros and Mali). This broad definition is
used, for example, in compiling trade statistics. For exchange control
purposes, the definition is narrower, excluding (3) and (4). Countries listed
under (1), (2), and (5) maintain operations accounts with the French Treasury
(see below), and there is in essence no exchange control applied by France
to these countries. Payments between them take place at fixed exchange
rates.[6]

4.3.2.   The French franc zone in Africa falls into two parts: the west African
zone and the Central African zone. Both zones possess a regional central bank.
The Banque Centrale des Etats de l'Afrique de l'Ouest (BCEAO) has its
headquarters in Dakar in Senegal. The Banque des Etats de l'Afrique Centrale (BEAC) has its headquarters in Yaounde in Cameroon. The framework of
the two zones is virtually identical. There is, in each case, a treaty among the
member countries in Africa and a treaty between each zone and France. There
is a second treaty between each zone and France concerning their respective
operations accounts with the French Treasury. Treaties of cooperation between the member countries in Africa provide for a common currency unit,
the CFA franc, (CFA stands for Communauté Française Africaine). The parity
is FFR 1 = CFA 50. They provide that CFA franc notes and coins should be
legal tender throughout the territory of the countries of each zone. Member
countries pool their reserves, which are held for their account by the central
banks in the region. The treaties of cooperation with France provide for the
unlimited guarantee by France of the money issued by the central banks and
for the deposit with the French Treasury of most of the exchange reserves
owned by member countries.

4.3.3.   The treaties concerning the operations accounts with the French
Treasury provide for the actions to be taken if the zone should go into debit,
and if the parity of the French franc should change against the unit of account.
In each case the unit of account is the CFA franc, at 50 CFA to 1 FFR.[7] The
zone is still developing. In January 1979, the BEAC and the Bank of Zaire
signed an agreement to establish the Central African Clearing House (see
below for clearing arrangements). In October 1979, the BEAC agreed to establish a money market in member countries during 1980, but limited progress
was made.[8]

SECTION 4. CLEARING ACCOUNTS

4.4.1. Clearing accounts are devices to ease international trade when a shortage of convertible foreign currency exists. As such, they were widely resorted to in the Western world just after the Second World War. They are still used in many cases between developing countries, and between certain developing countries and Socialist countries.[9] They are a device used to economize on scarce foreign exchange. The mechanism by which the bilateral payments agreements operated between the major industrial countries in the immediate postwar era was as follows:

"The central banks, as technical agents, supplied their own currency at a fixed rate of exchange against that of their partner up to a certain limit, which was often referred to as the 'swing,' since it was intended to afford room for minor fluctuations in commercial deliveries between the two countries; beyond the limits thus fixed settlements had generally to be made in gold or convertible currency."[10] This is in essence the arrangement still used today.

4.4.2. A development of these bilateral agreements evolved into a multilateral arrangement, the European Payments Union. This operated as follows: (1) Each month the union took over all bilateral surpluses and deficits of each of the members. Say, for example, during July 1950 Belgium ran a bilateral surplus with Britain. This would be treated as a surplus with the union in the case of Belgium and as a deficit with the union in the case of Britain. Britain would not be called on to settle directly with Belgium. (2) The monthly net positions of each member since mid-1950 were recorded by the BIS (the agent of the scheme), with the appropriate sign, and cumulated, so that at the end of each month each member had a "cumulative net position" within the union. (3) At the end of each month the change in a member's cumulative net position, compared with a month ago, had to be settled between the member and the union. (4) The main means of settlement were gold, U.S. dollars, and so-called "credits." The latter were in effect IOUs denominated in the borrower's currency. The lender undertook to accumulate them up to a certain ceiling. To some extent, these can be thought of as "swing credits" on top of the multilateral settlement of facility.[11]

4.4.3. So we see that the EPU operated as a truly multilateral settlement system. The device of cumulating the net monthly positions meant that even if Britain ran a deficit with Belgium during the month, a surplus with the Netherlands could be used to offset this. The system allowed a larger deficit against Belgium than might have been permitted under the swing credit arrangements.

4.4.4. Although such clearing accounts have largely disappeared from the industrialized world, they remain widespread both among Socialist countries, where they are extensively used between Comecon members, and also among the developing countries. In this case they are generally bilateral payments agreements with another country. But there are also a number of regional clearing arrangements.[12] Examples include the Central American Clearing House of Costa Rica, El Salvador, Guatemala, and Honduras and the multilateral clearing system of the Latin American Free Trade Association (LAFTA), grouping Argentina, Bolivia, Brazil, Chile, Colombia, the Dominican Republic, Equador, Mexico, Paraguay, Peru, Uruguay, and Venezuela. Payments are made through accounts maintained by the central banks of the various countries under reciprocal credit agreements within the framework of the clearing systems. The Asian Clearing Union linking Burma, India, Nepal, Pakistan, and Sri Lanka operates a rather similar system, and the West African Clearing House links Benin, The Gambia, Ghana, Ivory Coast, Liberia, Mali, Niger, Nigeria, Senegal, Sierra Leone, Togo, and Upper Volta.[13]

4.4.5. The restrictions built into such systems sometimes lead to switching possibilities. A number of houses specialize in putting together triangular, or even more complex, switch deals. For example, a company selling shoes to Egypt might be credited with dollars in an account designated as being usable only for payments to Egypt for goods. It might use these dollars to purchase cotton, to be sold to some other company, in exchange for convertible currency.

SECTION 5. BLOCKED CURRENCY

4.5.1. Such deals are very like those seen in the case of a blocked currency regime. Blocked currency may arise from a clearing agreement, where the currency is available only for purchase of goods from the other party to the clearing agreement. Another frequent cause of blocked currency balances is the setting up of exchange controls by a country. For example, following the declaration of UDI (unilateral declaration of independence) by Rhodesia in 1965, the United Kingdom blocked various accounts belonging to Rhodesian companies and individuals in the United Kingdom. Transfers to or from these accounts required special authorization. Equally, following a change of government, it is not uncommon for other countries to block the accounts of individuals from certain countries, often as a reprisal for the seizure of their own nationals' assets in a country concerned. For example, for many years the United States blocked accounts of Chinese individuals and companies in the United States, in retaliation for Chinese seizure of U.S. citizens' assets in China during the Chinese revolution. Another case where blocked accounts may arise is where an individual emigrates from a country. Frequently his assets in the country from which he is departing are blocked, either temporarily or permanently.

4.5.2. An interesting hybrid case was the so-called blocked rand market. Foreigners who had invested in South Africa before 1961 found that after the

Sharpeville riots, the South African authorities set up exchange controls. These meant that although foreigners could still sell their local securities on the Johannesburg stock exchange, the proceeds from such sales were blocked within South Africa. They were deposited in a blocked account in the name of the foreigner at a commercial bank. The proceeds could be taken abroad only under certain conditions. However, in order to allow foreigners a measure of freedom to take their blocked rand balances out, the latter could be used to buy quoted shares on the Johannesburg stock exchange and exported abroad to be sold, say, in London. As a result, a market in blocked rand balances developed in London, with dealers quoting the blocked rand at a fluctuating discount to the official rate. More recently, this system has been transformed into a system closer to the so-called two-tier system (see Section 6).[14]

SECTION 6. TWO-TIER EXCHANGE RATE SYSTEMS

4.6.1. A two-tier exchange rate system has been in operation in Belgium for over 15 years, and has on occasion been used by France, Italy, Spain, the Netherlands, and the United Kingdom (for 30 years, in the shape of the investment currency premium); it is now also used in South Africa. The two-tier exchange rate mechanism is one in which certain transactions, mainly on capital account, are required to pass through a financial exchange market, where exchange rates are floating. Other transactions are required to pass through an official market in which exchange rates are frequently pegged to some other standard.[15]

4.6.2. The two-tier system is in fact a special case of multiple exchange rate systems, which are officially banned under Article VIII, Section 3 of the IMF's Articles of Agreement. "No member shall engage in, or permit any of its physical agencies . . . to engage in, any discriminatory currency arrangements or multiple currency practices . . . except as authorised under this Agreement or approved by the Fund." However, for many years the IMF has tacitly conceded the need for such arrangements in certain countries. Indeed, multiple currency systems are extremely common in Latin America and also in certain other developing countries. However, the two-tier system is the most common example of this type seen in the major currencies. The system is almost always used to split capital account transactions from other transactions, as in the case of Belgium, France (under the *devises-titres* system) and—until October, 1979—the United Kingdom. As the United Kingdom case shows, however, such a two-tier system does not of itself guarantee stability of the normal exchange rate level, since in many cases capital flows can equally be achieved by adjustments in the timings of commercial payments (leads and lags) or other mechanisms. Equally, a wide divergence between the capital account rate and the current account rate normally prompts attempts to switch funds appropriate to one market into the other. Thus, extremely tight policing of the exchange control regulations can be required, and considerable administrative expenses may be involved.

NOTES

1. OECD, *Experience with Control on International Portfolio Operations in Shares and Bonds*, Paris, 1980, p. 8. This report includes a full survey of restrictions then in operation in OECD member countries.

2. *Report to the Council and the Commission on the Realisation by Stages of Economic and Monetary Union in the Community*, reprinted in Supplement to Bulletin 11—1970 of the European Communities in Luxembourg, 1970.

3. A succinct history of the snake from an official viewpoint is given in the *Deutsche Bundesbank Monthly Report*, January 1976: "The European System of Narrower Exchange Rate Margins." Good general discussions abound; for background, see L. Tsoukalis, *The Politics and Economics of European Monetary Integration*, George Allen & Unwin, London, 1977, and R. Hellman, *Gold, the Dollar and the European Currency Systems*, Praeger, New York, 1979. Technical analyses can be found in H. W. Mayer, "The Anatomy of Official Exchange Rate Intervention Systems," *Princeton Essays in International Finance no. 104*, May 1974, and in M. Barratt, *Floating Jointly: the Mechanics of the European Community's Currency Arrangements*, Federal Reserve Bank of New York Research Paper no. 7325, October 1973.

4. L. Tsoukalis, *The Politics and Economics of European Monetary Integration*, pp. 143–150.

5. See, for example, T. de Vries, "On the Meaning and Future of the EMS," *Princeton Essays in International Finance no. 138*, September 1980; R. Masera, "The Operation of the EMS: A European View," *Economia Internazionale*, November 1979; P. A. Trezise (ed.), *The European Monetary System: Its Promise and Prospects*, Brookings Institution, Washington D.C., 1979.

6. IMF, *Annual Report on Exchange Arrangements and Exchange Restrictions*, 1981, under "France."

7. A. Liddell, Financial Cooperation in Africa—French Style," *The Banker*, London, September 1979; an updated article by the same author with the same title appeared in *The Banker* in January 1982.

8. IMF, *Annual Report on Exchange Arrangements and Exchange Restrictions*, 1980, p. 27.

9. There is a good discussion in B. Tew, *International Monetary Cooperation: 1948–70*, Hutchinson, London, 1970.

10. BIS's *18th Annual Report.*

11. See B. Tew, "International Monetary Cooperation: 1948–70," Hutchinson, London, 1970.

12. *IMF Annual Report on Exchange Arrangements and Exchange Restrictions*, 1980, pp. 24–28.

13. E. Osagie, "West African Clearing House, West African Unit of Account and Pressures for Monetary Integration," *Journal of Common Market Studies*, March 1979.

14. R. M. Gidlow, "Exchange Control and the Blocked Rand Mechanism," *South African Journal of Economics*, vol. 44, no. 1, 1976.

15. P. Rushing, "The Two-Tier Exchange Rate System," *New England Economic Review*, Federal Reserve Bank of Boston, March/April 1974. See also V. Barattieri and G. Ragazzi, "An Analysis of the Two-Tier Foreign Exchange Market," *Banca Nazionale del Lavoro Quarterly Review*, December 1971, and E. F. Limburg, "Two-Tier Foreign Exchange Markets," *Amsterdam-Rotterdam Bank Economic Quarterly Review*, March 1973.

5

LINKS BETWEEN FOREIGN EXCHANGE AND MONEY MARKETS

This chapter explores the links between foreign exchange and money markets. We start by explaining how the two interlink at the level of an individual trader's position. Then we look at what this means for arbitrage. Then we look at how central banks intervene in the foreign exchange market, and in the domestic money market; and finally we examine the repercussions that foreign exchange intervention can have in the domestic money market.

SECTION 1. HANDLING AN EXPOSURE: FOREIGN EXCHANGE OR MONEY MARKET ROUTE

5.1.1. This chapter looks at the connection between foreign exchange and money markets. It explains why there is a connection, and how it is used by corporations and banks (Sections 1 and 2). It explains the intervention techniques used by central banks in the foreign exchange and money markets (Sections 3 and 4) and looks at some of their effects (Section 5).

5.1.2. We begin with the point of view of a corporation with foreign exchange exposure in a currency. As long as a currency has developed spot and forward exchange markets and money markets, and as long as exchange controls permit, an exposure can always be hedged in either market.

5.1.3. Suppose the treasurer of a British subsidiary of a U.S. company has a deutsche mark payment coming in, due in 90 days. Suppose he needs the funds now to send to the United States. Then he can borrow deutsche marks against his receivable and convert them into U.S. dollars now. Or, he can sell the deutsche mark forward against U.S. dollar and borrow U.S. dollars against the foreign exchange. The choice between the two will depend on the rates involved (see Table 5.1).

5.1.4. A dealer in a bank has the option of handling his positions in the same way. If he received a SFR deposit for 90 days, and is lending sterling for 90 days, he will have the option, again, of choosing the money market or the foreign exchange route. He can on-lend the Swiss francs, or do a foreign exchange deal. He would buy sterling to on-lend, and sell the sterling forward against SFR to repay his SFR deposit at maturity. Table 5.2 shows how his T-accounts would look.

SECTION 2. GENERAL COMMENTS ON ARBITRAGE

5.2.1. It follows from Table 5.1 and 5.2 that there is a very close connection between the interest rate and the forward exchange rate. For example, suppose the Swiss franc is at a premium forward against sterling—in other words the SFR is more expensive in the future than it is now. Common sense tells us that the dealer who is selling Swiss francs spot and buying them forward at a more expensive price in order to lend sterling will need to make more on his sterling lending than he would on his Swiss franc lending. Otherwise it would not be worthwhile switching his funds into sterling. From these thoughts, we can derive a few rules of thumb. (The exact calculations are set out in Chapters 9 and 10.)

5.2.2. First, the currency with the lower interest rate will sell at a premium in the forward market against the currency with the higher interest rate. Sup-

TABLE 5.1. Financing a DMK Receivable: Money Market Route versus Foreign Exchange.

Money Market Route		Day	Foreign Exchange Route	
Cash In	Cash Out		Cash In	Cash Out
		DMK		
DMK loan proceeds	Convert to US$	Day 1	—	
Receivable	Repayment of DMK loan	Day 90	Receivable	Pay to bank to settle forward FX deal
		US$		
DMK loan proceeds	Remit to HQ	Day 1	US$ loan proceeds against FX	Remit to HQ
—	—	Day 90	Proceeds of forward deal	Repay US$ loan
Step 1. Borrow DMK.			Step 1. Sell DMK forward against US$.	
Step 2. Buy US$ and pay U.S. parent.			Step 2. Borrow US$ and pay U.S.	
Step 3. Receive DMK and repay loan.			Step 3. Receive DMK and settle forward deal.	
			Step 4. Use proceeds of forward to repay loan.	

TABLE 5.2. Matching a Swiss Franc Liability and a Sterling Asset.

Money Market Route

Day	Cash In	Cash Out
SFR		
Day 1	SFR deposit	On-lent to market
Day 90	Repay SFR deposit	Receive repayment from market
£STG		
Day 1	Borrow from market	Make £STG lending to customer
Day 90	Repay market	Customer repays

Step 1. Take SFR deposit; on-lend SFR to market.
Step 2. Lend £STG to customer; borrow £STG in market.
Step 3. Receive SFR repayment from market and repay customer deposit.
Step 4. Receive £STG repayment from customer and repay market.

Foreign Exchange Route

Day	Cash In	Cash Out
SFR		
Day 1	Receive deposit	Buy £STG
Day 90	Receive SFR from forward deal	Repay deposit
£STG		
Day 1	Proceeds of SFR sale	Lend to customer
Day 90	Customer repays	Pay for SFR forward purchase

Step 1. Take SFR deposit and swap it for £STG.
Step 2. Lend £STG to customer.
Step 3. Receive £STG repayment from customer and use it to settle forward SFR purchase.

pose that US$ three-month deposits yield 20% and DMK three-month deposits yield 10%. Then the deutsche mark must sell at a premium in the three-month forward market. Suppose it did not: suppose it sold at a discount. That means, conversely, that the dollar is at a premium against the deutsche mark. So a German investor could buy dollars spot and sell them forward at a profit. In addition, he picks up 10% interest differential. In a free market, this situation could never last. Investors would buy U.S. dollars spot and sell them forward until the weight of forward selling had driven the U.S. dollar to a discount—that is, the forward deutsche mark would show a premium.

5.2.3. The second rule is that this premium (on an annualized basis) will tend to equal the interest difference. Suppose, in our example again, it did not, and that it were only 5% per annum. Then it would cost a German investor only 5% per annum to buy spot dollars and sell them forward: yet he would receive a 10% interest improvement, so there is still a net profit of 5%. Again, in a free market this situation would not last. Funds would move out of deutsche mark into dollars until there were no net profit in doing so. That is, until the forward margin (premium or discount) in annual terms equaled the interest differential.

5.2.4. Third, it follows from the equality of interest differentials and forward margins that if one changes for any reason the other will move to offset it. In practice, the interest differential tends to be the dominant factor, because the vast bulk of activity in the forward exchange market is conducted interbank on a swap basis (see Chapter 1, Section 2). This relationship can be summed up like this: *If the interest differential moves in a currency's favor, the forward margin moves against it.*

5.2.5. To continue our example, suppose German interest rates rise from 10% to 15% while the U.S. dollar rate remains at 20%. Interest rates have moved in the deutsche mark's favor. So the forward premium on deutsche mark will *fall* from 10% to 5% per annum so that it equals the new interest differential of 5%. Conversely, suppose now that U.S. dollar rates also fall to 15%. The interest differential has moved *against* the US$, so the forward margins move in *favor* of the US$: the premium on deutsche marks (i.e., discount on US$ against DMKs) disappears entirely as both interest rates are now at 15% and the differential is zero.

5.2.6. It should be stressed that "interest differential" is very crude. To be strictly accurate, one should use something like "net accessible interest differential." In other words, the interest rate should apply to borrowing and lending which are accessible to the international market—unaffected by exchange controls. To take a classic case, during the period of heavy upward pressure on the Swiss franc in 1977 to 1979, interest rates on the domestic Swiss money market were running at around 2 to 3% per annum. But those interest rates were not available to nonresident holders of the Swiss francs. They were, on the contrary, charged a negative interest rate of—at its peak—10% per quarter, or rather more than minus 40% per annum. Domestic Swiss rates were not "accessible" to the market.

5.2.7. Secondly, the interest rate should be "net": it should be adjusted for any reserve requirement factors, interest withholding taxes, or other adjustments applicable to nonresidents. For example, before the introduction of IBFs (see Chapter 1, Section 4), a U.S. bank was able to pay a better interest rate on a dollar deposit with its branch in London, compared with the rate it could pay for a deposit with its head office in New York, because the latter was subject to the full range of Federal Reserve System reserve requirements.

5.2.8. Equally, if a nonresident were placing funds in a center where an interest withholding tax is levied on nonresidents, he would need to allow for this tax before comparing an interest rate on a deposit in another currency which does not attract withholding tax. It is possible that the withholding tax could be reclaimed under a double tax treaty between the depositor's country and the country in which the deposit is made. But against this must be set the extra cost and inconvenience of processing the claim, and so forth. Also, many of the countries which are Euromarket centers have a rather limited network of double tax treaties. If withholding tax has to be taken into account, the necessary adjustment formula is given in Chapter 13.

5.2.9. Finally, it should be mentioned that the relationship between the net interest differential and the swap market permits a bank's dealer to "create" a forward market if a deposit market is available. For example, if a dealer is asked to quote a forward price for a small amount of five-year Austrian schillings, he has a problem. The Austrian forward schilling market does not stretch that far forward and there is no real Euro-Austrian schilling deposit market. But if he can obtain deposit quotes for five years in the domestic Austrian market, and if he feels safe in assuming that these are in line with what would prevail in the Euroschilling market if there were one, he can manufacture a swap price using the formula given in Chapter 10, Section 4. Naturally, this is a very rough-and-ready procedure. It would only be safe to do it for a small-sized deal and then only if adequate margin were taken.

SECTION 3. FOREIGN EXCHANGE INTERVENTION

5.3.1. Intervention by central banks in foreign exchange markets, in its "pure" form, consists of purchases/sales of foreign currency against domestic currency in the spot or forward markets. Other forms of intervention are indirect, such as money market operations, changes in reserve requirements, and so on (discussed in Section 4), or exchange controls (discussed in Chapter 4). In its "pure" form, then, intervention can be divided into spot, swap, and out-right forward operations.

5.3.2.   A spot purchase or sale of foreign currency against domestic cur-rency tends to have an immediate effect on the spot exchange rate. If the deut-sche mark is rising, and the Bundesbank appears in the market to sell deutsche marks and buy U.S. dollars, this will tend to depress the deutsche mark spot rate. It will also increase the Bundesbank's foreign exchange reserves by the amount of U.S. dollars bought. It may affect the German money supply, de-pending on who buys the deutsche mark and whether he invests the deutsche mark in bank deposits or government bonds or is forced (as in 1970) to place the deutsche mark in a special deposit with the Bundesbank.[1] In the last two cases the inflow is "sterilized" but in the first case it feeds through into the money supply. (See Section 5 for a discussion of this problem.)

5.3.3.   An outright forward purchase or sale of foreign currency against do-mestic currency tends to have an immediate effect on the margin between the spot and forward rate. The effect on reserves does not show up until maturity, when it is the same as outlined in the last paragraph. The Bank of England in-tervened in this way during 1964 through 1967. The aim was to support the forward sterling rate and so reduce the discount on forward sterling. This would cut the cost of forward cover on sterling assets and so encourage invest-ment in sterling assets. At the same time, operating on an outright rather than a swap basis meant the Bank did not have to supply spot sterling to the market. But the devaluation of 1967 meant that these forward operations cost the Bank £350 million,[2] and they were then abandoned.

5.3.4.   A swap operation also alters the margin between the spot and the forward rate. But it has an immediate impact on the spot market as well. The counterparty receives funds on his account now. Hence, if the Bank of England had intervened in the swap instead of the outright market, it would have been selling sterling spot and buying it back forward. The counterparties would have been long of spot sterling, which they would probably have sold off. That was why the Bank dealt outright forward. But swaps have been used by some central banks to affect the cost of forward cover: a notable example is the Bundesbank which had amounts outstanding of up to $2.7 billion in 1958–69 and 1971.[3] However, experience tended to show that these swap in-terventions were being "misused by the combination of interest rate arbitrage and Bundesbank swap transactions to carry on 'roundabout transactions' by which it was possible to obtain interest rate profits without using additional funds."[4]

5.3.5.   Even so, the Bundesbank still deals in the swap market. During 1980 its swap deals with the market totaled the equivalent of US$ 16.8 billion.[5] The aim of these swaps was not, this time, to cut the cost of forward cover, but li-

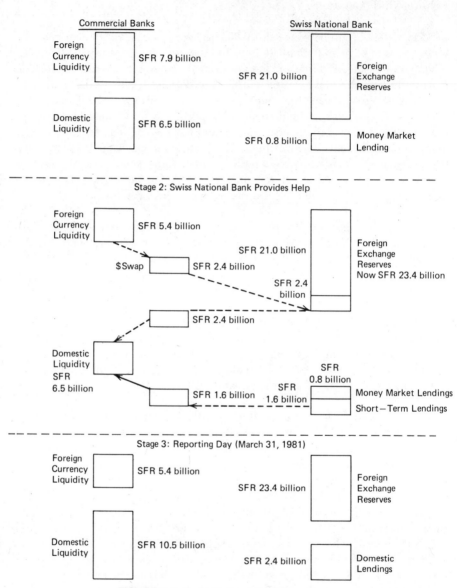

Stage 1: March 20, 1981

Commercial Banks — Swiss National Bank

Foreign Currency Liquidity — SFR 7.9 billion

SFR 21.0 billion — Foreign Exchange Reserves

Domestic Liquidity — SFR 6.5 billion

SFR 0.8 billion — Money Market Lending

Stage 2: Swiss National Bank Provides Help

Foreign Currency Liquidity — SFR 5.4 billion

SFR 21.0 billion — Foreign Exchange Reserves Now SFR 23.4 billion

$Swap — SFR 2.4 billion

SFR 2.4 billion

SFR 2.4 billion

Domestic Liquidity SFR 6.5 billion

SFR 0.8 billion

SFR 1.6 billion — SFR 1.6 billion — Money Market Lendings / Short—Term Lendings

Stage 3: Reporting Day (March 31, 1981)

Foreign Currency Liquidity — SFR 5.4 billion

SFR 23.4 billion — Foreign Exchange Reserves

Domestic Liquidity — SFR 10.5 billion

SFR 2.4 billion — Domestic Lendings

FIGURE 5.1. Swiss National Bank Intervention.

quidity management. This type of operation is common also in the Netherlands but the classical example is Switzerland.

5.3.6. Foreign exchange swaps are used regularly by the Swiss National Bank to manage liquidity in the domestic money market. The reason is that the domestic money supply (and available liquidity) is small compared with the size of the foreign currency market. A typical example occurred during March and April 1981. The Swiss National Bank's sight liabilities to other banks (the best available measure of money market liquidity) on March 20 totaled SFR 6.5 billion. On March 31, the quarterly reporting date, they had risen to SFR 10.5 billion. Then after the reporting date they fell again to SFR 6.3 billion on April 10.

5.3.7. The extra liquidity on the reporting date was provided first by the traditional credits from the Swiss National Bank—discounts and advances against security—and second by short-term foreign exchange swaps totaling SFR 2.4 billion. The way in which the liquidity was provided flows from the nature of the swap. Swiss banks sold dollars for spot value to the Swiss National Bank, receiving Swiss francs in exchange. These could be deposited with the Swiss National Bank in order to meet their liquidity requirements. At the same time the banks bought the dollars back in the forward market for a date after the reporting date. The counterpart to the extra liquidity held by the banks was a rise in the Swiss National Bank's foreign exchange reserves on March 31 to SFR 23.4 billion equivalent, compared with SFR 21.0 billion on March 20 and SFR 21.1 billion on April 10. To sum up, the Swiss commercial banks exchanged dollar liquidity for Swiss franc liquidity to meet the reporting requirements. It is worth knowing that the Banque de France has made a habit of doing similar swaps, not so much to manage banks' liquidity as to smooth (and conceal) changes in its reserves (see Section 1.7.5). (See Figure 5.1.)

5.3.8. Another example of the link between the foreign exchange and domestic money markets can be seen if we look at a drawing by the Federal Reserve Bank of New York on its swap network (see Chapter 3, Section 6) to finance sales of foreign currencies and stabilize the dollar. The drawing leads to two opposite and offsetting effects on bank reserves, under the Federal Reserve's current operating procedures.[6] First, the sale of a foreign currency for dollars by the Fed in the exchange market causes a fall in U.S. bank reserves. The U.S. bank (say, Citibank) receives foreign currency, paying over dollars to the Federal Reserve. This cuts its dollar reserves. Second, the reserves work their way back into the system. (See Figure 5.2 overleaf.)

5.3.9. The way in which this happens will vary. It depends on the course of action taken by the securities trading desk at the Federal Reserve. Consider a swap with the Bundesbank. To start with, the swap drawing results in a credit

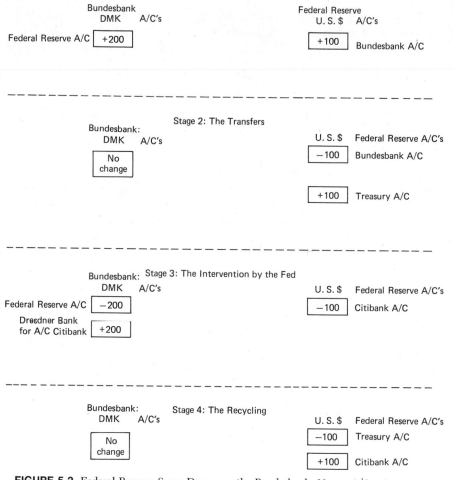

FIGURE 5.2. Federal Reserve Swap Drawn on the Bundesbank. NOTE: A/C = Account.

of deutsche marks to the Federal Reserve's account at the Bundesbank. It also results in a credit of U.S. dollars to the account of the Bundesbank at the Federal Reserve. The latter account is then debited with these dollars which are invested in a special U.S. Treasury certificate of indebtedness. As a result, Treasury cash balances at the Reserve Bank increase. Under normal circumstances, the U.S. Treasury will then spend these dollars in the course of its operations, putting reserves back into the system, so the original reserve draining is offset. By comparison a direct intervention by the Federal Reserve in the foreign exchange markets to sell an existing balance of deutsche marks—that is, its own holding rather than the proceeds of a swap drawing—will have an

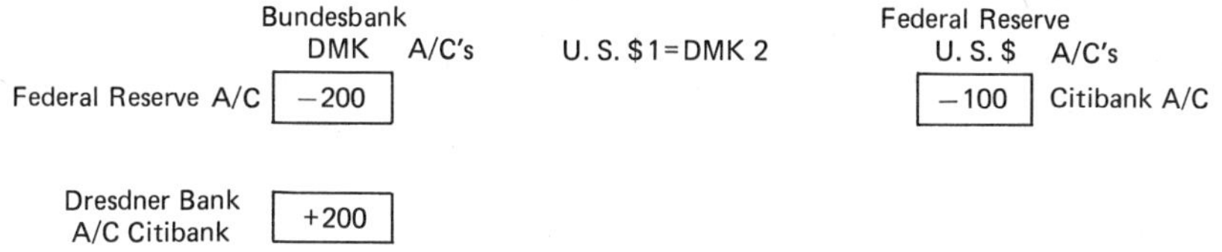

Bundesbank
DMK   A/C's   U. S. $1=DMK 2   Federal Reserve
                                             U. S. $ A/C's

Federal Reserve A/C | −200 | | −100 | Citibank A/C

Dresdner Bank
A/C Citibank | +200 |

FIGURE 5.3. Intervention Financed by Federal Reserve Balances.

immediately draining effect on bank reserves, unless offset by other action. (See Figure 5.3)

SECTION 4.   MONEY MARKET INTERVENTION TECHNIQUES

5.4.1.   Central banks will also try to influence the exchange rate by intervening in the money market. For example, during the 1960s, when the pound was under pressure, speculators outside the United Kingdom would borrow sterling. They then sold it against a stronger currency, such as the deutsche mark. If the pound were devalued before the sterling borrowing matured, the sterling repayment would become cheaper in terms of deutsche marks. So the Bank of England often used its money market operations to force up short-term interest rates very sharply. This made it costly to continue sterling borrowings when the currency was not actually devalued.

5.4.2.   Apart from changes in official interest rates, open market operations are the main way in which central banks try to manage the money markets. The simplest operation consists of a straightforward purchase of Treasury bills or government stock by the central bank from the banks. The banks' holdings of cash will rise, while their holdings of securities will fall. For example, in the United Kingdom, if the money market is in shortage, the first sign will normally be that the clearing banks withdraw funds which have been placed at call with the discount market. This will restore their own cash position, leaving the discount market with a shortage; the shortage can be filled by a purchase by the Bank of England of Treasury or commercial bills from the discount market. In the United States, a money market shortage might be met by the Federal Reserve by outright purchase of government securities from banks or dealers, or by sale and repurchase agreements (repos).

5.4.3.   The effect of these operations will depend on the reserve ratios on banks' liabilities. To see why this is so, consider an imaginary country called Home. Its currency is Home currency (HC). Assume that there is only one bank, call it Barclays, and the only other means of payment is cash. Suppose the government prints HC 1 million and pays it to Home Machine Company in exchange for machinery. HMC pay the cash into Barclays, whose balance sheet now becomes (assuming nil balances to start with):

Liabilities	Assets
HMC deposit HC 1 million	HC 1 million cash

Suppose that the government requires Barclays to hold 10% of its assets in cash. Then Barclays can lend the other HC 900,000 to General Motors Company. They proceed to mark a credit limit for GM who draw this down, by taking out cash. Barclays' balance sheet is now:

Liabilities	Assets
HMC deposit HC 1 million	HC 100,000 cash
	HC 900,000 GM loan

GM hands the cash over to Shell in exchange for oil. Shell deposits the cash with Barclays:

Liabilities	Assets
HMC deposit HC 1 million	HC 1 million cash
Shell deposit HC 0.9 million	HC 0.9 million GM loan

Barclays can now lend 90% of HC 0.9 million, that is, HC 0.81 million to ICI. They will pay the money to Ford, who will deposit it with Barclays, and so on.

5.4.4. In fact, the system keeps expanding until the original HC 1 million in cash represents 10% of Barclays' total assets, which will total HC 10 million. At this point, Barclays won't lend any more money, because if it did, the ratio of cash to assets would fall below 10%, and the government would object. In other words, the 10% ratio means that an extra HC 1 million of cash can support deposits of HC 10 million. The deposits created are 10 times the original cash. As a matter of fact, if the reserve ratio is R, the multiplier is $1 \div R$—in our example $1 \div 0.1$ equals 10. It follows that if we lower the reserve ratio to 5% the multiplier rises from 10 to 20. The smaller the reserve ratio, the bigger the multiplier.

5.4.5. Equally, a draining of reserves from the system will force it to shrink by the same ratio. So, open market operations can be a very powerful force by which the central bank can influence the level of the banking system's activity. But, other factors must also be taken into consideration. The assets used for open market operations are mostly government debt of some kind. So the central bank must be careful that its open market operations are not conducted indiscriminately. That would make it hard to keep selling government debt to the public. Also, the interaction of reserve ratios and other controls (such as the "corset" in the United Kingdom when it was in operation) can sometimes have unpredictable results because of the complexity and sophistication of today's financial markets. Accordingly, open market operations are not always as simple, nor as powerful, as the pure theoretical model would indicate.

5.4.6.   Other techniques of money market intervention include varying the reserve requirement. (In the United States, the Federal Reserve has imposed marginal reserve requirements, but in the past was inhibited by fears that banks might leave the system; in the United Kingdom, the fixed reserve asset ratio has been more or less abolished, though the Bank of England can call for special deposits from the banking system. Other central banks, particularly the Bundesbank, have made much more frequent use of this instrument.) The effect of raising this, of course, is to force the banking system to lay hands on reserves which can be placed with the central bank. At the same time it reduces the total amount of credit which a given quantity of reserves can support.

5.4.7.   In Germany, another tool has also been used. This is control of the rediscount quota—the amount of paper banks were allowed to sell to the Bundesbank at the official discount rates. More recently the rediscount quota has been replaced by Special Lombard credits. Lombard credits are loans against the security of paper rather than actual discounting of the paper. The Special Lombard credit's main feature is that the Bundesbank remains completely free to decide the cost, amount, and maturity of its lending. (It was suspended in May 1982.) And, as we saw in Section 3, another tool of money market intervention is the use of foreign exchange swaps. These are used regularly by the Swiss, German, and Dutch central banks, and occasionally elsewhere. Repurchase agreements constitute important tools of open market intervention in the United States, France, and to a lesser extent Germany; they are occasionally used in the United Kingdom. (The various central banks' intervention methods are set out in more detail in Chapter 3.)

5.4.8.   Finally, it is worth mentioning that there is one enormous money market, the Euromarket, which escapes reserve requirements and open market intervention entirely; this is discussed at greater length in Chapter 1.

SECTION 5.   FOREIGN EXCHANGE MARKET INTERVENTION AND THE MONEY SUPPLY

5.5.1.   At various points in this chapter we have touched on the links between foreign exchange and money markets, and how these are used by participants in the market, particularly by central banks when intervening. It is important to understand the wider effects of these links, because they affect the way in which central banks and governments operate their policies. For instance, a central bank which is committed to intervening in defense of a fixed exchange rate cannot control its money supply. If it does want to control money supply, it cannot intervene in unlimited amounts. To see why, we need to look at some examples of what happens when intervention takes place. The exact effects can be complex. They depend on our definitions of the money supply and the assumptions we make about how flows involved are financed. Very roughly, things work like this. If the authorities refuse to intervene in the foreign exchange market, an inflow of foreign currency will not change the country's foreign exchange reserves. Hence the inflow need not necessarily change the domestic money supply. But if the authorities intervene to buy the foreign currency, there will be an effect on the reserves. All other things being equal, this will affect the domestic money supply.

5.5.2. Perhaps the country which has had greatest experience of foreign currency inflows, and where these inflows have made most impact, is Switzerland. Figure 5.4 shows the monthly changes in official reserves as a percentage of average monthly exports for the period 1978 to 1979. We can see that because of Swiss support for a weakening dollar, Switzerland's reserves rose in December 1978 to 150% of average exports. That figure compares with 50% for the previous month. The change for the United States and for the United Kingdom during this period was negligible. As a result, the Swiss money supply, which had grown by less than 1% on average during 1977, grew by 19.8% during 1978.[7]

5.5.3. It became clear to the Swiss authorities that this process could not be continued indefinitely. During 1979 the degree of dollar support was sharply reduced. That allowed a much more restrictive monetary policy. The money supply was actually reduced during 1979 by 1.2%. This was achieved at the price of a firm exchange rate. From an average of US$ 1 = SFR 2.4035 during 1977, the Swiss franc strengthened to average 1.7880 during 1978, and 1.6627 during 1979. But a price was paid for this policy. The effects of the very rapid growth of money supply during 1978, and the subsequent weakening of the exchange rate during 1980 and 1981, were seen later in the consumer price index. This had risen by 0.8% on average during 1978, but rose 3.7% during 1979, 4.0% during 1980, and by March 1981 had risen by 6.4% compared with the same month of the previous year.

5.5.4. The detailed interrelationships are perhaps best understood by taking another case study. An interesting example occurred in the United Kingdom during 1977. The pound sterling was extremely firm during most of 1977. Sterling benefited from the arrangement of a medium-term standby facility for the Bank of England by the Bank for International Settlements in January 1977 and the decision by the Wilson Government to raise medium-term external finance from the IMF. Until October of 1977, the Bank of England sold sterling to stop the pound from rising. As a result, the United Kingdom's external reserves rose. This tended to boost the money supply. To understand what actually went on, we will look again at our country called Home.[8] (See 5.5.9. for

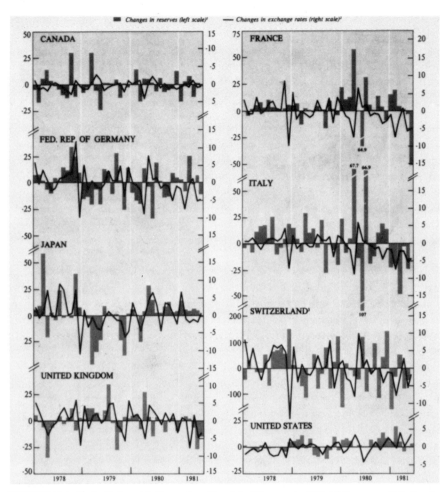

FIGURE 5.4. Eight Industrial Countries: Monthly Changes in Official Reserves Relative to Exports and in Exchange Rates, January 1978—June 1981 (in Percent). Source: IMF *1981 Annual Report*, p. 48.

[1] Changes in reserves are defined here as the total of changes in foreign exchange holdings, reserve positions in the Fund, and holdings of SDRs, minus changes in the use of Fund credit and cumulative SDR allocations. In calculating these changes, foreign exchange holdings are valued in U.S. dollars and are corrected for valuation changes, and all changes in SDR-denominated reserve components are converted into U.S. dollars at average monthly exchange rates. The figures for 1979–81 have been adjusted by excluding the value of ECUs issued against gold holdings of EMS members. For each country, the change in reserves is expressed as a percentage of average monthly exports for the period 1978–79.

[2] The exchange rate at the end of each month is measured in U.S. dollars per unit of domestic currency for all countries except the United States, for which the effective exchange rate derived from the Fund's multilateral exchange rate model is used.

[3] The left scale for Switzerland is different from that used for the other countries because of the exceptionally large magnitudes of reserve changes relative to exports.

a summary.) We start by making certain assumptions. First, all payments to Home residents from abroad are made in Home currency (HC). Second, the banks do not themselves hold foreign currency, nor do they lend Home currency abroad. Third, the public sector has no foreign currency transactions. Finally we assume that nonresidents' Home currency deposits are excluded from the definition of the money supply.

5.5.5. We start with the way in which foreign exchange is taken into or paid out of the official reserves. The reserves are held by the Exchange Stabilization Fund. The ESF's working balances in Home currency are held in Treasury bills. When the ESF buys foreign currency it sells these Treasury bills back to the government. In exchange it receives Home currency with which it can then pay the seller of foreign currency. In order to finance the payment to the ESF, the government is forced to borrow elsewhere. In effect, government securities are switched from the ESF to other holders.

5.5.6. Consider the case of a Home exporter who is owed HC 100 for an export delivery. Assume the overseas customer does not already hold Home currency. Then he will have to sell foreign currency for HC and pay the proceeds to the HC account of the exporter. Under our assumptions, the bank receiving the foreign currency will sell the currency immediately to the ESF. In order to buy the foreign currency from the bank, the ESF sells its Treasury bills to the government. This forces the latter to borrow elsewhere. In the absence of any other buyer, the government borrows from the banks. In effect, Home currency claims on the government are switched from the ESF to the banks. As there is a rise in the Home exporter's HC deposits, the money supply increases. The transactions associated with this change, as they affect the balance sheets of the banks and the ESF, and the balance of payments, are shown in Table 5.3.

TABLE 5.3.   Effects of a Home Current Account Surplus.

Sector	Liabilities	Assets
Home Banks		
Private sector HC deposits	+ 100	
HC claims on Treasury		+ 100
ESF		
Official reserves		+ 100
HC claims on Treasury		− 100
Balance of Payments		
Current account: exports		+ 100
Capital account		—
Change in reserves (increase, −)		− 100

TABLE 5.4.   Effects of a Home Capital Account Surplus.

Sector	Liabilities	Assets
Home Banks		
Nonresidents' HC deposits	+ 100	
HC claims on Treasury		+ 100
ESF		
Official reserves		+ 100
HC claims on Treasury		− 100
Balance of Payments		
Current account		—
Capital account		+ 100
Change in reserves (increase, −)		− 100

5.5.7.   On the other hand, an inflow may also take the form of a rise in Home currency bank deposits held by overseas residents. This will not affect the money supply. In this case, the overseas resident sells foreign currency to a Home bank and places the proceeds in an HC account. The bank again immediately sells the foreign currency to the ESF. The ESF sells Treasury bills back to the government, which borrows HC from the bank. So the bank has effectively taken an HC deposit from a nonresident in order to on-lend it immediately to the government. However, this time there is no increase in the money supply, as nonresidents' HC deposits are not included in the definition. The transactions are set out in Table 5.4. All of this has worked on the assumption that the ESF buys all foreign currency which is offered to it. Assume the ESF never intervenes, and assume still that neither Home banks nor the Home private sector hold foreign currency. Then it is clear that any foreign currency sold to Home residents is immediately sold back to nonresidents, because we have assumed that Home people never hold foreign currency. The exchange rate must move until nonresidents are willing to buy back the Home currency. It is the exchange rate which now takes the strain. The reserves do not change.

5.5.8.   Let us now allow for residents' foreign currency holdings. They only affect the Home money supply when Home residents switch foreign currency into Home currency. To prove this, assume a Home current account surplus of HC 150 (see Table 5.5). Suppose that HC 50 of this is actually paid to the Home private sector in foreign currency. Suppose this foreign currency is deposited with the banks (who on-lend it to nonresidents). A further HC 60 worth is paid to Home residents in foreign currency and immediately sold for Home currency. The ESF finances its purchases of foreign currency by selling Treasury bills which are bought by the bank. The rest is financed by a fall in foreigners' HC bank deposits of HC 30 and a fall of HC 10 in overseas holdings

TABLE 5.5.　Effects of Home Current Account Surplus When Intervention Takes Place.

Sector	Liabilities	Assets
HC deposits of private sector	+ 100	
HC deposits of nonresidents	− 30	
HC claims on public sector		+ 70
Foreign currency deposits of private sector	+ 50	
Foreign currency loans to nonresidents		+ 50
Balance of payments		
Private sector current account surplus which is used to finance:		+ 150
Foreign currency lending by Home banks (increase, −)		− 50
Overseas HC deposits with Home banks (increase, +)		− 30
Overseas lending to Home public sector (increase, +)		− 10
Change in reserves (increase, −)		− 60

of public sector Home currency debt. We assume this is sold to the banks. So bank lending to the government rises by the HC 10 of public sector debt, and HC 60 which the banks lend to the government to finance the increase in reserves. That makes a total of HC 70. This feeds straight through into Home money supply. So does the HC 30 fall in foreigners' HC bank deposits which are paid to U.K. residents. So there is a net rise in Home's money supply of HC 100. This is equal to the private sector current and capital account surplus on the balance of payments *less* the increase in Home private sector foreign currency holdings. In other words the HC 50 paid to Home residents in foreign currency, which was not switched into Home currency, had no effect on Home's money supply.

5.5.9.　Let's now boil this lot down to what matters. Foreign currency inflows and outflows can affect a country's money supply. That can happen only if the Exchange Stabilization Fund, in our example, is intervening in the foreign exchange market on a *net* basis. That is, the ESF must not just buy and sell in the market to smooth exchange rate movements, but must be supplying foreign currency to the market, or absorbing currency from the market. If intervention is taking place, the effect on the money supply need not be the same as the amount of intervention. As we saw in 5.5.7, if the inflow produces a rise in nonresidents' deposits, the money supply need not be affected. Equally, the effect on the money supply depends on how the ESF finances its interventions. In our example in 5.5.6, if the ESF's Treasury bill holdings could be refinanced from overseas, the effect on money supply would be offset. In other words, foreign currency flows will tend in general to affect the money supply, but not always; it depends on what else is happening. But, as a rule of thumb: if Home central bank supports Home Currency, it drains funds from Home money market; if it supports another currency, it adds funds to the Home market.

NOTES

1. See, for example, Dr. O. Emminger, "The D-Mark in the conflict between Internal and External Equilibrium, 1948–75," *Princeton Essays in International Finance no. 122*, p. 28.

2. E. B. Chalmers (ed.), *Forward Exchange Intervention: The British Experience 1964–7*, Hutchinson Educational, London, 1971, p. 11.

3. E. Blumenthal, "Forward Interventions of the Deutsche Bundesbank," in P. Coulbois (ed.), *Le change à terme*, Editions Cujas, Paris, 1972.

4. Ibid. p. 149.

5. *Deutsche Bundesbank Annual Report*, 1980 English translation, p. 69.

6. See R. M. Kubarych, "Monetary Effects of Federal Reserve Swaps," *Federal Reserve Bank of New York Quarterly Review*, Winter 1977–78.

7. Figures from IMF, *International Financial Statistics*, March 1981, series 34B.

8. This section is adapted from C. M. Miles and P. A. Bull, "External and Foreign Currency Flows and the Money Supply," *Bank of England Quarterly Bulletin*, December 1978.

6

ECONOMICS AND THE MARKETS

This chapter sets out some of the economic knowledge that a trader needs to understand what is going in the markets. The first section explains some of the pitfalls in economic statistics. The next section explains why monetarism has become so important. The next three sections explain the problems central banks have in choosing, fixing, and meeting monetary targets; Section 6 looks at the results of their efforts, and Section 7 explains the different definitions of money supply that are used. The next section explains what fiscal policy is, and how it works. Section 9 looks at the problems of measuring what fiscal policy is doing, while the next section looks at some of the political processes involved in budget making in the United States, the United Kingdom, Germany, France, and Japan. Section 11 shows how tax flows can affect domestic money markets. The next two sections explain what the balance of payments is, and the policies that governments use to keep it under control.

SECTION 1. LIES, DAMNED LIES, AND STATISTICS

6.1.1.   The aim of this chapter is to make clear what lies behind government and central bank policy. It will be short and simple. More detailed studies of these subjects are listed in the reading list. The first step is to note some points about interpreting statistics when they are published. Many of these points are obvious but easily get overlooked in the heat of the moment (or in politicians' statements).

6.1.2.   The first questions, as far as the markets go, are "Is this figure in line with what the market expected? How much is already discounted in the present price?" Next is, "Is this number good or bad?" The answers to the last question get complicated, but we start with some general points.

6.1.3.   First, "Is the figure seasonally adjusted?" A lot of statistics, like money supply, exports and imports, industrial production, and so on are influenced by the season of the year. A bad unemployment figure in December does not mean much if the ground is frozen hard so all building workers are laid off temporarily. So we should look to see if the figure is adjusted to take account of the season.

6.1.4.   Then, too, all seasonal adjustment is guesswork. Most statistical series are adjusted by the so-called U.S. Bureau of the Census X-11 method. This relies on a long run of past data. The movements in the data are then split into four components: trend, cyclical, irregular, and seasonal. The point is that to do this needs several years of data. So if the series is fairly new—say, the U.S. M1 series, which used to be M1B—the seasonal adjustment may not be very reliable.

6.1.5.   Another obvious point is the base date of the series. Often, just before an election, a politician will announce that inflation is running at x%. He does not say whether he took last month's increase and multiplied it by 12 to put it on an annual basis; the last three months multiplied by 4; or whatever.

6.1.6.   And yet another point is to check whether a figure is "real" or "nominal." That is, does it include inflation? Few people would think the statement "GNP grew by 10% last quarter" meant much without knowing whether price effects were included. But it is surprising how often monthly retail sales figures in nominal terms are taken to be in real terms, and vice versa.

6.1.7.   Finally, there are always two ways of looking at a statistic. An optimist will say that a glass is half full of water, a pessimist that it is half empty. So the market will interpret a statistic one way or another depending on whether it is confident of the economic management of the country or not. For every optimistic interpretation, in other circumstances there can be a pessimistic interpretation. Some examples of this are shown in Table 6.1. Let's turn now to looking at some of the important parts of economic policy that move the markets. In recent years, perhaps the most important single area has been that of monetary policy, to which we now turn.

SECTION 2.   MONETARY POLICY

6.2.1.   Monetary policy is important to the markets because it can affect the levels of (and expectations about) interest rates and inflation. So this section explains what lies behind the monetarism of recent years; how monetary policy is organized in certain countries; what the results have been; and what the problems have been.

TABLE 6.1. Lies, Damned Lies, and Statistics

Rising Statistics	Pessimistic View	Optimistic View
Consumer/wholesale prices	Inflationary; less competitive exports.	Monetary policy will be tightened and rates will rise
GDP, industrial production	Faster growth, higher inflation, and higher imports.	Economy is performing well. Interest rates may rise.
Interest rates	The authorities are aware of the currency's weakness.	The authorities are determined to bring inflation under control.
Money supply	Inflationary.	Interest rates will rise to correct it.
Trade deficit	Trade balance is out of control; devaluation needed to restore balance.	Deficit will be offset by capital inflows or is only cyclical.
Inventories	Stockpiling due to fear of rising prices; imports may rise.	Unsold stocks mean economy is slowing, inflation will ease.

6.2.2. Monetarism as a doctrine has been around for years. (We will be looking at some of the ideas involved later.) But as a practical policy, control of money supply and the use of money supply targets are fairly recent. In fact, it would be fair to say that this policy only really became a practical option when exchange rates were allowed to float in 1973. As we saw in Chapter 5, it is impossible to have a completely fixed exchange rate and to have complete control of the money supply at the same time, unless you are very lucky. The intervention needed to stabilize the exchange rate will usually show up somewhere in the money supply.

6.2.3. In late 1974, Germany became the first country to announce a formal money supply target for the year ahead. In early 1975, the United States followed suit, along with the Swiss and the Canadians. In 1976, France and the United Kingdom announced targets. Japan is one of the few major countries that has not. The Bank of Japan makes a short-term projection but this is not seen as a target.[1] In many cases informal money supply targets—not necessarily published—have also been used in other countries.

6.2.4. The original ideas behind monetarism came from the quantity theory of money. This started from a truism. The total money stock in a country circulates at a certain speed to finance the country's economic activity. To see what this means, imagine we are on an island with $500 in bills. The only production on the island is loaves of bread. Say 2,000 loaves are produced, and paid for, at 50 cents each. Then the annual value of production is $2,000 \times \$0.50 = \$1,000$. The turnover of the economy—its annual production value—equals the quantity of production (call it Q) multiplied by its price (call it P).

6.2.5. So we can see that every year the stock of money, $500, must turn over twice to pay for the turnover of the economy. If the island's children burn $250, so now there is only $250 in bills on the island, the money stock would have to circulate twice as fast—four times a year—to pay for the turnover. The number of times that money circulates in an economy every year is called its velocity. When the stock of money was $500, the annual velocity was 2. Now it has had to rise to 4.

6.2.6. The idea behind quantity theory was that velocity is usually fairly stable over time. In that case, a change in the quantity of money will show up in the prices or quantity of output. Suppose our islanders print another $250, so the money stock is now $500. But suppose velocity stays stable at 4. It does not change. Then our $500, turning over 4 times a year, is enough to finance annual turnover of $2,000 but production of loaves is only 2,000 (and cannot be increased). Then the extra supply of money can only end by bidding up prices—to the point where each loaf will cost $1. Because by assuming constant velocity, we assumed that people are just as inclined to spend money as before. If they get twice as much, they will spend twice as much. If there is only the same number of loaves to spend it on, the producers of loaves will be able to raise their prices.

6.2.7.   There are a lot of complications to this theory in real life which mean it does not really work the way I have stated it. (We will look at some of the complications in the section on money supply.) But the point is that many traders, and many central banks, believe that controlling the money supply is important in controlling inflation. If the market sees that a central bank has the money supply under control, that makes the market more confident about that currency. So, monetary policy is important for a trader to understand. Let's look now at how it works.

6.2.8.   The first question a central banker asks himself is: What do I want to control? There are at least a dozen different possible answers. For practical purposes he usually chooses monetary base, M_1, M_2, M_3, or some variant. Let's look at each in turn. Individual country definitions vary—we look at that in Section 7—but here is an outline. Monetary base is notes and coin in circulation plus banks' balances at the central bank. Looked at the other way around, we can describe it as the central bank's liabilities to the banks and to the general public, since notes and coin are also its liabilities. In other words, the monetary base is part of the central bank's balance sheet. So—in theory—it can keep the base under fairly tight control.

6.2.9. M_1 is usually defined as notes and coin plus demand deposits at commercial banks. That is, M_1 is what people use to make payments to each other. The issue gets complicated when people make payments using other accounts, like NOW or ATS accounts in the United States (NOW are negotiable orders of withdrawal, a kind of interest-bearing demand deposit; ATS is automatic transfer from savings—people can draw automatically from savings accounts if their demand deposit goes overdrawn.) More of these problems in Section 6.5.9.

6.2.10. M_2 is usually defined as M_1 plus small time deposits at banks. It usually aims to include money holdings that are partly means of payment and partly means of savings, but not to include money-market-type money. This is included in M_3, which is usually defined as M_2 plus large time deposits and CDs. Often a country will also have a very broad measure of liquidity (The Federal Reserve uses L, the Bank of England PSL_1 and PSL_2—private sector liquidity 1 and 2) which is M_3 plus other liquid assets such as investments in Treasury bills.

SECTION 3.   CHOOSING A MONETARY TARGET

6.3.1.   Not all of these measures are equally easy to control, and shifts can take place among them. So choosing the right target is not easy. In the United

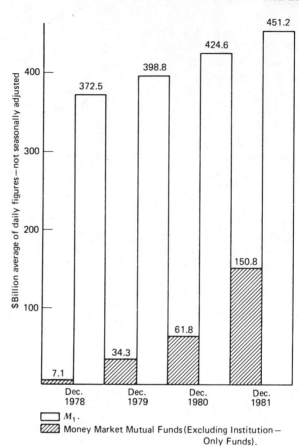

FIGURE 6.1. U.S. Money Market Funds in Relation to M_1. Source: *Federal Reserve Bulletin*, April 1982, p. A13.

States the Federal Reserve has gotten around this problem by setting a number of different targets for M_1, M_2, and M_3. In the United Kingdom, targets have been set in terms of sterling M_3 (i.e., M_3 defined to exclude foreign currency balances) and more recently M_1 and PSL_2 as well. In Germany, the target has been central bank money stock (that is, the monetary base, but adjusted to a constant-reserve-ratio basis as of January 1974. This allows for the fact that Germany quite often changes its reserve requirements).France sets its target in terms of M_2, while Canada sets it in terms of M_1. So in fact, no central bank has chosen the same target as any other. This, of course, is because each country's banking system is different. But, to put it mildly, it does suggest that there is no overwhelming agreement as to *which* money supply should be controlled.

6.3.2.   The issue is also made more complex by shifts among M_1, M_2 and M_3. These can happen in several ways. First, there can be changes in a country's financial system. A classic case is the growth of U.S. money market funds. They

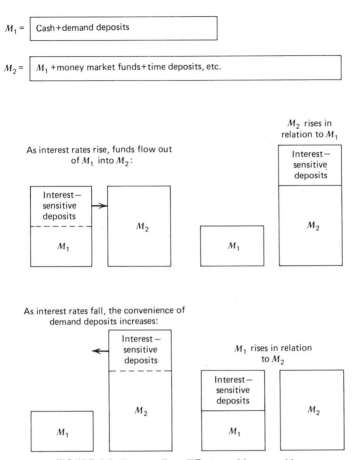

FIGURE 6.2. Interest Rate Effects on M_1 versus M_2.

are included in M_2 but not M_1. Their growth has been phenomenal (see Figure 6.1). This has held down M_1 growth, compared to M_2. A second problem, which is related, is concerned with interest rate movements. The higher the level of interest rates, the more a depositor loses by leaving money interest free on a demand deposit account. So as interest rates rise, money tends to flow out of M_1-type assets into M_2-type assets. Again, M_1 growth is held down compared with M_2. (See Figure 6.2)

6.3.3.   Another set of problems comes from the fact that the central bank faces a dilemma between the quantity of money it supplies and the price at which it supplies the money—interest rates. We saw in Chapter 5 that there was a similar dilemma with fixed exchange rates. If a central bank held the exchange rate rigidly fixed, it had to be prepared to intervene in unlimited quantities. If it did not intervene, it had to let the rate move free. There is a similar problem in the domestic market. The central bank cannot fix the inter-

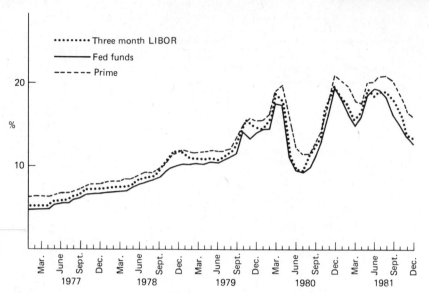

FIGURE 6.3. Prime, Fed Funds, and Three-Month LIBOR 1977–1981 (Monthly Averages in Percent). Source: Data Resources, Inc.

est rate at which it will supply money, and also the amount of money it supplies. It must choose one or the other. Again, the United States is a classic case. In October 1979, the Federal Reserve decided to aim at stricter adherence to money-supply targets. It decided to accept greater interest rate variability as a result. The results are well known (see Figure 6.3).

6.3.4. In the past, the problem of whether to fix interest rates or the money supply tended to be solved by fixing interest rates. First, as we have seen, there was a commitment to fixed exchange rates, which made it difficult to fix the level of money supplied. Second, particularly in the United Kingdom, it was believed that it was wiser to fix interest rates, since this helped meet another target, selling the government's debt. Also, another target which was often chosen was credit, rather than money supply. Central banks tend to control credit by interest rates, or direct credit controls. In France today, and in the United Kingdom during the 1950s and 1960s, credit ceilings have been used to fix the total level of credit available to the economy. The IMF also tends to impose targets for domestic credit expansion (DCE) on those countries who have turned to it to borrow money. The reason for this is that the money supply is not an accurate measure of the state of an economy when there are large inflows or outflows of currency.

6.3.5. DCE is the rise in the money supply adjusted for any change caused by a surplus or deficit on the balance of payments. The reason the IMF tends to prefer DCE over a measure of the money supply is that, when an economy is running a balance of payments deficit, the growth in the money supply is deceptively low. Currency is flowing overseas to pay for the balance of payments deficit. DCE is rising faster than the money supply, so that the money supply understates the true degree of overheating in the economy.

SECTION 4. FIXING THE TARGET

6.4.1. Having decided what target to fix, the central bank must ask itself how high it wants to set it. To see what is involved, let's go back to our island. Now that the islanders have understood the connection between money supply and inflation, they decide that for the year ahead, they can realistically expect to increase production of loaves by 10%, from 2,000 to 2,200. But because of the recent inflation, the bakers' workmen have been getting restless and are demanding an increase in wages. So it seems likely that the island will probably have inflation of about 5%.

6.4.2. The islanders appoint a central bank to deal with the problem. The central bank decides that velocity will probably remain stable, at around 4. It assumes that the price of a loaf will be 5% higher, namely $1.05. It assumes that production will be 2,200. So it expects that the value of turnover in the island—Gross National Product—will be $2,310 = 2200 × $1.05. So it knows that the money supply, circulating four times a year, must be enough to finance an annual turnover of $2,310. In other words, it concludes that the money supply must equal $577.50, since if this amount turns over four times during the year, it equals $2,310. In fact, the money supply must expand by just over 15%, to finance the 10% rise in production and 5% inflation.

6.4.3. Suppose, now, that the central bank decides that this is too high; it does not want inflation to be as high as 5%. Suppose it aims for 2½%. Then it will expect the price of a loaf at the end of the year to be $1.025. If it expects the growth in production of loaves to be unchanged, at 10%, this inflation figure implies a value of GNP equal to 2,200 × $1.025 = $2,255. If the velocity of circulation is still expected to be 4, this means that a supply of money of $563.75 will be sufficient. That is, the money supply must grow by just over 12½%, financing a 10% rise in production and 2½% inflation.

6.4.4. When it decided to squeeze inflation by squeezing the money supply, the central bank made two big assumptions. First, it assumed that inflation could be cut from 5% to 2½% without affecting production. But it might be that the bakers' workmen, who we said were restless, might not be prepared to produce 10% more loaves without getting a large increase in wages. They might go on strike, or they might not work as hard. In any event, production might not rise as fast as the central bank expects. In that case, its money supply target would be pitched too high, and inflation would rise higher than its intended 2½%, while production would fall below target.

6.4.5.   The second big assumption that the central bank made was that velocity would stay stable at 4. But suppose, for some reason, velocity fell to 3. Then the projected money supply of $563.75 would only be enough to finance a GNP of $1691.25. If prices rose to $1.025, production would have to fall to 1,650 loaves per annum; conversely, for production to remain steady at 2,200, the price per loaf would have to fall to 76.875 cents. What has happened, in fact, has been a collapse in demand.

6.4.6.   As we said earlier, if you assume a stable velocity, that means you assume that people are as likely to spend money when they get it as they did in the past. If velocity falls, that means people are no longer spending the money as quickly as they did. So when the central bank makes its forecast for the year ahead, it has to forecast not only inflation and production, but also how it thinks people's spending and saving habits are likely to move during the coming year. All this makes the process of fixing the target quite complicated.

6.4.7.   Coming back from our island to reality, let's look at how these problems were worked out in Germany. In 1977, the Bundesbank estimated for the year ahead[2] the growth of productive potential (estimated at 3%) and the desirable change in the use of potential (+2%). Combining these two, the Bundesbank arrived at a forecast of real GDP (gross domestic product) growth of around 5%. To this was added the "unavoidable" rate of price increase (+4%) and a rise in the velocity of circulation of 1%. So the target was set at 8% (5% + 4% less 1% rise in velocity).

6.4.8.   Similar calculations are made by most central banks in setting their money supply targets. In most cases, central banks have become a little more flexible over time in setting their targets; Germany and Switzerland began by publishing single-figure targets and have now moved to a range, while the United Kingdom and the United States have always set their targets in the form of a range, in the U.S. case usually between 2½ to 3% wide. Many central banks have tried to set their targets at a gradually lower level over time, in order to try and squeeze inflation out of their economies.

6.4.9.   An important question is the choice of base for the target. The best example is the United States. In the beginning, the Federal Reserve rolled its targets forward every three months. If the target was overshot, no attempt was made to adjust for this during the next target period. This meant that the target effectively legitimized the previous excessive growth. This became known as base drift: the base on which the targets were set tended to drift up over time. The process is illustrated in Figure 6.4.

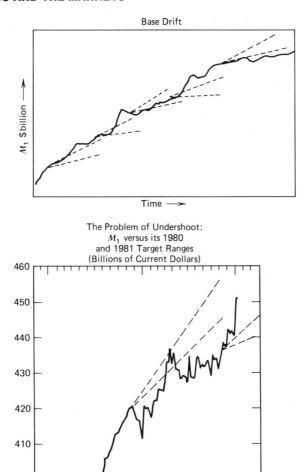

FIGURE 6.4. Base Drift and Undershoot. Source: *Data Resources, Inc. Review.*

6.4.10. With the advent of the Humphrey-Hawkins Act in 1978, the Fed was required to set targets on an annual basis. This cut back some of the problem of base drift, since the target was set on the basis of the fourth quarter of the previous year. It did not remove it entirely, though, since if the fourth quarter growth was excessively high, the base could be moved up too high. Equally, as happened during 1981, if the fourth quarter was unusually low, that meant that the target for the succeeding year would be unusually tight (see Figure 6.4).

SECTION 5.   MEETING THE TARGETS

6.5.1.   This section discusses how central banks try to meet their targets. We looked at some specific cases for the major countries in Chapter 1; this section is concerned with the general mechanics. We need to understand how a change in policy is transmitted through the financial system and affects the money supply. There are two main ways of looking at this process. One side looks at the liabilities of the banking system, and the other looks at the assets.

6.5.2.   Monetarists tend to look at the liabilities side. The view which focuses on the assets side has been described as the "European (and IMF) view of money creation."[3] Of course, both views must be true. The liabilities of the nation's banking system must always equal its assets. It is a question of which is primary. Just as some banks are inherently lenders, needing deposits with which to fund themselves, and other banks are inherently deposit-takers, needing places to lend, one side or other of the national balance sheet can be seen as the driving force. And on your view of which side is primary, depends your view of the effectiveness of the individual policy tools we will look at. It depends on whether you think that the central bank should aim to control the markets for credit, or the markets for money.[4]

6.5.3.   Nowadays (although perhaps not in the past), monetarists tend to think that interest rates do not really matter for controlling the money supply. Professor Milton Friedman, the high priest of monetarism, criticized the United Kingdom for trying to control the money supply in 1980 via fiscal policy and interest rates. He argued strongly that it was far better to control the level of money supply by controlling the amount of reserves available (see 6.5.5). On the other hand the "European" view would argue that raising interest rates reduces the demand for credit. That cuts down the growth of the assets of the banking system, and therefore its liabilities. Against this it can be argued that in times of high inflation, borrowers will be prepared to pay high interest rates, since in real terms the interest rates are low. Also, in today's economy, ways around the problem may be found.

6.5.4.   For example, banks might be persuaded to "roll up" interest payments; that is, they might lend the borrower the money to pay the interest. Another alternative is for borrowers to accept the burden of higher interest payments but to reduce the effect on their cash flow by trying to stretch the maturity of their loans. Experience in the United Kingdom has tended to suggest that, to quote Professor Kaldor, "The experience of using interest rates as the central instruments for the control of monetary aggregates has not been a happy one ... the net affect of interest changes on a broad definition of the 'money stock' was perverse—a rise in interest rates appears to have led to the 'money stock' rising faster than money income, not lagging behind it."[5]

6.5.5. Monetarists generally accept that interest rates are not very effective as a means of controlling the money supply (as Friedman argued above). They therefore argue for direct control on the liabilities side of the balance sheet. They would control the supply of reserves available to the banking system. As we saw in Chapter 5, a change in the reserves of the banking system changes its liabilities in proportion to a multiplier. So by controlling total reserves, the central bank can control total bank deposits. The Federal Reserve adopted this approach in October 1979. As we have seen since then (see Figure 6.4) the price of this approach is greater instability in interest rates.

6.5.6. Another problem arises from the effect of changes in the mix of deposits that the public holds. In the United States there are different reserve requirements on different types of deposits. So the amount of reserves that will support a fixed level of the money stock will change, depending on the kind of deposits the public holds.

6.5.7. Finally, there is the problem of what in the United Kingdom is known as Goodhart's Law (after Charles Goodhart of the Bank of England). This law asserts that when the authorities attempt to control any monetary total, then the activities of the financial system in creating substitutes will change the demand for it, so its behavior will not reflect conditions accurately. This, again, fits in with the view referred to earlier as the European view of money creation. On this argument, controlling the supply of reserves to the banking system to stop it granting credit will mean that borrowers will look elsewhere. They will borrow either from near-banks, who do not have to keep reserves with a central bank, or from overseas, or through "disintermediation"—in the United States, for example, by issuing more commercial paper. This argument applies whether the supply of reserves is controlled by open market operations or by reserve requirements.

6.5.8. Direct controls on bank lending, if tight enough, mean that the target can be achieved almost automatically. But, once again, Goodhart's Law comes into play. If the banks are unable to lend, they are less able to compete for deposits. Nonbank financial institutions will bid for the deposits, which will disappear from the money supply, and will use them to lend to companies. So unless the central bank is always widening the network of its controls over lending, its money supply targets will become less and less useful. During the 1960s, when the Bank of England tried to run similar direct controls on bank lending, all that happened was that nonbanks took up the slack demand for credit.[6]

6.5.9. We have talked about the ways central banks try to meet their targets, and looked at some of the problems that each method raises. There are problems which are common to all of these methods. Of these, we need to look at four, which are interconnected: external flows, velocity shifts, market instability, and how soon a target miss should be corrected.

6.5.10.   External flows can have a major impact on a monetary policy target. We have seen in Chapter 1, Section 9 and Chapter 5, Section 5 how great an impact they had in Switzerland. In fact, the Swiss were forced to abandon their monetary targets in 1979 in the face of the vast foreign exchange flows into the country. This did not lead the Swiss National Bank to abandon its money supply targets, though: "The decision only indicates that a policy aimed at price stability is made more difficult if the rest of the world does not pursue a similar policy. The conclusions drawn from the foreign exchange market developments last autumn, therefore, would be not to abandon our money stock target, but to recommend countries with high inflation rates to adopt a similar target. . . ."[7]

6.5.11.   Germany and the United Kingdom have had the same problems from time to time. It is possible that the impact of foreign currency flows is linked to our next topic, the instability of velocity. There is some evidence that the velocity of circulation in Germany and Switzerland dropped sharply in 1977 and 1978 partly because of flows into these countries of U.S. dollars; and that partly because of these shifts, U.S. velocity rose above trend during that period.[8]

6.5.12.   As we saw earlier, the central bank faces a major problem if velocity is unstable. Figure 6.5 shows that velocity has varied considerably in France, the United Kingdom, the United States, and Germany; France has shown perhaps the most consistent trend, and the United States the least. Of course, where there is a clear trend, the central bank has no problem. It is when there are unexpected changes that problems begin. For example, in the United States, the shift to NOW and ATS accounts during 1978 to 1980 caused the Federal Reserve great problems. Recently, too, it has been argued that the velocity of money is less stable than the velocity of credit, so that the Federal Reserve should concentrate on the latter.[9]

6.5.13.   Questions of velocity are a little academic. But a very practical problem arises when we ask how quickly the central bank should move to correct a temporary overshoot or undershoot of its target. If the target is exceeded for a month, does it matter? If it is exceeded for six months, does it matter? How quickly should the central bank try to get the money supply back within its target range? Can it get the money supply back within the target range that quickly without disrupting the markets? Let's look first at the question of whether it matters if the money supply temporarily overshoots or undershoots. General consensus is that it does not. What is not yet clear is what everybody means by temporary.

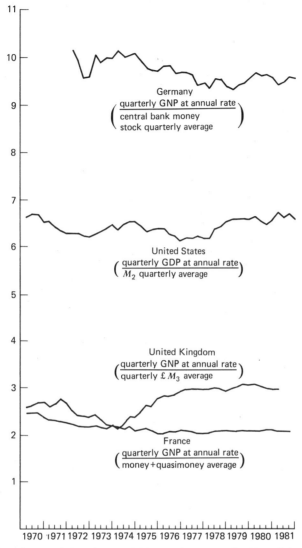

FIGURE 6.5. Velocity of Circulation of Money: Germany, the United States, the United Kingdom, and France. Source: Data Resources, Inc.

6.5.14. A recent Federal Reserve staff study found that variations in money growth above or below targets lasting a quarter or so are not likely to have substantial economic effects, provided they are later offset.[10] In the same study the Federal Reserve found that an overshoot had to be brought back into line with the target within about three months to be reasonably sure of hitting a one-year target.[11] Trying to bring the overshoot back into line more quickly would not greatly increase the success rate in hitting the one-year target, but

would cause great instability of interest rates. (This is a very convenient finding; the period for which the overshoot can be tolerated is about the same as
the time it takes to bring it back into line. It doesn't bear thinking about what
would happen if the tolerable period were shorter than the time it took to
correct the overshoot.)

6.5.15.   Let's stop for a minute to summarize. Although there is a good deal
of debate about whether they should aim to control money supply or credit,
most major central banks have now adopted annual money supply targets.
To reach their objective, they usually have three main tools: interest rates,
control of the supply of reserves, and credit controls. The main problems
that they face are changes in velocity, the effect of flows of foreign currency (in some countries), and the question of how far they can afford to
tolerate short-run deviations from their target, and how quickly they can
bring the money supply back to the target area without disrupting the markets
too much.

6.5.16.   From the point of view of the markets, in my own personal opinion,
nobody really cares which targets are chosen, so long as the markets are convinced that the authorities are determined to keep the situation under control
in the medium term. This situation is best illustrated by the Swiss case, where
the money supply targets were abandoned entirely in 1979, without affecting
the market's belief in the long-term determination of the Swiss National Bank
to hold inflation down.

SECTION 6.   THE RESULTS

6.6.1.   We can see from Table 6.2 that the experience with targeting has
been fairly mixed. The United States has met some targets, and not others;
Germany, after overshooting its targets for four years in a row (at least in part
because of foreign currency flows), then proceeded to undershoot targets.
Switzerland has in general tended to overshoot targets (spectacularly in 1978)
while France has also fairly consistently overshot, although less so than the
United Kingdom, whose record has been consistently poor.

6.6.2.   There are, though, other criteria. Table 6.3 shows the average inflation performance before and after adoption of monetary targets, compared
with the world average from 1970 to 1975 (about when most targets were
adopted) and 1976 to 1981. Once again, the record is rather mixed. Switzerland's performance improved substantially after adopting monetary targets;
that of the United Kingdom and France worsened. Before adopting targets, all
countries except the United Kingdom were below the world average, which
was equally the case after adopting targets. On this basis, an admittedly casual
test, one can only say that the results are "not proven."

TABLE 6.2. Monetary Policy: Targets versus Results.

United Kingdom

Date	$\pounds M_3$	
	Target	Result
April 1976–1977	12[a]	9.5
April 1976–1977	9–13	7.2
1977–1978	9–13	16.4
1978–1979	8–12	10.4
October 1978–1979	8–12	13.1
April 1979–1980	7–11	17.6
February 1980/April 1981	7–11	19.7
April 1981–1982	6–10	n.9

United States

Date	M_1		M_2		M_3	
	Target	Result	Target	Result	Target	Result
1975 II:1976 II	5–7½	5.4	8½–10½	9.6	10–12	12
1975 III:1976 III	4–7½	4.6	7½–10½	9.3	10–12	11.5
1975 IV:1976 IV	4½–7½	5.8	7½–10½	10.9	9–12	12.8
1976 I:1977 I	4½–7	6.4	7½–10	11.0	9–12	12.8
1976 II:1977 II	4½–7	6.8	7½–9½	10.8	9–11	12.4
1976 III:1977 III	4½–6½	7.9	7½–10	11.1	9–11½	12.7
1976 IV:1977 IV	4½–6½	7.9	7–10	9.8	8½–11½	11.7
1977 I:1978 I	4½–6½	7.8	7–9½	8.8	8½–11½	10.5
1977 II:1978 II	4½–6½	8.1	7–9	8.5	8½–11	10.0
1977 III:1979 III	4–6½	7.1	6½–9	8.6	8½–11	9.6
1977 IV:1978 IV	4–6½	7.3	6½–9	8.8	8–10½	9.4
1978 I:1979 I	4–6½	5.5	6½–9	7.2	7½–10	8.5
1978 II:1979 II	4–6½	5.0	6½–9	7.3	7½–10	8.4
1978 III:1979 III	2–6	4.8	6½–9	7.6	7½–10	8.3
1978 IV:1979 IV	1½–4½	5.5	5–8	8.3	6–9	8.1
1979 IV:1980 IV	4–6½[b]	7.1	6–9	10.0	6½–9½	10.2
1980 IV:1981 IV	3½–6	5.7	6–9	8.4	6½–9½	11.8
1981 IV:1982 IV	2½–5½	n.a.	6–9	n.a.	6½–9½	n.a.

Germany

Date	Target	Result
Dec. 1974–Dec. 1975	8	10.1
1976 annual average	8	9.2
1977 annual average	8	9.1
1978 annual average	8	11.5
1978 IV–1979 IV	6–9	5.5
1979 IV–1980 IV	5–8	4.9
1980 IV–1981 IV	4–7	3.6
1981 IV–1982 IV	4–7	n.a.

TABLE 6.2. *(Continued)*

Switzerland

	M_1		Monetary Base	
Date	Target	Result	Target	Result
1975 annual average	6	4.3	6	5.4
1976 annual average	6	8.0	6	2.0
1977 annual average	5	5.4	—	3.1
1978 annual average	5	16.2	—	14.9
1979 annual average	5	− 2.8	—	7.5
1980 annual average	—	− 0.9	—	− 6.0
1981 annual average	—	− 2.9	4	− 1.4

France

	M_2	
Date	Target	Result
1977	12½	12.3
1978	12	13.2
1979	11	13.4
1980	11	11.6
1981	10	14.7[c]
1982	12½–13½	—

[a] M_3 (i.e., £M_3 + foreign currency balances) target announced July; in December £M_3 target set.

[b] M_1B.

[c] First nine months at an annual rate.

TABLE 6.3. Inflation Before and After Adoption of Monetary Targets.

Country	(1) Average from 1970 to First Year of Target	(2) In Year Preceding First Target	(3) Average Since Setting Up First Target
United Kingdom	13.5	13.7	15.3
United States	7.5	11.3	9.0
Canada	6.6	10.4	8.9
Germany	6.7	5.9	4.6
Switzerland	8.0	8.0	3.6
France	8.9	9.9	11.07
World average 1970–1975	9.3	1975–1981	12.6

SOURCE: M. D. K. W. Foot, "Monetary Targets, Their Nature and Record in the Major Economies," in B. Griffiths and G. E. Wood, *Monetary Targets*, Macmillan, London, 1981, p. 30, and IMF, *IFS Yearbook*, 1980, and *IFS* December 1981.

SECTION 7. MONEY SUPPLY FIGURES

6.7.1. Table 6.4 gives definitions of the main measures of money supply in seven major countries. Those for the United States are easily the most complex, reflecting the sophistication of that country's financial institutions (and perhaps an obsession with detail in measurement). Interestingly, nonresidents' (apart from banks' and official institutions') holdings of U.S. dollars are included in the money supply.

6.7.2. This is not the case for the U.K. definition, where nonresidents' holdings of sterling are excluded, as also are U.K. residents' holdings of foreign currency (except for the broader M_3 definition). The German definition also excludes nonresidents' deposits, and all German definitions exclude holdings of foreign currency. The Swiss definitions also exclude holdings of nonresidents, but residents' sight deposits in foreign currency are included in M_2 (and thus, of course, M_3). Aside, too, from the international differences in definition, it is important to know that the different statistics for money supply are of varying degrees of reliability, in the sense that some statistics are prepared more quickly than others. This is not a subject which is set out very often in the official statistics, but in January 1979 the Federal Reserve published some estimates of how up-to-date statistics for money supply, on the then current definitions and on its new proposed definitions, could be expected to be.[12]

6.7.3. These are set out in Table 6.5. They show that at that time three-quarters of M_1 figures were available within one week but that a quarter had to be estimated; less than half of the M_2 figures were available within one week of the date for which the figure was compiled, but over 80% were available within six weeks of the date. These lags help to explain why large revisions in money supply figures can often be made at a later date, and why it is so dangerous to rely on only one or two weeks' figures.

SECTION 8. FISCAL POLICY

6.8.1. We turn now to the other major area of policy which interacts with monetary policy: fiscal policy. This can be crudely defined as the government's tax and spending policy. The dealer needs to understand two aspects of fiscal policy: first, its impact on the economy as a whole—on money supply, public sector borrowing, inflation, economic activity, and the balance of payments—and, second, its effect on flows of tax payments through the markets.

6.8.2. Most traders automatically think of fiscal policy as being government deficit spending, and therefore almost automatically inflationary. To show why this need not be so, we have to look at why governments started using fiscal policy to manage their economies after the war. During the worldwide slump

TABLE 6.4.   Money Supply Definitions.

United States[a]

M_1 = average of daily figures for (1) demand deposits at all commercial banks *other than* those due to domestic banks, the U.S. government, and foreign banks and official institutions *less* cash items in the process of collection and Federal Reserve float; (2) currency outside the U.S. Treasury, Federal Reserve Banks and the vaults of commercial banks; (3) travelers checks of nonbank issuers; (4) negotiable order of withdrawal and automated transfer service accounts at banks and thrift institutions, credit union share draft accounts, and demand deposits at mutual savings banks.

M_2 = M_1 + savings and small denomination time deposits (including "retail" term repurchase agreements) at all depository institutions, overnight repurchase agreements at commercial banks, overnight Eurodollars held by U.S. residents (other than banks) at Caribbean branches of member banks, and money market mutual fund shares (excluding money market funds for institutions).

M_3 = M_2 plus large denomination time deposits at all depository institutions and "nonretail" term RPs at commercial banks and savings and loan associations plus money market funds for institutions.

L = M_3 plus other liquid assets such as term Eurodollars held by U.S. residents (other than banks), bankers' acceptances, commercial paper, treasury bills and other liquid treasury securities, and U.S. savings bonds.

United Kingdom[b]

M_1 = notes and coin in circulation with the public + U.K. private sector sterling sight deposits at U.K. banks (less 60% of items in transit).

M_2 = M_1 less interest-bearing private sector sterling sight bank deposits + private sector interest-bearing retail sterling bank deposits.

Sterling M_3 = M_1 + U.K. private sector sterling time deposits + U.K. public sector sight and time deposits.

M_3 = sterling M_3 + U.K. residents' deposits in other currencies.

Private sector liquidity:

PSL_1 = money + money market instruments + certificates of tax deposits.

PSL_2 = PSL_1 + deposits at building societies, trustee savings banks and National Savings Bank + British Savings Bonds.

Money = sterling M_3 less public sector deposits and time deposits of over two years' maturity.

Money market instruments = Treasury bills, bank bills, deposits with municipalities and with finance houses.

Certificates of tax deposit: issued by government against advance payments of tax.

Germany

Central bank money stock = cash in circulation outside banks + minimum reserves on domestic liabilities (calculated at January 1974 levels: 16.6% for sight deposits, 12.4% for time deposits, 8.1% for savings deposits).

M_1 = cash in circulation outside banks + sight deposits of domestic nonbanks (private and public sector).

M_2 = M_1 + time deposits of domestic nonbanks (private and public sector).

TABLE 6.4. *(Continued)*

$M_3 = M_2$ + savings deposits of domestic nonbanks (private and public sector).
All four definitions exclude holdings of foreign currency.

France[c]

M_1 = notes and coins in circulation outside the banks + sight deposits at banks, post offices, savings banks and the Treasury.

$M_2 = M_1$ + term deposits and deposit bonds (*bons de caisse*) at banks + savings accounts at banks + bonds issued by the Caisse Nationale de Credit Agricole + time deposits at the Treasury.

Japan[d]

M_1 = notes and coin in circulation outside the banking sector + demand deposits at commercial banks, mutual savings banks, credit associations, Agricultural Bank, Small Business Bank, Bank of Japan, and Foreign Exchange Fund.

$M_1'= M_1$ + quasimoney held by private corporations.

Quasimoney = all deposits less demand deposits.

$M_2 = M_1$ + all quasimoney.

$M_3 = M_2$ + deposits at post offices and all cooperative banks, labor credit associations, money trusts, and loan trusts of all banks.

Published series are for M_1, M_1', M_1' + CDs, M_2 + CDs, and M_3 + CDs.

Switzerland[e]

Monetary base = notes and coin in circulation + Swiss National Bank's liabilities on giro transfer accounts to banks, commerce, and industry. (Monetary base does not include required reserves as these were suspended in 1977.)

M_1 = notes in circulation and sight deposits at banks and post offices of residents.

$M_2 = M_1$ + term deposits in Swiss francs of residents + residents' sight deposits in foreign currencies.

$M_3 = M_2$ + savings deposits of residents.

Canada[f]

M_1 = currency in circulation outside banks + privately held demand deposits less private sector float.

M_1B = currency + all checkable deposits.

$M_2 = M_1B$ + all notice and personal time deposits.

$M_3 = M_2$ + all other privately held chartered bank deposits (in all currencies).

---

[a] SOURCE: *Federal Reserve Bulletin*, January 1982, and Federal Reserve H.6 press release, February 5, 1982.

[b] SOURCE: *Bank of England Quarterly Bulletin*, December 1981; CSO *Financial Statistics Explanatory Handbook*, 1981 edition.

[c] SOURCE: *Bulletin Trimestricl de la Banque de France*, September 1981, Tables 1 and 2.

[d] SOURCE: *Bank of Japan Economic Statistics Monthly*, October 1981, pp. 19–20.

[e] SOURCE: *Bulletin mensuel de la Banque Nationale Swisse*, April 1981 and "Revision de la statistique concernant la masse monitaire," *Bulletin, Mensuel*, August 1975.

[f] SOURCE: *Bank of Canada Review*, March 1981.

TABLE 6.5. Timing of Final Data Availability, Proposed and Current Monetary Aggregates, Based on Data for June 1978.

	Percent of Actual Data Available by Lag		
Aggregate and Component	One Week[a]	Four to Six Weeks[a]	Four Months[b]
Proposed			
M-1 = currency and checkable deposits	75.4	0.6	24.0
Savings deposits component of M-1 +	69.3	0.1	30.6
M-1 + = M-1 plus bank savings	72.9	0.4	26.6
Savings deposits component of M-2[c]	30.5	55.5	13.7
M-2 = M-1 plus all savings deposits[c]	49.1	32.7	18.0
Time deposits component of M-3	36.1	48.7	15.2
M-3 = M-2 plus all time deposits[c]	43.4	39.7	16.8
Current			
M-1 = Currency and bank demand deposits	76.9	0.0	23.1
Savings and checkable deposits in M-1 +	68.4	0.0	31.6
M-1 + = M-1 plus checkable deposits at thrift institutions and commercial bank savings	73.6	0.0	26.4
Time and savings deposits component of M-2	63.8	0.0	36.2
M-2 = M-1 plus commercial bank savings and time deposits excluding large negotiable CDs	69.3	0.0	30.7
Thrift institution component of M-3	0.0	100.0[d]	0.0
M-3 = M-2 plus thrift institution deposits	40.8	41.2	18.1
Large negotiable CDs at large commercial banks	100.0	0.0	0.0
M-5 = M-2 plus large negotiable CDs at large commercial banks	44.1	38.9	17.0

SOURCE: Reproduced from *Federal Reserve Bulletin,* January 1979.

[a] Estimates of all monetary aggregates are made one week after the Wednesday close of the week based on past patterns of behavior and, in some cases, early estimates from a sample of institutions. Most of the data available in four to six weeks are from thrift institutions and foreign-related banking institutions.

[b] Most of the data available with a four-month lag are from quarterly condition statements submitted by nonmember banks. Earlier estimates of these data are made from member bank data and benchmark ratios from the latest condition report.

[c] In the proposed M-2 and M-3 aggregates, percentages sum to slightly less than 100 because one part of the savings deposit component is available with a six-month lag.

[d] Very good estimates of total deposits at savings and loan associations and mutual savings banks are available one week after the end of the month. Final data become available four weeks after month-end for savings and loans, and six weeks after month-end for mutual savings banks.

of the 1930s, most people felt that fiscal policy was not a good way of boosting an economy out of a slump. Keynes showed that they were wrong. He argued that if the government spent an amount equal to the shortage of demand in an economy, it would create the extra demand without causing excess demand.

6.8.3. So long as the government did not spend more than the amount of the "deflationary gap," this need not cause inflation. On the contrary, the government was simply making use of slack resources in the economy. For some years after the war, this approach worked quite well in several countries. But of course the real world is very complex, and people's expectations tend to rise over time. So if the government is always seen to be supporting the economy like this, political pressure tends to build up to provide too much support, which tends to produce inflation.

6.8.4. More recently, people have argued that to add government spending to private spending is misleading. Private spending, they said, tends to be "crowded out" by government spending. So extra government spending does not change the volume of demand in an economy, but only its composition. All these issues are still controversial and unresolved. For our purposes, we need to look at how the effects of fiscal policy are transmitted to the economy.

6.8.5. Suppose we have the following: the U.S. banking system in total has liabilities of $10,000 million, and assets of: cash, $800 million; Treasury bills, $1,000 million; and loans, $8,200 million. Suppose in the next quarter the Government runs a deficit of $280 million. That $280 million is paid to people who deposit it with the banks. Suppose that all of the deficit is financed by issuing Treasury bills. Suppose that the banks are the only buyers of Treasury bills. Then the $280 million extra in deposits that the banks receive is entirely invested in Treasury bills. So at the end of the quarter, we have a new balance sheet for the banking system of liabilities $10,280 million, and assets of: cash, $800 million; Treasury bills, $1,280 million; and loans, $8,200 million.

6.8.6. It looks as if nothing has changed, except that the balance sheet of the banking system has grown by $280 million on both sides. It is almost like a conjuring trick. What has happened is that the government has spent more, the proceeds have come into the private sector's hands, which has lent the money to the banks, who have lent it back to the government. It is a more or less instant recycling. The key link is the fact that the government's "promise to pay" is regarded by the banks as being a completely safe investment. The circle can only be completed if the banks have confidence in the government's promise, and invest all their extra deposits in Treasury bills.

6.8.7. Though it seems that nothing has changed, three things have in fact happened. First, the incomes of companies or individuals have risen by $280 million. So, other things being equal, their spending will tend to go up. This will push up someone else's income, and so on. Second, the public is now more liquid. It holds $280 million more bank deposits than it used to. If it has a planned ratio of bank deposits to total assets, the actual ratio will now be higher than planned. The public will start to shift assets out of bank deposits into other assets. Third, the banks hold more Treasury bills. If they have a planned ratio of Treasury bills to total lending, they will want to expand their lending.

6.8.8.   So a rise in the government's deficit tends to expand the public's income, expand the public's holdings of bank deposits, and allow the banks to lend more. The effect of these changes on the rest of the economy depends on several things. If there is a great deal of unemployment, the effect will be different than if the economy is already fully stretched. Another question is the effect of the deficit on individuals' expectations about the future. If all other things are equal, though, we can say in general that a rise in the government's deficit tends to increase both economic activity and inflation.[13]

SECTION 9.   MEASURING FISCAL POLICY

6.9.1.   We have seen why fiscal policy is used in the way that it is, and why people in the markets think that it is important. Now we need to look at how we can measure exactly what is happening. The first question is what is included in fiscal policy. In federal nations, such as the United States and Germany, it may be right to split the fiscal effects of the central government and the social security system on the one hand from state and local governments on the other. In countries with important nationalized industries, such as the United Kingdom and France, we ought also to look at these. This is especially true if their investment, pricing, or employment policies are determined by political rather than commercial factors.

6.9.2.   The next important thing to look at is the difference between policy changes and automatic changes. The former include changes in tax rates, or public spending. The latter include social security commitments (such as unemployment benefits) which are automatically available to those who qualify. If unemployment rises, unemployment benefit payments will rise, so government spending rises, without any specific fiscal policy change by the government. Often, people look at policy changes in a budget to assess its effect. But if the budget is certain to produce such a large change in unemployment that spending on social security drastically rises or falls, it might be right to take account of some of the budget's automatic effects as well as its policy changes.

6.9.3.   Economists have dreamed up different ways to measure fiscal policy to take account of these complications. The simplest measure of all, of course, is the forecast change in the actual budget deficit or surplus. But as we saw,

TABLE 6.6.   Government Deficit/Surplus (Calendar Year Basis) as Percent of GNP.

Year	United States	United Kingdom	Germany	France	Japan	Canada
Average 1950–1959	− 0.25	− 1.07	− 0.85	− 4.44	− 0.25[a]	+ 0.42
Average 1960–1969	− 0.66	− 0.93	− 0.62	− 1.02	− 0.93	− 1.00
Average 1970–1979	− 2.06	− 3.68	− 1.37	− 0.46	− 3.01	− 2.66
1970	− 1.16	+ 1.30	− 0.08	+ 0.47	− 0.43	− 1.17
1971	− 2.33	− 1.1	− 0.18	− 0.39	− 0.22	− 2.01
1972	− 1.48	− 2.5	− 0.44	+ 0.64	− 1.57	− 1.64
1973	− 0.61	− 3.17	− 0.31	+ 0.65	− 1.61	− 1.38
1974	− 0.77	− 4.15	− 1.03	+ 0.34	− 1.33	− 1.10
1975	− 4.93	− 7.97	− 3.30	− 2.96	− 4.74	− 3.80
1976	− 3.33	− 5.42	− 2.67	− 1.75	− 1.97	− 2.59
1977	− 2.69	− 3.13	− 1.86	− 0.76	− 6.13	− 4.35
1978	− 2.08	− 5.11	− 1.99	− 0.80	− 6.82	− 4.56
1979	− 1.19	− 5.52	− 1.87	0.01	− 5.31	− 4.00
1980	− 2.59	− 4.99	− 1.93	− 0.01	n.a.	− 3.52

[a] 1955/9 only

SOURCE: International Monetary Fund, *International Financial Statistics Yearbook*, 1981, Lines 80, 99a.

NOTE: Share of general government tax revenue accounted for by central government (as a proxy for central government's relative importance): U.S., 60–70%, U.K., 80–90%, Germany, 60–70%, France, 90–95%, Canada, 50–60%, Japan, 50–60% (this estimate for 1974 based on expenditures). Source: IMF, *Government Finance Statistics Yearbook*, 1981, pp. 24, 326–328.

changes in unemployment will also affect the level of government spending. So some economists adjust the level of the actual budget balance on the basis of a fixed output or employment rate.

6.9.4.   One approach is to measure what the budget deficit would be if the economy were at full employment. Another approach is to look at the long-term past average output level of the economy. This gives a cyclically adjusted budget balance, that is, what the budget balance would be if the economy were at the average output level of the past.[14]

6.9.5.   Another way of looking at budget deficits, which is often used, is to look at them as a percentage of the country's Gross National Product. Table 6.6 shows the figures for some of the major countries, and a longer trend is illustrated in Figures 6.6 and 6.7. A word of caution is in order. For each country, the comparison of the deficit as a percentage of GNP over time should be fairly consistent. But it is dangerous to compare the percentages of different countries, because the figures show the operations of central government only. State and local governments' importance varies considerably among countries and ought to be taken into account.

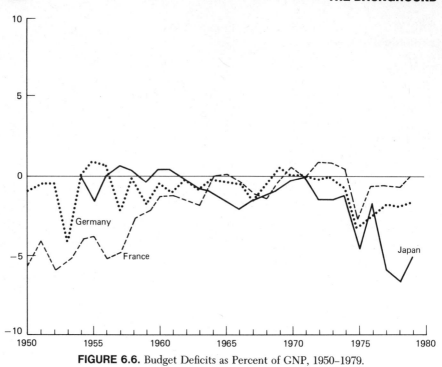

FIGURE 6.6. Budget Deficits as Percent of GNP, 1950–1979.

6.9.6. The footnote to Table 6.6 gives a rough indication of the relative importance of local government in different countries. In order of centralization, the countries run: France, the United Kingdom, the United States, Germany, Canada, and Japan. Obviously, a large central deficit offset by a large surplus at other levels of government is less critical than a large central government deficit which is reinforced by a deficit elsewhere in the system. With that in mind, it is interesting to look at the trend over time. For the first few years after the war, of course, all government finances were rather distorted. Then, from the second half of the 1950s to around 1970, central government deficits tended to be small and fluctuating.

6.9.7. After the 1970–1971 recession, deficits started to expand, and exploded when the oil crisis pushed all major economies into recession. Some countries, such as the United States and France, pulled back quickly toward balance; others, such as the United Kingdom and Japan even more so, continued to run large deficits. In many ways, these figures show up the reverse of popular demonology. The United States, for example, about whose budget deficits there has been enormous concern in recent years, is shown up as having consistently run a smaller deficit than Japan on average during the 1970s, whereas Germany's has usually been larger than that of France, which has a less fiscally "respectable" image.

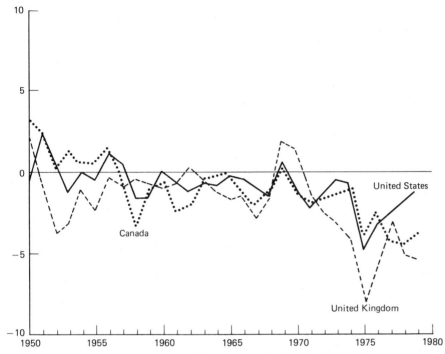

FIGURE 6.7. Budget Deficits as Percent of GNP, 1950–1979.

SECTION 10.   MANAGING FISCAL POLICY

6.10.1.   This section discusses the ways in which various countries put together their budgets. Before discussing individual countries, though, it is useful
to look in comparative terms at the structure of their budgets. The reason is
that government budgets are becoming dominated by "automatic" expenditures. This is spending on social security and the like, where the payment is not
made by a specific decision, but comes as of right. The higher the proportion of
such spending, the less direct control a government has over its budget—unless it chooses to attack the problem at its roots by cutting back on social security or other entitlements. Table 6.7 shows some of the key items of central
government revenue and expenditure in some of our major countries.

6.10.2.   Interestingly, some of our normal stereotypes take a knock when we
look at the figures. The supposedly hard-working, self-denying Germans spend
almost 70% of their budget on health and social security; the effete British
spend the lowest proportion of all, 39%. Once again, it should be said that
comparisons of this kind are risky; still, the picture is probably fairly accurate.
To see how governments manage these revenues and expenditures, we turn
now to the individual countries.

TABLE 6.7. Key Items of Central Government Revenue and Expenditure.

	As Percent of Total Revenue			As Percent of Total Expenditure	
	1972	1979		1972	1979
United States:					
Income tax	59	58	Defense	32	21
Social security	24	28	Health and social security	41	44
Other	17	14	Other[a]	27	35
United Kingdom:					
Income tax	39	39	Defense	17	15
Social security	15	16	Health and social security	37	39
Value Added Tax (VAT), etc.	27	24	Other	46	46
Other	19	21			
Germany:					
Income tax	20	20	Defense	12	10
Social security	47	52	Health and social security	64	69
(VAT), etc.	28	24	Other	24	21
Other	5	4			
France:					
Income tax	17	17	Defense	n.a.[b]	7 (1978)
Social security	36	43	Health and social security	n.a.	59
(VAT), etc.	37	32	Other	n.a.	34
Other	10	8			
Canada (1974)			(1971)		
Income	54	53	Defense	11	8
Social security	9	11	Health and social security	44	40
Sales taxes, etc.	16	14	Other	45	52
Other	21	22			

SOURCE: IMF, *Government Finance Statistics Yearbook.* Japanese figures not available on a comparable basis. Country Tables A, Lines I and IV 1, IV 2, IV 5; B, Lines I and 2, 4 and 5.
[a] "Other" mainly consists of housing, education, transport and communications, debt interest, and general transfer payments.
[b] n.a. = not available.

6.10.3. Of the countries we shall look at, the United States has the weakest government control of the budget. Of recent years, control of the budget has increasingly passed to Congress. A major exception to this was in 1981, when President Reagan succeeded in imposing his draft budget almost wholesale on the Congress. But, more and more, detailed provisions of taxation and spending are settled by congressional committees. This makes for very disorderly budget making, so what we shall say here represents more an ideal than the reality.

6.10.4. In theory, though, the schedule is as follows: The budget is made for a fiscal year which begins in October of the preceding year. FY 1982 started in October 1981. For the FY 1983, initial plans began in spring 1981. During the autumn and winter of 1981–82 these plans were finalized, and at the start of February 1982 the FY 1983 budget was presented by the president to Congress. By March 15, Congress standing committees must report to the House and Senate budget committees. By April 1, the Congressional Budget Office must submit its fiscal policy report to the House and Senate budget committees. By April 10, the president must submit revisions, if any, to the budget. By May 15th, Congress must adopt its first concurrent budget resolution. This sets targets for total receipts, outlays, and the budget authority. The budget authority consists of the amounts that agencies are allowed to lend or commit. During the summer, the president revises plans to meet current developments, and by September 15, Congress must pass its second concurrent resolution. This sets binding budget figures.

6.10.5. In fact, during the 1981 session, things did not work out quite like that. The Reagan administration submitted its FY 1982 budget on March 10, 1981, forecasting a FY 1982 deficit of $45 billion. In July, it reduced that estimate to $42.5 billion, anticipating "reconciliation" savings ordered by the first fiscal 1982 budget resolution. The reconciliation package was finally passed on July 31, cutting $35.2 billion from planned FY 1982 spending. But as the economy slackened during the summer, the forecast deficit figures jumped dramatically. In September, President Reagan asked Congress to approve a further $16 billion package of spending cuts and revenue increases. Congress could not agree to this, and in order to permit the government to continue functioning until the budget was settled, a temporary "continuing appropriations" resolution was passed. This permitted government spending to continue at current levels until November 20.

6.10.6. As it turned out, Congress could not agree in time on a revised version of the budget that was satisfactory to the president. The final version put to him was vetoed, and, for a day, the federal government was closed down. Once again, a temporary resolution was passed, providing funding through to March 31 for government departments whose regular appropriations bills had not been enacted. In summary, therefore, despite the neat schedule laid down in the Budget Act of 1974, the U.S. budget process is a bit of a shambles.[15]

6.10.7. In the United Kingdom, the budget process is in some ways far more efficient than the American; in other ways, it is far less consistent. The main merits of the U.K. approach are that the budget is, in practice, effectively decided by the Chancellor of the Exchequer and his Treasury team, on their own, without the distracting haggles of much parliamentary or cabinet involvement. Of course, the Chancellor takes into consideration the political factors. But, in the end, the budget is primarily his and the Prime Minister's.

6.10.8. Compared with the U.S. method, this gives great speed and flexibility in decision making. A major policy reversal can be announced overnight, and can take effect immediately. On the other hand, the U.K. system has a major weakness: expenditure and tax decisions are made separately. The traditional April budget is almost entirely concerned with revenue decisions. Spending decisions are made at different times, presented in different documents, and (until recently) calculated in different units of account.

6.10.9. The usual timetable runs something like this: During the early summer, the Public Expenditure Survey Committee reviews existing public spending volume plans, and submits a report to cabinet. During the late summer and autumn, cabinet decides on public spending plans up to four years ahead on the basis of the PESC exercise. It focuses mainly on the coming financial year, and the next one. In December or January, a public expenditure White Paper is published setting out spending plans for the next four years. During January and February, the White Paper is considered by parliamentary select committees, followed by a report, and during March, a one- or two-day debate in the House.

6.10.10 During March or April, the budget is presented, showing how the government proposes to finance its spending. The main Supply Estimates, detailing amounts of money to be spent by the government in the coming year, are published. After a debate on the budget, the Finance Bill containing the tax proposals is published, and debated in Parliament during March or April through to July. All being well, the Finance Bill is enacted in July or August, together with a Supply Resolution and Consolidated Fund (Appropriation) Bill, which provides the government with formal authority to spend the amounts detailed in the Supply Estimates.

6.10.11 Supplementary Estimates are presented as needed during the rest of the fiscal year, to cover any spending that becomes necessary.[16] The major benefits of this system are that tax changes can be made with immediate effect when the Chancellor thinks it is right to do so, and, if necessary, enacted retroactively by Parliament; the major problem is making tax decisions fit spending decisions.

6.10.12 German management of fiscal policy is, like much else in Germany, controlled by a specific group of laws. These, like all others in Germany, flow from the Basic Law. This lays down that the *Länder* (provinces) should perform all government tasks other than those reserved for the *Bund* (federal government). The main laws controlling the budget process are the Stabilitäts-und-Wachstumsgesetz, the Haushaltsgrundsätzegesetz, and the Bundeshaushaltsordnung (abbreviated StWG, HGrG, and BHO respectively; their titles in English are: Stability and Growth Law, Budget Basic Principles Law, and Budget Regulations). The Basic Law lays down that revenue from income and corporation taxes and turnover taxes accrue jointly to the *Bund* and the *Länder*. The law also lays down that the *Bund* and *Länder* must agree how much of the revenue from turnover tax is given to the *Bund* and how much to the *Länder*. This can lead to difficult negotiations. For 1979–1980, the *Bund* received 67.5% and the *Länder* 32.5% of turnover tax revenue. The *Bund* wanted a higher proportion but was unable to force it through against the resistance of the *Länder;* as a result, the *Bund* had to finance 13% of its expenditure by borrowing, against only 7% for the *Länder* in 1979.[17]

6.10.13. The Basic Law and the Budget Regulations do not lay down a fixed timetable for the passage of the budget. In 1976, for example, the federal budget for that year was not approved by the Bundestag (lower house) until May, whereas the 1978 budget was passed in January; the 1982 budget was passed, after a great disagreement, in January 1982. If the budget is not passed in time, Article 111 of the Basic Law authorizes the federal government to make necessary payments to continue existing operations, and if need be, to borrow to finance this (up to 25% of the total amount of the previous budget).

6.10.14. The actual procedure for the budget proccess is laid down in the Budget Regulations. Government's draft budget proposals are laid before the Bundestag and the Bundesrat simultaneously (The Bundestag is an elected lower chamber; the Bundesrat is in effect a "chamber of ambassadors" since its 41 members are appointed by the governments of the *Länder*. They are members of the *Land* governments which they represent, and are bound by the orders of their governments. All legislation which affects the *Länder* financially can be passed only if the Bundesrat gives its assent.) The first reading of the budget takes place in the Bundestag, while simultaneously the Bundesrat debates the proposals. The Bundesrat must give its opinion within six weeks.

6.10.15. The second reading of the budget in the Bundestag takes place after the budget committee of the Bundestag has worked through the proposals, and cannot take place until the Bundesrat has given its opinion. After further discussion in the Bundestag, the third reading takes place. The bill is then sent back to the Bundesrat. If the latter cannot agree with the shape of the bill, a reconciliation committee (*Vermittlungsausschuss*) is called in to mediate between the two houses. If changes are agreed, the bill must then pass again through the Bundestag. (The reconciliation committee procedure was needed, for example, in December 1981 to settle the final shape of the 1982 budget.)[18]

6.10.16. The German system is not quite as flexible as the British, but considerably more so than the American, particularly when it comes to supplementary budgets. Quite often, two or three of these are passed in a year. As well as this, the Stability Law of 1967 allows the federal government to spend more than budgeted for, if the economy requires it. The funds needed are taken from special reserves which the *Bund* has to deposit with the Bundesbank when the economy is growing too fast. (In practice, this provision is less important these days.)

6.10.17.   The management of French fiscal policy is, like that of Germany, regulated by a basic law: in this case, the "Organic Law" of 1959. Many of the details of the budget system are regulated by the Ordinance of January 2, 1959.[19] The main point about these is that they were brought in just after the takeover by General de Gaulle. Before him, the finances of France had been collapsing because of political instability and inability by the Parliament to control policy steadily. So, the 1959 arrangements strongly centralized control of the budget.

6.10.18.   Article 40 of the constitution forbids members of Parliament to "reduce public revenues or create or enlarge an item of public expenditure." On items of detail within the budget, Article 42 of the Organic Law is even stricter, as it forbids amendments to the budget proposal, except for those which would "prevent or reduce an item of expenditure, create or increase a revenue, or increase control over public spending." So, in complete contrast to the U.S. system, the French Parliament has very little control indeed over the budget system.[20]

6.10.19.   The actual timetable runs something like this. During January, the budget and forecasting departments of the Ministry of Finance start preparing a draft budget, which is presented to the cabinet around mid-February. Discussions among the various ministries then start to take place, while at the same time the Ministry of Finance sets up three sets of documents. These are the *budget voté* (a detailed layout of the current year's budget, as voted by Parliament at the end of the preceding year); the *services votés* (basically, this year's cost of last year's services); and planned new measures. By July, the interministerial discussions should produce a draft budget, which must then be presented to Parliament by the first Tuesday of October.

6.10.20.   Parliament is allowed 70 days for discussion of the budget, which comes into effect on the first of January. If Parliament fails to vote the budget before that date, the government has the right to put the budget into effect by decree. If, on the other hand, the government is late in submitting the budget for some reason, so that Parliament's 70 days finish after the start of the new budgetary year, the government depends entirely on Parliament for legal authority to receive revenue.[21]

6.10.21.   It could save confusion to know that the French traditionally refer to the various budgetary documents by the color of their cover. The blues are the documents which have to be deposited with Parliament in October, consisting of the lists by ministry of *services votés* and new measures, together with the special accounts of the Treasury, the draft finance law and various other documents. The yellows are supplementary annexes deposited at the same time. The whites crosscast the budget into the form of programs by ministry. The greens are the *budgets votés*, the legal documents voted by Parliament which contain the detailed authority for all expenditure.[22]

6.10.22.　Like the German and the British governments, the French government has the freedom to introduce supplementary budgets if it decides that the economy is not behaving in the way that it expected. These take the form of *lois de finances rectificatives*, one or two of which are often introduced during the year. As well as the general budget which we have been discussing, French fiscal policy is transmitted through certain supplementary budgets and the special accounts of the Treasury.

6.10.23.　The most important supplementary budget (*budget annèxe*) is that for the posts and telecommunications, which accounted for FF 100 billion, and the social assistance for agriculture (*budget des prestations sociales agricoles*—BAPSA), which accounted for FF 41 billion; these two between them account for FFR 141 billion of the total supplementary budgets of FFR 147 billion. The special accounts of the Treasury were, between the wars, a very important means by which the governments of the day managed to finance themselves while concealing the extents of their deficits. Hence, today, they are very tightly controlled.

6.10.24.　The major items—apart from road funds and the like—are loans to various development funds, and loans to the departments and communes, which are repaid when local taxes are gathered. This account totals about half of the value of the special accounts: in 1979, the figure was FFR 60 billion out of a total of FFR 112 billion. This account normally goes more and more heavily overdrawn—the Treasury lends to the local authorities—until October, when funds start flowing in. During 1979, for example, the Treasury lent out about FFR 24 billion during the first 10 months of the year, and received FFR 22 billion during the next two months.[23]

6.10.25.　Finally, it is worth mentioning that a great deal of state activity has been "debudgetized." That is, a good deal of spending has been moved outside the budgetary framework. The duty of financing these items has been transferred to bodies which are independent (for example the Caisse des Dépôts et Consignations, Crédit Foncier, and similar bodies). The accounts of these bodies are not submitted to Parliament (in contrast to the U.K. Public Accounts Committee). The official reason given for this is a simple one: they have a legal personality which is separate from that of the state, which cannot therefore determine their financial activity. In fact, of course, government control is fairly tight. It takes the form of technical and financial "sponsorship" (*tutelle*) exercised beforehand, and control afterward through a Commission de Vérification des Comptes.

6.10.26.　Fiscal policy in Japan is largely set by the central government. Local governments and the social security system have relatively little independence. The budget falls into three parts: the general account budget, special account budgets, and government-affiliated agencies, including the Fiscal Investment and Loan Program (FILP). Preliminary work on the budget starts early in the year, culminating in reports from the various ministries to the Minister of Finance by August 31, on their individual budget plans. During the autumn, the budget bureau of the Ministry of Finance starts to coordinate these plans, and the Ministry of Finance prepares a budget draft around the end of December.[24]

6.10.27. After discussion in cabinet, the budget is usually presented to the diet in January, together with the budgets of about 15 government-affiliated agencies, and the FILP. The fiscal years runs from April 1 to March 31, and if the ordinary budget is not expected to be approved before the start of the fiscal year, a provisional budget is presented to the diet. When the regular budget is approved, the provisional budget is absorbed into the regular budget. (This is quite a common procedure—it has happened 12 times since the war, 6 times during the 1970s: 1970, 1972, 1973, 1974, 1976, and 1977.) Also, if the government decides to change the balance of fiscal policy during the year, it will present another supplementary budget.

6.10.28. The 38 special account budgets cover specific projects, such as the postal services, social security, foreign exchange reserves, foodstuffs control (price management of staple commodities—the third largest special account, after the national debt consolidation fund and the special account for transfers of local taxes; the welfare insurance account is considerably smaller).[25] The FILP is one of the most important special accounts. It owes its importance partly to the days of the Dodge Line—the balanced budget law imposed by the United States after the war. The FILP allowed the central government to finance investment and other activities, without necessarily seeming to incur a deficit on the general budget, which would have broken the Dodge Line. In 1980, the FILP totalled ¥ 18 trillion, compared with the total general account budget of ¥ 43 trillion. So when the Japanese budget is presented, it is important to look not just at the general account budget, but also at the FILP and the other special accounts.

SECTION 11.   TAX FLOWS AND THE MONEY MARKET

6.11.1. Another area in which government fiscal policy affects the market is the mechanical impact of tax flows. Whether or not these have any effect depends on the success of any smoothing operations carried out by the central bank. If tax flows drain funds from the market, but these funds are replaced at once by some kind of open market operation by the central bank, then there need be no net effect. Certainly, though, the effect of these tax flows makes monetary management in the very short run more difficult for the central bank if the effect of the tax revenue is large. For one thing, the open market operations caused by the tax flows may be misread by the market as a signal of a change in basic policy.

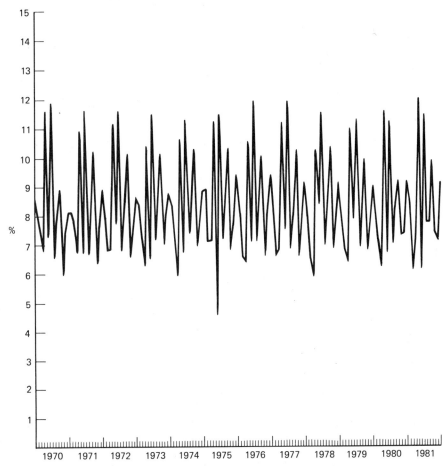

FIGURE 6.8. U.S. Tax Revenue: Month as Percent of Year.

6.11.2. A glance at Figures 6.8 to 6.12 shows how the importance of each month in the tax year has moved over the last decade. In most countries, there is a strong and fairly stable pattern, which is largely due to the timing of corporate tax payments. Individual tax payments, of course, are now fairly smoothly made in most countries through a standard monthly deduction; it is the payment of corporation taxes, which depends of course, on profits, that tends to vary. The U.S. pattern is dominated by the fact that corporations must estimate and pay taxes on a pay-as-you-go basis, with payments generally due in quarterly installments on the 15th day of the 4th, 6th, 9th and 12th months of the fiscal year. Since, on average, most corporations use the calendar year as their fiscal year, this tends to produce tax revenue peaks in April, June, September, and December.

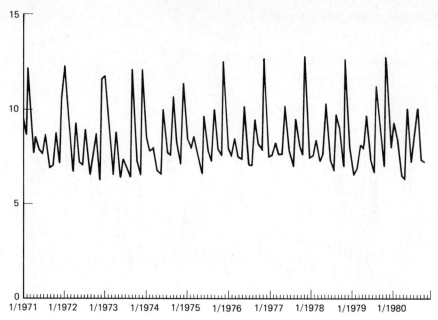

FIGURE 6.9. U.K. Tax Revenue: Month as Percent of Year.

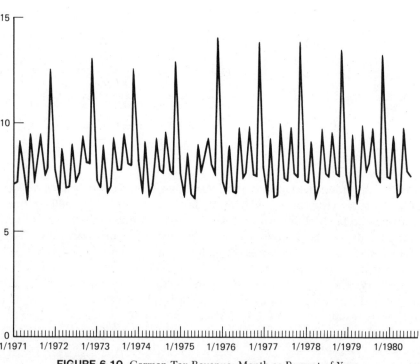

FIGURE 6.10. German Tax Revenue: Month as Percent of Year.

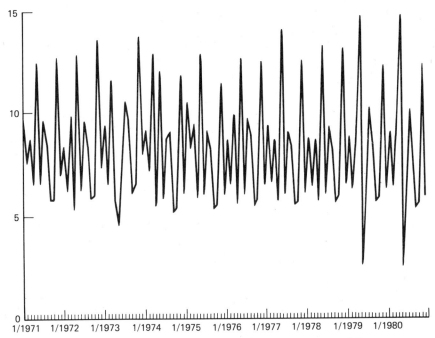

FIGURE 6.11. Japanese Tax Revenue: Month as Percent of Year.

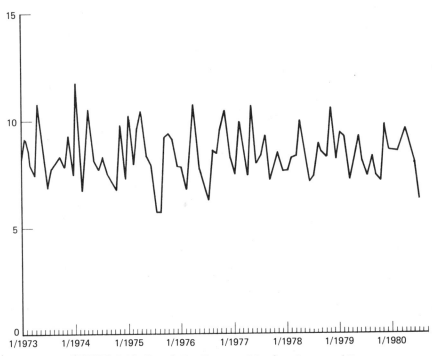

FIGURE 6.12. French Tax Revenue: Month as Percent of Year.

173

6.11.3. Similarly, the U.K. system is dominated by heavy payments in January and February, since payments are usually made about nine months in arrears, and a high proportion of companies have fiscal years ending on March 31, in line with the government's fiscal year. There is a secondary peak in October, caused by corporations whose fiscal year ends in December, and similarly in July for those whose year ends in September. Also, of recent years, there has been a buildup of tax receipts in March and September, owing to the petroleum revenue tax, which is payable at those dates. The 1982 budget introduced a provision to spread this more evenly. The German system is classically regular in appearance on the chart, with a major peak in December, and secondary peaks in March, June, and September. The pattern has not changed for over a decade.

6.11.4 In Japan, the major tax peak now occurs in April (shifting from May after 1978), with subsidiary peaks in July and November. The French pattern is much less clearly distinguishable than the others. However, there tend to be local peaks in September, December, and May, with February sometimes also an important month. Income tax, apart from pay-as-you-earn, is payable by provisional settlement in February, with a second provisional settlement in May, and settlement (in certain cases) of the final balance in September, alternatively by mid-December. Major tax dates for corporation tax are March 15, April 15 (final settlement of previous year's balances), June 15, September 15, and December 15.

SECTION 12.   THE BALANCE OF PAYMENTS

6.12.1. The balance of payments can be described as a record of a country's international economic accounts. That is, it records the goods and services that the economy has sold to and bought from the rest of the world, and the changes in the country's claims on and liabilities to the rest of the world. Because the balance of payments consists of double-entry bookkeeping, its components must necessarily balance, just like those of a corporation.

6.12.2. It is meaningless to say that a balance of payments is not in balance, just as it is meaningless to say that the accounts of a corporation do not balance. When concern is expressed over a country's balance of payments, what is usually meant is that part of the balance—for example the current account—is behaving in a way that puts strain on other parts of the balance that are needed to finance it. Hence the foreign exchange markets usually look at the behavior of the trade account or current account of a country to assess the likely pressure on a currency arising from the need to finance any deficit. But in theory the behavior of any one part of the balance of payments is irrelevant. Some other component in the balance will move to offset it.

6.12.3. In fact, the United States Advisory Committee on the Presentation of Balance of Payments Statistics, which issued its report in June 1976, recommended against trying to identify an overall surplus or deficit in the balance of payments. It went so far as to recommend that the terms "surplus" and "deficit" be deleted from official references. As a result, there is some difference of approach between the U.S. official statistical presentation of the balance of payments and that of most other countries. Professor R. M. Stern has remarked that "the rest of the world, by its continued reliance upon outmoded balance-of-payments concepts, is apparently out of step with the United States."[26]

6.12.4. Unfortunately the foreign exchange markets regard the professor's view as academic, and still focus on the trade and current account of the countries whose currencies they are dealing in. So we shall now look at these in some depth. For the sake of comparability, we shall concentrate on the presentation used by the IMF in its *Balance of Payments Manual.* The balance of payments breaks down into two main components: the current account, referring to goods, services, income, and transfers; and the capital account, covering financial assets and liabilities.

6.12.5. The current account itself can be broken down into the trade balance and other current items. The trade balance is the difference between exports and imports of goods. The other items in the current account include earnings from shipping and the like, spending on travel, income from investment (in the form of interest and dividends, or reinvested earnings which are left invested in the country where they were earned), and other goods and services. They also include transfers—which can be either migrants' transfers or other transfers including official spending. The capital account can be split into four main sections. The first is direct investment: purchases of factories overseas and the like. Next is portfolio investment in shares or bonds. Then come other capital movements—borrowings and lendings, changes in the credit terms given or taken by firms in international trade. Finally, there are movements in the country's official reserves.

6.12.6. These ideas can best be understood by looking at a specific case. Table 6.8 shows a simplified balance of payments for our old friend, Home Country. Home has earned a surplus on its trade accounts, because its exports at 190 were larger than its imports, at 165. So its trade balance shows a surplus of +25. It has had to pay away interest and dividends to companies overseas which have invested in it, so that there is a transfer on current account outwards—that is, minus—of 15. Quite a few workers from Home have gone abroad to work at better paying jobs, and they are sending money back to their families; so that transfers from abroad back to Home show up as a surplus of +40 in the balance of payments. Goods coming into Home tend to be shipped

TABLE 6.8.   Home Country Balance of Payments.

Exports	190
Imports	165
Trade balance	+ 25
Interest and dividends	− 15
Transfers	+ 40
Shipping, etc.	− 10
Current account	+ 40
Capital account	
Direct investment	+ 200
Net lending	− 100
Portfolio investment	− 30
Change in reserves (− rise)	− 110

in foreign ships, so Home has to pay away 10 on shipping and transport account.

6.12.7.   When we add these three items to the trade balance, we find that Home has a current account surplus of +40. In a sense, that represents an inflow of cash. To show what happens to this cash, we look at the capital accounts. We see that firms from overseas are buying factories in Home, so that there is an inflow on direct investment account of 200. Home's banks have tended to prefer to lend abroad, so on net lending there is an outflow of 100, and similarly Home's investors tend to buy foreign stocks, so that there is an outflow on portfolio investment of 30. If we add up what we have so far—current account +40, direct investment +200, net lending −100, portfolio −30— we come to a total of +110.

6.12.8.   The current account and the balance of capital accounts so far have meant a cash inflow of 110. The Home government adds these to its foreign currency reserves. To make the double-entry system balance, a rise in reserves has to be negative. If we stop to think about it, we will see why this is. Basically, any government's foreign exchange reserves are held—by definition—in foreign currency. Usually, these foreign currency reserves are held in Treasury bills or similar instruments overseas. In effect, the Home government is lending money to other governments by placing its reserves in these countries. So a rise in reserves has to be treated just the same as a net lending by Home's banks abroad.

6.12.9.   With this simple example in mind, we will look briefly at a more complicated case. We will look at the U.S. balance of payments for 1980. (The

TABLE 6.9.   U.S. Balance of Payments, 1979–1980 (in Billions of US$).

	1979	1980
Exports	182.1	221.8
Imports	− 211.5	− 249.1
Trade balance	− 29.4	− 27.4
Military transactions	− 1.3	− 3.3
Investment income	32.5	32.5
of which: Direct	32.0	28.0
Other services	3.1	5.2
Remittances, etc.	− 5.7	− 6.9
Current account	− 0.8	+ 0.2
Net private capital flows	− 5.0	− 39.8
Net official asset flows	− 15.4	8.0
Other items	− 2.7	− 3.9
Errors	+ 23.9	+ 35.5

figures are set out in Table 6.9.) We can see from the table that the trade deficit fell slightly in 1980, because exports (benefiting from the lagged effects of the dollar's depreciation in 1977–1979) improved faster than imports. This trade deficit was large, but it was more than offset by net income on nontrade current account items. Of these, the largest was investment income.

6.12.10.   Most of this comes from receipts from direct investment—earnings by companies and factories abroad which are owned by U.S. corporations, as distinct from investments in bonds or shares. These fell slightly in 1980, largely because of the world recession. On the other hand, other investment income rose substantially, to around $4.5 billion, because of the higher interest rate levels of 1980 which improved earnings on investments. These earnings, together with their net surplus on other service transactions (banking, insurance, shipping, etc.) of $5.2 billion, helped to finance a deficit on military transaction of $3.3 billion and net remittances abroad (of pensions and other similar transfers) of $6.9 billion. The total combined to produce a balance on current account of $0.2 billion; for practical purposes, we can say that the current account was in exact balance, given the size of transactions involved.

6.12.11.   That was the easy part. The capital account is much more complex. First, there is a very large error element in the U.S. balance of payments accounts. Part of this comes from errors and omissions in the reporting of current account transactions. But people think that most of the error is from unrecorded flows of private capital. In 1980, this unrecorded inflow was very large. It almost offset the large recorded outflow through banks. The banking outflow happened because in much of 1979 and in the first quarter of 1980, during the domestic credit squeeze, U.S. banks had borrowed heavily from their own offices in foreign countries, so as to fund loans in the United States.

6.12.12.   When credit restraints were imposed in March 1980, U.S. economic activities slowed down. So U.S. banks repaid about $20 billion in borrowings from their own offices abroad, and lent more to other foreigners. Apart from these private flows, there was an official inflow. That is, foreign countries' reserve assets in the United States grew by $16 billion in 1980. The United States built up its own reserves by $8 billion, so that the net official reserve asset flows show an inflow of $8 billion.

6.12.13.   Most of the inflow from abroad came from OPEC members, with only a very small rise in reserves held by industrial countries. The latter, indeed, reduced their reserves sharply during the first quarter, because they were selling dollars to defend their currencies. To a great extent, these reserve movements reflect the fact that the United States benefits from being the world's only major reserve currency. Increases in foreign official reserve assets in the United States are, in effect, involuntary lending by foreign governments to the United States.

6.12.14.   Even within the figures that we have shown, there are many possible complications. For example, a very important source of capital flows can be changes in the terms of credit granted by firms in international trade. But the important point to realize is that the balance of payments consists of a whole set of interconnected flows. As we said earlier, these must always balance; the critical question is whether or not the balancing is achieved without strain.

6.12.15.   We can think of the balance of payments as being like a company's accounts. There is a cash flow element—the current account—and there are the changes in balance sheet items that show up as capital flows. If we think of it this way, we can see that it is not necessarily a good or bad thing to be running a surplus or deficit on current account. A current account surplus is equivalent to a positive cash flow, and a deficit equivalent to a negative cash flow. If we compare a country with a company, a company can be having a negative cash flow for many reasons, some good, some bad. It may have a negative cash flow because it is buying inventory so as to produce goods from inventory to sell later. Or it may be buying investment equipment from abroad, again with a view to building up production.

6.12.16.   But, just like a company, a country cannot run a negative cash flow forever. It can only do it as long as other people are willing to lend to it. Hence the foreign exchange market's concern about the current and trade accounts. These give a quick and easy indication of how the country's cash flow is doing. But it is also important to look at the balance sheet side, the capital flows.

6.12.17. For instance, during 1974, the United Kingdom's balance of payments deficit trebled from the 1973 level (from £1.1 billion to £3.3 billion), because of the effects of the oil crisis. But because the OPEC countries invested quite a lot of their earnings in sterling (for lack of other markets outside the United States in which to invest funds at that time), and because the British government borrowed abroad, the United Kingdom's official reserves rose during 1974, and sterling stayed fairly stable. A bank which looked only at the current account, and not the capital flows, would have lost money by selling sterling short.

SECTION 13.   BALANCE OF PAYMENTS POLICY

6.13.1.   In this section, we look at those government policies that affect the balance of payments. The most important of these are policy on the exchange rate, policy on borrowing from abroad, and trade policy. Exchange rate policy will be affected by many factors. But to put them in context, let us look at a simple case. Once again, we look at our Home Country. Home's exports per year are running at 100 widgets, while it is importing 200 widgets. The balance of widget trade, therefore, is in heavy deficit. Home's dictator is getting worried, so he orders a devaluation of the currency. In the past, Home's currency was set at HC 2 = US\$ 1. The dictator announces that henceforth the parity will be HC 3 = US\$ 1.

6.13.2.   Since all Home's widget exports are priced in Home currency, buyers of Home's widgets find that they are cheaper. Suppose that in the past the widget was priced at HC 2.0, so that the price to the foreign buyer was US\$ 1. Suppose that Home's widget exporters keep their widget prices fixed in Home currency. Then, the foreign buyer finds that he has only to pay US\$ 0.67 per widget that he buys from Home instead of US\$ 1 as in the past. Home's exports are now one-third cheaper, and hence more competitive in international terms. Foreign buyers will buy more Home widgets, and less from elsewhere, so that Home's exports will rise.

6.13.3.   Now let us look at Home's imports of widgets. Suppose that foreign sellers of widgets to Home priced their widgets in dollars. Suppose that they priced each widget at US\$ 1. Then each widget was costing the Home importer HC 2 to buy. But after the HC devaluation, assuming that foreign sellers of widgets keep their prices fixed at US\$ 1, the Home importer finds that each widget now costs him HC 3. Clearly, he is going to tend to prefer to buy his widgets domestically, rather than from the world market. So Home's imports should also fall.

6.13.4.   The net result of all these changes should be an improvement in Home's trade balance. This, of course, is the classical argument for devaluation of a currency. Conversely, the classical argument for a revaluation is when the trade surplus is excessive; revaluing the currency makes exports from the country more expensive, and imports into it cheaper, so it tends to reduce the trade surplus.

6.13.5.   Of course, the real world is not so simple. The first point is that a devaluation of a currency usually increases domestic inflation. To see why, let's look again at Home's imports from abroad. We saw that the effect of the devaluation made imports more expensive. We assumed that this meant that Home people would cut back their imports of widgets. But part of Home's imports probably consist of essential raw materials, like oil, or metals, which are used in the production of widgets.

6.13.6.   So, the effect of the devaluation will be to increase the costs of these essential imports, and push up domestic widget production costs. The devaluation will also push up the price of imports of food and other consumption goods. That will probably lead Home's trade unions to ask for more wages. So a devaluation tends to be inflationary. In some countries, where there is a very high level of essential imports from abroad, such as the United Kingdom, it has been suggested that the effect of a devaluation is washed out after a couple of years by the domestic inflation that results from it.

6.13.7.   We should also notice the effect on domestic production. We saw that a devaluation of the Home currency made Home's exports more competitive in the world markets. We said this would lead to an increase in Home's exports of widgets. But if Home's producers of widgets were already working flat out at full capacity, they would not produce more for exports. To be fully effective, a devaluation is best made when there is surplus domestic production capacity that is available to meet the extra world demand for exports that the devaluation creates.

6.13.8.   Another complication is that very often exporters work on the basis of orders for some months or years ahead. So the effects of a devaluation or revaluation will not show up immediately in export or import volumes. What would happen to Home's balance of payments if the volumes of exports and imports did not change? Clearly, widget exports of 100 units now earn less in foreign currency, because their U.S. dollar price has fallen from $1 to $0.67.

6.13.9.   So instead of earning $100 from abroad, Home only earns $67. Conversely, the import price of widgets is still fixed at US$ 1, so Home is still spending $200 a year to buy widgets from abroad. So, the first effect of a devaluation is to *worsen* the trade deficit. Earnings from exports fall; imports cost the same in dollar terms as they did before. This is often called the J-curve effect. The reason is that the trade balance looks like a J: To start with, it goes down the first part of the curve of the J, and then it goes up again later.

6.13.10.   As to how long each stage lasts, economists and econometricians have been spending a long time trying to find out. The answer is, of course, that it varies a great deal among the countries and over time. A fairly recent survey for the United Kingdom found that the average contract periods for U.K. exports were just under six months, while those for imports were just under four months. This, together with the fact that the bulk of U.K. exports are invoiced in sterling (nearly 75% according to the survey) and only about 30% of imports are invoiced in sterling, suggests that the negative J-curve effect for the United Kingdom should be quite large, for at least six months, although there are no very precise figures.[27]

6.13.11.   Another complication in real life is that if an exporter is invoicing in foreign currency when his own currency is devalued, he has two choices: he can either cut his foreign currency price, in which case his exports become more competitive and he sells more; or he can keep his price the same and sell the same volume but make more profit. If he keeps his foreign currency price unchanged, the effect of the devaluation simply feeds through to corporate profits. It does not produce any immediate improvement in the balance of payments (although, of course, because exporting is now more profitable, it will probably tend to increase the number of exporters over time).

6.13.12.   Another area of balance of payments policy, of course, is trade policy. A government can discourage imports by tariffs, or by nontariff barriers. These latter are especially important in certain countries, such as Japan. (For example, traditionally, Japanese testing requirements for automobiles meant that it was very difficult to sell cars to Japan. This, of course, tended to improve Japan's trade balance.) Another way in which a country can try to reduce imports is by import deposits. These have often been used, for example, in Italy when the government wants to bring the balance of payments under control. An importer has to put down, say, 50% of the value of the goods that he wants to import. The money has to be deposited, interest free, at the central bank.

6.13.13.   This has two immediate effects: first, the importer has to find half of the cost of his imports "up front," rather than relying on the exporter to give him credit for payment; second, it costs him money because he has to pay interest on his borrowing, or, if he has the funds already, he loses the interest that he could earn on it. The effect is that imports become more difficult to finance and more expensive. Other countries impose more complicated systems, like import taxes, or separate exchange rates for imports which are considered "undesirable," such as luxury goods. These multiple exchange rate systems are much more common in developing countries.

6.13.14.   Finally, a very important part of balance of payments policy is its financing. We saw earlier how important capital flows can be in affecting a country's balance of payments. A country will have no problem running a current account deficit if it has easy access to international credit. That access partly depends on how much it has already borrowed, and partly on its balance of payments prospects. To find out how much a country has already borrowed is quite a complicated job, and many banks spend a great deal of time on it as part of their country risk assessment procedures.

6.13.15.   There are a number of international reporting systems, which can be divided into three main types: debtor reporting systems; creditor reporting systems; and other systems. The main debtor reporting system is the World Bank's *Debt Reporting Systems* (DRS). This covers the total long-term external public debt—and, for some countries, also the long-term external private debt—of all those countries that have borrowed from the World Bank or the International Development Association. On the creditor reporting side, the main sources are the BIS *Statistics on Banks' International Lending,* the OECD *International Capital Market Statistics,* the World Bank's *Capital Markets System* (CMS), and the OECD *Development Assistance Committee Statistics.* The main international statistics of the third type are the IMF statistics. They cover governments' external borrowing, the external assets and liabilities of countries' financial institutions, and the capital accounts of countries' balances of payments.[28] The IMF figures are published (in part) every month in its *International Financial Statistics,* which is the most convenient place to get a quick look at a country's external position, although the figures are not always as up-to-date as one would want.

6.13.16.   We have looked now at some of the main economic factors that influence the foreign exchange markets, and some of the ideas behind them. Our next job is to tie these "fundamental" factors in with other ways of looking at what influences an exchange rate's movements. These other factors are often loosely referred to as "technical analysis." We put these two ways of looking at an exchange rate together in the next chapter.

NOTES

1.   B. Griffiths and G. E. Wood (eds.), *Monetary Targets,* Macmillan, London, 1981, pp. 14–16.
2.   Cited by M. D. K. W. Foot in B. Griffiths and G. E. Wood, *Monetary Targets,* p. 20, who

refers to H. Bockelmann, "Quantitative Targets for Monetary Policy," pp. 11–24, in *Actes du seminaire des Banques Centrales*, proceedings of a conference held in Paris in April 1977 and published by the Banque de France in 1977.

3. W. D. McClam, "U.S. Monetary Aggregates, Income Velocity and the Euro-dollar Market," *BIS Economic Papers* no. 2, BIS, Basle, 1980, p. 8.

4. There is a vast literature on these topics, extensively referred to in B. Griffiths and G. E. Wood, *Monetary Targets*, among others. For the credit versus money supply approach in the U.S., for example, see R. G. Davis, "Broad Credit Measures as Targets for Monetary Policy," *Federal Reserve Bank of New York Quarterly Review*, Summer 1979, on the one hand, and Henry Kaufman's testimony before the House of Representatives Committee on the Budget (February 6, 1978) on the other. In the United Kingdom a similar debate has gone on since the time of the Radcliffe Committee.

5. N. Kaldor, "Monetarism and U.K. Monetary policy," *Cambridge Journal of Economics*, vol. 4, no. 4, December 1980, pp. 315, 289.

6. A good discussion of this issue in the U.K. context is M. H. Miller, "Monetary Control in the U.K.," *Cambridge Journal of Economics*, March 1981, vol. 5, pp. 71–9.

7. K. Schiltknecht, "Targeting the Base—the Swiss Experience," p. 224 in B. Griffiths and G. E. Wood, *Monetary Targets*.

8. B. Brittain, "International Currency Substitution and the Apparent Instability of Velocity in Some Western European Economies and in the United States," *Journal of Money, Credit and Banking*, vol. 13, no. 2, May 1981.

9. W. D. McClam, "U.S. Monetary Aggregates," 26–9.

10. P. Tinsley et al., *New Monetary Control Procedures, Volume II*, Federal Reserve Staff Study, Board of Governors of the Federal Reserve System, Washington D.C., 1981, p. 20.

11. P. Tinsley et al., "Money Market Impacts of Alternative Operating Procedures."

12. "Redefining the Monetary Aggregates," *Federal Reserve Bulletin*, January 1979.

13. There are many books setting out these theories. One I have found useful is J. Fleming, *Inflation*, Oxford University Press, 1976.

14. See *OECD Economic Outlook Occasional Studies*, "Budget Indicators," Organization for Economic Cooperation and Development, Paris, July 1978, and the references cited there for a general discussion of these topics. For the United States, see in particular F. de Leeuw et al., "The High-Employment Budget: New Estimates 1955–80," *Survey of Current Business*, U.S. Department of Commerce, November 1980; for Germany, see, for example, the OECD 1980 report on Germany.

15. See, for example, *Congressional Quarterly: Weekly Report*, February 13, 1982.

16. For some of the issues involved, see "Budgetary Reform in the UK," *Report of the Armstrong Committee*, Oxford University Press for the Institute of Fiscal Studies, 1980.

17. Presse u. Informationsdienst der Bundesregierung, *"Bonner Almanach 1980/81,"* Bonn, 1981, pp. 168–169.

18. Bundesministerium der Finanzen "Der Bundeshaushalt," Bonn, December 1978. See also D. Coombes et al., *"The Power of the Purse,"* Political & Economic Planning, London, 1976, for a general (albeit dated) discussion of parliamentary control of the budget.

19. See P. Lequeret, "Les techniques de preparation et de controle du budget de l'État," *Notes et études documentaires*, La Documentation Française, Paris 1973; and Ministère du Budget, "Eléments d'information sur la procédure budgetaire," Paris, undated (1978?), Note bleu no. 3713; "Du Budget Voté au Budget Exécuté," Paris, 1979, Note bleu no. 4104.

20. See D. Coombes et al., "The Power of the Purse," pp. 118 and 105–162.

21. Ibid. pp. 114–115.

22. Ministere de l'Economic, "Le budget de 1981," in *Statistiques et études financières*, Paris 1981, p. 12.

23. Ministere de l'Economic, "Les rhythmes d'execution du budget de l'Etat," *Statistiques et études financières*, Paris, November–December 1980, p. 8.

24. Budget Bureau, Ministry of Finance, *The Budget in Brief*, Tokyo 1979, pp. 69–76.

25. *Quarterly Bulletin of Financial Statistics*, September 1980, Ministry of Finance, Japan.

26. R. M. Stern et al., "The Presentation of the US Balance of Payments," *Princeton Essays in International Finance*, no. 123, August 1977.

27. S. Carse, J. Williamson, and G. E. Wood, *The Financing Procedures of British Foreign Trade*, Cambridge University Press, United Kingdom, 1980, pp. 103–9.

28. All these are described in: Bank for International Settlements, *Manual on Statistics Compiled by International Organisations on Countries External Indebtedness*, Basle, March 1979.

7

TRADING THEORIES

This chapter sets out some of the theories that are used in forecasting exchange rate movements. It explains three "fundamentalist" theories: relative money supply, purchasing power parity, and the portfolio theory. Then we look at "technical" methods: charting, moving averages, and filter rules.

SECTION 1. FUNDAMENTAL THEORIES

7.1.1.   There are many people who claim to know how to forecast exchange rates. The stock response is, "If you're so clever, why aren't you rich?" Of course, some people can forecast currency movements, but it is very hard to do consistently. This chapter doesn't offer solutions to the problem, but it tries to give guidelines on the methods people usually use. Basically, theories can be divided into two sets: fundamentalist and technical. The former type rest on "fundamental" factors affecting an exchange rate; they look at economic and political events in the country. Technical theories, by contrast, only look at the movement in the exchange rate itself. They do not look at the fundamental factors which might be behind the movement.

7.1.2.   Let's start with the fundamentalist theories. We can subdivide them into three categories. The first sees the exchange rate determined by the relative price of monies; the second by the relative price of goods; and the third by the relative price of assets. An example of the first type would be the relative money supply growth theory; of the second, the purchasing power parity theory; of the third, the portfolio theory. There are many other fundamentalist theories, of course, mainly hybrids of these three elements.

7.1.3.   The approach which looks at relative growth of the money supply has its source in the "monetary approach to the balance of payments" theories. These were developed at the start of the 1970s as part of the general growth of monetarism that we saw in the last chapter. Under fixed exchange rates, this approach argued that if the demand for money and the initial supply did not balance, spending would diverge from income. This would work through to change the balance of payments surplus. It would carry on until the stock of money held was equal to the quantity demanded. The argument under floating exchange rates was that a rise in the money supply, other things being equal, makes people less willing to hold the domestic currency compared with overseas currencies. They had enough to begin with. This leads to a depreciation in the exchange rate of the currency because they buy other currencies.[1]

7.1.4.   Efforts have been made to test this theory. Some have been successful within their own terms; others have suggested that the theory is not valid. It is important to note that the theory depends critically on a stable velocity of circulation of money. We saw in the last chapter that it is very hard to prove statistically that this stability exists.

7.1.5.   A second kind of theory sees the exchange rate as being concerned with the relative price of goods. This line of reasoning is a very old one, and was reformulated by Cassel in 1923 as the purchasing power parity theory. The theory is normally specified in one of two forms. The absolute purchasing power parity theory says that the "equilibrium" exchange rate is set by the ratio of the country's price level to that of the foreign country. The relative PPP theory looks at the ratio of the "equilibrium" exchange rate in a current period (*t*) to the "equilibrium" exchange rate in a base period (*o*). It says that this is determined by the ratio of the domestic country's price index in period *t* to the foreign country's price index in period *t*, where both indexes are measured relative to period *o*. Let's put this another way. The absolute purchasing power parity theory says that if automobiles cost more in the United States than they do in Germany, the U.S. dollar is overvalued relative to the deutsche mark. The relative theory says that if automobile prices have risen faster in the U.S. than they have in Germany, then the dollar is overvalued relative to the deutsche mark compared with some set base date.

7.1.6.   There are many problems with this theory. An overwhelming objection (for our purposes) is that as a matter of practical fact PPP failed to predict the movements of exchange rates in the last few years. The PPP theory may well apply over a period of five or ten years, but equally it can fail disastrously over the one- or two-year period. This is the furthest forward that the normal trader or investor will be looking.[2]

7.1.7. A third approach says that the exchange rate is part of the choice of assets. This is an extension of the portfolio theory, originally developed by James Tobin. It says that investors have a tradeoff between return and risk. Currencies which are seen as having a higher risk must pay a higher return in interest rates. If not, investors will not be prepared to hold them. Changes in expectations about interest rates, inflation, current account movements, or other factors will affect investors' preferences. They will result in shifts among currencies.[3]

7.1.8. The major problem with this is that we don't always know exactly which expectations we are to be concerned with, or what other factors may cause investors to change their minds. The theory is very flexible. It can accommodate changes in expectations resulting from unrest in Poland, uncertainty in Saudi Arabia, or changed views about inflation because of a major labor strike. But at the same time it does not give us a very clear definition in advance of what factors will or will not affect exchange rates. To that extent, of course, it is more realistic, but at the same time woolier.

7.1.9. In practical terms, those of us in the marketplace who must predict exchange rates have to accept that no single theory will determine the movement of a currency. At any one time, it may be a comparison of purchasing power parity, relative money supply growth, relative desirability of assets in different currencies, expectations of the movement of inflation or the trade balance, or many other factors which will influence a currency. During the period 1977 to 1979, the foreign exchange market was obsessed with the behavior of the U.S. trade balance and the inability of the United States to respond to the growing energy deficit or to manage economic policy. So funds flowed into deutsche marks and yen, in particular, currencies where the current account was better. The overall economic management was also seen as better.

7.1.10. The move by the U.S. authorities in October 1979 to tighten sharply domestic money supply caused a major psychological shift. The foreign exchange market began to look at the level of relative interest rates. Any rise in inflation in the United States or the United Kingdom (where a similarly "monetarist" policy was in place) was seen as meaning that interest rates would be raised to control inflation. So higher inflation tended to produce a strengthening currency. This was a total reversal of the traditional market pattern, where funds tended to flow out of high inflation currencies.

7.1.11. In the real world, no matter how much one might wish to set forth an economic theory, much of exchange rate behavior can be summed up in one word: confidence. If international asset-holders have confidence in the management of a currency, and the prospects of the country, the exchange rate will tend to be firm. Theoretically this is not a very satisfactory position, but it is the nature of the real world.

SECTION 2.   TECHNICAL METHODS

7.2.1.   We now turn to the second major type of exchange rate trading theory. This is the technical approach. The technical approach was first used in the commodity markets. When exchange rates began floating, though, certain traders decided that they should look at a currency as just another commodity. The technical approach began to be applied to currencies. Chartists or technicians say that history repeats itself. They are more interested in the fact that a contract breaks its historical support level than the reason for it. They look for unusual volumes of trading and breakouts, rather than the fundamental factors behind the markets. In essence, technicians or chartists say that a price reflects the consensus of everyone in the market. They look at the movement of the herd, and believe in its statistical regularity. The chartist approach is the most widely known of the technical approaches, but there are others. They include the use of moving averages (and their more sophisticated variants, Box-Jenkins techniques), filters, price–volatility relationships, price momentum indices, and other techniques.

7.2.2.   We begin with charting techniques. One of the most popular charting techniques is the bar chart. Generally, a bar chart records a price or rate daily, with a vertical line representing the daily price trading range. A small horizontal bar is often used to identify the closing price on a particular day. One studies the trend of these movements in an effort to find patterns. If a price repeatedly reaches a level without being able to break through it, that becomes the resistance area. If, later, the resistance area is penetrated upward, a significant price rise is expected. The signal is especially strong if the breakout happens when trading is active. Similarly, if a price seems to bounce off a floor price level, it is considered a sell signal if the price later falls through this level. These patterns may be seen in Figure 7.1.

7.2.3.   A second pattern which analysts look for is a trend line. By definition, a trend line requires a number of observations before it can be established. It is identified by successive daily levels which are continually higher or lower than the previous day's level. For example, a clear uptrend occurs when each day's low is reached at a higher level. When those are connected for an extended time, they form a trend line. Closing prices may occur at random above the line, but none should occur below the trend line. Equally, a downward trend is seen from successive daily highs that are lower than the previous ones. If the lines connecting the daily lows and those connecting the daily highs are parallel, this implies that the volatility of the market is not changing

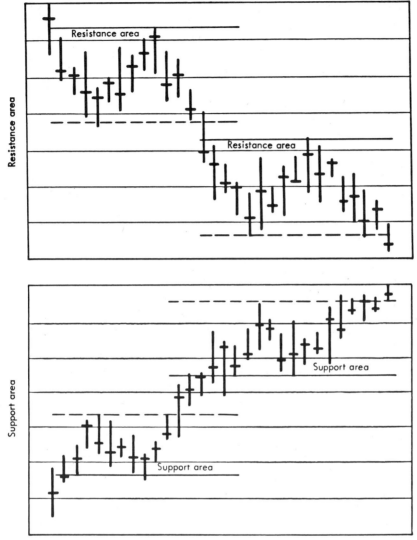

FIGURE 7.1. Basic Bar Chart Formations. Source: *Commodity Trading Manual*, © 1977, Chicago Board of Trade. Reproduced from Edward W. Schwartz, *How to Use Interest Rate Futures Contracts*, Dow Jones-Irwin, Homewood, Illinois, 1979, p. 86.

and a channel has been created. A breakout from a channel is considered a strong technical signal for a major uptrend or downtrend. A channel is illustrated in Figure 7.2.

7.2.4. Another important pattern is the head and shoulders formation. Essentially it consists of four distinct periods: the left shoulder, the head, the right shoulder, and an abrupt penetration through the level of the neck. This is

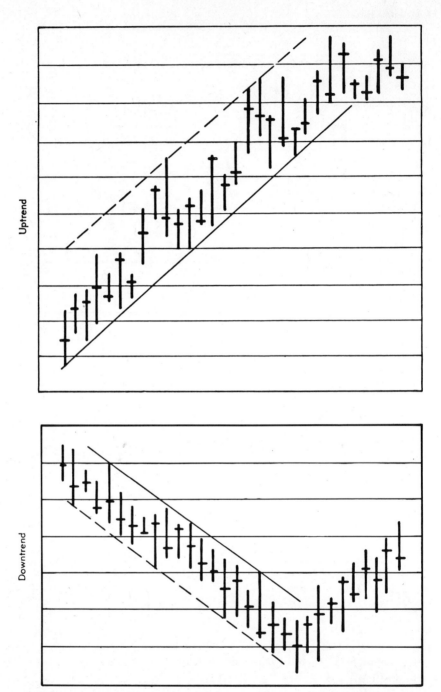

FIGURE 7.2. Channels. Source: *Commodity Trading Manual*, © 1977, Chicago Board of Trade. Reproduced from Edward W. Schwartz, *How to Use Interest Rate Futures Contract*, Dow Jones-Irwin, Homewood, Illinois, 1979, p. 88.

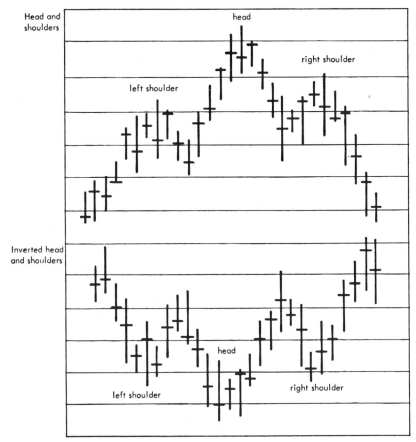

FIGURE 7.3. Head and Shoulders Formations. Source: *Commodity Trading Manual,* © 1977, Chicago Board of Trade. Reproduced from Edward W. Schwartz, *How to Use Interest Rate Futures Contracts,* Dow Jones-Irwin, Homewood, Illinois, 1979, p. 89.

illustrated in Figure 7.3. If the neck level is not broken through, the formation is normally considered meaningless.

7.2.5. Another important formation is the double top. This usually signals the end of a rally. Often, the second top is sustained for a shorter period than the first one. The formation is illustrated in Figure 7.4.

7.2.6. Both the head and shoulders formation and the double top formation may be reversed, in which case they are referred to as the inverted head and shoulders and the double bottom. In both cases, of course, the formations signal the reversal of a previous downward movement.

7.2.7. Several of these concepts are used in another form by technical analysts who do not rely primarily on charts, but purely on the price series

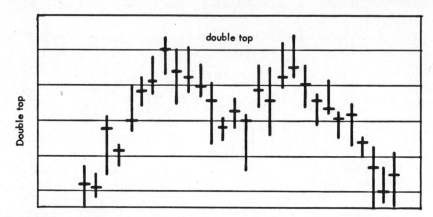

FIGURE 7.4. Double Tops and Bottoms. Source: *Commodity Trading Manual,* © 1977, Chicago Board of Trade. Reproduced from Edward W. Schwartz, *How to Use Interest Rate Futures Contracts,* Dow Jones-Irwin, Homewood, Illinois, 1979, p. 90.

itself. For example, the channel concept can be used as part of a computer model.[4]

7.2.8. We can define the ideas formally in this way. The highest and lowest closing price of the last N days are found. We get a sell signal if a price on day $(N + 1)$ is lower than the lowest close of the last N days. Stop orders are used to take action when the signals are given. Only one position can be signaled per day. We always have a position, be it long or short. We are never "square." When we get a new buy or sell signal, the old position is cut out at the same time. This method takes away any element of judgment. If the high and low of the day are equal, then we assume that the market is locked limit. Nothing is done on that day. The trade will be done at the opening on the first day the market is not locked.

7.2.9. This set of rules defines an intraday closing price channel. A parallel definition can be made for an interday closing price channel. In this case, we only get a buy signal if the *close* on day $(N + 1)$ exceeds the highest close of the last N days. We then deal at the next day's opening. Using these methods, a computer simulation showed that during the period 1970 to 1976 cumulative profits could be generated by using the price channel method.[5] But the same study also showed that a more consistently successful method was the cross-over method, sometimes called the moving average method. This is completely independent of charting concepts. We work out two moving averages from the price. One is a shorter-term average, and one a longer-term. If the short-term average is above the long-term average, one should be long, and if the short-term average is below the long-term average, one should be short. Actually this theory boils down to the bandwagon technique: Go long if the market has gone up, short if it has fallen.

7.2.10. The method works like this. The average of M days' closes and N days' closes are calculated where $M < N$. The M index, then, is the short-term index, and N the long-term. People often use 5, 10, 15, or 20 days for the averages, for instance, a 5-day and a 15-day or a 10-day and 20-day average. The averages include today's close and use only business days. If the average of series M (the short-term) is above the average of series N, a buy order is placed on the opening the next day. Conversely, if it is below, a sell order is placed on the opening the next day. As before, the aim is always to hold a position, be it long or short. When we get a new buy or sell signal, the old position is cut out at the same time. If the high and low of the next day are equal, then again we assume that the market is locked limit, and a trade cannot be made on that day. The trade will be done on the first day that the market is not locked.

7.2.11. Using this method, 11 of 14 commodities tested showed crossovers to be the most consistently successful model. The exceptions were silver, pork bellies, and soybean oil, where price channel methods were more successful. The crossover technique was most successful in the case of the sugar price, generating a cumulative profit of $335,843; the largest string of losses using this technique was $13,851. A total of 311 trades were made, of which 109 were profitable.

7.2.12. These figures illustrate two main points. First, the crossover method, provided it was followed successfully, would have generated substantial profits over the period 1970 to 1976. However, the ratio of profitable trades to unprofitable was under 50%, and at certain points substantial cumulative losses could have been made. So "a speculator must be able psychologically to cope with a series of losses in order to take advantage of possible profits. In summary, a mechanical approach means a well-disciplined trader." In real life one cannot run the losses forever: one has to use stop-loss limits to protect one's capital.[6]

7.2.13. Another technical method of analysis is the so-called filter rule. Investors following an X percent filter rule take a long position in a currency that has risen X% from its most recent low point. They hold the position until the currency falls by X% from the highest level reached since the position was opened. Suppose we use a 2% rule. When a currency rises 2% from its recent low, we buy. When it falls 2%, we sell. The signal to sell is also a signal to go short. The short position is then held until it is closed out on the next buy signal. One test found that for five currencies over two and a half years, "for the whole sample the one, three, and five percent filters are remarkably profitable."[7] In one case, for example, the one percent filter rule for the French franc would have yielded an annual rate of return of 16% over the two-and-a-half-year sample period. The successfulness of the filter rule suggested the likelihood of a bandwagon effect in the markets, which if followed by adhering to a filter rule would generally produce profits.

7.2.14.   So there is a wide range of trading theories from which to choose, both fundamental and technical. Of course, we want to know how we find the best method. If I knew for certain I wouldn't bother to write this book: I would have retired on the proceeds. But we do need to try to find a sensible way. So, first, we have to set criteria for choosing the best. Really, we need to know which theory is going to anticipate the future more accurately than the market will. This raises the question of what the market's anticipation is, since the forward rate cannot strictly be taken as the market's anticipation, being dominated by interest differentials. However, there is no other clear-cut measure of expectations, short of conducting a regular sample poll. Also, the forward rate is relevant for the corporate treasurer, in that he has to decide whether or not to hedge a position. The current forward rate represents the alternative to taking an open position. So the forward rate is about the best option. But using the forward rate as a bench mark is only applicable if a method produces explicit forecasts. If, like most technical services, it simply produces a buy or a sell signal, another test is to work out the total return which would have been earned by slavishly following the service's signals.

7.2.15.   A recent test[8] suggested that several of the forecasting services can "beat the market." However, another recent study[9] suggested that technical analysis was a more successful technique than the forecasting services, although the basis of comparison was limited to one fundamental forecasting service.

7.2.16.   In the end, both of these attempts at measuring the successfulness of forecasting or technical services rely ultimately on track record, but the potential user should be clearly aware that track record of itself is no guarantee of future performance. A second qualification which I would make from a personal point of view is that in committing oneself to a technical service, one must not be prepared merely to accept possibly long strings of losses (see the quotation concerning trading discipline above), but one must also be prepared to accept as an act of faith the technical method now being used in the belief that it is the best of all possible methods at this point in time. It is essential, therefore, that the trader or speculator who is following these services be prepared to accept a substantial commitment of capital in the event of an initially unfavorable long series of losses, in the hope that the tide will turn eventually. Against this, however, it must be said of the fundamentalist services that the market's view of fundamentals changes unpredictably.

NOTES

1.   See for example H. G. Johnson, "The Monetary Theory of Balance of Payments Policies," in *The Monetary Approach to the Balance of Payments,* J. A. Frenkel and H. G. Johnson (eds.), Allen & Unwin, London, 1976.

2.   L. H. Officer, "The Purchasing Power Parity Theory of Exchange Rates: A Review Arti-

clc," *IMF Staff Papers*, 1976; "Purchasing Power Parity: A Symposium," *Journal of International Economics*, May 1978.

3. M. P. Dooley and P. Isard, "The Portfolio-Balance Model of Exchange Rates," *International Finance Discussion Paper 141*, Board of Governors of the Federal Reserve System, May 1979; R. Dornbusch, "Exchange Rate Economics: Where Do We Stand?," *Brookings Papers on Economic Activity* no. 1, 1980.

4. This discussion draws heavily on F. H. Hochheimer, "Channels and Crossovers," in P. J. Kaufman (ed.), *Technical Analysis in Commodities*, John Wiley & Sons, 1980.

5. Ibid.

6. Ibid., p. 65.

7. M. P. Dooley and J. R. Shaefer, "Analysis of Short-Run Exchange Rate Behavior—March 1973 to September 1975," Board of Governors of the Federal Reserve System, *International Finance Discussion Paper No. 76*, February 1976.

8. R. N. Levich, "How to Compare Chance with Forecasting Expertise," *Euromoney*, London, August 1981.

9. S. Goodman, "Technical Analysis Still Beats Econometrics," *Euromoney*, London, August 1981.

PART **2**

DEALING
CALCULATIONS

8

SPOT

This chapter sets out the basics of a spot deal: where the settlement is made, when it is made, what the quotations mean, how cross spot rates are worked out.

SECTION 1.   SETTLEMENT COUNTRY

8.1.1.   A foreign exchange trade is an exchange of two currencies. When the deal has been agreed upon, the parties to the deal arrange settlement. This takes place in the two countries whose currencies are being used. For example, a deal exchanging U.S. dollars for deutsche marks is settled by a payment of U.S. dollars in the United States against a payment of deutsche marks in West Germany. For convenience I shall apply the term *settlement country* to the country where the actual transfer of funds is made.

8.1.2. The place in which the deal is made—the dealing center—need not be in one of the settlement countries at all. For example, it is possible to trade French francs against deutsche marks in New York. A company making a FFR/DMK deal with a bank in New York may think that its francs and deutsche marks are being transferred in New York. This will seem especially plausible if the bank is running accounts for the company in New York denominated in the two currencies. But the bank's own currency holdings which correspond to those accounts will be held in the settlement countries. So the rules applying to such transactions—for instance, with respect to settlement dates—will be the same as for deals conducted in the normal way (Cf. 14.2.9).

SECTION 2.   SPOT SETTLEMENT

8.2.1. A spot foreign exchange deal is defined as one made for settlement in two working days' time. Thus under normal circumstances a deal done Monday is settled on Wednesday.

8.2.2. A working day is defined as one in which both banks are open for business in both settlement countries; *except* that if the deal is done against the U.S. dollar, if the first of the two days is a holiday in the United States but not in the other settlement country, that day is also counted as a working day.

8.2.3. In the case of a US$/DMK deal, done on Monday, we would normally have settlement Wednesday. This would not be affected by a U.S. holiday on the Tuesday. But it would be affected by a German holiday on the Tuesday. In the latter case, the spot date would be postponed until Thursday, provided that both centers were open Thursday. If Tuesday were a normal day, but Wednesday were a holiday in either the United States or Germany, then the spot day would be Thursday (if both centers were open that day).

8.2.4. In the case of a US$/DMK deal done, say, in London, the occurrence of U.K. bank holidays during the spot period is entirely irrelevant. This is because all bank account transfers are made in the settlement country rather than the dealing center, as discussed in Section 1. However, in the deposit market it would not be customary to deal for a date which was a holiday in the dealing center. (See 11.1.10.)

8.2.5. In certain countries, such as the United States or Germany, bank holidays may affect only part of the country (depending on whether it is a local state holiday, or, if religious, whether the area is mainly Catholic or Protestant, etc.). In this case the date for settlement could vary according to the regional location of the bank accounts involved. This complication will generally be ignored in this book.

8.2.6. Settlement of both sides of a foreign exchange deal should be made on the same working day. Because of time zone differences, settlement on any given working day will take place earlier in the Far East, later in Europe, and later still in the United States.

8.2.7. This implies a risk. To continue the US$/DMK example, a bank selling deutsche marks may deliver them in Frankfurt before receiving the dollars in New York. If the recipient in Germany goes bankrupt before delivering the dollars (as happened in the case of Herstatt Bank), losses may arise. (See 17.6.6). The principal that the two sides of the deal should be completed on the same day is referred to as the principle of *value compensee* or compensated value.

8.2.8. The only exception to the principle of compensated value arises for deals in Middle Eastern currencies for settlement on Friday. This is a holiday in most Middle Eastern countries. When this happens, the person buying the Middle Eastern currency (say, Saudi riyals) makes payment (say in U.S. dollars) on Friday. Delivery of the riyals takes place on Saturday, which is a normal business day in the relevant countries (see Appendix 5, on Islamic Value Dates).

SECTION 3. QUOTED AND BASE CURRENCIES; DIRECT AND INDIRECT QUOTATION

8.3.1. The term "quoted currency" is used to mean the currency which is variable in an exchange rate quotation; the term "base currency" is used to mean the currency which is fixed. Thus if £STG 1 = US$ 2.2550, sterling is the base currency and the U.S. dollar the quoted currency. In this book I shall write exchange rates as base/quoted (in this case £STG/US$).

8.3.2. Direct quotation takes the form of variable amounts of domestic currency against a fixed amount of foreign currency. The foreign currency is the base currency. A Swiss bank quoting 85.5 Swiss francs per 100 deutsche marks would be quoting direct; a variable amount of Swiss francs against a fixed deutsche mark amount. Many people say "normal" for direct currencies.

8.3.3. Indirect quotation, conversely, takes the form of fixed amounts of domestic currency against varying amounts of foreign currency. A British bank quoting £1 = DMK 4.1325 is quoting "indirect." Many people in the market say "reciprocal" for indirect currencies.

8.3.4. In the United States, both types of quotations are used: for domestic business "U.S. terms" are often used, that is, normal direct quotation (DMK 1 = US$ 0.5525). For international business U.S. banks use "European terms," or reciprocal indirect quotation (US\$ 1 = DMK 1.81). The reason for this is the international market's habit of dealing against the U.S. dollar, using direct terms. U.S. banks have fallen into line with international market practice.

SECTION 4.   SELLING AND BUYING RATES

8.4.1.   Where the currency's exchange control regulations permit, a bank will normally quote a "two-way price" in the currency. So a bank might quote the exchange rate as US\$ 1 = DMK 2.2550/60. This conventional way of writing the rate shows that the bank will sell DMK 2.2550 in exchange for US\$ 1; it will buy deutsche marks at 2.2560. The lower rate is the selling rate for deutsche marks; the maxim is, "Sell low, buy high."

8.4.2.   The reason for this apparent perversity is that the bank's "income" from a sale is fixed at \$1; it tries to sell as few deutsche marks as possible in exchange for the \$1. To test the maxim, suppose the bank sells DMK 2.2550 million, receiving \$1 million. It then uses the \$1 million to buy DMK 2.2560 million, netting a final profit of DMK 1,000. Clearly, the narrower the spread between the selling and buying rates, the less the bank's profit.

8.4.3.   The conventional quotation needs explaining when the "big figure" (of 2.25 in our example) is being straddled. Say we have a selling rate of 2.2495 and the buying rate is 2.2505. Normal market convention is to write this as 2.2495/05. The "big figure" on the left is 2.24; on the right hand side it is understood as being the next "big figure" up, 2.25.

SECTION 5.   CROSS-RATES

8.5.1.   A cross-rate may be defined as an exchange rate which is calculated from two other rates. For example the DMK/SFR rate can be derived as a cross-rate from the US\$/DMK rate and the US\$/SFR rate.

8.5.2.   The practice in the world foreign exchange market at present is that currencies are mainly dealt against the U.S. dollar. If Bank A asks Bank B for its deutsche mark rate, that rate will be quoted against the U.S. dollar unless otherwise specified. Since the vast bulk of dealings are done against the U.S. dollar, it follows that the "market rate" for a currency at any moment is most accurately reflected in its exchange rate against the U.S. dollar. Thus a bank asked to quote £STG/DMK would normally calculate this rate from the £STG/US\$ and US\$/DMK rates, if an exact market rate is required.

8.5.3.   So I will use the rule that an exchange rate between two currencies, neither of which is the U.S. dollar, will be referred to as a cross-rate. The term

TABLE 8.1. Calculating Cross Rates.

	Both Normal	Both Reciprocal	One Normal, One Reciprocal
Currency we want to show in the cross-rate as			
Quoted	US$ 1 = SFR 1.6230/40	CAN$ 1 = US$ 0.8950/53	£STG 1 = US$ 2.2530/40
	divide by	divide into	multiply by
Base	US$ 1 = DMK 1.8110/20	£STG 1 = US$ 2.2530/40	US$ 1 = DMK 1.8110/20

"exchange rate" will normally refer to the rate for a currency against the U.S. dollar, unless otherwise specified.

SECTION 6. CALCULATION OF CROSS-RATE

8.6.1. There are three cases to consider: both exchange rates quoted direct or normal, both indirect or reciprocal, and the case where one is direct and the other indirect.

8.6.2. Let's look first at the case where both are normal. For example, US$ 1 = DMK 1.8110/20 and US$ 1 = SFR 1.6230/40. The U.S. dollar is the base currency in both cases. We want to find the selling and buying rates for Swiss francs in terms of deutsche marks (the deutsche marks will be our base currency).

8.6.3. If we are selling Swiss francs we must be buying deutsche marks. So we take the US$/SFR selling rate, 1.6230, and divide it by the buying rate for deutsche marks, 1.8120. (We divide by the currency which is to be the base, in this case the deutsche mark.) The selling cross-rate therefore is 89.56 SFR per 100 DMK after rounding in the bank's favor. Similarly the buying rate is found by taking the SFR buying rate, 1.6240, and the DMK selling rate, 1.8110, to give 89.68.

8.6.4. A parallel procedure is followed when both currencies are reciprocal: the U.S. dollar is the quoted currency in both cases. For example, we have £STG 1 = US$ 2.2530/40 and CAN$ 1 = US$ 0.8950/53. We want the cross-rates, using sterling as the base currency. The rate at which we sell U.S. dollars against sterling (we buy sterling) is 2.2530. We buy US$ against CAN$ (we sell Canadian dollars) at 0.8953. Because we are dealing with indirect currencies, we divide by the quoted currency. So we sell Canadian dollars against sterling at 2.5164.

8.6.5. When one rate is normal and the other reciprocal, the procedure is the same but we multiply (alternatively we may convert the reciprocal currency to normal by taking reciprocals and then dividing by the base currency). Suppose we have £1 = US$ 2.2530/40 and US$ = DMK 1.8110/20. The rate at which we sell DMK against US$ is 1.8110; the rate at which we buy sterling against U.S. dollars (sell US$ against £STG) is 2.2530. Multiplying these gives selling rate for DMK against £STG of 4.0801, and a buying rate of 4.0843. The calculations are summarized in Table 8.1.

9

FORWARDS I—OUTRIGHTS

This chapter explains what a forward contract is, and what premium and discount mean. It explains how to work out the cost of hedging, option forwards, cross and reciprocal forwards, and the value date for a forward contract.

SECTION 1. DEFINITION

9.1.1. A forward exchange contract is an agreement between a bank and another party to exchange one currency for another at some future date. The rate at which the exchange is to be made, the delivery date, and the amounts involved are fixed at the time of the agreement.

9.1.2. Such a contract is to be distinguished from a foreign exchange futures contract. These are discussed in more detail in Chapter 15. However, for comparison, a definition is given here.

9.1.3.   A futures foreign exchange contract is a contract between two parties for the exchange of a certain amount of foreign currency at a future date. The amount and the date are normally standard. For instance, in the case of the International Monetary Market of Chicago's sterling contract, the contract is for £25,000. Delivery is normally the third Wednesday of the contract month (March, June, September, or December). A futures contract need not involve a bank as counterparty. A forward contract is normally completed by delivery of all or part of the sum involved. This is unusual in the case of a futures contract which is normally "closed out" by a contract in the reverse direction before the maturity of the original futures contract.

SECTION 2.   PREMIUM AND DISCOUNT

9.2.1.   Suppose a quoted currency is more expensive in the future than it is now in terms of the base currency. Then the quoted currency is said to stand at a premium in the forward market, relative to the base currency. Conversely, the base currency may be said to stand at a discount relative to the quoted currency.

9.2.2.   Take the U.S. dollar as the base currency and the deutsche mark as the quoted currency. We may have a spot rate of US\$ 1 = DMK 2.2500. The rate quoted by a bank today for delivery in one year's time (today's one year forward rate) may be US\$ 1 = DMK 2.2150. In this example the dollar buys fewer deutsche marks in a year's time than it does today. The dollar stands at a discount relative to the deutsche marks. Putting it in converse terms, the deutsche mark stands at a premium relative to the dollar.

9.2.3.   The size of the dollar discount or deutsche mark premium is the difference between 2.2500 and 2.2150, that is, 3½ pfennigs. The convention in the foreign exchange market is normally to quote in terms of "points," or hundredths of a unit. Hence 3½ pfennigs would normally be quoted as 350 points.

9.2.4.   It will be clear from the above (9.2.1) that in order to arrive at the forward price, the deutsche mark premium or dollar discount must be *subtracted* from the spot. Conversely, a deutsche mark discount or dollar premium is *added*.

9.2.5.   As in the spot market, banks in the forward market will normally quote a selling and a buying rate. As in the spot market, the convention is that the selling rate for the quoted currency (the buying rate for the base currency) is quoted first. In our example, the spot rate might be quoted at 2.2500/10 and the one year forward discount for US\$ (or DMK premium) at 350/340. In other words, if the dealer is buying U.S. dollars forward he will charge a discount of 350 points, but if he is selling he will give away only 340 points' discount. In European terms, he will sell deutsche marks at a premium of 350, but only buy at a premium of 340.

9.2.6. There is an apparent inconsistency in this quotation. The spot is quoted at 2.2500/10, that is, low/high, and the deutsche mark premium/dollar discount at 350/340, that is, high/low. In both cases the convention of Section 8.4.1. is followed; that is, the selling rate for the quoted currency is given first. The apparent inconsistency flows simply from the fact that the deutsche mark premium/dollar discount is to be *subtracted* from the spot rate. So the selling price for delivery in three months' time (often referred to as the outright three-month price) is 2.2500 less 350 points, that is, 2.2150. Now the buying price is 2.2510 less 340 points, that is, 2.2170. So we can quote the three-month outright as 2.2150/70, which matches the way in which the spot is quoted.

9.2.7. It follows from the above that a price of 350/340 indicates a premium for the quoted currency in the forward market and a discount for the base currency; conversely, a price of 340/350 would indicate a discount for the quoted and a premium for the base.

9.2.8. This can be summed up as: **High/low = subtract. Low/high = add.** In premium/discount terms in the United States:

High/low: discount for the dollar
Low/high: premium for the dollar

Elsewhere the tag is reversed as the market there looks at the rates in currency terms:

High/low: premium
Low/high: discount

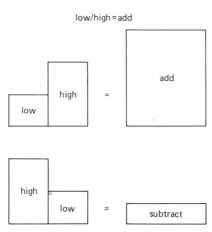

FIGURE 9.1. Treatment of Forward Margin.

9.2.9. Occasionally on a Reuters Monitor or a table of rates the forward price may be quoted as "−5/+5" or "5P5." This indicates that the forward is "round par." This term means that the middle rate for a currency in the spot market is identical to the middle price available in the forward market: the forward price is at par with the spot. Thus the dealer will buy dollars against the currency at a discount and sell at a premium; in European terms he will charge a premium to sell the currency, and will only buy at a discount. It follows that a quotation of "−5/+5" or "5P5" applied to our spot rate example of 2.2500/10 would produce a forward price of 2.2495 selling rate and 2.2515 buying rate.

9.2.10. Equally, a quote of 20/00 (or 20/P) may be seen, indicating a forward dollar discount or currency selling premium of 20, but that the bank only buy at par. A quote of 00/15 (or P/15) indicates sales made at par, purchases at a dollar premium or currency discount of 15.

SECTION 3. HEDGING COSTS

9.3.1. We often need to work out a percentage cost per annum of a forward contract. This varies according to whether our calculations are based on the spot price or the outright forward price (see 10.3.1). Views differ on this; my own view is that the choice should vary according to the underlying deal. If one is hedging a forward commitment, then the outright rate should be used. Thus a firm needing to buy forward DMK 1 million against US$ for the purchase of machinery should use the outright rate. This is the important rate for its business: it determines the amount of dollars required. In other cases it may be more appropriate to use the spot rate. If we are considering an investment, we would probably want to express the hedging cost or profit as a percentage of our original investment, so we would probably use the spot rate. It is like the money market difference between a discount rate and an ordinary interest rate. Suppose again that we have a spot rate of 2.2500/10 and a three months' forward rate of 350/340. Then, working on middle rates of 2.2505 and 345, we can calculate that the approximate hedging cost for three months is 0.0345 divided by 2.2505 or 0.0153. (We might prefer to use the market's selling rates of 2.2500 and 350). Multiplying by 100 to express this in percentage terms, we find this is 1.53% for three months. We multiply this by four to gross it up to annual terms of 6.13%. (This is slightly inaccurate. If we really needed to be exact to six places of decimals or so we would gross it up by compounding.)

9.3.2. The formula, therefore, is:

$$\text{Hedging cost} = \frac{\text{forward premium}}{\text{outright or spot}} \times \frac{12}{n} = \frac{F}{O} \times \frac{12}{n} \text{ or } \frac{F}{S} \times \frac{12}{n}$$

where n = number of months in forward contract.

SECTION 4.   OPTION FORWARDS

9.4.1.   Under the normal forward contract discussed earlier (9.1.1.), the exchange rate, the amount of currency involved, and the delivery date are all agreed upon when the deal is made. But the bank's customer may be uncertain exactly when he can deliver his funds. He may not know when he will be paid for his exports, or he may not know when his imports will arrive. In this case he may take out an option forward contract.

9.4.2.   An option forward contract is defined as a forward contract where the delivery date is at the customer's option. It is not like a stock market option, where the customer is paying for the option to a deal at a certain price. In a foreign exchange option contract, the deal is done, and the rate is fixed. The option applies only to the delivery date.

9.4.3.   As in a normal forward contract, the parties to an option contract agree at the time of the deal on the amount of currency and the exchange rate involved. The delivery date is fixed as being between two dates. So a contract may be "option from spot until December 6," or "option between 9 and 10 months."

9.4.4.   In fixing the rate at which a deal is made, the bank will bear in mind the possibility that the customer may deliver at the worst possible time, and the rate will have to be quoted accordingly.

9.4.5.   Suppose we have US$/DMK rates as follows:

Spot: 1.8100/10
Three months: 300/290
Six months: 590/580

The bank's customer wants to buy deutsche marks, option from spot until the six-month date. Suppose the bank sells them at the spot price, and the customer does not take up delivery until six months' time. Then the customer has effectively avoided being charged the discount on his dollars, or paying the premium on deutsche marks, for a six-month-forward purchase. So the bank assumes the worst, and charges the full six months' dollar discount/deutsche mark premium, making the outright 1.7510.

9.4.6.   But suppose the bank were buying the deutsche marks from the customer, option from spot until the six months date. What if the bank gave the customer the full six months' dollar discount/deutsche mark premium, and the customer delivered on the spot date? Then the bank would find it had made an expensive purchase. It could buy deutsche marks for spot value in the market at a better price. Accordingly, it takes the worst view and pays the customer only the spot price. In this case it would benefit the customer to try to narrow the option period, say, to "option between three and six months." Then the bank would give the customer three months' dollar discount/deutsche mark premium.

9.4.7. The general rule is that the bank gives the customer the worst rate ruling during the option period. So we have:

1. Dollar discount/currency premium:
   a. Bank sells currency, buys dollars; discount on dollar/currency premium is charged to the last date.
   b. Bank buys currency, sells dollars; option from spot—no dollar discount/currency premium given. Option between two dates—dollar discount/currency premium given to first date.
2. Dollar premium, currency discount:
   a. Bank sells currency, buys dollars; option from spot—no dollar premium/currency discount given. Option between two dates—dollar premium/currency discount given to first date.
   b. Bank buys currency, sells dollars; dollar premium/currency discount charged to the last date.
3. Currencies which move from premium to discount or vice versa:
   a. Bank sells currency, buys dollars; the highest dollar discount/currency premium during the period is charged.
   b. Bank buys currency, sells dollars; the largest dollar premium/currency discount during the period is taken.

9.4.8. Here are some examples using the following rates:

	US$/DMK	US$/LIT	US$/DKR
Spot	1.8100/10	831.00/50	5.1920/30
Three months	300/290	200/300	100/200
Six months	590/580	400/600	150/50

The bank sells DMK option from spot to three months at 1.8100-0.03 = 1.7800; buys DMK option from spot to three months at 1.8110; buys DMK option between three and six months at 1.7820; sells DMK option between three and six months at 1.7510. The bank sells LIT option from spot to three months at 831.00; buys LIT option from spot to three months at 834.50; sells LIT option between three and six months at 833. For DKR, where the three months is in currency discount/dollar premium, and the six months is in currency premium/dollar discount, the bank will sell DKR option spot to three months at 5.1920; buy DKR option from spot the three months at 5.2130; sell DKR option between three and six months at 5.1770, and buy DKR option between three and six months at 5.2130.

SECTION 5.   CROSS AND RECIPROCAL FORWARDS

9.5.1.   A typical cross forward calculation arises when a customer needs a sterling/deutsche mark forward. For this to be exact, it should be worked out from the professional interbank prices, which of course are against the U.S. dollar. We have £STG/US$ spot 2.2500/10 and US$/DMK spot 1.8100/10. The three-month £STG/US$ price is 350/340, while the three months US$/DMK price is 300/290.

9.5.2.   We first find the outright three-month £STG/US$ price, 2.2150/70, and the outright three-month US$/DMK price, 1.7800/20. We then find the cross spot and three-month outright prices along the lines of paragraph 8.6.5. (i.e., multiplying in this case). This gives us a three-month outright price of 3.9427/3.9507 and a spot of 4.0725/4.0766.

9.5.3.   The forward premium for deutsche marks against sterling is then found by subtracting the three-month outright from the spot, giving us a premium of 1298/1259.

9.5.4.   Let's take an example with a currency where the dollar is at a premium (the currency is at a discount). Suppose the French franc spot against the dollar is 4.2500/20 and the three-month is 100/200, that is, dollar premium, franc discount. Then against sterling, using the same £/US$ rates we get a spot of 9.5625/9.5713, and a forward margin of 1266/1002; that is, the franc is at a premium against sterling although at a discount against the U.S. dollar (because sterling is at an even greater discount against the U.S. dollar).

9.5.5.   Reciprocal forwards are sometimes needed when a currency is quoted both direct and indirect. An example is the Canadian dollar against the U.S. dollar, which can be quoted for instance, as either 91.22/25 or 1.0958/63; a forward quote may need to be turned around also. A similar case arises with the Irish pound, which is quoted in the market indirectly against sterling, for instance, IEP 1 = £STG 0.9625/35. If we want to turn around a forward quote for the Irish pound, for example, we go about it like this. Suppose we have a spot and three months price using the Irish currency as the base and sterling as the quoted currency. Suppose the spot is IEP 1 = £STG 0.9410/20 and the three-month margin is 150/120. We want to quote with sterling as the base.

9.5.6.   First we find the three-month outright, with the Irish pound as base, that is, 0.9260/0.9300. Then we work out the reciprocals, obtaining 1.0615/1.0627 for the spot and 1.0752/1.0800 for the forward. (Note that the lower, or selling price in Irish terms of 0.9410 produces the higher, or buying price in sterling terms of 1.0627.) The last step is to find the forward margins by subtracting the spot price from the three-month outright, yielding 137/173. Thus in Irish terms we have a spot of IEP 1 = £STF 0.9410/20 and sterling at a three-month premium of 150/120; in sterling terms, a spot of £STG 1 = IEP 1.0615/27 and the Irish pound at a discount of 137/173.

SECTION 6.   FORWARDS EXPRESSED AS OUTRIGHTS

9.6.1.   The use of margins in forward quotations is convenient because the margins tend to move much less quickly than the spots, and because it is the margins which are relevant in the swap market. But certain currencies, such as the Venezuelan bolivar and various others, have limited or nonexistent swap markets, so that banks will often quote the forwards in outright form. Certain banks also quote other currencies, such as the South African rand or the Spanish peseta, in this form.

SECTION 7.   CALCULATION OF FORWARD VALUE DATES

9.7.1.   The first step in finding the standard forward value dates for periods of one, two, three months, and so on, is to fix the spot date (see Chapter 8, Section 2). The standard forward date will normally be the same date in the relevant month. So, if spot is October 3, one month is November 3, two months, December 3, and so on.

9.7.2.   If the date so found is a holiday, then the date is rolled onward to the next day in which banks are open for business in both centers. Say we are dealing US$/DMK for one month, November 3 is a weekend, or a holiday in New York or Frankfurt. Then we roll the date onward to the 4th, if that day is a business day in both centers. If it is not, then we keep rolling the date onward until such a day is reached.

9.7.3.   Exceptions to this rule arise in the case of month-ends. A month-end date is the last day of a month where banks are open for business in the two settlement countries. In a US$/DMK deal, if November 30 is a U.S. holiday, then month-end would be November 29, provided that day is a business day in both centers.

9.7.4.   There are two exceptions to the standard rule of 9.7.1, both of which are concerned with month-ends. The first is the so-called "end-end" rule. This says that if the spot value date is a month-end, then all forward value dates are also month-ends. Suppose the October month-end is October 28, the 29th and 30th being a weekend and October 31 a public holiday. Then if spot is October

28, that is, the month-end, the end-end rule makes the one-month date November 30 (if that is the November month-end), *not* November 28.

9.7.5. The second exception is that forward value dates must not be rolled on beyond the month-end. Suppose the one-month date would normally be March 31, but that date is a holiday. We do not roll the one-month date on to April 1, but instead roll it backward to March 30.

10

FORWARDS II—SWAPS

In this chapter we look at swaps. After explaining how swaps are used to switch exposure between currencies and over time, we look at how they are used to "manufacture" interest rates. Then we look at how interest rates affect the swaps. Next we look at the use of medium-term swaps. Then we see how forward forward swaps work. Finally, we look at the use of swaps in extending contracts and in working out broken dates.

SECTION 1.   THE NATURE OF A SWAP

10.1.1.   A typical swap trade might be the sale of £STG 1 million against US$ 2.2 million for spot value, coupled with the purchase of £STG 1 million for delivery in three months' time against US$ 2.17 million. In general, a swap is an exchange of one currency for another on one day, matched by a reverse exchange on a later day. In our example we swapped £1 million into dollars: we sold £1 million and bought it back three months forward. The swap rate is the difference between the rates of exchange used in the two trades. In our example, where the spot trade is done at 2.2000 and the forward at 2.1700, the swap rate is 0.03 or 300 points.

10.1.2.   In most swap deals, the two exchanges are made at the same time with the same counterparty. But this need not necessarily be the case. One could buy spot from one counterparty and sell outright forward to another. Such a trade may be called an "engineered" swap to distinguish it from the more usual, or "pure" swap.

10.1.3.   Clearly in the pure swap the *spot* rate used is not very important. (But see 10.9.2.) What matters is the *swap* rate: the premium or discount received for the forward sale of dollars which are bought spot. The market tends to use a spot rate which is close to the current market rate, but chosen so as to make calculation easy.

SECTION 2.   USING SWAPS—FIRST EXAMPLES

10.2.1.   Swaps have two basic uses: (1) to switch a deal from one currency to another, and back again, on a hedged basis; and (2) to move a given currency deal forward or back in time.

10.2.2.   An example of the first kind of swap could be if a bank had to lend Eurolire. Because of the Italian exchange controls and other problems, the "natural" market for Eurolire is thin, to the point of nonexistence. So to provide Eurolire a bank will normally borrow U.S. dollars, buy lire in the spot

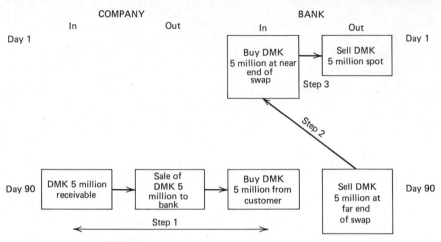

FIGURE 10.1. Bringing an Exposure Nearer in Time.

market, and sell them back in the forward market. It "manufactures" Eurolire from Eurodollars.

10.2.3.   An example of the second type of deal is when a customer makes an outright forward sale of, say, DMK 5 million six months forward to a bank. The bank will hedge this by a spot sale and a forward swap, rather than an outright deal. This is because interbank outright deals are very rare. They are regarded as too risky. It is different for the customer. From the point of view of the customer, his outright forward transaction—normally—hedges a commercial exposure. For example, the company may be expecting to receive a payment of DMK 5 million in six months' time. Not to sell forward would leave that exposure open.

10.2.4.   However, from the point of view of the bank, it is now exposed on an outright forward basis by its DMK 5 million purchase, without an underlying transaction in the opposite direction. This position is risky. Yet it may be difficult to find a counterparty willing to take such a risk, since most interbank forward trading is not done on an outright basis—precisely because of the high degree of risk. So the bank will sell the DMK 5 million in the *spot* market. It will then do a swap, buying DMK 5 million spot, and selling them forward. (The steps are set out in Figure 10.1.) The swap carries no exchange risk, and it is much easier to find a counterparty. So the swap market helps to bring a forward exposure nearer, so that it can be closed out more easily. Equally it can be used to push an exposure away in time.

10.2.5.   Suppose I am an exporter with a steady stream of French francs coming in. Suppose the franc is very weak, so that I am not inclined to sell my francs now, because I expect the currency to recover. Then I could, if the ex-

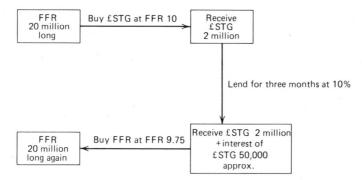

FIGURE 10.2. Pushing an Exposure Further Away in Time.

change control system in my country permits it, swap my francs for three or six
months, let us say into sterling if I am based in the United Kingdom. I am still
long of francs, but instead of switching out of francs I am effectively lending
them and borrowing sterling against them. When the deal unwinds I receive
my francs back again and can—I hope—sell them at a better rate. Figure 10.2
shows this in simple terms. Equally, a bank might want to run a basic long position in francs without showing it in the spot book. To do this it could swap
the position out into the forward book. (We saw in Chapter 5 how a dealer
would look at the foreign exchange and money market route to solve his problem. See also Chapter 12, Section 4 on swapping out a position in the "short
dates.")

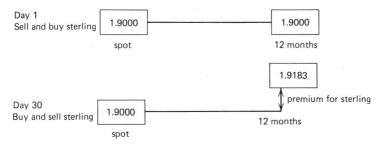

FIGURE 10.3. Taking a Forward Position.

10.2.6.   Another important use for swaps, of course, is as a straight trading
operation. Swaps let us take a view on interest rates. Remember the rule of
5.2.4: if the interest differential moves in a currency's favor, the forward margin moves against it. So let's look at a situation where the one-year US$ and
£STG rates are both 10%. The forward margin will be near zero (if you're not
sure why, read over 5.2.1.–5.2.5.). So a U.S. investor pays no premium for

forward sterling. Suppose he thinks that in one month's time the 11-month rate for sterling will be below the 11-month US$ rate. That means that forward sterling will be at a premium. So it makes sense to buy forward sterling. And to do this without incurring an exchange risk, he can deal in the swap market. That is, he sells sterling spot and buys it 12 months forward, believing that in one month he can sell the sterling at a premium. The steps are set out in Figure 10.3 (see also Section 8).

SECTION 3.   SWAP RATES IN PERCENTAGE TERMS

10.3.1.   We often need to express the swap rate in percentage terms, usually to compare it with an interest differential. The choice of base—either the spot price or forward outright price—will depend on circumstances (see 9.3.1); in most professional deals the relevant rate will be the outright forward rate. So in our earlier example (10.1.1), with the spot at 2.20 and the forward at 2.17, the hedging cost for three months (90 days) would be 0.03/2.17 or 1.38%; if the spot is used as a base, the cost is 1.36%. These rates are normally annualized by multiplying by four (i.e., number of days in a year—360—divided by number of days in swap period—90). (The 360-day year is used to compare with Eurorates. See 11.1.2. A 365-day basis could of course be used also.)

10.3.2.   This process can be summed up:

$$\text{Swap rate in \%} = \frac{\text{swap rate in points}}{\text{spot or outright in points}} \times \frac{360 \times 100}{\text{number of days in swap}} = \frac{F}{S \text{ or } O} \times \frac{360 \times 100}{N}$$

For a reciprocal currency like sterling, using the outright price gives higher swap costs if the hedged currency has a forward discount because then the outright is a smaller number than the spot. It works the other way around if it is at a premium. In our case, where sterling was being sold spot and bought forward at a discount, the hedging cost rises from 1.36% using the spot rate for calculations, to 1.38% if the forward rate is used. Conversely, if forward sterling is at a premium, resulting in an outright forward rate of say 2.23, then the hedging cost would fall to 1.35% (=0.03/2.23) on the outright basis.

SECTION 4.   FINDING INTEREST RATES FROM SWAP RATES: INTEREST UNHEDGED

10.4.1.   We need the calculation of the swap yield if we must compare interest rates between currencies. Suppose we want to find the cheapest way to borrow Eurodeutschemarks. We can either borrow deutsche marks directly or borrow another currency (typically Eurodollars) and swap into deutsche

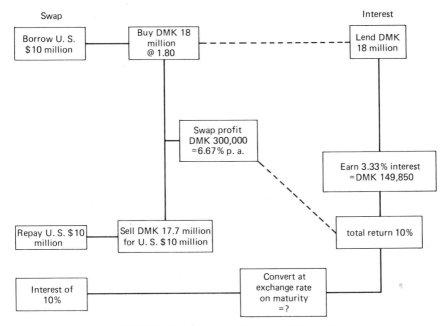

FIGURE 10.4. Arbitrage: Interest Unhedged.

marks. We have to find the cheapest rate at which a bank could lend deutsche marks.

10.4.2. The quickest, crudest measure of the cost of the deal is like this. We take the Eurodollar interest rate and subtract the swap yield (be it positive or negative). Suppose we have a middle US$/DMK spot of 1.80 and that dollars are at a three-month discount (deutsche marks are at a premium) of 300 (middle). Suppose it costs us 10% to borrow three-month Eurodollars. We need the swap yield. As we saw above, if F is the margin, S the spot, and O the outright, the swap yield is F/S or F/O depending on circumstances. (As a matter of fact, when we work out the exact formula, we will see that the yield works out as F/S for normal or indirect currencies such as the deutsche mark and F/O for reciprocal or direct currencies such as sterling.)

10.4.3. So we take the swap yield here as $0.03/1.80 = 0.01667$. This is 0.0667 if we multiply by four to put it on an annual basis. Putting it in percentage terms, we have 6.67%. This is the swap profit. Because the bank is buying its forward dollars at a discount (receiving a premium on the forward deutsche marks it is selling), the swap yield is positive. The profit on the swap can be used to offset its Eurodollar costs. So the "manufactured" deutsche marks cost 10% less 6.67%, i.e., 3.33%. We can then compare this with the cost of raising Eurodeutschemarks directly. The formula for this is set out in Figures 10.4 and 10.5.

$$R_2 = R_1 \pm \left(\frac{F}{S} \times \frac{360}{N} \times 100 \right)$$

where

R_1 = interest rate on currency borrowed
R_2 = interest rate on currency lent ("manufactured")
F = forward margin in points
S = spot rate in points
N = number of days

In words:

Second currency interest rate =
$$\text{first currency interest rate} \pm \left(\frac{\text{swap}}{\text{spot}} \times \frac{360}{\text{days}} \times 100 \right)$$

For an investor looking at the interest differential between the two currencies we would write:

$$\text{Interest differential} = \pm \frac{\text{swap}}{\text{spot}} \times \frac{360}{\text{days}} \times 100$$

If the actual differential is bigger than the amount implied by the swap calculation, the switch is worth making.

FIGURE 10.5. Crude Arbitrage Formula.

10.4.4.   If the currency being produced is at a discount in the forward market, F will be negative. Then R_2 will be greater than R_1. If the currency is at a premium, so F is positive, R_2 will be less than R_1. Effectively, R_1 is the direct interest cost, and F/S is the swap yield adjustment.

SECTION 5.   FINDING INTEREST RATES FROM SWAP RATES: INTEREST HEDGED

10.5.1.   But this formula ignores the foreign exchange exposure on the interest payable on the deal. If there is a large swing in rates during the life of the deal, this could wipe out any profit. Suppose our rates are: spot DMK 2.35 one year 1141/1121, US$ deposits one year 14.75%. Then on the crude formula we have a deutsche mark yield of about 10%. But if at maturity the mark has weakened to 2.50, the realized yield is only 9%. (The deutsche mark interest earned is now worth less in dollar terms.) So the bank needs to have a formula which works on a fully hedged basis. This is set out in Figure 10.6. To find it,

The formula is slightly different when we deal with a reciprocal exchange rate than when we deal with a normal exchange rate. The normal formula is used, for instance, when borrowing US$ (first currency) and lending DMK (second currency):

Interest hedged formula: normal exchange rate

$$R_2 = R_1 \times \frac{B_2}{B_1} \times \frac{(S - F)}{S} + 100 \times \frac{B_2}{N} \times \frac{F}{S}$$

$$\begin{array}{c}\text{Second currency}\\ \text{interest rate}\end{array} = \begin{array}{c}\text{First currency}\\ \text{interest rate}\end{array} \times \frac{\text{Second basis}^a}{\text{First basis}^a} \times \frac{\text{outright}}{\text{spot}}$$

$$+ 100 \times \frac{\text{second basis}^a}{\text{days}} \times \frac{\text{swap}}{\text{spot}}$$

This formula is exactly the same as the crude one *except* that the first currency's interest rate is multiplied by a factor to allow for the cost or benefit of selling the interest forward. The reciprocal formula is the same except that the adjustment factors change; it is used, for example, when borrowing US$ (first currency) and lending £STG (second currency):

Interest hedged formula: reciprocal exchange rate

$$R_2 = R_1 \times \frac{B_2}{B_1} \times \frac{S}{(S - F)} + 100 \times \frac{B_2}{N} \times \frac{F}{(S - F)}$$

$$\begin{array}{c}\text{Second currency}\\ \text{interest rate}\end{array} = \begin{array}{c}\text{First currency}\\ \text{interest rate}\end{array} \times \frac{\text{Second basis}^a}{\text{First basis}^a} \times \frac{\text{spot}}{\text{outright}}$$

$$+ 100 \times \frac{\text{second basis}^a}{\text{days}} \times \frac{\text{swap}}{\text{outright}}$$

The factor used to allow for the cost of hedging interest is inverted, and the swap yield is expressed as a percentage of the outright.

Note also that if we are going "backward"—that is, into dollars—the formulae are reversed. If a normal currency is being borrowed to produce dollars we would use the "reciprocal" formula; if a reciprocal currency is borrowed, we use the "normal" formula.

[a] 360 or 365, as the case may be.

FIGURE 10.6. Formula for Fully Hedged Interest Arbitrage. © JK Walmsley. The Foreign Exchange Handbook.

we work through a deal step by step. The steps are set out in Figure 10.7, overleaf, which you should glance at first.

10.5.2. We will use the rates from our first example (10.4.2). That is, US$ 1 = DMK 1.8000 three-month forward dollar discount, DMK premium 300, and three-month Eurodollars (90 days) cost 10%. The bank borrows $10 million to

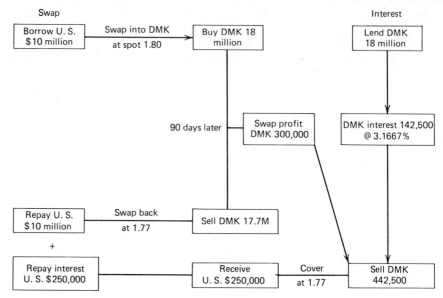

FIGURE 10.7. Fully Hedged Interest Arbitrage.

swap into deutsche marks. It receives DMK 18 million spot and pays away DMK 17.7 million in three months' time. So the profit on the swap is DMK 300,000. Now we know that in 90 days the bank must pay interest of US$ 250,-000. It will cover this interest by selling its deutsche mark earnings forward at 1.7700. So we know it will need DMK 442,500 (= 250,000 × 1.77) in 90 days. It has made DMK 300,000 on the swap, so to break even, its DMK interest earnings must total DMK 142,500. These earnings are on a principal of DMK 18,000,000, so over the three-month period the interest rate is 142,500/18,-000,000 = 0.79166%. Putting that on an annual basis, we multiply by four, getting 3.1666%.

10.5.3.   This compares with the 3.33% we worked out in 10.4.3. The reason that this rate is slightly lower is that the bank bought forward its dollar interest payable against its DMK interest earnings as well as swapping the DMK principal. Because the dollar was at a discount (the deutsche mark was at a premium) forward it made an extra profit. This meant it could lower the deutsche mark interest rate at which it lent, and still break even. Conversely, if the dollar were at a premium and the currency were at a discount—for example, the Italian lira,—its lending rate would have to be higher to compensate it for the extra cost of covering its LIT interest receivable.

10.5.4.   To be absolutely accurate, our formula should take account of the spread in the spot rate, since the principal amount is swapped but the interest is sold forward outright (i.e., using the other side of the spot). But the effect is very small. With the sort of rates we have used, a 10-point spot spread means 0.008% difference in the rate.

10.5.5.   The formula we have set up can be used to value a deal that is not hedged. To value the deal, we must predict the rate at which the interest earnings are sold off when they are received. To plug this assumed rate into the formula we replace $(S - F)$—the rate at which we would sell off the interest if the deal were hedged—in the first term. So the normal formula is:

$$R_2 = R_1 \times \frac{B_2}{B_1} \times \frac{\text{assumed rate}}{S} + 100 \times \frac{B_2}{N} \times \frac{F}{S}$$

and the reciprocal formula is:

$$R_2 = R_1 \times \frac{B_2}{B_1} \times \frac{S}{\text{assumed rate}} + 100 \times \frac{B_2}{N} \times \frac{F}{(S - F)}$$

To revert to our example in 10.5.1, if we plug in an assumed rate of 2.50, we see that to break even the bank must earn 10.99% rather than the 10.07% shown by the formula; in other words, if it lends at 10%, it ends up by losing nearly 1%. The calculation is:

$$R_2 = 14.75 \times \frac{360}{360} \times \frac{2.50}{2.35} - 100 \times \frac{360}{365} \times \frac{0.1121}{2.35} =$$

$$15.6915 - 4.7049 = 10.99$$

10.5.6.   Several variations of the formula in Figure 10.6 exist, usually simplified to ignore the possibility of a 365 = day basis and sometimes only applicable when going out of US\$ into another currency. For example:

$$\text{Interest differential} = \frac{\left[\dfrac{360}{\text{Number of days}} + \dfrac{\text{US\$ cost}}{100} \right] \times \left[\text{Swap} \times 100 \right]}{\text{spot}}$$

SECTION 6.   FINDING SWAP RATES FROM INTEREST RATES

10.6.1.   We have seen that the swap rate and the interest differential between two currencies are closely linked. In our examples so far, we have taken the swap rate as given and used it to derive interest rates. We now reverse the process and derive swap rates from interest rates.

10.6.2.   The term "interest rates" contains a number of problems which will be dealt with in Chapter 11. In this chapter, "interest rate" is taken to mean "interest rate available to participants in the international market, adjusted for special factors such as reserve asset costs and withholding taxes," in other words, to borrow a phrase, "net accessible interest rates."

10.6.3.   We begin with the simplest formula, ignoring spreads and the hedging of interest. We have, say: $S = 2.0950$; $R_1 = 10.875\%$; $R_2 = 15\%$; $N = 92$; $B_1 = 360$; $B_2 = 365$ where S = middle spot rate; R_1 = interest rate on dollars; R_2 = interest rate on sterling; N = number of days in the deal; B_1 = number of days in $ interest basis; and B_2 = number of days in sterling interest basis.

10.6.4.   Suppose we have £1 million to invest in either sterling or dollars; we want to know the forward margin which would make the two deals equivalent. We start by putting the interest rates on a common basis. For the sake of convenience, we shall put them on the 365-day basis, which means multiplying R_1 by 365/360 to produce, say, 11%.

10.6.5.   Now, if we swap into dollars, there is an interest loss of 4% for 92 days on $2,095,000 which must be compensated for by a profit on the swap. The exact loss is:

$$\frac{2,095,000 \times 4 \times 92}{360 \times 100} = \$21,415.55$$

10.6.6.   We must therefore make at least $21,415.55 on our swap, so £1 million sold spot for $2,095,000 must cost only $2,095,000—$21,415.55 = $2,073,584.50. Hence our break-even outright forward rate is 2.073584, say, 2.0736, making the break-even margin 214 points.

10.6.7.   Notice that if our principal had been only £1, we would have had:

$$\frac{2.0950 \times 4 \times 92}{360 \times 100} = 0.0214$$

from which we can deduce a formula:

$$F = \frac{S \times (R_2 - R_1) \times N}{B \times 100}$$

where we have S = spot in points; F = forward margin in points; N = number of days; and B = common interest basis.
In words:

$$\text{Forward margin} = \frac{\text{interest difference} \times \text{spot} \times \text{days}}{\text{interest basis} \times 100}$$

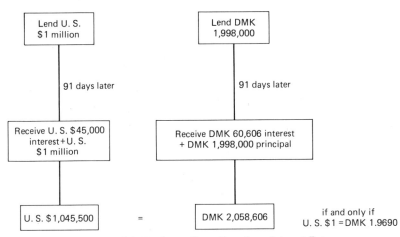

FIGURE 10.8. Finding a Swap Rate from Interest Rates.

10.6.8. The crude formula above is convenient for quick calculations. To find the exact formula, we work through an example. The steps are set out in Figure 10.8, which you should glance at first. We have US$/DMK 1.9980/90, three-month (91-day) DMK interest rate is 12%, US$ interest rate is 18%. Suppose we have a principal amount of $1 million. If we place the US$ we have interest of $1,000,000 \times 18/100 \times 91/360 = \$45,500$. The DMK principal is DMK 1,998,000 earning DMK 60,606. The outright rate that we need is the one which equalizes principal and interest on both sides—$1,045,500 and DMK 2,058,606, that is, $2058606/1045500 = 1.9690$. So the swap rate is 290.

10.6.9. To turn this into a formula, we write the interest rates as R_1, R_2, the spot as S, number of days as N, interest bases as B_1, B_2, principal amounts as P_1, P_2, and the outright as O. We have $R_1 = 18$; $R_2 = 12$; $B_1 = 360$; $B_2 = 360$; $P_1 = 1,000,000$; $P_2 = 1,998,000 = P_1 \times S$; $S = 1.9980$; and $N = 91$. Our dollar interest is $1,000,000 \times 18/100 \times 91/360$ or $P_1 \times R_1/100 \times N/B_1$.
So our dollar total including principal is:

$$P_1 \left[1 + \frac{R_1 \times N}{100 \times B_1} \right]$$

Similarly, our DMK total is:

$$1,998,000 \times \frac{12}{100} \times \frac{91}{360} \text{ or } P_2 \left[1 + \frac{R_2 \times N}{100 \times B_2} \right]$$

Because our DMK principal is $1,998,000 = 1,000,000 \times 1.9980$, that is, $(P_2 = P_1 \times S)$, we can write the second bracket as $P_1 \times S \left[1 + R_2 \times N/(100 \times B_2) \right]$
To get the outright we divide one into the other:

$$O = \frac{P_1 \times S \left(1 + \dfrac{R_2 \times N}{100 \times B_2}\right)}{P_1 \left(1 + \dfrac{R_1 \times N}{100 \times B_2}\right)}$$

Canceling out P_1, we finally have:

$$O = S \times \frac{\left(1 + \dfrac{R_2 \times N}{100 \times B_2}\right)}{\left(1 + \dfrac{R_1 \times N}{100 \times B_1}\right)}$$

To get the swap rate, of course, we subtract the spot rate from both sides. To test the formula we plug in our numbers:

$$O = 1.9980 \frac{\left(1 + \dfrac{12 \times 91}{360 \times 100}\right)}{\left(1 + \dfrac{18 \times 91}{360 \times 100}\right)} = 1.9980 \times \frac{1.03033}{1.0455} = 1.9690$$

10.6.10.   The formula just given is for normal indirect currencies. Once again, it has to be amended for reciprocal (direct) currencies. Suppose we have the same dollar rates as before but we are looking at sterling. We have $R_2 = 16$; $B_2 = 365$; $S = 2.3555$; and $P_2 = P_1/S = 424{,}538.31$. As before, our dollar interest is:

$$P_1 \times \frac{R_1 \times N}{100 \times B_1} = \$45{,}500$$

Our sterling interest is:

$$P_2 \times \frac{R_2 \times N}{100 \times B_2} = \frac{P_1}{S} \times \frac{R_2 \times N}{100 \times B_2} = \pounds 16{,}935.01$$

Our sterling total is:

$$\frac{P_1}{S}\left[1 \times \frac{R_2 \times N}{100 \times B_2}\right] = 441473.31$$

Because the exchange rate is quoted the other way up, we divide the dollar amount by the sterling amount to get O:

$$O = \frac{P_1 \left(1 + \dfrac{R_1 \times N}{100 \times B_1}\right)}{P_1/S\left(1 + \dfrac{R_2 \times N}{100 \times B_2}\right)} = S \times \frac{\left(1 + \dfrac{R_1 \times N}{100 \times B_1}\right)}{\left(1 + \dfrac{R_2 \times N}{100 \times B_2}\right)} = \frac{1045500}{441473.31} = 2.3682$$

Normal formula:

$$F = S \left| \frac{1 + \dfrac{R_2 \times N}{100 \times B_2}}{1 + \dfrac{R_1 \times N}{100 \times B_1}} - 1 \right|$$

$$\text{Swap} = \text{spot} \left| \frac{1 + \dfrac{\text{second currency interest rate} \times \text{days}}{100 \times \text{second interest basis}}}{1 + \dfrac{\text{first currency interest rate} \times \text{days}}{100 \times \text{first interest basis}}} - 1 \right|$$

Reciprocal formula:

$$F = S \left| \frac{1 + \dfrac{R_1 \times N}{100 \times B_1}}{1 + \dfrac{R_2 \times N}{100 \times B_2}} - 1 \right|$$

$$\text{Swap} = \text{spot} \left| \frac{1 + \dfrac{\text{first currency interest rate} \times \text{days}}{100 \times \text{first currency interest basis}}}{1 + \dfrac{\text{second currency interest rate} \times \text{days}}{100 \times \text{second currency interest basis}}} - 1 \right|$$

where: F = swap rate
$\quad\quad\;\; S$ = spot
$\quad\quad\;\; R_1$ = first currency interest rate
$\quad\quad\;\; R_2$ = second currency interest rate
$\quad\quad\;\; B_1$ = first currency interest basis
$\quad\quad\;\; B_2$ = second currency interest basis
$\quad\quad\;\; N$ = number of days

FIGURE 10.9. Calculation of Swap from Interest Rates: Formula.

giving a swap of 137 discount for dollars or 137 premium for sterling. The formula is identical, therefore, except that R_1, B_1 change places with R_2, B_2. They are set out for convenience in Figure 10.9. It is worth noting that if we go back now and apply this formula to the rates we used for the crude formula in 10.6.3—6, the swap rate thrown up by the exact formula is 202 compared with 214 points—a difference of 12 points, which is proportionately quite large. So it is well worth using the exact formula.

10.6.11. This formula produces a swap rate that is consistent with the fully hedged arbitrage formula. That is, if we take a US$ borrowing rate of 18%, DMK spot of 1.998, and swap of 290, we can produce DMK on a fully hedged basis at 12% for 91 days. It is worth going through the formula by hand to convince oneself of this.

SECTION 7.   MEDIUM-TERM DEPOSITS/LOANS

10.7.1.   We often have to deal with questions like: Is it more attractive to deposit (or borrow) five-year Swiss francs at 8% or five-year U.S. dollars at 13%? At what exchange rate will we break even? Or: If we borrow five-year U.S. dollars at 15% and lend five-year deutsche marks at 9%, will we make a profit? Or: If five-year sterling costs 14⅝% and the five-year swap is 300/500, at what rate can we lend U.S. dollars?

10.7.2.   Working out the answers is a little more complicated than it appears at first blush. They involve several interest payments and several swap rates. So we have several unknowns but only one equation. To get farther, we must make some assumptions, or go by trial and error. There is not a straightforward formula as we had in Sections 5 and 6.

10.7.3.   We will begin by supposing that we have the choice of depositing Swiss francs at 8% for five years or U.S. dollars at 13%. Suppose our principal amount is $1 million and the spot rate is 1.8500. To begin with we will make a simplifying assumption. We will assume that the Swiss franc interest receivable, and the dollar interest receivable, can both be reinvested on receipt, at the going rate (i.e., 8% or 13%). We also assume that we as investors are willing to leave these intermediate interest payments in their respective currencies; that is, we are not eager to cover the Swiss franc interest receipts back into dollars, or vice versa.

10.7.4.   On this basis, we ask: What five-year swap rate equalizes these two deals? Our assumptions mean that we can treat this deal exactly like the one in Section 6. That is, we calculate cumulative interest plus principal in the two currencies and divide one into the other to get the break-even outright rate.

10.7.5.   We have the figures for this situation set out in Table 10.1.

10.7.6.   But all this only applies on our original assumptions. Let's relax our assumption about the reinvestment rate. We can no longer guarantee that the Swiss francs can be reinvested at 8% or the dollars at 13%. We see at once that we now have to make some assumptions about what reinvestment rates apply. Alternatively, we can get hold of the one- to five-year interest rates for each currency, and work out a set of forward forward rates: one year against five years, and so on. This is fairly laborious and depends on our being able to deal at these rates. But it has the benefit that if we can, then we can tie up the deal completely on Day 1, without uncertainty about the actual reinvestment rates that apply when the time comes.

10.7.7.   What difference does this make? For the sake of argument, suppose that all other rates are as before but the dollar reinvestment rates are higher (because there is a downward sloping yield curve in the one- to five-year area).

TABLE 10.1.   Calculation of Medium-Term Swap from Deposit.

Item	Amount
Year 1 US$ interest	US$ 131,805.56
SFR "	SFR 150,055.56
Principal and interest	US$ 1,131,805.56
at end of Year 1	SFR 2,000,055.56
Year 2 US$ interest	US$ 149,178.26
SFR "	SFR 162,226.73
Principal and interest	US$ 1,280,983.82
at end of Year 2	SFR 2,162,282.28
Year 3 US$ interest	US$ 168,840.78
SFR "	SFR 175,385.12
Principal and interest	US$ 1,449,826.60
at end of Year 3	SFR 2,337,667.40
Year 4 US$ interest	US$ 191,094.96
SFR "	SFR 189,610.80
Principal and interest	US$ 1,640,919.54
at end of Year 4	SFR 2,527,278.20
Year 5 US$ interest	US$ 216,282.31
SFR "	SFR 204,990.34
Principal and interest	US$ 1,857,201.85
at end of Year 5	SFR 2,732,268.55

NOTE: The implied outright forward rate is given by the ratio of principal and interest at the end of year five, that is, 2,732,268.55/1,857,201.85 = approx 1.4712. Remembering that the spot rate was 1.8500, this gives us a five-year swap rate of 3788 (Swiss franc premium, dollar discount). In fact, we could apply this method to each of the intervening years, too. This would give us an annual swap rate of 828, 1620, 2376, 3098, and 3788.

Say they are 16%, 15½%, 14½%, 14%, and 13% respectively. The Swiss franc rates are 8% flat all the way through. Then we find swap rates of 1291, 2421, 3345, 4153, and 4795 respectively. We no longer have the fairly smooth progression of 10.7.5. The early swaps are proportionately much larger than the later, because the interest differential is higher.

10.7.8.   Of course, this type of situation (or its converse) is much more common than our first assumption of a dead flat yield curve. But a yield curve consisting of several different rates rather than just one brings in several more unknowns. We can handle that as long as we stick to our original assumption that we are content not to hedge the interest flows. But if we relax that, we find that the only way to solve our general problem is by trial and error (or, as computer people say, by iteration), unless we are given every single piece of information to begin with.

10.7.9.   Let's look at a case where we are given all the information to begin with. We estimate that we can borrow five-year sterling at 14⅝%. We can lend five year dollars at 15³/₁₆%. We have the following spot and forward rates:

Spot	$1.7800/10
One year	200/275
Two years	300/400
Three years	350/450
Four years	400/500
Five years	400/500

10.7.10. We look at a principal of £10 million. With this we buy $17.8 million. We know that our dollar interest receivable annually is $2,740,921.88 and our sterling interest payable is £1,462,500. We know that our dollar interest, sold forward for sterling at the market's buying rate for dollars (i.e., the right hand side of the swap) will yield:

Year 1 £1,516,415.98
Year 2 £1,506,001.03
Year 3 £1,501,875.00
Year 4 £1,497,771.52
Year 5 £1,497,771.52

so our profit in sterling is:

Year 1 £53,915.98
Year 2 £43,501.03
Year 3 £39,375.00
Year 4 £35,271.52
Year 5 £35,271.52

and our profit in US$ terms:

Year 1 $97,453.13
Year 2 $79,171.87
Year 3 $71,859.38
Year 4 $64,546.88
Year 5 $64,546.88

where the dollar equivalents are calculated at the relevant forward rates of 1.8075, 1.82, 1.825, 1.834, 1.83. (We use the left-hand side of the spot, because it is a swap deal rather than an outright.)

10.7.11. We assume (for simplicity) that these profits can also be lent out at the dollar lending rate of 15 3/16%, from the date that they accrue until the maturity of the deal. This produces cumulative earnings from each year as follows:

Year 1 $171,560.45
Year 2 $121,000.45
Year 3 $ 95,344.17
Year 4 $ 74,349.93
Year 5 $ 64,546.87

10.7.12. The total over the five years is thus $526,801.87. On the other hand, we know that to hedge our principal amount of £10 million, we have to buy back £10 million five years hence at a sterling premium (dollar discount) of 500 points, which will cost us $500,000 at the far end. So the profit over the deal is $526,801.87—500,000 = $26,801.87. (Given the size of the principal amount, and the fact that lines are being tied up for five years, that is, it is not a particularly attractive deal.)

10.7.13. It is worth exploring the sensitivity of this deal to different assumptions. If we rework the figures on the assumption that accrued profits can be reinvested at only 14³⁄₁₆% rather than 15³⁄₁₆%, for example, the total profit falls from nearly $27,000 to $15,500. But a 1% change in the sterling interest rate is much more powerful: if the dollar rate (and reinvestment rate) are held unchanged at 15³⁄₁₆%, but the sterling rate is raised to 15⅝%, the deal swings from a profit of nearly $27,000 to a loss of over $1.2 million. The reason is that this interest rate is acting on the whole principal, rather than just the annual profits or losses as the reinvestment/refunding rate is. Equally, a rise of 100 points in the first year's swap rate cuts the profit from nearly $27,000 to about $1,000 whereas the same change in Year 4 cuts the profit much less, to $10,000, because the dollar receivable is worth less in sterling terms in Year 1 and that cumulates over time. The impact in Year 4 is not cumulated over so long a time.

10.7.14. But the same rise of 100 points in Year 5 makes a difference of $100,000; because again it is applied to the whole principal, rather than the annual profits or losses which are much smaller. Summing up, then, the reinvestment rate and the intervening year's swap rates are not particularly critical compared with the five-year interest rates and the five-year swap rate. However, this does not mean they can be ignored. If the funding cost of the early losses in the deal were ignored, there would be an apparent profit of about $122,000 which does not in fact exist.

SECTION 8. FORWARD FORWARD SWAPS

10.8.1. A forward forward is a swap deal between two forward dates. It might be done to take a view on the swap rates (further ahead than we did in Section 2) or to offset other flows. For instance, the treasurer of Zum Beispiel

GmbH might have DMK 5 million due in six months' time, but she might also have a DMK 5 million payment to make in one month. If she wants to lock in today's swap rates, she would do a forward forward deal.

10.8.2.   Suppose we have:

> DMK spot 2.1500 − 10
> DMK one month 50/40
> DMK six months 280/260

She knows that she must buy dollars for deutsche marks in six months, for which she will benefit from a dollar discount (receive a deutsche mark premium) of 260 points. She knows also that she must sell dollars for deutsche marks in one month for which she will pay a dollar discount (deutsche mark premium) of 50 points. The forward forward rate is the difference between the two: 210 points. If the deals were done as outrights, the one-month deal would be done at 2.1450 and the six-month at 2.1250 for a net benefit (dollar discount, deutsche mark premium) of only 200 points. Doing the deals separately is more expensive because it adds the cost of dealing on both sides of the spot rate.

10.8.3.   A common use of forward forward rates is to take a view on interest rate movements. Suppose we have the following £STG/US$ rates:

Spot	1.8980/90
One month	20/10
Two months	30/20
Three months	40/30
Six months	40/30
Twelve months	30/20

10.8.4.   This pattern happens when U.S. rates are slightly below U.K. rates for all periods, but rather less so at the far end. Suppose we think the market has got it wrong. We think that in the next six months U.K. rates will fall but U.S. rates will not change very much. We think that in six months' time the six-month swap will be 100/200; that is, U.K. rates will be significantly below U.S. rates for the period. (Remember the rule of Chapter 5: When the interest differential goes against a currency, the swap goes in its favor.) So we decide to take a forward forward position "sixes against twelves."

10.8.5.   We think sterling will go from discount to premium in this period (dollars will go from premium to discount). So we want to be long of sterling (short dollars) at the far end, vice versa at the near end. So we sell sterling at the near end for a discount of 40 and buy it back at the far end at a discount of 20. The whole operation costs us 20 points.

10.8.6. Suppose we get it right. In six months' time the swap has moved to 100/200. We have to buy sterling at the near end and sell it at the far end. For this we get 100 points premium on our sterling at the far end against the 20 points discount we paid, netting 120 points in total. Of course, 120 points is small compared with the probable movement in the spot, but as a forward forward dealer we are much less exposed than if we took an outright position. "Our net exchange position will be only marginally affected by the spot rate's movements, but there will be a cash flow difference — there will be a profit/loss to be invested/funded over the period till the position unwinds".

10.8.7. Let's look at the arithmetic of the position.

Day 1:	spot	1.8980/90
	six months	40/30
	twelve months	30/20
Day 180:	spot	1.7500/10
	six months	100/200

On Day 1 we sell sterling and buy $5 million in the six-month period at 1.8940, making £2,639,915.5. We sell $5 million and buy £2,637,130.80 at 1.8960 in the one-year date. On Day 180 we have to buy sterling at $1,7510, costing $4,622,492.08 and sell it forward at $1.7610, receiving $4,643,987.34. So we have a profit today of $377,508, the difference between our sale of $5 million for sterling and what we have to pay to cover it. "On the far date we sold $5 million and bought sterling but only receive $4643987.34 for the sterling we now sell back, giving us a loss at the far end of $356012.66 and a net profit on the whole deal of $21,496".

10.8.8. What would have happened if the forwards had moved the same way but the spot had gone the opposite way, to $2.0300/10? It costs us $5,-361,668.30 to buy sterling at the near end—that is, spot. But at the far end we get $5,393,763.1 for our sterling, giving us a profit on the whole deal of $32,-094.8—about $1,000 more than before, but at the far end of the deal this time. The 28-cent movement in the spot hardly made any difference. "But it does make a difference when we take into account the interest cost of funding the loss which we now have at the near end of the deal when we close it out."

10.8.9. Forward forward deals often crop up when a trader decides to cover a slightly different period from his natural interest. Let's look again at Zum Beispiel GmbH's treasurer, who has a South African rand receipt due in 13 months. She calls her bank late in the afternoon and is quoted (bear in mind that the rand is reciprocal: rand 1 = US$ 1.0200/10):

Spot	1.0200/10
12 months	350/340
13 months	450/440

She asks why the 13-month dollar premium/rand discount is proportionately so high and is told that the South African prime rates have just risen after the close of business in Johannesburg (which is an hour ahead of Frankfurt). Since the interest differentials have gone in the rand's favor, the forwards move to offset this by going further into discount. She is told that the forwards are expected to rise again tomorrow and no one is eager to deal 13 months as it is an awkward period.

10.8.10. She decides to deal today but thinks it would not be worth paying the 100 points extra for the 13th month. She thinks that if she waits a month the situation will have settled. So she deals for 12 months which creates a forward forward position, "twelves against thirteens." She expects that if she waits a month her position—which will then be "elevens against twelves"—can be closed out for about 20 points.

10.8.11. If she is right, she has locked in her forward cover for the period at a total cost of 370 points instead of 450, because she avoided paying the extra cost of dealing into an "awkward" period.

SECTION 9. EXTENDING MATURING CONTRACTS

10.9.1. A further common use of a swap is where, say, a forward sale of deutsche marks has been made to cover an export receivable. As maturity approaches, it is found that the funds will not be received in time. A swap has to be done to adjust the maturity date.

10.9.2. At this point we must allow for accumulated profit or loss. Suppose we use the original contract's spot rate as the "spot" rate on which the new swap is based (see 10.1.3). For example, suppose the corporation originally sold the bank deutsche marks two months forward against U.S. dollars; suppose the deal was done off a spot rate of 1.8000 and a DMK premium/dollars discount of 200, making an outright of 1.7800. Assume we now have to extend for a further two months owing to payment delays, and that the two-month DMK premium is now 220. If we use the original outright rate of 1.7800 as the "spot" for our new extension, the new outright rate will be 1.7580. But suppose in the meantime the deutsche mark has strengthened to 1.7000. The firm has made a loss — or less profit than it might have — by selling forward when it did.

10.9.3. Hence, if the bank lets the old deal mature, and does a new deal based on today's rates, the customer will be delivering deutsche marks sold to the bank at 1.7800. But he will have to buy them from the bank in order to deliver them, and must pay 1.7000 for them. Then he will sell them back to the bank at 1.700–0.0220 = 1.6780. The steps are set out in Figure 10.10. Suppose his original sale had been DMK 5 million. At the original rate, this would have produced $2,808,988.76. But to buy in DMK 5 million for the extension at

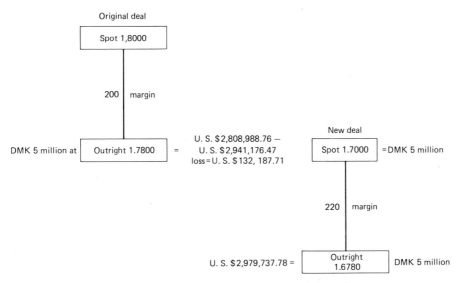

FIGURE 10.10. Extension of a Contract at Current Rate.

1.7000 will cost him $2,941,176.47—crystallizing a loss of $132,187.71. The deutsche marks are now sold forward at the current outright rate of 1.6780, yielding $2,979,737.78 at the new maturity. If at this postponed maturity date it were necessary again to extend the deal, and the spot had moved back up to 1.8000, the extension would now crystallize a profit; and so on.

10.9.4. On the other hand, if the deal is extended at the original rate, the extension would not throw up any cash difference. (See Figure 10.11.) But there would be a hidden loss which could continue to accumulate indefinitely. This is an inherently undesirable possibility for both sides; the bank is providing an unsecured loan, and the corporation's books are not reflecting its true position. Hence it is generally recommended that all extensions of forwards be made at current market rates. The drawback for a firm whose business requires many changes in delivery dates—such as a commodity trader—is that this method continually throws up a string of small profits or losses which have to be taken into or out of the normal cash flow of the business. So the choice of the correct rate on which to base the extension of forwards is largely one of philosophy. In summary: management control requires extensions to be made at current market rates; cash flow simplicity requires that they be carried out at the original rates.

10.9.5. If a forward contract is in fact extended at the historic rate, then the bank should adjust for the fact that it is lending the customer his loss (or taking his profit as a deposit). This has to be worked back into the swap rate. We look at how this is done in the next section.

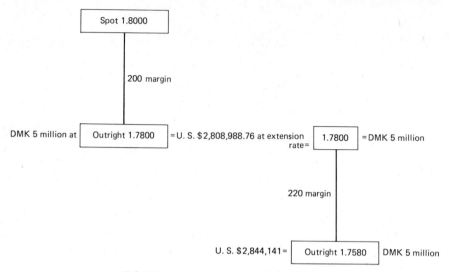

FIGURE 10.11. Extension at Original Rate.

SECTION 10.   EXTENSIONS AT HISTORIC RATES

10.10.1   This section looks at how to extend a maturing contract using historic rates. Using current rates the calculation is straightforward; we saw it in 10.9.4–5. DMK 5 million sold forward at an outright rate of 1.7800 were extended at the new forward rate of 1.6780. The old forward was closed out by a spot purchase of DMK 5 million at 1.7000. This threw up a loss of $132,187.71.

10.10.2.   But suppose for some reason the contract is extended off the historic rate. The customer buys DMK 5 million to close out the old contract as before. But he does it at 1.7800, so his cash loss does not show up. It only shows up in a smaller dollar inflow at the maturity of the new contract. The bank has lent him his loss until the new maturity. How do we adjust for this?

10.10.3.   We start by realizing that this is a special case of the formula in Section 6 of this chapter. That is, we have to get a swap adjustment from the interest the bank will charge its customer for lending it the loss (or taking the profit on deposit). It is a special case of the formula for swap rates from interest rates: one of the interest rates is zero. There is a loan of U.S. dollars to the customer but no deutsche mark deposit by the customer. So we take the formula:

$$F = S\left[\frac{\left(1 + \dfrac{R_2 \times N}{B_2 \times 100}\right)}{\left(1 + \dfrac{R_1 \times N}{B_1 \times 100}\right)} - 1\right]$$

We see that the bottom half of the fraction is one, because $R_1 = 0$. So we now have:

$$F = S \left[\frac{R \times N}{B \times 100} \right]$$

where

F = adjustment needed
S = current spot rate
R = dollar interest rate (say 10%)
N = days in new contract
B = 360

Using the rates we had earlier,

$$F = 1.7000 \left[\frac{10 \times 60}{36000} \right] = 0.0283 = 283 \text{ points}$$

10.10.4.   This would be the adjustment if the bank lent the whole of the principal amount to the customer. But of course it is only lending the loss, so the adjustment has to be weighted accordingly. To find the dollar amount of the loss, we take the difference between the new rate (1.7000) and the old (1.7800) as a percentage of the new rate, and apply this to the dollar amount of the old forward contract (being the dollar equivalent at maturity of the old forward). In our example:

$$\frac{1.7000 - 1.7800}{1.7000} \times 2,808,988.76 = 132,187.71$$

10.10.5.   To generalize this into a formula, we say that the dollar amount at the maturity of the original contract was $1. Then the dollar loss is given by:

$$\$1 \times \frac{1.7000 - 1.7800}{1.7000} = \frac{\text{new rate} - \text{old rate}}{\text{new rate}}$$

If we designate the new spot rate S_N and the old S_O we can write this as:

$$\frac{S_N - S_O}{S_N}$$

and the whole formula is:

$$F = \frac{S_N - S_O}{S_N} \times S_N \left[\frac{R \times N}{B \times 100}\right] = \frac{(S_N - S_O) \times R \times N}{B \times 100}$$

where

F = adjustment to forward

S_O = old contract rate

S_N = new spot rate

R = interest rate on currency being received by customer at maturity (here, dollars)

B = interest basis for interest rate

N = number of days in new contract

10.10.6. When we plug in the numbers from our example, we have:

$$F = \frac{(1.7000 - 1.7800) \times 10 \times 60}{360 \times 100} = -0.0013 = 13 \text{ points against customer}$$

So instead of showing 220 points in the customer's favor in the new forward, the bank will show only 207. Clearly, if the rates had moved in the customer's favor, F would be positive and the swap would be adjusted in the customer's favor.

SECTION 11. BROKEN DATES

10.11.1. A forward (or a deposit) transaction which is not for certain standard dates—normally 1, 2, 3, 6, or 12 months, and in some cases 1, 2, 3, 4, 5, 6, 7, 8, 9, 10, 11, or 12 months—is referred to as a "broken" or "odd" date. Calculation of the outright forward price for such a date is made by using the swap rates. Suppose that we are buying deutsche marks against sterling, the spot rate is DMK 4.0, and the two-month premium is 300 while the three-month premium is 450. Suppose that we are dealing on April 3 (spot 5th) for June 15 for a date which is two months and 10 days ahead. A convenient method of calculation is as follows. The third month—between June 5 and July 5—has 30 days in it; so we take 10/30ths, or ⅓rd, of the third month's premium (which is 450 less 300, that is, 150 points), totaling 50 points. This is added to the two month premium of 300, to produce a total of 350; so our outright rate for June 15 would be $4.000 - 0.0350 = 3.9650$.

10.11.2. This "pro rata" method of calculation is acceptable for normal maturities where no special factors (e.g., days of peak interest rates) are involved (see Chapter 13, Adjustments). The pro rata method is not always acceptable for shorter maturities, however (see Chapter 12, Short Dates).

11

MONEY MARKET CALCULATIONS

This chapter sets out some of the basic calculations in the money market area. We explain the conventions used and the kinds of deposit traded, and then there is a section setting out what the yield curve is. Then we look at mismatching and the profit and risk involved. Section 5 explains how to work out broken dates, which ties in with the next section on forward forward rates. Then we explain CDs, and some basic CD calculation. Section 9 discusses other markets that a Euromoney market trading room might be involved in, and Section 10 explains the calculations used in discount securities. Finally, Section 11 looks at combining money market paper and a foreign currency swap.

SECTION 1.   CONVENTIONS

11.1.1.   Throughout this chapter, all comments relate (unless otherwise stated) to the Euromarket, that is, deposits traded outside the country of origin. Deposits traded in the country of origin are referred to as domestic.

11.1.2.   The Euromarkets use two bases for calculating interest. These are the 360-day year and the 365-day year. The 365-day year is used for sterling, the Irish pound, the Kuwaiti dinar, and the Belgian franc. All other currencies are dealt on a 360-day basis. The Belgian franc is also dealt on a 360-day basis if both parties to the deal are non-Belgian. Sometimes the Canadian dollar is dealt on a 365-day basis with customers, but interbank Euro-Canadian is usually 360. Of course, any basis can be used, given mutual agreement.

11.1.3.   The method of calculation for 360-basis is as follows. Suppose the deal is for 91 days, the interest rate 10%, the principal amount US$ 1 million. Then interest is calculated from:

$$\frac{10}{100} \times \frac{91}{360} \times 1,000,000 = 25,277.78$$

Because this method uses actual days elapsed and a 360-day year, it is sometimes called a 365/360 basis.

11.1.4.   The calculation method for 365-day basis is similar. We replace 91/360 by 91/365:

$$\frac{10}{100} \times \frac{91}{365} \times 1,000,000 = 24,931.51$$

Note that for the same nominal interest rate of 10%, the 365-day basis produces a lower interest amount. Thus a 10% Eurodollar rate (360-day basis) compares with a 10.13889% Eurosterling rate on a 365-day basis. Equally, a 9.863% Eurodollar rate, 360 basis, is equivalent to 10% Eurosterling on a 365-day basis. This method is sometimes called the 365/365 method.

11.1.5.   Another method of calculating interest rates is used in certain European countries for domestic deposits. It can be described as the Continental, or 360/360 method compared with the Euromarket (365/360) or the sterling (365/365) method. The two latter methods compute interest on the actual days elapsed, whereas the Continental method treats the year as consisting of 12 30-day months. Thus a deal running from December 5, 1980 to December 5, 1981 would be treated as a 360-day deal. A deal running from December 5, 1980 to May 12, 1981 would be treated as having 157 days (5 × 30 + 7) instead of the actual 158 days. Note that the result of this method is to produce a lower effective rate, for a given nominal rate, than the 365/365-day sterling method, which in turn is lower than the 365/360 Euro or U.S. method.

11.1.6.   Market practice is to pay interest at the maturity of the deal, except where periods of over one year are involved. In that case interest is paid annually on the "anniversary" of the deal. Let's look at a two-year deal done on December 5, 1980. Interest would be paid on December 5, 1981. Interest would be paid again, and the principal repaid, on December 5, 1982. A two-

and-a-half year deal done on the same date would pay interest on the same dates, with a final interest payment (and repayment of principal) on June 5, 1983. If the anniversary is not a business day, the procedure adopted is the same as in the forward market (see Chapter 9, Section 7); it will be rolled forward to the next business day, providing this does not take us into the next month.

11.1.7.   The deposit market quotes two rates for a given period. The offered rate is the rate at which the dealer is prepared to lend money. The bid rate is the rate at which he is prepared to borrow. Normal U.S. practice is to quote the bid rate first. Normal London market practice is to quote the offered rate first. Hence "7¼–½" in the United States, "7½–¼" in London, both mean "I lend at 7½%, borrow at 7¼%."

11.1.8.   A large amount of Eurocurrency lendings involve LIBOR. LIBOR is the London Interbank Offered Rate. It can be defined in two ways: (1) the rate at which funds are offered to a first-class bank in London for the maturity period in question: (2) the rate at which a first-class bank in London offers funds to another first-class bank in London. In either case, LIBOR attempts to measure the cost to a bank of raising new funds from the market in order to on-lend. It is the basis of almost all variable-rate lending in the Euromarkets. In view of its importance, it should be stressed that the LIBOR concept is purely judgmental. For example, three-month LIBOR for US\$ 1,000 million will very likely differ from three-month LIBOR for US\$ 5 million. For we are considering the dealer's judgment of what it would cost him to raise that amount for on-lending. It may well be that he judges that it would cost him more to raise the larger amount, because it will move the market against him. Hence normal practice for any given loan is to calculate LIBOR as the average of the rates quoted by several "reference banks" selected for the purpose. The rates published in the financial press reflect a consensus of often diverse views. LIBOR is usually fixed at a time specified in the original loan agreements (normally 11:00 A.M. London time). It is quoted for deposits starting from the spot date (see 11.1.10) for various periods, of which the most common are three and six months.

11.1.9.   The LIBOR convention has spawned many variations. These include, SIBOR (Saudi or Singapore Interbank Offered Rate), NIBOR (New York), KIBOR (Kuwait), ADIBOR (Abu Dhabi), HKIBOR (Hong Kong), MIBOR (Madrid), and so on. In all cases the concept attempts to measure a bank's funding costs for a loan, though the details vary from center to center. If no other details are given, it is normal to infer that the rate is for US\$ deposits traded in that center. It is quite possible to apply the concept to other Euro-deposits or domestic deposits (e.g., many domestic U.K. loans are linked to sterling LIBOR). Table 11.1 shows examples for 1981. Table 11.2 compares three-month LIBOR with the US prime rate (see also figure 6.3).

TABLE 11.1.   Different Euromarket Interest Rate Options.

Type of interest rate[a]	Number of tranches 1981	Number of tranches 1980	Amount (Millions of $) 1981	Amount (Millions of $) 1980
London Interbank Offered Rate	928	731	85,128.19	65,815.45
London Interbank Offered Rate/ US Prime Rate	71	10	45,321.40	3.410.00
Fixed Rate	173	235	11,336.67	13,591.38
US Prime Rate/London Interbank Offered Rate	6	2	5,750.00	311.30
US Bankers Acceptances	8	—	5,662.00	—
US Prime Rate	26	12	5,080.00	2,275.50
US Prime Rate/CD adjusted secondary market rate	7	—	3,310.00	—
Guarantee Commission	31	—	1,710.93	—
Hong Kong Interbank Offered Rate	35	12	1,400.56	608.77
Japan Long Term Prime Rate	25	5	1,234.23	323.14
Canadian Prime Rate	10	5	1,225.90	625.90
Sterling Acceptances Commission	10	—	1,171.66	—
CD adjusted secondary market rate	1	—	1,000.00	—
SDR Deposit Rate	4	—	770.70	—
Letter of Credit Commission	15	—	724.71	—
Singapore Interbank Offered Rate	19	14	678.06	320.30
Madrid Interbank Offered Rate	7	2	555.84	27.03
Bahrain Interbank Offered Rate	19	7	505.85	442.90
Hong Kong Prime Rate	10	4	494.80	329.50
London Interbank Offered Rate/ Canadian Prime Rate	1	1	459.50	100.00
US Prime Rate/Bankers Acceptances	1	—	375.90	—
Kuwait Interbank Offered Rate	6	4	361.21	138.70
London Interbank Offered Rate/ Bankers Acceptances	1	—	225.00	—
ECU Interbank Rate	1	—	204.70	—
London Interbank Offered Rate/ CD adjusted secondary market rate	1	—	170.00	—
Other	17	5	466.59	67.60
Total	1432	1049	175,324.40	88,387.47

[a] Joint rates refer to borrowers' or lenders' option.

SOURCE: Reprinted from "Annual Financing Report," *Euromoney*, March 1982.

TABLE 11.2.   Difference between Prime and Three-Month Libor, 1977–1981.

	Monthly Average (in Percent) Prime–Libor
1977 High	1.2 (February)
Low	0.46 (October)
Annual Average	0.83
1978 High	0.72 (February)
Low	− 0.37 (October)
Annual Average	0.39
1979 High	1.02 (June)
Low	− 0.05 (October)
Annual Average	0.68
1980 High	4.67 (May)
Low	− 0.12 (November)
Annual Average	1.27
1981 High	3.21 (November)
Low	0.85
Annual Average	2.04

SOURCE: Data Resources, Inc.

11.1.10.   The spot convention for deposits is the same as that for foreign exchange (see Chapter 8, Section 2), that is, two working days. However, a difference may arise in the case of a holiday. Consider a situation where New York and Frankfurt were open, but London closed, on a given day. Then the foreign exchange market would normally deal US$/DMK for that day, but London would not normally deal Eurodeposits maturing on a day on which it was closed. It would be possible in theory to do so but would generally be inconvenient.

SECTION 2.   TYPES OF DEPOSITS

11.2.1.   A call deposit is defined as a deposit which is repayable "at call." In practice, due to time zone considerations, and the need to transmit confirmations between countries, such deposits may be repayable at up to two days' notice, unless special arrangements have been made. The situation varies according to currency, and indeed the ability to take call funds from a customer depends on the currency. In some currencies there is not a well-developed call money market which makes it difficult to lay off funds.

11.2.2.   An overnight deposit is defined as a deposit made today which is repaid (or replaced) on the next business day. Overnight deposit trading is also complicated by time zone considerations. A Hong Kong bank can deal U.S.

dollar deposits overnight without difficulty, since New York will normally be 13 hours behind, giving plenty of time for instructions to be processed in Hong Kong and acted on in New York. However, London cannot normally deal overnight deutsche mark deposits as deals have to be in the Frankfurt clearing by 8:00 A.M. Effectively this means that processing and confirmation among the placing bank, the accepting bank, the placing bank's German correspondent, and the accepting bank's German correspondent would have to be completed by 8:00 A.M. on the same day as the deal, which is not really practical.

11.2.3. The time zone problem is less pressing for deposits starting tomorrow and maturing on the next business day, usually referred to as "tomorrow/next" or "tom/next." (It will be noticed that tom/next deals mature on the spot date.) It is possible to deal tom/next in most currencies that have a well-developed Eurocurrency market, but because of the time zone problem the market tends to dry up very early.

11.2.4. As in the foreign exchange market, the deposit market quotes spot/next (from spot to the next business day), spot/week, and so on.

11.2.5. A period deposit is defined as a deal starting on the spot date and maturing on some fixed and predetermined date. The phrase "the periods" usually refers to some or all of the "standard" periods of 1, 2, 3, 6, 9, or 12 months (see 9.7.1). Value date conventions for period deposits are the same as for foreign exchange, with the exception that it would be possible (though in practice unusual) to deal for a value date on which the dealing center was closed but the settlement center was open. That is, suppose (as in 11.1.10) that New York and Frankfurt were open, but London closed, on a given day. The foreign exchange market—and London—would deal US$/DMK for settlement on that day, but London would not normally deal Eurodollars or Euromark deposits for maturity on that day.

SECTION 3.   YIELD CURVE

11.3.1. A yield curve is a graph which plots interest rates against time. To make it meaningful, the different interest rates should be for comparable instruments. In this chapter, that means interest rates for deposits with a bank or CDs issued by a bank. In other contexts, we might plot the interest rates for Treasury bills maturing, say, in one, three, six, and twelve months' time and talk of a Treasury bill yield curve. Because of possible capital gains on a security (or a CD) and the differing taxation treatment of interest earnings and capital gains, constructing a true yield curve for securities can be quite complex. But for "clean" deposits the question of capital gain does not arise, so the yield curve concepts are quite simple.

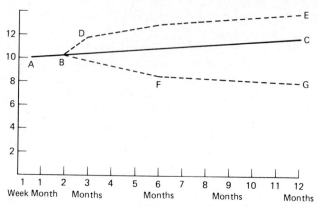

FIGURE 11.1. Yield Curves.

11.3.2.   Suppose we have the following set of rates: 1 week, 10%; 1 month, 10¼%; 2 months, 10½%; 3 months, 10¾%; 6 months, 11%; 9 months, 11½%; and 12 months, 12%. Then we can draw a simple yield curve as in Figure 11.1. (line AC). We can see that is slopes upward to the right. This is called a normal, upward-sloping, or positive yield curve. It is normal, because under normal circumstances a lender requires a slightly higher rate to compensate him for locking away his funds for a longer period. Equally, a borrower will be prepared to pay slightly more for the benefit of insulating himself against interest rate movements for a longer time.

11.3.3.   If the market thinks that rates are about to rise, the curve will rise more steeply; lenders will require extra compensation before they will lock in at today's rates. For they believe that rates will soon be higher, and so they would be better off to wait until rates rise before they lend. In this situation, it might be that the three-month rate is 12%, 12 months, 13%. We could draw a yield curve like the dotted line ABDE in Figure 11.1.

11.3.4.   Or it might be that the market expects rates to fall. In this case lenders will be happy to lend now for longer periods at rates below today's rates. For they fear that if they wait before they lend, the rate they receive will be lower still. In this case the 12-month rate might be only 8%, with the 6-month rate 9% and the 2-month rate 10½%. We could draw the dotted line ABFG in Figure 11.1.

11.3.5.   So looking at a yield curve tells us a lot about where the market thinks rates are going. If we look at Figure 11.1 we can see that, if today's yield curve is ABDE, the market expects rates to rise—but not for a couple of months, since AB is only sloping up gently in line with the normal pattern. If the yield curve were ABFG, equally, the market is expecting rates to fall after a couple of months. Also, the slope of the curve suggests that between two and six months hence—BF on the curve—the market expects quite a sharp fall, which will steady off later: FG is flatter than BF. The yield curve is telling us visually about the implied forward forward rates (which are discussed in Section 6). The forward forward rates are indicated by the *slope* of the yield curve. If the slope between any two points is upward, the forward forward rate for the period between those points is above the current rates; if it is downward, it is below.

11.3.6. A technique used by many investors is called "riding the yield curve." Suppose in the shorter maturities the slope of the yield curve is positive (and is expected to remain so). This means that, say, a six-month CD yields more than a three-month CD. Then, if rates do not change drastically, an investor can pick up extra yield by buying the six-month CD and selling it in three months' time to reinvest the proceeds in the six-month CD. In effect, he is collecting the premium for staying long in a market where a premium is paid for staying long. Of course, if rates have risen sharply in the meantime— as has often happened in recent years—he has earned less than he could have by staying short.

SECTION 4. MISMATCH

11.4.1. This line of thinking brings us to the question of mismatch. Mismatch happens when a trader borrows or lends money for a longer or shorter period than would be needed to match his commitment. If a bank lends money for six months, and funds the lending initially with a three-month deposit, it is mismatched. There are two kinds of mismatch: interest mismatch and funding mismatch (see Chapter 17). In our example, there is an interest mismatch of three months. If after six months the loan is repaid, then the funding mismatch is also three months; if the six-month loan is a roll-over loan whose final agreed maturity is, say, five years, then the funding mismatch is four years and nine months—the remaining period during which money must be raised to fund the loan.

11.4.2. Mismatching is the justification for a bank's existence. The origin of banking, after all, was in taking deposits, repayable at demand, and lending them out for a slightly longer period. It also carries risks; the control of these risks is discussed in Chapter 17. In proportion to the risk, it carries the chance of profits.

11.4.3. Suppose we have one month (30 days), 10–10⅛%; 3 months, 10⅝–¾%; and six months (180 days), 10⅝–10¾%. The market expects a rise in rates in the next three months, followed by a leveling out. Suppose a customer borrows $10 million for six months from the bank, and the bank thinks the market has got it wrong, and rates will fall. Then it will fund itself, say, for one month at 10⅛%. It earns $10{,}000{,}000 \times 10.75/100 \times 180/360 = \$537{,}500$ for the six-month loan, paying $10{,}000{,}000 \times 10.125/100 \times 30/360 = \$84{,}375$ for the one-month funds. Suppose in a month's time the rate for five-month money (150 days) has fallen to 10%. Then to cover its remaining position it borrows at 10%, paying $10{,}000{,}000 \times 10/100 \times 150/360 = \$416{,}666.65$ (ignoring interest on interest—see Section 6). So its total costs are \$501,041.65 and its total earnings \$537,500, leaving a profit of \$36,458.35.

11.4.4.   This compares with the ⅛% that the bank would have earned if it had immediately been able to fund itself for six months at 10⅝%, which would have shown a profit of only \$6,250.00 if it had not run a deliberate mismatch. Of course, the \$30,000 odd extra profit from this mismatch could just as easily have been a loss if the bank had misjudged rate movements. During 1979–1980 a number of the world's largest banks lost tens of millions of dollars on mismatch positions: hence the need for tight controls (see Chapter 17).

SECTION 5.   BROKEN DATES

11.5.1.   Suppose we need a period deposit rate for a date which is not a "standard" one; for instance, suppose we have the following Euro-deutsche mark rates:

One month   12⅛–12¼% 30 days
Two months 12¾–12⅞% 62 days

We need a bid rate for one month and one week, that is, 37 days. The rough calculation is to take the bid rate for 30 days at 12⅛%, and assume that the one week beyond the 30 days should be reckoned at the two-month bid rate, namely 12¾%, so that all we have to do is average the two rates, weighting them by the number of days involved:

$$\frac{30 \times 12.125 + 7 \times 12.75}{37} = \frac{363.75 + 89.25}{37} = \frac{453}{37} = 12.243$$

This method is the method used by most people in the market for a quick approximation of a broken date rate. Then they will make a quick mental adjustment to cover any special factors, to which we now turn.

11.5.2.   For we need to think more carefully about the assumption that the seven days of the second month are "worth" 12¾%; this in fact is not so. To see why, let us look at an extreme example. Suppose we have US$ deposits:

One month (30 days) 10%
Two months (60 days) 20%

We need a 37-day rate again. Using our crude method, we get:

$$\frac{30 \times 10 + 7 \times 20}{37} = \frac{440}{37} = 11.8919\%$$

Now we calculate a 50-day rate:

$$\frac{30 \times 10 + 20 \times 20}{50} = \frac{700}{50} = 14\%$$

Now a 59-day rate:

$$\frac{30 \times 10 + 29 \times 20}{59} = \frac{880}{59} = 14.9\%$$

But we know that our 60-day rate should be 20%; it seems improbable that the 59-day rate will only be 14.9% and the 60-day rate 20%, unless there are some very special factors (which, by assumption, there are not in our example).

11.5.3.   In fact, what is happening is that the days in the second month are "worth" more than 20%. If you have earned an average return of 10% during the first 30 days, then in order to earn an average return of 20% over the whole 60 days, the second 30 days must be yielding more than 20%. Otherwise they cannot pull the average over the whole period up to the 20% required. In market jargon, the "forward forward rate for 60 days against 30 days" must be higher than 20%. In fact (see 11.6.2 below) it is 29.75196. If we now recalculate our 59-day rate, we find:

$$\frac{30 \times 10 + 29 \times 29.75196}{59} = \frac{1162.8068}{59} = 19.7086\%$$

which is clearly much more closely in line with what we should expect.

11.5.4.   Notice that we have made a simplifying assumption about the second 30 days: that they can be treated all the same. We said that the forward forward rate for the whole of the second 30 days was about 29¾%. This might not be the case if there were special dates within the period. Suppose that in the middle of our second month (Day 45) there was a special reporting date and as a result of balance sheet "window-dressing" the market was prepared to bid 100% for money running from Day 44 to Day 46. (This happens regularly in Swiss franc deposits over month- or quarter-end.) Then we would have to refine our forward forward rate calculations. In practice, most dealers will simply make a mental adjustment for this factor rather than make elaborate calculations. It is important to be aware of how it might affect the rate calculation, though.

SECTION 6.   FORWARD FORWARD RATES

11.6.1.   We turn now to the mechanics of calculating a forward forward rate. The simplest approach is to consider a specific case. A bank is lending for 60 days at 20% against a deposit which it has paid 10% for 30 days for. What is the break-even rate on the second period—that is, how much can it afford to pay for a deposit starting on Day 31 and maturing on Day 60? We assume the deposit and loan are for US$ 1 million and interest is paid on a 360-day basis. Then:

$$\text{Bank pays interest in first period of: } \frac{10}{100} \times \frac{30}{360} \times 1,000,000 = \$8,333.33$$

$$\text{Bank earns interest over lifetime of loan of: } \frac{20}{100} \times \frac{60}{360} \times 1,000,000 = \$33,333.33$$

However, in accordance with Euromarket convention, interest earned on the two-month loan is not paid to the bank until the end of the two months, whereas the bank must pay away interest on the one-month deposit at maturity. So for the second period it not only has to fund its $1 million principal amount but also the US$ 8,333.33 which it has paid away in interest. So the principal amount to be funded in the second period is $1,008,333.33.

11.6.2.   Now we know that the bank has earnings of $33,333.33 over the two months and costs (so far) of $8,333.33. So there is a net $25,000 which is available to pay the interest on our new principal of $1,008,333.33. So to calculate our forward forward interest rate we work the $25,000 as a percentage of the principal and annualize up from our 30-day period to a 360-day period:

$$\text{Forward rate} = 100 \times \frac{360}{30} \times \frac{25000}{1008333.33} = 1200 \times 0.0247933 = 29.75196\%$$

The formula is set out in 11.6.3–9; Figure 11.2 sets it out in words.

Forward-forward rate =

$$\frac{\text{(Long period rate} \times \text{days in long period)} - \text{(Short period rate} \times \text{days in short period)}}{\text{Days left in long period} \times \left[1 + \dfrac{\text{short period rate} \times \text{days in short period}}{100 \times 360} \right]}$$

In our example (11.6.1.) we have

$$\text{Forward rate} = \frac{20 \times 60 - 10 \times 30}{30 \times \left[1 + \dfrac{10 \times 30}{36000} \right]} = 29.75196$$

FIGURE 11.2. Forward Forward Interest Rate Calculation. © JK Walmsley. The Foreign Exchange Handbook.

11.6.3. In order to reduce this to a formula, we set up some definitions. Notice that we have two possible situations: (1) Bank lends long and borrows short. (2) Bank lends short and borrows long. We now set up some definitions:

R_1 = bid rate for shorter, first period
R_2 = bid rate for second period
R_3 = offer rate for first period
R_4 = offer rate for second period
N_1 = number of days in first period
N_2 = number of days in total second period, that is, including first
B = interest basis (usually 360)
P = principal amount
I_1 = interest earned if lending short
I_2 = interest paid if borrowing long
I_3 = interest paid if borrowing short
I_4 = interest earned if lending long
I_5 = interest residual case (2), that is, amount left to be earned in Period 2
I_6 = interest residual case (1), that is, interest we can afford to pay in Period 2

11.6.4. We deal first with case (1) (lend long, borrow short). Interest paid in first period is

$$I_3 = \frac{R_3}{100} \times \frac{N_1}{B} \times P_1$$

Interest earned in total period is

$$I_4 = \frac{R_2}{100} \times \frac{N_2}{B} \times P_1$$

(Notice we assume we lend at the market's bid rate, borrow at the offer.)

11.6.5. Hence interest available to fund our second-period borrowings, I_6, is

$$I_6 = I_4 - I_3 = R_2 \times \frac{N_2}{100} \times \frac{R_1}{B} - \frac{R_3}{100} \times \frac{N_1}{B} \times P_1 = P_1 \frac{(R_2 \times N_2 - R_3 \times N_1)}{100 \times B}$$

11.6.6. Our forward forward interest is calculated by working I_6 back into an annual percentage of the principal (notice that the principal is now $P_1 + I_3$):

$$\text{Forward rate} = \frac{100 \times B \times I_6}{(N_2 - N_1) (P_1 + I_3)} = \frac{P_1(R_2 \times N_2 - R_3 \times N_1)}{(N_2 - N_1) (P_1 + I_3)}$$

11.6.7.   If we set the principal amount equal to unity, the formula simplifies to

$$\text{Forward rate} = \frac{R_2 \times N_2 - R_3 \times N_1}{(N_2 - N_1) (1 + I_3)} = \frac{R_2 \times N_2 - R_3 \times N_1}{(N_2 - N_1)\left(1 + \dfrac{R_3 \times N_1}{100 \times B}\right)}$$

11.6.8.   By a corresponding process we arrive at the rate for the other side:

$$\text{Forward rate} = \frac{R_4 \times N_2 - R_1 \times N_1}{(N_2 - N_1)\left(1 + \dfrac{R_1 \times N_1}{100 \times B}\right)}$$

11.6.9.   It is perhaps worth noting that this formula is widely used in the market, but expressed in different ways, some of which are superficially very different. For example, I have seen the following method:

(1)   Convert the rates into a yearly basis, i.e., multiply the rate by the exact number of days and divide by 360.
(2)   Deduct the nearer factor from the further.
(3)   Divide the difference by the nearer factor plus 100.
(4)   Then multiply by 360 and divide by the number of days in the intervening period.
(5)   Multiply the result by 100.

11.6.10.   This method is equivalent to that set out in 11.4.7., for example, as we can see by following each step.
Step (1) calculates:

$$\frac{R_2 \times N_2}{360} \quad \text{and} \quad \frac{R_3 \times N_1}{360}$$

Steps (2) and (3) calculate:

$$\frac{\dfrac{R_2 \times N_2 - R_3 \times N_1}{360}}{100 + \dfrac{R_3 \times N_1}{360}}$$

and steps (4) and (5) produce:

$$100 \times \frac{360}{N_2 - N_1} \left[\frac{\dfrac{R_2 \times N_2 - R_3 \times N_1}{360}}{100 + \dfrac{R_3 \times N_1}{360}} \right]$$

By canceling out the 360s in the numerator and dividing the bottom bracket by 100 to produce $1 + R_3 \times N_1/360 \times 100$, we can see that the two formulae are identical.

SECTION 7.   CERTIFICATES OF DEPOSIT

11.7.1.   Some years after the birth of the Eurodollar market, the certificate of deposit concept was introduced to it. The CD has since become an important source of funds for banks. The CD was first issued in the U.S. domestic market in 1961 and in the Euromarket in 1966. Essentially, a CD is an instrument (normally negotiable) evidencing a time deposit made with a bank at a fixed rate of interest for a fixed period. CDs bear interest and CD rates are in general quoted on an interest-bearing (rather than a discount) basis (see 11.7.6). Normally interest on a US$ CD is calculated for actual days on a 360-day basis and paid at maturity. But for CDs issued with a maturity over one year, interest is paid annually on the anniversary of the issue in the Euromarket; on domestic U.S. CDs over one year, interest is normally paid semiannually. CDs are also available in sterling, Japanese yen, Hong Kong dollars, United Arab Emirate dirhams, Kuwaiti dinars, SDRs and ECUs.[1] In other countries, notably Germany and Switzerland, central banks have resisted the introduction of CDs. They wished to prevent foreigners from being able to invest in a flexible and negotiable instrument, since this would only compound the problem of reducing inflows of "hot money" into the currency. U.S. dollar CDs have also been issued in Nassau, Singapore, and Hong Kong, as well, of course, as in London.

11.7.2.   Only the sterling and yen CD markets are large, however, and the Japanese CD market is overwhelmingly a domestic one. In most other currency CDs, the markets are narrow and liquidity poor, although a determined effort has been made to promote SDR CDs in London by a group of banks (Barclays Bank International, Chemical Bank, Citibank, Hongkong & Shanghai Banking Corporation, Midland Bank International, National Westminister Bank, and Standard Chartered Bank).

11.7.3.   Sterling CDs are dealt on a basis comparable to that of US$ CDs except that interest is calculated on a 365-day basis. Interest is paid annually on the anniversary of issue for CDs of maturity over one year. Japanese CDs are issued to a specific buyer and registered in his name, so that the transfer must be notarized and the issuing bank advised. They are also potentially subject to withholding tax (depending on the relevant treaty). Both features have limited their attractiveness internationally.

11.7.4.   CDs are available in various types as well as various currencies. The first variation was the floating rate CD (FRCD). These were introduced in 1977. They have maturities, usually, of three to five years. Interest on FRCDs is normally payable semiannually, and is usually linked to six-month LIBOR. Thus the 1977 issue by Sanwa Bank paid ¼% over six-month LIBOR. Other FRCDs have been issued at different margins or at the "mean of bid and offer."[2]

11.7.5. In 1978, the "roll-over CD" (sometimes called the roly-poly) was introduced. Essentially it is a contract to buy a normal six-month CD every six months for a predetermined period, typically three years. For a floating rate roll-over CD, the interest rate is fixed at a margin above six-month LIBOR as with the FRCD. A fixed rate roll-over involves fixing the interest rate at the start of the contract. The roll-over CD is not negotiable in that the investor is contracting to buy CDs in the future and this contract is not a negotiable instrument.[3]

11.7.6. Another innovation is the discount CD. This was introduced early in 1981 in the U.S. domestic market[4] and subsequently in London. Here the CD does not pay a stated rate of interest. Instead, the certificate bears a wording along the following lines: "XYZ Bank certifies that a sum has been deposited with this bank, which together with interest solely in respect of the period to the maturity date will on the maturity date equal U.S. dollars X." The advantage of a discount CD is that its price can immediately be compared with other discount instruments such as Treasury bills. The disadvantage is that it cannot easily be compared with other CDs.

SECTION 8.   CD CALCULATIONS

11.8.1. Let's start by assuming that the life of the CD we are looking at is under one year, so that interest is due at maturity. Suppose we have a 15% CD for $1 million issued with 90 days to maturity. (As it is a US$ CD, it is dealt on a 360-day year.) What is the value at maturity? Clearly it is face value plus interest earned, calculated on a simple interest basis[5]:

$$\text{Maturity value} = 1{,}000{,}000 + 1{,}000{,}000 \times \frac{15}{100} \times \frac{90}{360} = \$1{,}037{,}500 =$$

$$\text{principal} \left[1 + \frac{\text{coupon}}{100} \times \frac{\text{days from issue to maturity}}{360}\right]$$

11.8.2. At any point before maturity this CD will have earned a certain amount of interest already—the "accrued interest." If we are buying a CD on a given day we will want to know the accrued interest, which is given by the following (we suppose we buy the CD on day 30):

$$\text{Accrued interest} = 1{,}000{,}000 \times \frac{15}{100} \times \frac{30}{360} = \$12{,}500 =$$

$$\text{principal} \times \frac{\text{coupon}}{100} \times \frac{\text{days from issue to purchase}}{360}$$

11.8.3. We need to know what price we should be prepared to pay for this CD, assuming that the general level of interest rates is unchanged since it was issued. That is, a 60-day CD will currently also be issued at a coupon of 15%, so we have the choice between buying a new CD or the "secondary" CD which has been outstanding for some time, both yielding a coupon of 15%. We know, from our formula in 11.8.1, that the new CD will at maturity be worth 1,000,-000 $1 + 15/100 \times 60/360 = \$1,025,000$. Clearly the amount we are prepared to pay for the old CD must be such as to produce an equal yield over the 60 days. That is, we must have:

$$\frac{1,037,500}{\text{price for old CD}} = \frac{1,025,000}{1,000,000}$$

for two yields to be equal. Hence clearly:

$$\text{Price for old CD} = 1,000,000 \times \frac{1,037,500}{1,025,000} = 1,012,195.12$$

This price is a little below the face value plus accrued interest so far, which we saw in 11.8.2 to be $1,012,500. The reason is that although interest has accrued, it is not yet payable. The buyer must wait to receive it, and so will require a discount on the price he pays for accrued interest.

11.8.4. Suppose now that the general level of interest rates has changed so that a new 60-day CD pays 10%. Then we know, from 11.8.1, that its value per $1,000,000 at maturity will be $1,016,666.67. We want to know the price that we should pay for an old 90-day 15% CD with 60 days to run. As before, the value of the old CD at maturity is $1,037,500, and as before we calculate the price by dividing the values at maturity into each other:

$$\text{Price} = \frac{\text{value of old CD at maturity}}{\text{value of new CD at maturity}} \times 1,000,000 =$$

$$\frac{1,037,500}{1,016,666.67} \times 1,000,000 = \$1,020,491.80$$

Clearly, what we are doing is bidding up the price of the old CD to the point where the yield when we buy the old CD is equal to the 10% coupon available on a new CD. Because the value of the CD at maturity is a function of the coupon and the days from issue to maturity, as we saw in 11.8.1, we can calculate the price of the old CD in terms of interest rates:

$$\text{Price} =$$

$$\frac{\text{principal}}{\text{amount}} \times \left[\frac{1 + \dfrac{\text{coupon on old CD}}{100} \times \dfrac{\text{days from issue to maturity}}{360}}{1 + \dfrac{\text{coupon on new CD}}{100} \times \dfrac{\text{days from issue to maturity}}{360}} \right]$$

11.8.5. We can apply this to the case when we want to value a CD which we intend to buy in the market. To do this, we have to change the bottom line of the formula: instead of writing "coupon on new CD" we can put "current yield on CD," and instead of using the number of days from issue to maturity we write the number of "days from purchase to maturity." This gives us:

$$\text{Price} = \text{principal amount} \times \left[\cfrac{1 + \cfrac{\text{coupon on CD}}{100} \times \cfrac{\text{days from issue to maturity}}{360}}{1 + \cfrac{\text{yield on CD}}{100} \times \cfrac{\text{days from purchase to maturity}}{360}} \right]$$

11.8.6. It follows from this formula that we can equally well calculate the yield on a CD if we know the price paid. By rewriting the formula above, we find that:

$$\text{Yield} = \left[\cfrac{\text{principal amount} \left(1 + \cfrac{\text{coupon on CD}}{100} \times \cfrac{\text{days from issue to maturity}}{360}\right)}{\text{price}} - 1 \right]$$
$$\times \left[\frac{360 \times 100}{\text{days from purchase to maturity}} \right]$$

This formula can be tested by seeing whether it works for the purchase of a CD on the issue date. In this case the days from issue to maturity equal the days from purchase to maturity and the price equals the principal amount, so that the yield equals the coupon as one would expect.

11.8.7. Let's look now at the case of a trader who thinks that rates are going to come down and so buys a 90-day CD, financing it with a 60-day deposit. The parallel case in the domestic U.S. market would be a CD financed by a term repo. Now clearly the price at which we sell the CD after 60 days must be enough to pay our funding cost; so we know that we must have:

$$\text{resale price} = \text{principal amount} \left[1 + \frac{\text{funding cost}}{100} \times \frac{\text{days held}}{360} \right]$$

Suppose the CD is for $1 million and is funded at 12% for the 60 days that we hold it; then we must have:

$$\text{Price} = 1,000,000 \times \left[1 + \frac{12}{100} \times \frac{60}{360} \right] = \$1,020,000.00$$

But we know from 11.8.6 that we can find the yield on the CD if we know the price which is paid on it, which we have just found; so by plugging the price calculation above into the yield formula of 11.8.6 we can see that we can find the break-even yield at resale:

$$\text{Break-even yield} =$$

$$\left[\frac{1 + \dfrac{\text{coupon}}{100} \times \dfrac{\text{days from issue to maturity}}{360}}{1 + \dfrac{\text{funding cost}}{100} \times \dfrac{\text{days held}}{360}} - 1 \right]$$

$$\times \left[\frac{360 \times 100}{\text{days remaining from sale to maturity}} \right]$$

11.8.8. Let's apply this formula to our 15% 90-day CD, assuming that we buy it on the issue date and we can finance it for 60 days at 12%. What yield can we afford to sell at, and still break even? Our formula says:

$$\text{Break-even yield} = \left[\frac{1 + \dfrac{15}{100} \times \dfrac{90}{360}}{1 + \dfrac{12}{100} \times \dfrac{60}{360}} - 1 \right] \frac{360 \times 100}{30} =$$

$$\left[\frac{1.0375}{1.02} - 1 \right] 1200 = 20.588\%$$

In other words, because we were making 3% profit for 60 days, we can afford to see rates move up a good deal in the secondary market before we make a loss.

11.8.9. If we are buying a CD in the secondary market rather than on the issue date, we have to change the formula. We have to use the yield at which we buy the CD rather than the coupon. The remaining life of the CD is no longer the period from issue to maturity, but the period from purchase to maturity. With these modifications the formula is now:

$$\text{Break-even yield} =$$

$$\left[\frac{1 + \dfrac{\text{yield}}{100} \times \dfrac{\text{days from purchase to maturity}}{360}}{1 + \dfrac{\text{funding cost}}{100} \times \dfrac{\text{days held}}{360}} - 1 \right]$$

$$\times \left[\frac{360 \times 100}{\text{days remaining from sale to maturity}} \right]$$

11.8.10. We have looked at finding out what yield we can afford to sell at in order to break even. The opposite question is: If I know the yield at which I bought the CD, and the yield at which I sold, how much did I make during the holding period? Clearly, the answer in general is that the holding period yield is (sale price − purchase price)/purchase price and it can be expressed as an annual interest rate by grossing it up by 360/holding period. The most general case is going to be that in which we buy a CD in the secondary market and then later resell it. The holding period yield on a CD bought at issue is a special case of this general case where the yield at purchase equals the coupon. We can solve this general problem by taking the formula we have just worked out in 11.8.9 and turning it around. We are not looking for the break-even yield on resale since we already know what we have sold the CD at. We are looking for the holding period yield, which must, if we are to break even, equal our funding cost. So we rewrite our formula and after some manipulation we get:

$$\text{Holding period yield} =$$

$$\left[\frac{1 + \dfrac{\text{yield when bought}}{100} \times \dfrac{\text{days from purchase to maturity}}{360}}{1 + \dfrac{\text{yield when sold}}{100} \times \dfrac{\text{days from sale to maturity}}{360}} \right]$$

$$\times \left[\frac{360}{\text{holding period}} \right]$$

11.8.11.   So far, all our calculations have been for CDs whose maturity was less than one year. Calculations for CDs over one year are much more complex because there are multiple interest payments. In general these calculations can only be done step by step, by "iteration," rather than by using formulae. A microcomputer or programmable calculator is desirable. The problem is the variable number of days involved which can be affected by holidays. Also annual interest payments on CDs in the Euromarket are affected by leap years. Semiannual payments (e.g., in the U.S. domestic market) are affected by the fact that the 365 days of the year are inherently impossible to divide equally into 182.5 days. The effect of holidays is also a complication.

11.8.12.   However, to show the underlying principles, let us assume that we are trading a CD with annual payments in a world with a 365-day year but no holidays and no leap years. Suppose it is a five-year half-million-dollar CD paying 10% interest annually on January 1. Interest is 500,000 × 10/100 × 365/360 = $50,694.44. Suppose we hold the CD for one year and 37 days and wish to know the resale price if we sell at 9%. We proceed as follows: Today's price is the discounted value of future proceeds. We know that at the end of Year 5 we will receive $500,000 plus interest of $50,694.44. We discount this sum back to the end of the fourth year at 9%:

$$\frac{\$550,694.44}{1 + \dfrac{9 \times 365}{100 \times 360}} = \$504,645.53$$

If the CD were sold on Day 1 of Year 5, we would receive this price plus the interest payable on that date. So we must now discount back to the end of Year 3 the total of interest payable plus the price at the end of Year 4:

$$\frac{\$504{,}645.53 + \$50{,}694.44}{1 + \left(\dfrac{9 \times 365}{100 \times 360}\right)} = \frac{\$555{,}339.97}{1.09125} = \$508{,}902.60$$

To this discounted rate at the end of Year 3 must be added the interest payable at that date, and the total must be discounted back to the end of Year 2:

$$\frac{\$508{,}902.60 + \$50{,}694.44}{1 + \left(\dfrac{9 \times 365}{100 \times 360}\right)} = \frac{\$559{,}597.04}{1.09125} = \$512{,}803.70$$

We then take this price and add it to the interest due at that date, making a total of \$563,498.14. We know that, as of Day 37 in Year 2 when we are selling the CD, this is the price we will receive if we hold the CD for another 328 days. So we discount this price over 328 days:

$$\frac{\$563{,}498.14}{1 + \left(\dfrac{9 \times 328}{100 \times 360}\right)} = \$520{,}793.10$$

which is the price we need.

SECTION 9.   OTHER MARKETS

11.9.1.   As a rule Euromarket trading rooms tend to concentrate on clean deposits and CDs. Exchange control, withholding tax, and other considerations tend to limit trading in other instruments. However, for completeness, this section gives an outline of certain domestic markets which are relevant internationally. They are, in the United States, Treasury bills, bankers' acceptances, commercial paper, and the repo market (Fed funds are discussed in Chapter 1); in the United Kingdom, Treasury bills and acceptances; German *Schuldscheindarlehen;* and the Japanese *gen-saki* market. The discussion will be very brief; readers requiring more detail are referred to the Bibliography.

11.9.2.   The U.S. Treasury bill market is the largest and most liquid in the world. A trade of \$50 million presents no particular problem. This makes it an attractive short-term investment vehicle. Also, discount income on Treasury bills of under six months' maturity is exempt from withholding tax. Interest payments on other Treasury securities, for example, notes and bonds, and discount on longer bills, attract withholding tax, although exemption can be obtained in certain cases. Treasury bills are issued in minimum denominations of $10,000. They are in book-entry form. That is, they are held in a computer—it is not possible to take physical delivery. Treasury bills for three and six months are auctioned weekly while one-year bills are auctioned monthly. Prices are calculated on the basis of actual number of days and 30-day months over a 360-day year, on a discount basis (see Section 10 on discount calculations). As well as the cash market, the Treasury bill futures market is very large indeed (see Chapter 15).

11.9.3. After Treasury bills—$245 billion outstanding at the end of 1981— commercial paper is the next important short-term market with $164 billion outstanding at that date. Commercial paper is a promissory note, usually un- secured and issued by a corporation for up to 270 days. (This limitation ensures exemption from SEC registration procedures, though a rating is still needed from an agency.) Typically the maturity is 15 to 35 days. CP is usually issued in multiples of $100,000. Large issuers place their paper directly, using a sales force if necessary. Others issue their paper through dealers. Either way, com- mercial paper is normally the cheapest and most flexible method of short-term corporate financing. CP calculations, like Treasury bills, are on a discount basis.

11.9.4. Bankers' acceptances outstanding at end-December 1981 were rather less than half the CP total, at $69 billion. Acceptances have the major advantage that they do not require the lengthy and expensive rating agency assessment required of CP issuers (since the investor's credit risk on accep- tances is the bank rather than the corporate borrower). A bankers' acceptance is a bill of exchange: an order by the drawer to the drawee (accepting bank) to pay the payee a specific sum of money on a certain date. After the bank has accepted the bill it may hold it or, more typically, sell it in the market. BAs are discounted instruments, traded on an actual days/360-day-year basis (see Sec- tion 10). They are generally in bearer form and normally in any given maturity up to 180 days—usually about 90 days. The market trades in minimum lots of $1 million but more typically $5 million. BAs may be eligible for rediscount at the Fed, or ineligible. The distinction makes little practical difference except that the ineligible market may be a little less liquid, and may cost a little more because a bank selling them incurs a reserve requirement cost.

11.9.5. Repurchase agreements are another large market, at around $80 billion. A repurchase or repo deal is a sale of securities with a commitment to repurchase them at a set date. The rate is an ordinary interest rate (i.e., add-on rather than discount) calculated on actual days/360-day year. So interest is calculated (assuming a discount security, and that sale and repurchase price are equal—the repo is "priced flat"):

$$\text{Interest due} = \begin{pmatrix} \text{principal} \\ \text{amount} \end{pmatrix} \times \begin{pmatrix} \text{repo} \\ \text{rate} \end{pmatrix} \times \frac{\text{(days repo is outstanding)}}{360}$$

The underlying securities are priced so as to give the lender (i.e., the buyer of the security) a margin to protect himself. In some cases the pricing is not flat, but set in terms of a sales price and a repurchase price chosen to give an equivalent yield. In this case of course the RP rate is given by:

$$\text{RP rate} = \left(\frac{\text{repurchase price} - \text{sale price}}{\text{sale price}}\right) \times \frac{360 \times 100}{\text{days RP is outstanding}}$$

and the interest due is then calculated as before. Alternatively, given the repo rate, the repurchase price is found (by simple manipulation of the previous equation) as:

$$\text{Repurchase price} = \text{sale price}\left[1 + \frac{\text{repo rate} \times \text{days outstanding}}{100 \times 360}\right]$$

(This formula can be compared with the Japanese *gen-saki* formula of 11.9.8 to see the impact of a securities sales tax.) If the security is not a discount one, but an interest-bearing one, things are more complex. Assume first that during the repurchase period no interest payment is made. Then all that happens is that both sales price and repurchase price have to be defined to include accrued interest. If, however, interest is paid during the life of the deal, street practice is to pay interest on the security price including accrued interest, until the next coupon date. Then the security is repriced "flat" to exclude accrued interest, and interest is paid on the flat price. Suppose we do a 30-day repo on a security whose price is 102⅜, including 2⅜ accrued interest. Suppose a coupon of 2½ is payable on Day 11. Then on Day 12 the security is repriced to 100. Suppose the repo is done at 10%; then the interest payable is given (if the principal amount were $100):

$$\frac{10 \times 102\tfrac{3}{8} \times 11}{100 \times 360} + \frac{10 \times 100 \times 19}{100 \times 360}$$

and the repurchase price is

$$102\tfrac{3}{8} + \frac{10 \times 102\tfrac{3}{8} \times 11}{100 \times 360} + \frac{10 \times 100 \times 19}{100 \times 360}$$

So the formula is

$$\text{Repurchase price} =$$
$$\text{Sale price} + \frac{\text{repo rate} \times \text{days till coupon} \times \text{sale price}}{100 \times 360} + \frac{\text{repo rate} \times \text{remaining days}}{100 \times 360} \times \text{flat price}$$

Since the collapse of Drysdale Securities, which generated capital by building up accrued interest, attitudes to this type of deal have become a great deal more cautious. But in general, repurchase agreements are attractive because of their flexibility of term; repos can be done, in theory, for any maturity. In practice, the bulk is overnight. Typically the overnight repo rate is below the Fed funds rate, because corporations and other lenders who have no direct access to the Fed funds market are lenders in the overnight repo market.

11.9.6. The main U.K. money market securities available to foreign investors free of withholding tax and in bearer form are—apart from CDs—Treasury bills and commercial bills of exchange (acceptances). Calculations in both cases are the same as those for their U.S. counterparts, except that a 365-day year rather than a 360-day year is used. Both markets are highly liquid. The Treasury bill market has shrunk in recent years as the U.K. government has funded more through National Savings and long-term debt, so that the total outstanding fell from £10.8 billion (say, $24 billion) in 1975 to £2.2 billion (say, $3.9 billion) at the end of 1981. But it remains an easy market to trade in size, as does the acceptance market, which has grown strongly as recent Bank of England policies have underpinned it (see 1.5.11–12). The total outstanding in February 1982 was £10.1 billion (say, $18 billion) and under normal conditions trades of £10 million ($20 million) present no problems, at least in the shorter maturities. For decades the acceptance was used to finance international trade; the "bill on London" was used all over the world. U.K. exchange controls inhibited this after World War II, but the 1979 removal of controls has reopened the market. A syndicated acceptance credit facility of £365 million was arranged for PEMEX in 1981, for example.

11.9.7.　In Germany, exchange controls and administrative policy have traditionally been directed at keeping short-term money market investors out. So the available range of instruments is not wide; Treasury bills are not really viable (see 1.6.6–9). Occasionally, however, Eurotrading rooms invest in *Schuldscheindarlehen* (see 1.6.10 and Table 1.10). These are medium-term and have restricted negotiability, though, so there is not a lot of active trading. They are issued at par and bear interest, which is calculated on a 360-day/360-day-year basis (see 11.1.5). Interest is normally payable annually.

11.9.8.　The main short-term market in Japan that is of interest to Eurotraders is the *gen-saki* market (see 1.8.7–8). This is a repurchase market and the calculations are exactly the same as those for the United States repo market, with two modifications, one being a 365- rather than 360-day basis. The other is required if the investor pays the securities transfer tax (which may be absorbed by his counterparty, but of course the rate will be adjusted to reflect this). The formula for a discount instrument is:

$$\text{Repurchase price} = \text{sale price} \frac{\left(1 + \dfrac{\text{repo rate} \times \text{days outstanding}}{100 \times 360}\right)}{1 - \text{tax rate}}$$

That is, the price has to be grossed up to allow for the tax (currently 0.1% of face value, so the bottom line would be 0.9999). Similarly for the formula allowing for interest payments.

SECTION 10.　DISCOUNT SECURITIES

11.10.1.　Treasury bills, commercial paper, bankers' acceptances, and various other instruments are dealt on a discount basis; and from time to time this applies also to CDs. In cases where local exchange control forbids forward exchange cover on interest payable, it may also be convenient to deal clean deposits on a discount basis. We will set out the calculations as for a bill; they can of course be applied to the other instruments mentioned. We will look at the calculations for price given discount rate; discount rate given price; conversion of interest rate to discount and vice versa; holding period yield; and the forward forward bill rate ("bill parity").

11.10.2. Suppose we have a bill for $1 million which is being discounted at 10% for 90 days using a 360-day year. Then the discount amount is $10/100 \times 90/360 \times 1,000,000 = \$25,000$.

Here it is as a formula:

Discount amount = discount rate/100 × discount period/360 × face value

Clearly the price today is the face value less the discount amount, $975,000 or:

$$\text{Price} = \text{face value} \left[1 - \frac{\text{discount rate}}{100} \times \frac{\text{discount period}}{360} \right]$$

11.10.3. To find the discount rate given the price or the discount amount we manipulate these formulae. If the discount amount is given we turn the first formula above around to get:

$$\text{Discount rate} = \frac{\text{discount amount}}{\text{face value}} \times \frac{360}{\text{discount period}}$$

Conversely, if we are given the price, we turn the second formula around to get:

$$\text{Discount rate} = \left[1 - \frac{\text{price}}{\text{face value}} \right] \times \frac{360}{\text{discount period}}$$

11.10.4. We have been using a discount rate rather than an interest rate. The difference is that a discount rate is applied to the principal at the far end of the deal (the face value); an interest rate is applied to the principal at the near end. In our example the face value is $1,000,000 and the principal at the near end is $975,000; so if we express the discount amount as a percentage of the near end we see that it is not 10% but 10.2564%. The formula for converting a discount rate to an interest rate is:

$$\text{Interest rate} = \frac{360 \times \dfrac{\text{discount rate}}{100}}{360 - \left[\dfrac{\text{discount rate}}{100} \times \text{discount period} \right]}$$

where the interest rate is on a 360-day basis. To make it a 365-day basis we put 365 in the top line. Conversely, to get the discount rate from the interest rate we turn this formula around to get:

$$\text{Discount rate} = \frac{360 \times \dfrac{\text{interest rate}}{100}}{360 + \left[\dfrac{\text{discount rate}}{100} \times \text{discount period}\right]}$$

11.10.5. Sometimes we need the holding period yield on a bill: the return earned by buying a bill and later selling it. Clearly the profit on the deal is sale price − purchase price, and in percentage terms it is:

$$\frac{\text{sale price} - \text{purchase price}}{\text{purchase price}} = \left[\frac{\text{sale price}}{\text{purchase price}} - 1\right]$$

To gross this percentage up to a 365-day interest rate we multiply by 365 divided by the holding period, so our final answer is:

$$\text{Holding period yield} = \left[\frac{\text{sale price}}{\text{purchase price}} - 1\right] \times \frac{365}{\text{holding period}}$$

To put this formula in terms of the yield at the time of sale and the yield at the time of purchase we would work out the sale price and purchase price in terms of yield by using the formula for price in 11.10.2. To put the holding period yield on a 360-day basis, of course we would gross up by 360 rather than 365 in the top line.

11.10.6. We sometimes need to decide between buying a long bill and buying a short bill. In these circumstances we need the forward forward ("bill parity") rate. Say we can buy a six-month bill or two three-month ones. Given the rate on the six-month bill and on the first three-month bill, what must we earn on the second three-month bill to make the two deals equal? We start by assuming that the same principal amount, $1 million, is invested in the six-month bill and the three-month bill. At the maturity of the longer bill we will receive a certain amount (in fact, the face value of the long bill). To break even, this must equal the face value of the later, second short bill. That face value must be equal to the proceeds of the investment in the first short bill (the face value of the first short bill) plus the discount earned on the second short bill. Hence:

$$\text{Discount on second short bill} =$$
$$\text{face value of long bill} - \text{face value of first short bill}$$

To express this as a discount rate we express it as a percentage of the amount at the far end, that is, the face value of the long bill, and to express it as an annual rate we gross it up by 360 (or 365) divided by the length of the second short bill, over which the discount is earned. So we have:

$$\text{Break-even rate} =$$

$$\left[\frac{\text{face value of long bill} - \text{face value of first short bill}}{\text{face value of long bill}} \right]$$

$$\times \left[\frac{360}{\text{days in second short bill}} \right]$$

This formula can be rewritten in terms of discount rates, but it then becomes a little complicated to lay out in words.[6]

SECTION 11.   LENDING OFF THE SWAP

11.11.1.   A bank sometimes needs to lend money using the swap market. This can happen when the currency being lent is not easily obtained directly—for instance, Eurolire or Eurobolivars. Or it can be done simply because it is cheaper—the arbitrage works out that way. Or it can occur indirectly if a corporation is tapping a source of funds in a currency which is not its own. For example, a German corporation might borrow in the U.S. bankers' acceptance market and swap back into deutsche marks. The bank is asked to quote an all-in rate for a deutsche mark loan based on its acceptance.

11.11.2.   In the case of Eurolire and the like, it is a straightforward deposit deal. The formulas of Chapter 10, Section 5 are used, since normally the deal will be done over the spot value date. The second case presents a complication. Settlement in the BA or commercial paper market is done on a same-day value basis. Unless the deal is done very early in the morning in New York, it is impossible to give good value in sterling for that day, because the cutoff for town clearing is 3:00 P.M. in London. And deutsche marks cannot be done at all, since the Frankfurt cutoff is 8:00 A.M. (see Chapter 20 on clearing systems). Hence the dollar proceeds have to be invested overnight (and the German company must fund itself in deutsche marks overnight). If the paper is issued on a Friday, of course, the delay is three days rather than overnight. In order to find the total cost, we need to go through the deal step by step.

11.11.3.   Suppose on Tuesday the German company issues a bankers' acceptance for 30 days for $5 million. The discount rate is 14⅛%. So the dollar proceeds received today are $4,941,145.83. These are invested overnight in the Fed funds market at 14⅜%, so that proceeds plus interest next day amount to

$4,943,118.86. Today (Tuesday) we swap these anticipated proceeds into deutsche marks, value tomorrow, with the swap maturing after 29 days from the start—that is, 30 days from today, to coincide with the maturity of the acceptance. Deutsche marks value tomorrow can be bought, say, at 2.3535 and the 29-day swap over tomorrow is a dollar discount/deutsche mark premium of 100 points, so the outright is 2.3435. So the deutsche mark value tomorrow, of the BA proceeds plus interest from the Fed funds investment, is 4,943,118.86 × 2.3535 = DMK 11,633,630.24. Now these funds will only be received tomorrow. To fund itself in the domestic market the German corporation must borrow overnight deutsche marks. It can borrow up to that amount, which with the interest cost will equal the sum available tomorrow from the acceptance deal. That is, the amount it can borrow today is equal to the deutsche mark proceeds of the acceptance, discounted back one day at the overnight deutsche mark rate (which is, say, 9%). So the amount it borrows is equal to:

$$\frac{11,633,630.24}{1 + \left(\frac{1 \times 9}{100 \times 360}\right)} = 11,630,722.56$$

(We wrote 1 × 9/100 × 360 to make it clear that this is an overnight deal. If the paper were issued on a Friday, the factor would be 3 × 9/100 × 360.)

11.11.4. This sum is the initial deutsche mark borrowing. The deutsche mark repayment value is the amount of deutsche marks required to repay the acceptance: that is, $5 million covered forward at 2.3435, making DMK 11,717,500. So the all-in deutsche mark cost is the difference between this figure and the initial deutsche mark borrowing, grossed up on an annual basis:

$$\frac{11,717,500 - 11,630,722.56}{11,630,722.56} \times \frac{360}{30} \times 100 = 8.9533\%$$

which can then be compared with the cost of raising deutsche marks directly.

SECTION 12.   COMPOUNDING AND INTEREST PAYMENT FREQUENCIES

11.12.1. The powerful effect of compounding of interest is well known. It is especially relevant in certain money market situations. We start by setting out the standard compounding formula in comparison with simple interest. On a simple interest basis, an investment of $1,000 repaid in a year's time together with $100 of interest has yielded 10% (on a 365-day basis). Suppose instead we place the funds in an investment account paying 10% but with interest compounded four times a year. Then the effective annual rate of interest (i°), given the simple rate (i) and the number of compounding periods (n), is given by:

$$i^\circ = \left(1 + \frac{i}{n}\right)^n - 1$$

where the interest rates are in decimal form. So in our case, with $n = 4$ and $i = 0.10$, $i^\circ = 0.1038$ or 10.38% on an annual basis.

11.12.2. But suppose now that we know we shall need the funds in 270 days' time. Then the number of compounding periods is not four, but three. And to compare the investment account with other 270-day investments (e.g., a CD) we should allow for the fact that there will be less benefit from compounding. To do this we should only compound as many periods as we will actually invest, and then gross up, so we use the formula:

$$i^\circ = \left[\left(1 + \frac{i}{n}\right)^{n\prime} - 1\right] \frac{365}{t}$$

where $n\prime$ = number of compounding periods during the investment period, and t = days in the investment period.

11.12.3. On this basis we can see that the 10% investment account offers an "annual yield over the 270-day period" of 10.2486%, say, 10¼%. So although if the funds were left in the account for a year we would get 10.38% p.a., the loss of a compounding date reduces the available yield; if we were offered a 270-day CD instead at 10.3% this would be a better bet than the account, even though the latter's effective annual rate is 10.38%—because that effective rate relies on a compounding date from which we shall never benefit.

11.12.4. Subject to this exception, of course, the more the compounding periods, the higher the effective annual yield. If an investment at 10% is compounded daily over 365 days, the effective annual rate is 10.52%. In fact, the effect tends to fall off with the number of compounding periods, as we can see from the following:

Number of Compounding Periods per Annum	Effective Rate
1	10
2	10.25
3	10.33
4	10.38
6	10.43
12	10.47
52	10.51
365	10.52

11.12.5. These compounding formulae only work if the interest rate remains constant. In our example, the investor was certain to get 10% on the investment account over the year. But usually we are not certain what we will earn when we come to invest the interest we receive. The only instrument on which the reinvestment rate on the interest is certain is one on which no interest is earned—a discount instrument which only pays interest at maturity. In the money market this will typically be a Treasury bill, commercial paper, or a bankers' acceptance. In the bond market, it is the zero-coupon bond.

SECTION 13.   NONSTANDARD AMORTIZATIONS

11.13.1. By definition we cannot cover every nonstandard loan funding problem here. But this section aims to show ways of thinking about funding an unusual loan. The normal Euroloan is a straightforward roll-over facility, and this presents no particular funding problems arising from amortization. All that happens is that the amount drawn at each roll-over date declines in line with the amortization schedule.

11.13.2. The most common nonstandard facility that a Eurobank is asked to provide arises in connection with a lease or mortgage. The bank may be asked to quote a fixed-rate loan to fund a borrowing which is repaid by equal installments. That is, the fixed payment is mainly interest in the early years, shifting toward being mainly repayment of principal in later years.

11.13.3. For simplicity's sake we will look at a three-year deal. Suppose the initial principal amount is $10 million. There is an annual payment (or "rental") in arrears. At what rate should this be charged? We assume that the bank matches its position on the deal. Suppose one-year money is 10%, two-year, 12%, and three-year 15%. We realize at once that we cannot work out our average funding cost over the three years without knowing how much we have to fund for each year. We cannot work that out without knowing the interest rate. So first of all we have to guess at the rate. Say it is 12%. Then we work out the amortization schedule. We get an annual payment of $4,175,-419.19. In Year 1 the interest amount is $1,216,666.67, while the principal repaid is $2,958,752.52; in Year 2, $856,685.11 and $3,318,734.08 respectively; and in Year 3, $472,905.80 and $3,722,513.39 respectively. So we have to fund about $3.7 million for three years, $3.3 million for two years, and $2.95 million for one year.

11.13.4. A weighted average for the three years, therefore, will be a shade higher, say 12⅛%. (Strictly, we ought to allow for interest-on-interest at this point. With an upward-sloping yield curve we should benefit, since our early interest earnings are above the cost of funds, but if the yield curve slopes downward, we would have to fund initial losses. But this requires a fairly elaborate computer program.) With our new weighted average rate, we go back and rework the amortization schedule. The payment now comes out at $4,184,497.37. If the yield curve were steeply sloping the revised amortization schedule might mean we would have to rework the average rate. In our case this does not apply. But the whole process can be laborious and does need a computer or programmable calculator.

11.13.5. Let's look at another more complex deal. A construction company needs finance on a mortgage basis (i.e., fixed rate, fixed annual payments which comprise decreasing interest amounts and increasing principal repayments, as in our last example). No repayments will be made for the first 2¼ years—the interest will be rolled up, or debited to the loan. Thereafter payment is in 10 annual payments. The loan is denominated in Swiss francs, but on draw-down the proceeds are converted into U.S. dollars. The exchange rate used for the spot conversion is also used to convert the annual repayments, which are made in dollars. Finally, the borrower requires a fixed dollar amount, so the size of the Swiss franc loan varies with the exchange rate.

11.13.6. So on top of the calculations in our previous example the bank must work out what exchange rate to apply to the whole loan and must also allow for the initial rolling-up of interest. The latter is straightforward as one simply calculates the principal outstanding at the interest date, charges interest accordingly, and adds it to the principal. The former is a little trickier, since we need really to take a weighted average rate. But the weighting depends in part on the size of the loan, which depends in part on the exchange rate. Once again, it is a matter of trial and error, or a computer program.

11.13.7. As I said at the beginning, one cannot possibly cover all the possible nonstandard amortization schedules that a Eurobank might have to fund. But I hope that these two examples have suggested some points to watch for. The main problems are compounding and interest-on-interest, together with proper weighting of any fixed-rate loan rate calculated from multiple funding periods.

NOTES

1. See *Mitsubishi Trust Report*, September 1979, "Introduction of Yen Negotiable CDs"; R. Urquhart, "Investing Surplus Cash in Hong Kong," *The Treasurer*, September 1981; R.C.B. Smith, "A Fledgling CD Market is Hatched," *Euromoney*, April 1980; R. Barry, "The ABC of FRN's and CD's in the Gulf," *Middle East Economic Digest*, August 1981.
2. See M. S. Dobbs-Higginson, *CSFB Investment Manual*, Credit Suisse First Boston, London, 1980, p. 59.
3. "The New Roly-Poly," *Euromoney*, London, November 1978.
4. See for example "Why Discount CD's are so appealing," *Business Week*, March 30, 1981.
5. This section draws heavily on M. Stigum, *Money Market Calculations*, Homewood, Ill.: Dow-Jones Irwin, 1981.
6. For details, see M. Stigum, *Money Market Calculations*.

12

SHORT DATES

In this chapter we look at the special features of deals done for value before spot. In particular we explain why for outright deals before spot the swap rate is *reversed*.

SECTION 1. DEFINITIONS

12.1.1. A short date forward or deposit rate is normally defined as one which is for a maturity shorter than one month. A stricter definition would be for up to one week; and an even stricter definition would include only rates before spot. However, the normal use is for rates up to one month.

12.1.2. We saw (Chapter 8) that under normal circumstances the spot date for exchange and deposit deals is two working days forward. This allows some dealing for value before spot; that is, value today or value tomorrow. These deals are normally tightly constrained by time factors. Deals done value today are only really possible for currencies whose time zone is substantially behind that in which the deal is being struck. For example, it is possible to deal dollar/sterling in London for value today, because the five- or six-hour delay between London and New York gives time to get the instructions processed in New York. But dollar/yen in New York cannot really be dealt value today because there will be no chance to get the deal processed in Tokyo, which has closed by the time New York opens for business.

12.1.3.   Subject to these constraints, therefore, it is possible to deal for value before spot for certain currencies in certain countries. Given that normally there are two days between today and spot, this gives us two margins: that from today until tomorrow (overnight or O/N) and that from tomorrow until the next business day (tomorrow/next, tom/next, or T/N). These margins parallel the deposit rates for the same period.

12.1.4.   The tom/next swap is the rate at which a currency can be bought or sold against the next business day, which is also the spot date. If a deal were maturing value tomorrow, and it had to be rolled over to the next day, the tom/next adjustment would be used to calculate the new rate. The tom/next market is, as is the deposit market, a bit less affected by time zone constraints than the overnight market. But it still tends to dry up during the course of the morning. Its importance lies in the fact that it is used to roll over a spot position (hence in the United States it is often referred to as "the roll-over") since it is the last business day before spot.

SECTION 2.   USING SHORT DATE SWAPS

12.2.1.   Short date swaps work just like any other swaps. The only difference comes when we use them to calculate outright rates before spot. Suppose we have a US$/DMK spot rate of DMK 2.2535/40. Suppose we have a swap rate from Wednesday to Thursday of 11/5. Suppose spot is Wednesday and we want Thursday's rate. This is a perfectly normal forward, so we have spot DMK 2.2535/40 and forward 11/5, making Thursday's rate DMK 2.2524/35 (remembering high/low = subtract). Notice that the spread has gone up from five points to eleven points. The spread on the outright equals the spread on the spot plus the spread on the forward.

12.2.2.   But suppose now that our spot rate of DMK 2.2535/40 is actually for Thursday. We want Wednesday's rate—a rate before spot. Our forward margins have to be worked *backward* in time to a date before spot. One's first thought is: To go from Wednesday to Thursday, we subtracted 11/5. So to come back from Thursday to Wednesday we should *add* 11/5. What happens? We get DMK 2.2546/45. Our spread has gone negative; our selling rate is higher than our buying. Clearly something is wrong.

12.2.3.   Let's look at this another way. We know that the forward margin of five points from Wednesday to Thursday is the bank's—and the market's—rate for buying DMK and selling US$. Suppose on Wednesday we want to buy DMK for value Wednesday and sell them for value Thursday. We have to sell DMK to the market at the market's *buying* rate for DMKs, that is, five points. Since the deutsche mark is at a premium, the dollar at a discount, we will earn five points. If we deal the opposite way around—sell DMK for value

Wednesday and buy them for value Thursday—it will cost us eleven points.

12.2.4. Now let's look again at our spot for Thursday, which is DMK 2.2535/40. The market sells DMK value Thursday at 2.2535. At what rate will a bank sell value Wednesday? It has to cover its Wednesday position by buying DMK for value Wednesday (so that it can sell them to its customer). So—as always in a forward—it will deal value spot and then swap to its desired date, in this case Wednesday. So it buys DMK value Thursday at 2.2535 from the market. Then in the swap market it buys DMK for value Wednesday, selling them off again on Thursday to square up its spot position. But we saw just now that it earns five points by doing this. So it can sell DMK value Wednesday at five points better than value Thursday; that is, 2.2540. Conversely, we saw that if it dealt the opposite way round, that is, bought DMKs value Wednesday, it would cost the bank 11 points to do the swap. So it has to add this to Thursday's buying rate of 2.2540, making 2.2551 its buying rate for Wednesday.

12.2.5. In other words, *when dealing outright before spot the margin must be turned around.* To go from Thursday's DMK 2.2535/40 to Wednesday we don't add 11/5—we add 5/11, to get Wednesday's DMK 2.2540/51. If you stop to think about it, it does make sense, because this is a "backward" margin, not a "forward." We are going backward in time from the spot rate. The rule is: Overnight and tom/next go backward, not forward, so you must turn them around to get the outright. But once again, *this applies only to outrights.* It is only then that you work backward from spot. If you are swapping from tomorrow to the next day, you are going forward, so you don't turn the rates around. It's only when you want to use the tom/next to bring a rate back from spot to tomorrow that you turn it around; not when you are doing a swap from tomorrow to spot. The second case is a perfectly ordinary forward.

12.2.6. Let's now look at a short date cross rate. Suppose we need a £STG/DMK tom/next margin. We have the following rates:

Spot US$/DMK	2.0510/15	Spot £STG/US$	2.2512/17
Tom/next	5/4		3/2

We reverse the two margins and apply them to the spot rates to get outright value tomorrow:

US$/DMK	2.0514/20	£STG/US$	2.2514/20

We then calculate the relevant cross-rates:

Value tomorrow:	4.6185/4.6211	Spot 4.6172/94	

This gives a margin from tomorrow to spot (i.e., tom/next) of 13/17, which must be reversed again to 17/13. Inspection confirms that this is correct, since 17/13 shows that the DMK spot is at a premium over tomorrow. This is true, since the selling rate value tomorrow at 4.6185 is higher than the spot of 4.6172, and similarly on the buying side. In fact, the mechanics of the calculation are exactly the same as those for any other cross forward calculation. The only difference is the need to reverse the margins before starting the calculation, and then to reverse them back again after completion.

SECTION 3.   OTHER SHORT DATES

12.3.1.   Another short date rate which is commonly quoted is the spot/next rate. This is used for swapping from spot value to the next business day. It is often needed in working out cross rate adjustments; see Chapter 13, Section 3. Of course, like other short date rates for value *after spot*, there is no question of turning the spot/next margin round in calculations. It is an ordinary forward.

12.3.2.   Other short dates often quoted include the one-week, two-week, and less frequently, three-week swap rates. (Of course, for all short dates after spot, there is no question of reversing the swap.) For rates between these dates one tends to calculate a rate on a pro rata basis. We take the rates for the standard periods before and after the date in question, and work out the daily average margin between these two dates. But short date rates are very heavily affected by special factors, most notably month-end dates, reserve asset "makeup dates," tax payment dates, or other days when reporting requirements or liquidity factors have a distorting impact. In this case the rate has to be worked out exactly from interest rates (see Chapter 10, Section 5). For example, since the end-of-month ("ultimo") Swiss franc deposit market is not uncommonly bid 100% or more for a day or two, it would be wrong to work out a swap rate on a pro rata basis if it included the ultimo date (see Chapter 10 and Chapter 13).

SECTION 4.   SWAPPING OUT A POSITION IN THE SHORT DATES

12.4.1.   The short date market is widely used for swapping out a position. Let's look at an example. We believe that the deutsche mark will be weaker in three months' time than today. We could sell outright forward DMKs in the three months' date. But we feel this is too risky. Accordingly, we do a swap; we buy spot deutsche marks (say DMK 1 million) and simultaneously sell the same amount forward in the three-month period. We are now overbought for value spot, and oversold for value three months hence. Unless further action is taken, the DMK 1 million that are due to arrive on our account two days hence, on spot date, will remain there, earning no interest, until the forward sale matures, when they will be paid away to our counterparty.

12.4.2. Hence we have two alternative courses of action. We can either lend the money out from the spot date to the three-month date, or we can ensure that the money does not arrive on our account on the spot date, by selling it off in the short date market. In other words, we buy and sell in the tom/next market (hence the tom/next is often called the roll-over in the United States). The sequence of actions looks like this:

	Sell	Buy
Tomorrow	—	DMK 1 million
Spot	DMK 1 million	DMK 1 million
Three months	DMK 1 million	

12.4.3. Essentially this operation amounts to lending the deutsche marks out day-to-day through the swap. We are undertaking a long-term forward liability and covering it on a day-to-day basis in the tom/next market. By contrast an outright forward sale in the three-month period would be completely uncovered. We have now shifted our position nearer in time so that it is less risky. If we want to go oversold on an outright basis we can now sell off our DMK 1 million which are due to arrive on the account tomorrow, knowing that funds will come into the account from our tom/next swap, which itself has squared off our three-month swap. The risk is much closer and more easily controllable. On the other hand, swapping a position out day-to-day means writing a lot of tickets if we run the position for a while, so there is an extra cost here. And the compounding factor also has to be considered. In this case it would work in our favor, but if we were selling a discount currency it would work against.

13

ADJUSTMENTS

In this chapter we explain how to adjust forward quotes for a nonstandard date. Then we show how to adjust cross prices for the effects of a holiday in one country. Next we show how to allow for payment today, and how to adjust a deposit quote for withholding tax and reserve requirements. Finally we show how to price the negotiation of a check.

SECTION 1. NONSTANDARD RUNS

13.1.1. A helpful way of approaching this topic is to break the swap margin down into individual days. Suppose today is April 8, spot 10th, and we are looking at a one-month US$/DMK swap from April 10 to May 10—a 30-day period. Suppose the swap is 105/90. Then we can say, crudely, that "the days are running at 3½/3"—that is, the daily average margin is the total margin in the period divided by the number of days. In order to get a swap from April 10 to May 9—a run of 29 days—we would reduce the swap by 3½/3, making it 101½/87.

13.1.2.   Equally, we might want to adjust this run by bringing its start date forward a day as well, to April 9. Suppose that the tom/next (see Section 12.1.4) is also running at 3½/3; then we would add this on to the margin to bring it back to 105/90. On the other hand, if the short date market were very tight, for instance, by reason of the U.S. Federal funds rate being very high, the tom/next rate might be 10/7, in which case we would adjust the run of April 10/May 9 at 101½/87 by adding on 10/7 to make the run April 9/May 9 a total of 111½/94.

13.1.3.   This case serves to show that the forward margin need not be the total of a uniform daily average rate of 3½/3 as we started by assuming. It might be that our original one-month swap of 105/90 concealed the fact that each week the Wednesday/Thursday swap premium was typically lower than other days. Suppose there were a weekly reporting procedure in Germany which induced banks to bid for deutsche marks value Wednesday to sell back Thursday. (This doesn't happen, but it does every month-end in Switzerland. And the classic example of this used to be Thursday/Friday dollars because of the New York Clearing House funds system.) Then our weekly swap might look like this:

Monday/Tuesday	3/2½
Tuesday/Wednesday	3/2½
Wednesday/Thursday	5/6
Thursday/Friday	3/2½
Friday/Monday	9/7½ (i.e., three "normal" days: Friday/Saturday, Saturday/Sunday, Sunday/Monday)

13.1.4.   So the way to adjust a standard forward run to a nonstandard one is to find the number of days' adjustment required at the start and end of the standard run. Then find the daily swap rate for those days (making allowance for special factors). Then add or subtract those individual margins from the standard rate.

SECTION 2.   NONSTANDARD FORWARD RUNS; EXAMPLES

13.2.1.   The following example is essentially a forward forward transaction (see Chapter 10), and indeed this applies in a sense to any calculation where we seek forward margins over a date different from spot.

13.2.2.   A customer has a forward contract maturing with a bank for value the day after spot. He wants to extend it, say for a month. Suppose that last month he sold the bank HFL for July 18; today is July 15, spot the 17th. He wants to extend to August 17 (today's one-month date). We have the following rates:

HFL/US$	2.3220/30	(Value July 17)
Spot/next	5/3	(July 17/18)
One month	85/75	(July 17–August 17)

13.2.3.   Assuming that we are renewing the contract at current market rates (see 10.9.5), the bank sells the HFL back to the customer at 2.3215 (2.3220–0.0005) for value July 18. The bank now needs to know the swap from July 18 to August 17. To do this it deducts the spot/next (July 17/18) from the one month (July 17/August 17) to give a margin of 80/72. So the bank pays the customer a further premium of 72 points for the swap from July 18 to August 17.

13.2.4.   Let's look now at the case where a customer has sold deutsche marks forward to his bank for value March 31 at 2.0120. Today is March 11, spot is March 13. His accounts people say that the deutsche marks will not be paid to him until April 17. As he prefers always to hedge his deutsche mark receivables immediately, he wants to change the maturity date of the existing contract at once. He therefore asks the bank to quote him a rate to adjust the maturity from March 31 to April 17.

13.2.5.   Suppose the rates are as follows:

Spot	2.0230/40	(March 13)
One month	110/100	(April 13)
Two months	200/180	(May 13)

We find the swap from March 13 to 31 on a pro rata basis (18 days out of 31) as 64/58; and we work out the swap from March 13 to April 17 as 122/110. We do this interpolating between the one- and two-month swap margins on a pro rata basis, to get 12/10 as the swap from April 13 to April 17 (4/30ths of 200 − 110 and 180 − 100) and adding the result to the one-month margin (see Section 10.11.1). So the swap margin from March 31 to April 17 is 58/52 (i.e., 122/110 minus 64/58). As the bank has already bought these deutsche marks from the customer, it will make a new swap over March 31 (the choice of spot rate on which the contract is to be based being determined according to 10.9.5.); it will sell back value March 31, and buy forward value April 17, paying a further premium of 52 points to the customer.

13.2.6.   A very common case is when we want a set of standard periods over spot and over tomorrow. We have the following rates for the Hong Kong dollar:

HK$/US$	5.0510/20 spot	(September 23)
	5/par tom/next	(September 22/23)
	130/120 one month	(September 23–October 23)
	5/2	(October 22/23)
	270/250 two months	(September 23–November 23)
	6/3	(November 22/23)

We need to find one and two months over tomorrow. Our quote for value to-morrow is 5.0510/25 (remembering that we reverse the tom/next). Our one-month quotation is 130/120 less the adjustment at the far end, of 5/2, plus the adjustment at the near end of 5/par, making 130/118. Our two-month quota-tion is 270/250 less the far end adjustment of 6/3, plus the near end 5/par, making 269/247. So we have:

HK$/US$	value September 22	5.0510/25
One month	Sep. 22–Oct. 22	130/118
Two months	Sep. 22–Nov. 22	269/247

SECTION 3.   HOLIDAYS

13.3.1.   These principles have to be used when the effect of holidays has to be taken into account in cross-rates. Suppose we are looking at a FFR/DMK cross-rate calculation. Today is April 6, and the US$/FFR rate is being quoted spot April 8. But the US$/DMK rate is being quoted spot the 9th, as the 8th is a holiday in Germany. We see from the rules of Chapter 8, Section 2, that the FFR/DMK spot date will be the 9th. So we must adjust the US$/FFR rate, in order to make it appropriate for the 9th, before working out the cross-rate. We therefore have to find the rate for the US$/FFR swap for the 8th against the 9th—which is of course the spot/next swap rate—and apply it to the FFR spot. Suppose we have the following rates:

FFR/US$ spot (8th):5.0210/20   DMK/US$ spot (9th): 2.0815/25
             spot/next (8th/9th): 15/10

We calculate the outright rate for FFR/US$ value the 9th as 5.0195/5.0210 (5.0210−0.0015: 5.0220−0.0010). We then find the cross-rate for value April 9 by dividing 5.0195 by 2.0825 to get a selling rate for FFR/DMK of 2.4103; Similarly we have 5.0210 divided by 2.0815 for a buying rate of 2.4122 FFR per DMK, value April 9.

13.3.2.   Equally, if in the above case it had been France which had been on holiday on the 8th, the DMK/US$ rate would have required adjustment. The rule, therefore, is: *Adjust the currency of the country which is not on holiday, until we get to the first date when both countries are working.*

13.3.3. A parallel procedure has to be applied in the case of the forward margins. Suppose we are again considering FFR/DMK rates, and this time today is May 7, spot May 9 for both currencies. We are considering a one-month deal, which would normally be June 9, but for the fact that France is on holiday that day. We therefore have:

FFR/US$	DMK/US$
5.0335/45 (value May 9)	2.0780/90 (value May 9)
120/100 (May 9–June 10)	300/290 (May 9/June 9)
	10/9 (June 9/June 10)

We adjust the DMK forward by adding on 10/9 to give us 310/299 for the period May 9 to June 10, giving us a cross of 2.4211/2.4228 and forward margins of 295/318.

13.3.4. The following situation would require some care. We are dealing £/¥ and today is February 25:

£STG/US$	1.7070/80	(February 28)
	30/40	(February 28–March 31)
¥/US$	211.50/60	(February 27)
	100/90	(February 27–March 27)

The United Kingdom is on holiday on February 27, and Japan is on holiday March 31. Notice that because the United Kingdom's spot is dealing for the end of the month, the forward rate is also (see Section 9.7.4). However, the Japanese forward is not: and because Japan is on holiday on March 31, the cross forward should theoretically be rolled into April—but this would contradict the over-month-end rule of 9.7.5. So the cross forward must be dealt for March 30, which means the sterling/dollar forward must be brought backward to March 30 by adjusting for the rate for March 30/31. And the yen must be rolled forward from March 27 by adjusting by the rate for March 27/30. Also, we must adjust the spot yen to February 28. Thus, we have, say:

£STG/US$	1.7070/80	(February 28)
	30/40	(February 28–March 31)
	2/3	(March 30–31)
¥/US$	211.50/60	(February 27)
	10/5	(February 27–28)
	100/90	(February 27–March 27)
	5/4	(March 27–30)

13.3.5. We proceed first to sort out the spot calculation, for February 28. This is a matter of adjusting the yen rate to 211.40/55 for value February 28. Next we find forward margins for the two currencies for the period February 28 to March 30. We start by adjusting the sterling rate to end on March 30 by removing the rate for the 30th to the 31st of March; thus the sterling forward margin becomes 28/37 for the period February 28–March 30. Turning now to the yen, we need a forward for the period February 28–March 30. Notice that the original margin was February 27–March 27. We start therefore by adjusting this to run over February 28 by removing the rate for February 27/28, that is, 10/5. This gives us a rate of 90/85 for February 28–March 27. We must then add in the rate at the far end, to extend the margin from March 27 to March 30: adding in the 5/4 quoted for that period gives us a forward rate of 95/89 for the period of February 28–March 30, so we now have:

£STG/US$	1.7070/80	(February 28)
	28/37	(February 28–March 30)
¥/US$	211.40/55	(February 28)
	95/89	(February 28–March 30)

Bearing in mind that the pound is quoted indirect so that we multiply (see 8.6.5.), we have:

£STG/¥   360.85/361.33 value February 28
          103/74   margin for March 30 over February 28

13.3.6.   Fortunately we don't often have to deal with such complex cases in practice. The complexity, though, arises simply from the number of adjustments required—and, in the instance given, the need to be on the alert for the value-date rules—rather than any intrinsic difficulty in the calculation.

13.3.7.   The formula required may be set out as follows:

M = cross margin required to be calculated
S_1 = spot rate for first currency, unadjusted
S_2 = spot rate for second currency, unadjusted
F_1 = forward rate for first currency, unadjusted
F_2 = forward rate for second currency, unadjusted
A = spot adjustment for first currency
B = spot adjustment for second currency ⎫ any or all of which
C = forward adjustment for first currency ⎬   may be zero
D = forward adjustment for second currency ⎭
$$M = [(S_1 - A) \times (S_2 - B)] - [((S_1 - A) - (F_1 - A + C)) \times ((S_2 - B) - (F_2 - B + D))]$$

In words, margin = adjusted spot for first × adjusted second spot − (adjusted first spot − adjusted first margin) × (adjusted second spot − adjusted second margin). This formula is set out in full to match the steps taken above in 13.3.5. (Of course, for two direct currencies, we would divide rather than multiply.) However, there is a shortcut in the right-hand brackets. Where we are calculating the cross outright forward, the spot adjustments are made both to the spot rate and to the forward rate. So they cancel each other out. This is equivalent to saying that we could have proceeded as follows: Calculate adjusted spot cross sterling/yen as before; adjust sterling forward as before; take unadjusted spot yen, and apply to it the forward margin adjusted only for the period March 27–30; that is, instead of applying a margin of 95/89 to 211.40/55 we apply 105/94 to 211.50/60. The end result is the same, and this shortcut method is perfectly acceptable, providing we understand why it is correct: The spot adjustment "washes out" because it is applied to both the spot and, in the opposite direction, the forward. Hence the shortcut formula is:

$$M = [(S_1 - A) \times (S_2 - B)] - [(S_1 - F_1 - C) \times (S_2 - F_2 - D)]$$

In words, margin = adjusted first spot times adjusted second spot minus (unadjusted first outright minus first forward adjustment) times (unadjusted second outright minus second forward adjustment).

SECTION 4. PAYMENT TODAY

13.4.1.   Depending on time zone, it is sometimes possible to deal for value today, with good value being given on both sides of the deal today. For instance, if at 11:00 A.M. London time a company sells a bank in London U.S. dollars, against payment of sterling, it is possible for both these payments to be made for value that day, as the London clearing does not close until 2:30 and there is a five-hour delay permitting the payment of U.S. dollars on the same day. However, if the same company sold the bank deutsche marks, good value in deutsche marks could not be given for value that day, as the Frankfurt clearing closes at 8:00 A.M. for value that day. The bank would be able to pay its customer sterling, but would not receive the deutsche marks until the next day.

13.4.2.   The practice in these circumstances would be for the bank to allow for the fact that it is "out of funds" overnight, until the deutsche marks arrive on its account in Frankfurt. Because it is left short of sterling, the bank will charge its sterling lending rate; the lending rate will be worked back into its DMK/£ rate to reflect its costs. This is a special case of the formula we worked out in Chapter 10, Section 6 for working out swaps from two deposit rates. In this case the deutsche mark rate overnight is zero, because the bank does not have the use of the money. So our original formula:

$$F = S \left[\frac{1 + \dfrac{R_2 \times N}{B_2 \times 100}}{1 + \dfrac{R_1 \times N}{B_1 \times 100}} - 1 \right]$$

simplifies to:

$$F = S \left[\frac{R_2 \times N}{B_2 \times 100} \right]$$

because the bottom line simplifies to one, as $R_1 = 0$. The rate to which the "forward" adjustment F is being applied is not the spot rate S, but the rate for tomorrow, call it T. So we can write:

$$\text{Adjustment} = T \times \frac{N}{365} \times \frac{R}{100}$$

where

T = rate for value tomorrow

N = number of days that the bank is "out of funds"—normally one, but three at weekends, etc.

R = lending rate for sterling overnight (or three days, etc.)

SECTION 5. EFFECT OF WITHHOLDING TAX, RESERVE REQUIREMENTS

13.5.1. The bulk of the text in this book which is concerned with rates, arbitrage calculations, and the like assumes that the interest rates used are "net accessible interest rates." The word "net" implies "net of all withholding tax and other tax adjustments, and net of all reserve requirement costs"; while the word "accessible" means "generally available to the international market," that is, taking into account the effects if any of exchange control regulations. Sometimes we must adjust for these factors.

13.5.2. The impact of a withholding tax can be summarized in the following formula:

$$\text{Adjustment} = 100 \times \frac{a}{100} \times \frac{b}{100} \times \frac{c}{12} \times \frac{d}{100}$$

where

a = interest rate charged on the loan made by the bank to the borrower whose country imposes withholding tax

b = rate of withholding tax

c = number of months between deduction of withholding tax by the borrower's country and the date tax is repaid to the bank

d = bank's domestic currency interest rate for the period

13.5.3. To take an example, suppose a U.K. bank lends at 10% for one year in June 1981 to a Swiss borrower who is required to deduct withholding tax on the loan at 35%. Swiss withholding tax is repaid at the end of the calendar year for which it is deducted, so the bank is out of funds on the withheld portion for six months (from June 1982 when the interest is paid and tax deducted till January 1983 when the tax is repaid). Suppose that the interest rate (forward forward) for June 1982 to December 1982 is today 13%. Then the adjustment needed is:

$$100 \times \frac{10}{100} \times \frac{35}{100} \times \frac{6}{12} \times \frac{13}{100} = 0.2275\%$$

13.5.4. Another adjustment is needed in domestic dealing to allow for the cost of reserve requirements. In the United States, for instance, loans tend to be made at prime which allows for reserve costs: but on the bid side, when taking funds by the issue of CDs, it may be necessary to adjust the bid rate for reserve costs. In the United Kingdom, domestic sterling loans to a nonbank are often made at LIBOR plus a margin plus reserve asset cost. The formula is complicated by the fact that there may be several kinds of reserve assets, some of which yield interest while others do not. The general formula is:

$$\text{Adjustment} = \frac{A_1 R_1 + A_2 (R_1 - R_2) + A_3 (R_1 - R_3) + \ldots + A_N (R_1 - R_N)}{100 - (A_1 + A_2 + \ldots + A_N)}$$

where

$A_1 =$ amount required to be held interest free (if not permitted to be netted against liabilities—see 13.5.6)

$A_2 =$ amount required to be held at first rate of interest

$A_3 =$ amount required to be held at second rate of interest

$A_N =$ amount required to be held at Nth rate of interest

$R_1 =$ interest rate the bank can earn on liquid assets (say, three-month deposit rate)

$R_2 =$ rate received on A_2

$R_N =$ rate received on A_N

13.5.5. In the U.S. case the formula simplifies to $A_1 R_1/100\text{-}A_1$ since there is only one class of reserve asset, namely balances at the Federal Reserve. Often dealers quote the all-in rate which of course is:

$$R_1 + \frac{A_1 R_1}{1 - A_1} = \frac{R_1 - A_1 R_1 + A_1 R_1}{1 - A_1} = \frac{R_1}{1 - A_1}$$

Hence if a bank issues a CD at 12% with a 3% reserve requirement, the adjustment is 0.371; the all-in cost is 12.371%. In the United Kingdom and other countries there are several classes of reserve asset, some of which bear interest. A suitable U.K. formula for reserve asset costs might be:

$$\text{Adjustment} = \frac{A_1 \, R_1 + A_2 \, (R_1 - R_2) + A_3 \, (R_1 - R_3)}{100 - (A_1 + A_3)}$$

where

A_1 = interest-free balances held at Bank of England

A_2 = secured deposits required to be held with the discount market

A_3 = amount of special deposits (if any) called for by the Bank of England

R_1 = three-month sterling interbank offered rate (i.e., the rate on lendings forgone)

R_2 = interest earned on deposits with the discount market

R_3 = interest earned on special deposits

Suppose $A_1 = 0.5\%$, $A_2 = 6\%$, and $A_3 = 2\%$, $R_1 = 12\%$, $R_2 = 10\%$, and $R_3 = 8\%$. Then:

$$\text{Adjustment} = \frac{0.5 \times 12 + 6(12 - 10) + 2(12 - 8)}{100 - (6 + 2)} = \frac{6 + 12 + 8}{92} = 0.28\%$$

13.5.6.   Notice that in the denominator (bottom line) of this formula, A_2 is not included. The reason is that reserve assets are required by the Bank of England to be held against net eligible liabilities. Secured deposits with the discount market are allowed to be netted off before calculating eligible liabilities, which does not apply to interest-free balances or Special Deposits at the Bank. If we think for a moment we see that the bottom line of the formula measures the total amount of assets the bank can use to earn enough to cover the cost of its reserves. If required interest-free balances at the Bank rise, say, to 2½% from ½%, the bank has 2% fewer interest-earning assets. But if the secured deposits requirement rises by 2% to 8%, the bank can raise 2% more eligible liabilities and lend them out in the market, because it can net off the extra 2% of discount market deposits before working out its required reserves. So the general formula of 13.5.4. has to be applied carefully as regards netting of reserve assets against liabilities.

SECTION 6.   NEGOTIATION

13.6.1.   A bank will often buy, or negotiate, a foreign currency check from one of its customers. The check will then be sent to the country in which it is payable for clearance. For example, a bookseller may sell books by post to a

Japanese customer, and receive in return a check drawn on a bank in Tokyo, expressed in Japanese yen. He will sell the check to his bank in exchange for his domestic currency, say dollars; the bank will then send the check to its Tokyo branch or correspondent, who will present it to the Japanese bank for payment.

13.6.2. The bank's foreign exchange rate for this transaction has to reflect—as in the similar case of payment today in 14.4.1—the fact that it pays away funds to its domestic customer before being credited with the Japanese yen. The length of time involved in such a transaction depends both on the distance between the bank and the overseas center—Tokyo in this case—and on the efficiency of the domestic clearing system in the overseas center. Hence the foreign exchange rate applied to the transaction must reflect the cost to the bank of being out of funds for the relevant period of time; the adjustment will depend on prevailing interest rates and on the number of days involved.

13.6.3. The formula to be applied is that used in 13.4.2. Examples of typical check negotiation loadings (which will vary according to interest rates and the countries involved) and the number of days allowed for, are:

Country	Loadings (in Units of Currency)	Number of Days
Holland	0.0130	7
West Germany	0.0115	7
Spain	0.80	12
Australia	0.0050	7

14

ARTIFICIAL CURRENCY UNITS

In this chapter we explain what an artificial currency unit is. Then we look at the two most important, the SDR and the ECU, and some other units. Then we look at the EEC's green currencies, and at the concept of a trade-weighted exchange rate.

SECTION 1.   DEFINITION

14.1.1.   Artificial currency units can be split into three main types. These are standardized units used in international monetary cooperation; units of account used in multinational agreements; and "currency cocktails" consisting of units created out of a number of national currencies.

14.1.2. Standardized units with the aim of helping international transfers have included the gold franc of the Latin Monetary Union (see 14.4.10) which nominally existed among Belgium, France, Greece, Italy, and Switzerland between 1865 and 1921, and the CFA franc of the Communaute Financiere Africaine (see 4.3.1). However, they have been generally rare.

14.1.3. Units of account have been widely adopted for the purpose of international agreements. Examples include the accounts of the BIS (see 3.3.1) which have been kept in "Swiss gold francs" since 1930; the Telecommunication Convention of 1932 (which adopted the gold franc of the Latin Union as its unit of account); the Convention for the Unification of Certain Rules Regarding Air Transport, 1929 (which adopted the so-called Poincare gold franc—see 14.4.10); and the EEC unit of account (which was defined as equal to the then gold equivalent of one U.S. dollar). This last has now been phased out in favor of the ECU (see 14.3.1). Their chief aim was normally to help the bookkeeping of a multinational organization such as the BIS or EEC, or (as in the case of the air transport convention) to lay down international standards of value for payments.

14.1.4. Currency cocktails have generally had a slightly different purpose, namely to protect borrowers or lenders from the effects of currency fluctuations. Hence they are primarily a post-1945 phenomenon. The first such cocktail was the European Unit of Account (see 14.4.9), which was launched in 1961 with a bond issue for SACOR of Portugal. However, this original version of the EUA was essentially a currency option; the investor had the option of taking payment in one of the 17 currencies of members of the European Payments Union.

14.1.5. Currency baskets consist of an average of a number of currencies. The first basket was the Eurco (see 14.4.6), but the concept was effectively launched by the IMF when in June 1974 it revalued its Special Drawing Rights (see 14.2.1) by setting one SDR equal to the sum of specified amounts of selected currencies. As these currencies fluctuated, so the value of the SDR fluctuated. In 1975 the EEC followed suit by setting up a new European Unit of Account, which in 1979 was superseded by the European Currency Unit.

SECTION 2.   SPECIAL DRAWING RIGHTS

14.2.1. The nature of the SDR is twofold: It constitutes an international reserve asset and also an international unit of account. The SDR was created by the First Amendment to the IMF's Articles of Association. This created a Special Drawing Account at the IMF. Member states were issued with Special Drawing Rights, permitting them to obtain convertible currencies from the Special Drawing Account under certain circumstances. Only member states, and certain designated official institutions, may at present legally hold SDRs (see 14.2.7). During 1970 the first tranche of SDR allocations was made, in three annual installments, totalling SDR 9,500 million approximately; allocations were made according to member states' quotas at the IMF. The valuation of the SDR at this time was defined in terms of the gold value of one U.S. dollar.

14.2.2.   However, in 1971 the U.S. dollar was devalued. The SDR did not devalue, and its value was set at SDR 1 = US$ 1.08571. Following the second dollar devaluation of February 1973, its value was set at SDR 1 = US$ 1.20635. The IMF recognized the arrival of a floating exchange rate system and on July 1, 1974 introduced a new SDR, consisting of 16 units of currency, whose values were added together to produce the value of one SDR. This was the so-called standard basket. (See Appendix 3 for a discussion of the mathematics of currency baskets.) The amounts were chosen to reflect the relative importance in world trade of the currencies involved, and were set so that the value on July 1, 1974 of the new and the old SDR was US$ 1.20635. The method used was to determine the percentage share of the basket to be held by each currency. These percentages are converted into units of currency on the base date. These then constitute the basket.

14.2.3.   The composition of the SDR basket was revised effective July 1, 1978. It was announced that this basket would be revised at five-year intervals. However, effective January 1, 1981 the IMF announced a new, simplified basket for the SDR consisting of:

Currency	Amount
US$	0.54
DMK	0.46
£STG	0.0710
FFR	0.74
¥	34

14.2.4.   The valuation method for the SDR may be illustrated as follows. We will calculate the value of the SDR against the US$ for convenience's sake; then, to express the SDR against any other currency, we would simply take the exchange rate in the market for that currency against the US$ and calculate the cross-rate against the SDR as if it were a normal exchange rate. We assume that there are no holiday complications.

14.2.5.   The calculation, therefore, is as follows: suppose we have the following exchange rates: DMK 2.0950/60 per US$; FFR 5.0750/60; ¥

211.20/30; £STG 1 = US$ 2.1540/50. Then our calculation is (using middle rates for convenience):

$$SDR\ 1 = US\$\ 0.54 +$$
$$\frac{0.46}{2.0955} + 0.0710 \times 2.1545 + \frac{0.74}{5.0755} + \frac{34}{211.25} = US\$\ 1.2192$$

In other words, the SDR is the total dollar value of the "bits" of national currency in the basket. To find the interest rate we would take a weighted average. Suppose we have US$, one month, 11%; DMKs, 6.5%; FFR, 12.5%; ¥, 6.5% and STG, 12%. Then we take the weights, which are each currency as a percentage of the US$ value of the SDR; so the dollar's weight is 0.54/1.2192 = 44.3% and the DMKs weight is 0.46/2.0955 × 1/1.2192 = 18.0%, and so on, to get SDR rate = 0.54/1.2192 × 11 + 0.46/2.0955 × 1/1.2192 × 6.5 + 0.0710 × 2.1545/1.2192 × 12 + 0.74/5.0755 × 1/1.2192 × 12.5 + 34/211.25 × 1/1.2192 × 6.5 = 9.90%.

14.2.6.   As we said in 14.2.1, private institutions may not legally hold SDRs, although they may deal in instruments linked to the value of the SDR (see 14.2.7). IMF member states, and certain designated official institutions, which include the BIS, the Swiss National Bank, the World Bank, the International Development Association, the Andean Reserve Fund, the Arab Monetary Fund, the East Caribbean Currency Authority, the International Fund for Agricultural Development, and the Nordic Investment Bank, are allowed to hold SDRs. The BIS itself has taken deposits denominated in SDRs from the IMF: these represented part of the profits derived from the sale of the IMF's gold, and were deposited pending their disbursement as loans to low-income developing countries. Official holders of SDRs are also permitted to use SDRs to obtain convertible currencies via the fund's Special Drawing Account and to transfer SDRs among themselves in settlement of financial obligations. They may use SDRs in loans, and in the provision of security for the performance of financial obligations, by means of either a pledge of SDRs or an agreement for transfer and retransfer of SDRs. In 1979, they were allowed to make SDR swaps among themselves, and to trade in forward SDRs. The IMF must be notified of such deals as it handles the bookkeeping for the transaction.[1]

14.2.7.   These changes have been introduced by the IMF as part of its plans to make the SDR more widely used in international finance; the simplification of the basket to five currencies was also a part of this process. Accordingly, private institutions have become more involved in the SDR market (although in point of fact, this should be referred to as "the market for currency instruments index-linked to the SDR" since the banks cannot legally own SDRs). For example, since 1975, and particularly since the introduction of the simplified basket in 1981, a market in deposits linked to the SDR has existed.

14.2.8.   The mechanics are as follows: A company wanting to make an SDR-linked deposit would deposit, say, US$ with a bank. These would be valued in terms of SDRs at a specified exchange rate, either a rate quoted by the bank, or the official IMF rate. On maturity of the deposit, the US$ equivalent of the SDR deposit would be calculated and repaid to the customer together with interest.

14.2.9.   Suppose the customer asks the bank for a three-month SDR price for SDR 1 million; payment to be made in US$. The bank has the following rates:

US$/DMK	2.2525/35	US$	three-month bid	14¼
¥	226.50/60	DMK	three-month bid	9½
FFR	5.9810/30	¥	three-month bid	6⅛
£STG	1.8110/20	FFR	three-month bid	15½
		£STG	three-month bid	13½

First, using the method of 14.2.5, the bank works out the spot rate for SDRs, that is, SDR 1 = US$ 1.1467. Then it works out the interest rate by taking a weighted average as in 14.2.5 to get 12.398%, say, 12⅜%. An alternative method is to work out the three-month forward SDR (in the same way as the spot, but using outrights). Then the forward margin can be used, combined with the US$ rate, to "manufacture" the SDR rate just as for any currency, by using the formula of Figure 10.6. (Many banks quote the SDR rate:

$$= \left[\left(1 + \left(\frac{E \times D}{360} + 100\right)\right) \times \frac{S}{F} - 1\right] \times \frac{360}{D}$$

where

D = number of days
E = Eurodollar offered rate
S = spot SDR
F = forward SDR

It can be shown that this equates to the formula of Figure 10.6.)

Incidentally it is worth noting that holidays can cause complications in SDR value dates (and even more so in ECU dates) as the market has to be open in all five currencies. It would be possible to have the following situation. On Tuesday, June 16:

	16	17	18	19	20 (Sat.)	21 (Sun.)	22	23	24
DMK					x	x	x		
FFR		x			x	x			
¥				x	x	x			
£STG			x		x	x			

where x indicates a holiday. In that case a deal done 16th is for spot 24th.

14.2.10. The company wishes to deposit SDR 1 million; it pays US$ 1,146,700 to the bank, which records that it owes the customer the US$ equivalent of SDR 1 million. The term of the deposit is three months (90 days) and the rate of interest 12⅜%. The SDR (and the ECU) are dealt on a 360-day basis. Then the interest rate due is the dollar equivalent of SDR 35476.03, and at maturity the bank must repay the dollar equivalent of SDR 1,035,476.03; of the exchange rate at maturity is SDR 1 = US$ 1.2565/75, the dollar amount will be US$ 1,301,075.63. From the customer's point of view, the operation is exactly the same as that of buying any other currency; instead of making a DMK deposit, he is making one in SDRs. The advantage to him is simply that the SDR, being a composite of five currencies, will probably be more stable than any one individual currency. Movements in its components will probably tend to offset one another. However, the story is not quite so simple for the bank, as it has to hedge its SDR risk and is unable to do so directly, unless it can find a borrower of SDRs. It will have to swap the dollars it receives into the component currencies of the SDR; so each SDR deal involves at least four exchange swap and deposit deals.

14.2.11. Another fairly long-standing SDR-based market has been in the Eurobond market, where certain borrowers, particularly from Scandinavia, have on occasions issued bonds whose repayment value is linked to the SDR. The first such issue was made by Alusuisse in 1975. The first Eurocurrency credit with a tranche denominated in SDRs was made on behalf of the Kingdom of Sweden in 1981. These markets, however, are beyond our scope.

14.2.12. The first CD denominated in SDRs was issued by Chemical Bank in June 1980, and in January 1981 a group of seven banks in London announced that they would issue and trade in secondary SDR CDs (see 11.7.1). The participating banks were Barclays Bank International, Chemical Bank, Citibank, Hongkong and Shanghai Bank, Midland Bank, National Westminster Bank, and Standard Chartered Bank.

14.2.13. A clearing system for SDR-linked deposits has been established by Morgan Guaranty's Brussels branch, along the lines of the Euroclear bond clearing organization managed by the same firm. The accounts involved are maintained in Brussels on a memorandum basis only, and have their counterpart in deposits in any one of the countries where a component currency of the SDR is the lawful currency. Thus they are subject in principle to Belgian law and to the law of the country where the counterpart deposit is located.

14.2.14. This arrangement shows some of the problems which may arise from SDR-linked deposits. Another problem is the possibility of a change in the composition of the SDR; this has already happened three times in seven years. Normal arrangements in the SDR market are that if this happens, existing deposits would be valued on maturity on the basis of the SDR composition existing when the deposit was placed. Subsequent renewals would take place on the basis of the new basket.

14.2.15.   The SDR-linked market is still developing, and conditions are not so standardized as in other markets; accordingly they may vary widely as a result of negotiation between the parties.

SECTION 3.   EUROPEAN CURRENCY UNIT

14.3.1.   The European Currency Unit has its origin in the EEC Unit of Account, which was created under the Treaty of Rome for the purpose of providing a unit of account for EEC institutions. It was then defined as equal to 0.88867088 grams of 0.9 fine gold, the official par value of the U.S. dollar. Following successive devaluations of the U.S. dollar the emergence of floating currencies, and the creation of the SDR basket concept (see 14.2.2), the EEC decided to introduce a basket unit of account for its own accounting. This was known as the European Unit of Account (not to be confused with the earlier, private European Unit of Account—see Section 4). It was defined as equal to the sum of the following amounts: FBC 3.66 + LuxFr 0.14 + HFL 0.286 + DKR 0.217 + DMK 0.828 + LIT 109 + FFR 1.15 + £STG 0.0885 + IEP 0.00759. The EUA was introduced first in 1975 in respect of the Lome Convention on development aid, and the European Investment Bank's balance sheet. It was subsequently introduced in respect of the European Coal and Steel Community's operational budget (1976), the General Budget of the European Communities (1978), and custom matters (1979).[2]

14.3.2.   The European Currency Unit was created in 1979 with a value identical to that of the European Unit of Account, and an identical composition (but with a revision clause permitting changes, unlike the EUA). It took over all the existing functions of the EUA and was also introduced as the unit of account for the European Monetary System (see 4.2.1), where it took over from the European Monetary Unit of Account, a slightly different unit of account used for the bookkeeping of the European Monetary Cooperation Fund previously. Under the European Monetary System, EEC members' currencies are linked to a central rate defined in terms of the ECU. (See Appendix 3 on the mathematics of currency basket parities.)

14.3.3.   As in the case of the SDR, private traders are not at present legally able to hold ECUs, which are cleared through the European Monetary Cooperation Fund as the SDR is cleared through the IMF. However, as in the case of the SDR, private institutions are able to trade deposits whose value is linked to that of the ECU. The calculations are similar in principle to those for the SDR. Such a market has developed only in a limited way in comparison to that for the SDR, which has wider international attractions. However, an ECU CD

was issued by Lloyds Bank in early 1981 and a number of bond issues denominated in ECU have been made. Also in July 1981 the Credit National
of France raised a Eurocredit of ECU 200 million as part of a larger loan,
and issued ECU notes of three months' maturity in August 1981. In November 1982 a group of banks announced plans to set up an ECU clearing system.

SECTION 4.   OTHER CURRENCY UNITS

14.4.1.   A very wide range of other currency units have been devised on
various occasions for various purposes. They include: Arab dinar, Arcru, Asian
Monetary Unit, Barclays B-Unit, Eurco, European Currency Unit (private,
non-EEC version also known as the European Monetary Unit), European Unit
of Account, Gold francs, and Islamic dinars.

14.4.2.   The Arab Accounting Dinar is used in the accounts of the Arab
Monetary Fund. It is equivalent to three SDRs.[3]

14.4.3.   The Arcru is a privately developed currency unit (Arcru stands for
Arab Currency Related Unit). Its value is linked to twelve Arab currencies: Al-
gerian dinar, Bahrain dinar, Egyptian pound, Iraqi dinar, Kuwaiti dinar, Leba-
nese pound, Libyan dinar, Oman rial, Qatar rial, Saudi Arabian rial, Syrian
pound, and UAE dirham. To value the Arcru on any given date, the two currencies among the twelve that had proved the strongest since the base date of
June 28, 1974 and the two weakest would be eliminated, and an average taken
of the change in value against the dollar of the remaining eight currencies.
This average movement since the base date, expressed in U.S. dollars, provides
the new value of the Arcru. Note that this concept differs from the SDR and
ECU not only in dropping certain component currencies but also in the fact
that it is calculated in terms of an index based on average percentage changes,
rather than fixed amounts of currencies.[4]

14.4.4.   The Asian Monetary Unit is used in the Asian Clearing Union which
settles payments imbalances among Bangladesh, Burma, India, Iran, Nepal,
Pakistan, and Sri Lanka. Its value is defined as equal to that of one SDR.[5]

14.4.5.   The Barclays B-Unit was developed by Barclays Bank International
to facilitate international trade and is defined as the sum of £STG 1, DMK 6.0,
US$ 2.40, FFR 11.5, and SFR 7.00.[6]

14.4.6.   The Eurco or European Composite Unit was introduced in 1973 in
a loan to the European Investment Bank. It was defined as the sum of DMK
0.9, FFR 1.2, HFL 0.35, FBC 4.5, DKR 0.2, LIT 80, IEP 0.005, ,STG 0.075, and
LuxFr 0.5. In this issue interest was payable in the currency chosen by the

borrower, while principal was repayable in the currency chosen by the lender.[7]

14.4.7.   The European Currency Unit in its private form was introduced in 1970. It sets up fixed exchange rates among the currencies of the six member states of the EEC at that time (e.g., ECU 1 = DMK 3.2225). Thus in effect it set up a currency option arrangement rather than a true unit of account. Since the investor could ask for repayment of principal in the strongest of the six currencies, the concept was very attractive to lenders, but less so to borrowers. It was also used under the title European Monetary Unit.[8]

14.4.8.   The European Monetary Unit of Account was used in the book-keeping of the European Monetary Cooperation Fund before the introduction of the European Currency Unit. One EMUA was defined as equal to DMK 3.21978, FBC 48.6572, DKR 7.57831, FFR 5.55419, and HFL 3.35507. It was designed to guarantee the exchange value of outstanding balances in the fund.[9]

14.4.9.   The European Unit of Account, in its private version, was introduced in 1961 for a bond issue by the Portuguese company SACOR. The initial formula (which was changed subsequently in various ways for various issues) was that the EUA was set equal to the then gold value of the U.S. dollar, 0.88867088 grams of fine gold. The bond contract defined 17 reference currencies (those of the members of the then European Payments Union), whose currencies in turn had gold par values. Thus the cross rates among the 17 reference currencies were determined by their gold par values. The EUA's gold value would only change if (1) all reference currencies had changed in the same direction; and (2) at least two-thirds had changed in the same direction. These complex rules ensured that no change in the EUA's gold value took place between 1961 and 1971 when the U.S. dollar devalued against gold. The EUA was then linked to the EMUA (see 14.4.8) and then, following the launch of the European Currency Unit (see 14.3.1), to the latter unit. The EUA was set equal to ECU 1.1972258. This value of the EUA in terms of the ECU will remain constant until (1) all currencies of the ECU which are in the EMS (at the time of writing, all the EEC currencies other than sterling and the Greek drachma) change their central rates (par values) against the ECU; and (2) a majority of such changes are in one direction. If both these conditions are satisfied, the value of the EUA to the ECU will be changed in the same direction as the majority have changed, to the extent of the smallest percentage change of this majority group. Detailed provisions have also been made in bond issues using the EUA in the event of reference currencies not having clearly defined values and so forth.[10]

14.4.10.   Gold francs have been used as units of account for many years, and a number of different varieties exist. Perhaps the first was that of the Latin Monetary Union which linked certain European countries between 1865 and

1921. This gold franc was subsequently adopted as the basis for the Telecommunication Convention of 1932. Its value was defined as 10/31 of a gram of gold 0.900 fine. A second gold franc, known also as the Poincare franc, was used in the Convention for the Unification of Certain Rules Regarding Air Transport of 1929 and related conventions; it was defined as equal to 65½ milligrams of gold 0.900 fine. (This was replaced by the SDR under the Montreal Protocol of 1975.) The statutes of the Bank for International Settlements provide that the authorized capital of the bank shall be 500 million Swiss gold francs, equivalent to 145,161,280.32 grams fine gold; and the annual accounts of the BIS are maintained in these gold francs.[11]

SECTION 5.   GREEN CURRENCIES

14.5.1.   Reference is occasionally made to "Green" currencies. These are the notional rates of exchange used by the EEC in the management of its Common Agricultural Policy. As such, they cannot be dealt in directly. However, they do impinge on the foreign exchange operations of corporations involved in EEC agriculture.

14.5.2.   In 1962 the EEC issued its Regulation 129/62 setting up a unit of account for agricultural purposes. Its value was declared equal to 0.88867088 grams of fine gold—equivalent to US$ 1 at the time (see 15.3.1). This gave rates of exchange ("Green rates") of u.a.1 = DMK 4.0 = FFR 4.93706, for example. Hence, when the EEC set a price of u.a. 212.30 per ton for white sugar, this was equivalent to DMK 849.20 and FFR 1048.14.

14.5.3.   However, in 1969 the French franc devalued, changing its parity against gold so that its value against the unit of account moved to FFR 5.55419. This would have resulted in a rise in the price of white sugar to 212.30 × 5.55419 = 1179.15, a rise of 12.6%—which would have been paralleled in all other agricultural commodities. The inflationary effects of this were unacceptable to the French government, which arranged to postpone the devaluation of the Green rate.

14.5.4.   This meant, however, that white sugar sold in France still for FFR 1048.14: if exported to Germany, the French exporter would receive DM 849.20, for which his bank would give him FFR 1179.15. So it was necessary to prevent cheap French exports from swamping the German market. The EEC decided to place a tax on French exports to the rest of the EEC, and to subsidize French imports from the EEC. These taxes and subsidies were referred to as Monetary Compensatory Amounts, or MCAs.

14.5.5.   The move to floating exchange rates during 1971 through 1973 forced the EEC to move toward a corresponding system of floating MCAs to offset exchange rate movements. This came in a series of regulations of which the most notable were 974/71, providing for variable MCAs, and 509/73, providing for a weekly variation in MCAs to cope with the floating of sterling. By this stage telegrams from the EEC Commission to member states, setting out new MCAs, averaged 40 to 50 feet in length.

14.5.6.   In order to simplify matters, a new system was devised in June 1973 (Regulation 1463/74). The unit of account on which the system depended was no longer linked to the U.S. dollar but to the central rates of the "joint float" currencies of the EEC (see 4.2.2). This meant that for member currencies, MCAs were fixed provided central rates were unchanged, even if the joint float varied against the dollar. For nonmember currencies, such as sterling, variable MCAs continued in force.

14.5.7.   Following the entry into force of the European Monetary System (see Chapter 4) on March 12, 1979, the unit of account laid down for calculating agricultural prices was the ECU. The EEC wanted to maintain the common level of prices. So it was decided that the price levels in old units of account would be multiplied by an adjustment coefficient. This factor came to 1.208953.

14.5.8.   Summing up crudely, we can say that Green rate of exchange + MCA = market rate of exchange. It follows that, since firms actually trade in market rates of exchange on a daily basis, and MCAs are (at present) fixed on the basis of average rates of exchange during the previous week, there is some scope for profitable activity by firms able to forecast the likely level of the MCA.[12]

SECTION 6.   CALCULATION OF TRADE-WEIGHTED EXCHANGE RATES (EFFECTIVE EXCHANGE RATES)

14.6.1.   While not strictly an artificial currency unit, the calculation of a trade-weighted index for a currency is related to the concept and so is included here. Before the advent of floating rates, a devaluation or revaluation of a currency occurred against all other currencies simultaneously. A 5% revaluation of the deutsche mark against the U.S. dollar implied a 5% revaluation against the French franc, and so on. With the advent of floating rates, however, the impact of a 5% revaluation against the U.S. dollar coupled with a 2½% devaluation against the Swiss franc is not clear-cut. Hence attempts were made to take account of the average change of a currency against all others.

14.6.2.   Clearly a 20% depreciation of the Argentine peso against the deutsche mark is less important to Germany than a 10% depreciation of the French franc, since France is a much more important trading partner for Germany than Argentina. So the various currencies' changes need to be weighted by taking account of the share of a country's trade held by a partner currency.

14.6.3. Such a trade-weighted index may be called a "simple average" trade weighted index. Suppose we have four countries, A, B, C, and D. Suppose we are constructing a trade-weighted index for A and that A's exports and imports are conducted with B, C, and D in the following proportions: B, 50%; C, 30%; D, 20%. Suppose in Period 1 we have the following exchange rates for one unit of A's currency against the others: A $1 = B\ 2 = C\ 2.5 = D\ 3$. Suppose in Period 2 A revalues against B by 10%, devalues against C by 20%, and revalues against D by 15%. Then we can weight the percentage changes and add them: $+ 10\% \times 0.5 - 20\% \times 0.3 + 15\% \times 0.2$. The weighted change is 2%: so if we express the index for Period 1 as 100, that for Period 2 is 102.

14.6.4. However, this simple index takes no account of the effects of the exchange rate on changes in third-country trade. Thus, because A has devalued against C by 20%, it is now able to encroach on C's trade with B, and so on. To take full account of these effects requires a matrix of cross-elasticities in international trade, and this is the approach adopted by the IMF in its Multilateral Exchange Rate Model and by the U.K. Treasury in its index for sterling.[13]

14.6.5. The exact method of calculation is complex and varies from country to country. A widely used index is that calculated by Morgan Guaranty Trust Co. of New York which is a geometric index of exchange rates weighted by proportions of trade.[14] Morgan also calculates a "real" effective exchange rate. This makes an adjustment to take account of inflation to attain the "real" effective exchange rate. Suppose that taking 1977 as a base, the U.S. dollar has appreciated in effective terms from 100 to 107.5. Suppose that inflation over this period has been 22.5%: the "inflation-adjusted" or "real" effective index will total 130. The Japanese yen may have appreciated in effective terms over the same period by 12%, but if inflation in Japan over that period has been only 15%, the real effective exchange rate index will have risen only to 127. A difficulty in interpretation here is the choice of correct index to apply: export prices, domestic retail prices, or wholesale prices, for example. The inflation-adjusted index produced by Morgan Guaranty uses wholesale prices of nonfood manufacturers.[15]

SECTION 7. OTHER CURRENCY BASKETS

14.7.1. Many countries peg their currencies to a notional basket of currencies weighted in accordance with their pattern of trade. Usually this basket's makeup is not disclosed; but by looking at trade patterns, and the way the authorities react to rate changes, a fairly good estimate can be made.

14.7.2. For example, an article in August 1981[16] published estimates of the Australian currency basket's weighting of which the main items were:

US$	0.4019
¥	0.2299
£STG	0.0758
DMK	0.0486
NZ$	0.0404
Other	0.2034
Total	1.0000

14.7.3. The index, expressed in terms of May 1970 = 100, stood at 89.7 on May 7, 1981, for example. If the authorities had decided to push the Australian dollar up, they might announce on the following day that the index was 89.8 and intervene against the U.S. dollar as needed to maintain this level.

NOTES

1. See J. J. Polak, "The SDR as a Basket of Currencies," *IMF Staff Papers*, December 1979. An excellent survey of legal developments can be had from J. Gold, *SDRs, Currencies and Gold*, IMF Pamphlet no. 36, Washington, D.C., 1981 (and earlier pamphlets 19, 22, 26, and 33). For a more cynical view, see J. S. Carroll, "A Dollar is a Rose is an SDR," *Euromoney*, London, August 1981.

2. See, for example, International Bureau of Fiscal Documentation, "Further Changes in the Units of Account," *European Taxation*, 1979; and J. Gold, *Floating Currencies, Gold and SDRs*, IMF Pamphlet no. 19, Washington, D.C., 1976, pp. 40–45.

3. See J. Gold, ibid., p. 58.

4. See the September 1974 and July 1975 issues of *Euromoney*, London.

5. J. Aschheim and Y. S. Park, "Artificial Currency Units," *Princeton Essays in International Finance* no. 114, 1976.

6. *Currency Cocktails*, Barclays Bank International, London 1974.

7. J. Gold, *Floating Currencies, Gold and SDRs*, IMF Pamphlet no. 19, Washington D.C., 1976, pp. 40–45.

8. See Aschheim and Park, "Artificial Currency Units."

9. *Deutsche Bundesbank Monthly Report*, January 1976, March 1979.

10. *The European Unit of Account*, Kredietbank, Brussels, 1967. See also *Investment Manual*, Credit Suisse First Boston Ltd., London, 1980.

11. See F. A. Mann *The Legal Aspects of Money*, Clarendon Press, Oxford, 1971, and J. Gold, *Floating Currencies, Gold and SDRs*, IMF Pamphlet no. 19.

12. The MCA system is well described in R. W. Irving and H. C. Fearn, *Green Money and the Common Agricultural Policy*, Wye College, University of London, 1975.

13. See R. R. Rhomberg, "Indices of Effective Exchange Rates," *IMF Staff Papers*, Washington, D.C., March 1976.

14. See *World Financial Markets*, Morgan Guaranty Trust Co. of New York, August 1976.

15. *World Financial Markets*, May 1978.

16. B. Hilliard, "How the Australian Currency Basket Works," *Euromoney*, London, June 1981.

PART **3**

RELATED
ACTIVITIES

15

FINANCIAL FUTURES

In this chapter we look at how the markets for financial futures work and why they have grown so fast. Then we look at key contracts: Treasury bills and bonds, foreign currencies, CDs, and Eurodollars. Then we explain hedging, cross hedging and weighted hedging, and we look at the leverage effect on futures contracts. Next we look at straddles and spreads and then at the key concepts of basis, cheapness, and the strip yield curve. Then we explain the interpretation of open interest and volume. Finally we touch on regulatory and accounting issues.

SECTION 1.   OVERVIEW

15.1.1.   No market is more difficult to assess dispassionately than that for financial futures. It generates a great deal of "hype." The enquirer is met not with facts but with glossy brochures. Most of them use terms which mean nothing to banks or most corporations. Books on the subject are usually written by people from one exchange, and convey the impression that no other exchange has contributed anything to the industry; if not, they tend to have titles like *How to Make a Million in Financial Futures*.

15.1.2.   But clearly financial futures are here to stay, so traders need to know about them. Also, they are growing fast. The CBOT Treasury bond contract was introduced in August 1977. Trading turnover was US$ 3.2 billion in that year. In 1981, trading volume was $1,391 billion. One cannot deny that that market has been one of the fastest-growing markets on earth in the last few years; but one cannot help wondering if this speed of development will bring problems. Still, a market with that turnover obviously makes for good trading, so it is worth looking in more depth at financial futures. To begin with, we need to define a futures contract (cf. Chapter 9, Section 1).

15.1.3.   It is a standardized agreement made and traded on an exchange that is licensed to serve as a trading arena in specific futures contracts. Whereas forward contracts in foreign exchange or money markets are normally specifically negotiated with a view to making delivery, delivery is rare with futures contracts. Instead, most buyers of futures will close out the position before the contract matures by making an offsetting sale or purchase. The major differences between futures and forward contracts are summarized in Figure 15.1.

	Forward	Futures
Size of contract	Negotiable	Standard
Delivery date	Negotiable	Standard
Deal method	Private, usually telephone	Usually open outcry on market floor
Commissions	Negotiable	Flat rate for small deals; otherwise negotiable
Security	Credit risk assessed case by case	Margin required
Clearing	Direct settlement with counterpart	With clearing corporation
Regulation	Self-regulated or by central banks	In U.S., by Commodity Futures Trading Commission
Delivery	Over 90% delivery rate	Less than 1% delivery
Price fluctuations	No limit	Daily limit set by exchange
Liquidity	Provided by banks, corporations	Provided by banks, corporations and individuals
Leverage	Nil	Very high

FIGURE 15.1. Comparison of Futures and Forward Markets.

15.1.4. The development of financial futures is recent. The International Monetary Market in Chicago opened futures trading in seven foreign currencies in May 1972. In December 1974, the IMM and other major U.S. futures exchanges started trading in gold futures contracts. In April 1975, regulation of financial futures came under the authority of the Commodity Futures Trading Commission. (This had been created in 1974 by Congress following a wave of concern over regulation of the commodity markets, which previously had been largely self-regulated.) In October 1975, the Chicago Board of Trade introduced its GNMA mortgage-backed certificate futures contract. This was followed by the IMM's introduction in January 1976 of its 91-day Treasury bill contract. In August, 1977 the CBOT introduced futures contracts based on U.S. Treasury bonds, followed in September 1977 by 90-day commercial paper, and in September 1978 by a second version of the GNMA contract. In the same month, the IMM introduced a one-year U.S. Treasury bill contract, which was followed by the CBOT's introduction of 30-day commercial paper in May 1979, and U.S. Treasury notes in June 1979. The IMM introduced a four-year U.S. Treasury note contract in July 1979. During 1980, CD contracts were introduced on the IMM and CBOT, and in 1981 the IMM introduced Eurodollar time deposit contracts.

15.1.5. So the development of financial futures is very recent, but it has spawned a good many new contracts in a short time. This is due to two things. The first has been the competition between the IMM and the CBOT, to say nothing of other, smaller, and less successful exchanges such as the New York Futures Exchange. Second, and more important, the new contracts introduced in the 1970s filled a need. The volume of trading in them grew very fast. (Nil at the start of the decade, by the end of the decade financial futures were accounting for more than one-third of all futures contracts traded in the United States. Table 15.1 shows the main contracts.) This very fast growth has come from two factors: increasing demand for hedging, because of the growing volatility of financial conditions; and the excellent liquidity of the financial futures market (at least, the interest rate futures). This liquidity meant that those who wanted to hedge their positions could find traders on the opposite side of the market to take them out of the position.

15.1.6. As I said earlier, hard information on the structure of the markets is not that widely available. Some interesting points show up, though, in a survey conducted by the Commodity Futures Trading Commission of the United States in November 1977.[1] The survey covered all traders holding open contracts on November 30. The contracts covered were GMMA mortgage-backed certificates, U.S. Treasury bonds, and commercial paper on the Chicago Board of Trade, together with the U.S. Treasury bill contract and contracts in Canadian dollars, Swiss francs, deutsche marks, British pounds, and Japanese yen, on the IMM.

TABLE 15.1. Main Financial Futures Contracts Trading Volume, 1977–1981 (in Thousands).

Contract	1977	1978	1979	1980	1981
CBOT					
GNMA mortgages (CD & CDR)	422	953	1,371	2,337	2,293
T-bonds	32	555	2,059	6,489	13,907
Domestic CD	—	—	—	—	159
CME					
British pound	79	240	514	1,264	1,491
Canadian dollar	161	207	399	601	475
Deutsche mark	134	400	450	922	1,654
Japanese yen	82	361	329	575	960
Swiss franc	107	321	494	828	1,518
Gold	908	2,812	3,558	2,543	2,518
90-day T-bills	322	769	1,930	3,338	5,631
Domestic CD	—	—	—	—	423
Eurodollar	—	—	—	—	15
COMEX					
Gold	982	3,742	6,541	8,001	10,373
Silver	3,540	3,822	4,080	1,058	1,240
Copper	1,070	1,408	2,301	1,848	1,647

SOURCE: *Volume of Trading*, Futures Industry Association, Washington D.C., 1981.

15.1.7. In each of the markets there were a good many more speculative traders than hedgers. In a number of the markets, though, hedgers held the majority of open contracts on one or both sides of the market. In Treasury bonds, for example, hedgers held nearly 57% of the long side of the market, and almost 62% of the short side of the market. Only in Treasury bills, GNMA certificates, and Canadian dollars did speculative open interest exceed hedging open interest on both sides of the market. Even in these three markets, the hedging interest was appreciable. The survey confirms the view that the currency contracts are thinly traded and speculative. What hedgers there are tend to be heavily one way. For example, in the sterling contract, 784 traders were described as speculative, against 28 hedgers. The speculative traders held long positions of 4,713 and short positions of 2,002 contracts, while the hedgers were long of 771 contracts and short of 3,481 contracts.

15.1.8. The CFTC regularly collects information on the hedging/speculative classification of larger traders in agricultural futures markets. The survey showed that the general level of hedging in financial futures is about the same as that in the more traditional agricultural contracts which were included in the past surveys. In the GNMA futures contract, Chicago-based traders dominated the market with nearly one-third of the commitments on both sides, while traders in New York accounted for over 25% of both sides of the Treasury bond market. Traders from Switzerland tended to be the most active foreign participants. Only in the Swiss franc market and the Japanese yen market did traders from a single country (Switzerland) control more than 5% of either side of the market. (It is quite possible that these were U.S. deals channeled through Switzerland for anonymity's sake.)

15.1.9. The success of financial futures in Chicago spawned imitations in New York, which failed, in Toronto, in Hong Kong and Singapore (under discussion in both centers), and Sydney. (The latter trades U.S. dollars, yen, and sterling against Australian dollars and also has an apparently thriving market in 90-day bankers' acceptances.) The futures markets in Hong Kong and Singapore are run by the International Commodities Clearing House, which for years has run the London commodity clearing system. ICCH is now owned by the four major British clearing banks, together with Standard Chartered Bank. ICCH is also running the London International Financial Futures Exchange which opened in September 1982. The LIFFE trades a three-month Eurodollar contract, a three-month sterling interest rate contract, a 20-year gilt-edged contract, and four currency contracts (sterling, deutsche mark, Swiss francs, and yen against the U.S. dollar).

15.1.10. At first, many in the older financial markets such as foreign exchange were rather cool toward futures, first, because of the speculative nature of the markets—best summarized by saying that it is quite common for a trader to wander over from the frozen pork bellies pit and start trading deutsche marks—and second, because of a feeling that the markets were rather thin and narrow, dominated by "bandwagons," so a trader would find it difficult to "do the amount" without moving the market. This is probably still true of the foreign exchange currency contracts on the financial futures markets. But it is much less true of the established interest rate futures contracts, which have proven liquidity and depth. The importance of liquidity cannot be overstressed. If you can't do the amount, the market is useless.

SECTION 2.   ORGANIZATION OF THE MARKETS

15.2.1. Before discussing the financial futures contracts themselves in more detail, let's begin with the organization of the markets. The following description, in outline, applies to the CBOT, the IMM, and other similar institutions. Essentially, the membership of the market can be divided into two categories: brokers and locals. Brokers trade for nonmember customers and for other members. Locals trade for themselves. The locals are essential for the liquidity of the market. They are usually involved in three types of trading.

15.2.2. First, there are position traders. They will take a position, sometimes very large, and keep it until something causes them to change their mind. Position traders are relatively long-term traders, particularly compared to scalpers. These are floor traders who are constantly buying and selling. Often, scalpers keep positions for only a matter of minutes or seconds. Their contribution to the market is continuous moment-by-moment liquidity. The third type of local is the spreader. They concern themselves with the relative value of one contract month against another. They are arbitraging one period against another. Their contribution to the market is to give liquidity to the more distant periods. The other main source of liquidity is the very large number of small, individual speculators who trade on the exchange through the brokers. Although each may trade only one or two contracts, there are many thousands trading on the exchange, who again contribute to liquidity.

15.2.3. Trading takes place in the pits during specific hours. There is a separate trading area for each contract, so there is a gold pit, a corn pit, and so on. Orders are received on the trading floor by telephone or telex, and passed to the broker in the pit. Traders shout out the quantity and the price at which they want to buy or sell. They also use standard hand signals, especially when trading is noisy. The process is shown in Figure 15.2.

15.2.4. At the close of each day's trading, every member submits a trade confirmation record for every deal done on behalf of the firm or its customers. Every one of these trades must be "cleared," that is, verified and guaranteed, by the clearing house. The clearing house settles the account of each member firm at the end of the trading day. It matches each of the day's purchases and sales. It collects all losses and pays all profits. Its contribution to the safety of the market is to be the buyer from every seller and the seller to every buyer. A sale of Treasury bill contracts by A to B becomes a sale (by A) to the clearing house and a purchase (by B) from the clearing house.

15.2.5. This is a key safeguard for users of the exchanges. There is no need to worry who has taken the other side of the trade. The exchange clearing house itself guarantees the performance of every trade because it is the exchange itself which takes the opposite side to every contract. However, the exchange will not deal directly with public customers, but only with its clearing members.

15.2.6. In effect, the exchange does business only with its clearing members and the clearing members do business with all others. For example, the exchange sets margins for its clearing members and its clearing members in turn set margins for their customers. Thus, customer margins flow directly to the clearing member who, in turn, must settle with the exchange at the close of business each day. Each day the exchange requires a cash settlement from the clearing member based on the day's market positions and activity. This is regardless of the status of the member's customer margin money. A clearing member might let a customer be short of margin for a period of time, but this

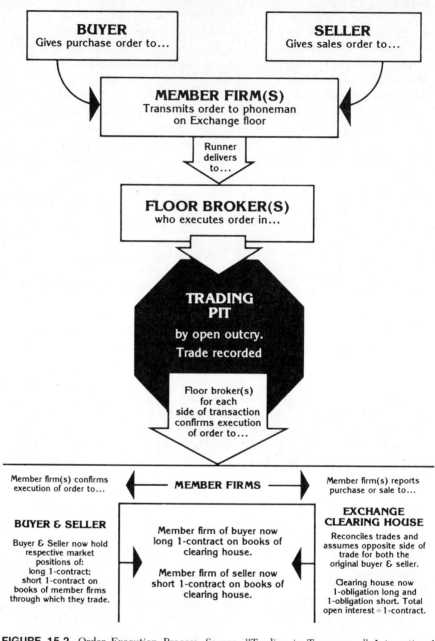

FIGURE 15.2. Order Execution Process. Source: "Trading in Tomorrows," *International Monetary Market*, Chicago, p. 11.

would have to be funded at its own expense. For the clearing house would not allow a clearing member to be undermargined overnight. Also, the exchange will supervise the financial status of its clearing members. So far, these arrangements appear to have been successful in preventing major problems; both the CBOT and the IMM state that there has never been a financial loss due to default on a futures contract on their exchanges.

SECTION 3.   TREASURY BILLS AND BONDS

15.3.1.   We turn now to the various instruments traded in the futures markets. (Gold futures are discussed in the chapter on gold.) Probably the main instruments for our purposes are the interest rate futures contracts, as the foreign currency contracts are less widely traded. Of the interest rate futures, perhaps the most liquid short-term contract at present is the 90-day U.S. Treasury bill. The standard contract is for 13-week U.S. Treasury bills having a face value at maturity of US$ 1 million. The delivery unit on the IMM is Treasury bills maturing 90 days hence. At the seller's option, he can deliver 91- or 92-day bills. (In point of fact, the vast majority of deliveries are made in 91-day bills.) The price is quoted in terms of the IMM index, that is, the difference between the actual yield and 100. Thus a Treasury bill yield of 10% is quoted in index form as 90.00. (Note that Treasury bills are traded on a discount basis.) Prices are quoted in multiples of 0.01 (US$ 25). The maximum daily price movement is 0.50 above or below the settlement price of the day before.

15.3.2.   Exceptions to this rule are the last day of trading in a contract, when there is no daily limit, and the "expanded daily price limits." These expanded limits come into effect whenever, on the successive days, any contract month closes at the normal daily price limit in the same direction. Contracts for the 90-day Treasury bill are currently traded for March, June, September, and December. Trading in the contract normally ends on the second business day after the 13-week Treasury bill auction of the third week of the delivery month.

15.3.3.   The Treasury bond contract on the Chicago Board of Trade is less directly relevant to us, but it is a very important contract. In fact, according to statistics produced by the Futures Industry Association for 1981, trading volume in the Treasury bonds contract of the CBOT was 13.9 million, making it the most traded contract in the United States. By comparison 2.1 million Treasury bond contracts were traded in 1979.

15.3.4.   The unit traded in this contract is U.S. Treasury bonds with a face value of US$ 100,000. The deliverable grade is U.S. Treasury bonds maturing at least 15 years from the date of delivery if not callable; or, if callable, the contract requires that there be at least 15 years remaining to the call. (Callability refers to the fact that some bonds are issued with a provision that any time after a certain date—the call date—the Treasury can call the bond back, before maturity, by paying principal and interest on the bond to the investor. For example, the 11¾% Treasury bond 2005/10 matures on February 15, 2010, but is callable after February 15, 2005.) The bond futures contract specifies delivery of an 8% bond. If a bond with a coupon other than 8% is delivered, it is priced, by a conversion factor, at an effective 8% yield. Because a US$ 100,000 11¾% coupon bond pays $11,750 in income annually versus US$ 8,000 annually for an 8% coupon bond, any comparison between the two has to reflect the 11¾% coupon's greater value. If each instrument is priced to yield 8%, the 11¾% coupon's price (conversion factor) as a decimal is 1.3974 ($139,740). The convention is to quote the bond price in 32nds: 68 − 16 means 68 16/32, that is, 68½.

15.3.5.   For financial markets in general the T-bill and T-bond contracts are the two most important financial futures contracts, aside from the gold (and silver) contracts which are discussed in the chapter on gold. But for traders in money and foreign exchange, the foreign currency contracts and the recently introduced CD and Eurodollar contracts are more directly relevant, and we turn to them now.

SECTION 4.   FOREIGN CURRENCIES, EURODOLLARS, AND CDS

15.4.1.   The best-established foreign currency contracts are those on the IMM. These include contracts in the Canadian dollar, deutsche mark, Swiss franc, Japanese yen, and pound sterling. Delivery is made on the third Wednesday of the contract month. If that day is not a business day in the country of delivery, delivery is made on the next business day. So for the Canadian dollar March contract, delivery would be made on the third Wednesday in March.

15.4.2.   The Canadian dollar contract is traded in units of 100,000 Canadian dollars. The minimum price fluctuation is in multiples of $0.0001 per Canadian dollar, that is, 1 point. The daily price limit is 75 points ($0.0075) above or below the previous day's settling price. Trading in a contract ends on the day before the delivery day of the contract month. Thus, in the case of the March contract, trading would end on the Tuesday before the third Wednesday in March.

15.4.3.   By way of comparison, the deutsche mark contract is traded in units of DMK 125,000. The minimum price fluctuation is the same, that is, $0.0001 per deutsche mark. The daily price limit is smaller at 60 points ($0.0060), but otherwise the conditions are the same. Trading in the contracts ends on the second day before the delivery date of the contract month, rather than the last day before the delivery day as in the case of the Canadian dollar. The reason is the ability to trade Canadian dollars in the "funds" markets, as against the normal spot delivery for other currencies (see Chapter 8, on spot trading).

15.4.4. We can see from Table 15.1 that these currency contracts have grown over time, but not nearly so spectacularly as some of the other financial instrument contracts. The very broad, liquid, and sophisticated bank market in foreign exchange has meant that futures contracts have usually been used only in a small way by those wanting to speculate in a currency. The bulk of natural commercial hedging activity is still channeled through the bank market, so the foreign currency futures markets are dominated by short-term speculative and technical considerations. This does not mean, however, that they are unimportant. Quite often the New York and even the Continental European market will be affected by movements on the futures markets if these are heavy and one-way.

15.4.5. We now turn to the relatively newly established CD and Eurodollar contracts. The IMM CD contract is the more widely traded, so we begin with this. The CD contract is different from the other futures contracts we have looked at because the buyer does not know what he will receive if he chooses to take delivery. All he knows is that the CD will be issued by an "approved delivery bank." Each month the IMM samples at least seven dealers from a list of at least ten dealers who trade actively in the domestic CD market. They are asked to name those banks whose CDs have the highest liquidity, lowest credit risk, and trade at identical yields. The current month's list is made up from those banks whose names appear on at least five lists (assuming that they have agreed that their CDs can be deliverable under the contract). The deliverable names are announced two days before the first delivery date.

15.4.6. The delivery unit is a CD having a fixed maturity value between $1 million and $1.2 million. On a normal CD, maturity value is principal plus interest; on a discount CD—see 11.7.6—it is the principal. The CD must have no interest payments falling due between delivery dates and maturity date. Its maturity can be between 2½ and 3½ months, and it can be delivered between the 15th and the end of the month. The reason for this spread of dates is to make sure there are enough deliverable CDs at any one time. Its effect, in comparison with the fixed delivery periods for Treasury Bills is shown in Figure 15.3.

15.4.7. Delivery amount is calculated as follows:

$$\text{Amount} = \frac{\text{maturity value}}{\left(1 + \dfrac{\text{days to maturity}}{360} \times \dfrac{[100 - \text{IMM price}]}{100}\right)}$$

This, of course, is the formula of 11.8.1, only turned around and using the current yield rather than the coupon on the CD which is expressed as (100 − IMM price) because of the IMM convention that yield equals 100 minus price.

15.4.8.   Trading volume in the IMM CD contract was $424 billion in 1981 (423,700 contracts at $1 million each), and volume in January 1982 was $128 billion, so the CD futures market has started to grow quite rapidly. The bulk of the trading, though, is in the near contracts. At the moment, liquidity at the far end is poor, although it is early to tell. It is even earlier to tell how the other new IMM introduction, the Eurodollar contract, will perform. This contract is again different from all the others, in that no cash delivery takes place. (This greatly simplifies settlement but raises a potential tax problem in that Eurodollar futures are apparently not covered by certain provisions of the 1981 Tax Act concerning commodity straddles.) The settlement price is fixed by the IMM Clearing House. It calls 12 major London "reference" banks for their perception of the LIBOR rate at which prime banks can raise three-month deposits (see 11.1.8), both at the end of trading and at a random time in the last 90 minutes of trading. After eliminating the two highest and the two lowest quotes, the average of the remaining eight is taken as the LIBOR rate. As with other instruments, the price is quoted as an index; 100 minus the yield. So a rate of 10.2% would be quoted 89.8. Delivery months are March, June, September, December, and the current month. Delivery date is the third Wednesday of the contract month. Trading in a contract ends at 3:30 P.M.

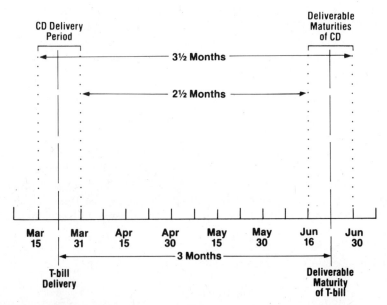

FIGURE 15.3. Delivery Periods for CDs and 90-Day T-Bills. Source: "Inside CD Futures," *International Monetary Market*, Chicago, p. 10.

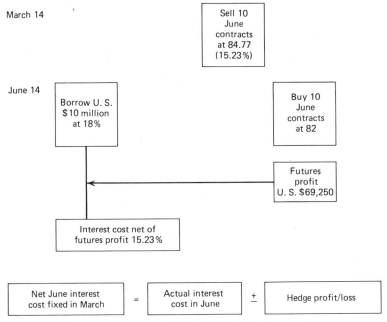

FIGURE 15.4. Fixing an Interest Rate by Hedging.

(London time), on the second London business day before the delivery date. The new LIFFE contract introduced in September 1982 has become a major force in the Eurodollar futures market.

SECTION 5.   HEDGING

15.5.1.   Having given this broad outline of some of the contracts involved, we can look at how they can be used. For convenience, we divide users into hedgers, arbitragers, and speculators. Let's look first at a short hedge. Suppose that a corporation has agreed to borrow Eurodollars on a three-month roll-over basis. It fears that interest rates are about to rise. It wants to lock in current interest rate levels on its borrowings. It will then sell Eurodollar futures contracts to the amount required. This is a "short" hedge. The mechanics are described in 15.5.2–4 and in Figure 15.4.

15.5.2.   Suppose today is March 14, 1982. Three month Eurodollar LIBOR is 15¼%. Three-month Eurodollar futures for delivery June 16 are 84.77 (i.e., 15.23%) but the firm fears that by June three-month LIBOR on its $10 million borrowing could be 18%. That would mean that the spot contract in June would be 82.00. So the firm sells 10 June contracts at 84.77. If its fears are correct, and the June contracts do go to 82.00, it buys back the contracts on June

14 (last trading day for the contract) at 82.00 and makes a profit of 2.77 per contract, that is, 277 basis points. Each basis point on a $1 million contract is worth $25, so its profit is $25 × 277 × 10 = $69,250. It now borrows for three months (say, 91 days) at 18%, costing:

$$\frac{18}{100} \times 10,000,000 \times \frac{90}{360} = \$450,000$$

15.5.3.   From this can be deducted the profit on the futures, making a total cost of $380,750, which produces an effective rate of 15.23% which the borrower has locked in today for three months hence. In other words, he has locked in today's futures rate for his borrowing. (In fact, it would be lower if we also allow for the fact that interest will be earned on the futures profit, since that profit is received at the start of the loan. But we cannot be certain of the investment rate we receive on the profit, since the amount is too small to be hedged itself by a futures contract; a forward forward placement with a bank would be difficult to arrange, since the amount is uncertain.)

15.5.4.   What would have happened if the interest rate had gone the other way, say, to 12%? Then the Euro contracts would have traded at around 88. Closing them out would have cost 3.23 per contract, so the loss would be 323 × 25 × 10, that is, $80,750. The interest cost on the LIBOR loan would be $300,000 to which would have to be added the loss on the futures contract of $80,750 which brings the total cost back to 15.23% (although a small adjustment for interest on interest would be needed). In other words, the cost is insensitive to interest rate movements.

15.5.5.   What we have just said is broadly true. However, the hedge will not always be as perfect as this, for a couple of reasons: first, basis risk (see 15.10.1 below), and second, variation in the LIBOR period. Suppose that the LIBOR period over June 16 is not 90 days as we assumed but 92 days, all other figures remaining the same. Then if the LIBOR rate has fallen to 12% our total cost works out at 15.16%, around 1/16% lower than before. Conversely, if LIBOR had risen to 18%, our all-in cost would be 15.29%, just under 1/16% the other way. At first sight it is hard to see what difference the two extra days makes. But in fact what is happening is that the profit or loss on the future is being spread over a longer time and so has a lesser cushioning effect than before. If LIBOR falls, the loss on the futures contract fails to offset all the cash saving from the lower LIBOR and our all-in cost falls slightly; conversely if LIBOR rises. The effect would be the opposite if the LIBOR period were ever less than 90 days.

15.5.6.   As an example of a long hedge, consider an institutional investor in U.S. Treasury bonds (see Figure 15.5). On April 1, 1982 he expects that in three months he will receive US$ 1 million, which he plans to invest in Treasury bonds. The investor suspects that rates are at or near their peak. At this point,

April 1, 1982

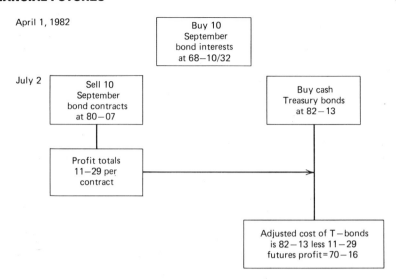

FIGURE 15.5. Hedging a Bond Holding.

20-year 8¼% Treasury bonds are yielding 12.26%. The investor wants to lock in today's yield level, in case it falls in the course of the next three months, before he receives his funds. His first step is to buy 10 September bond futures contracts. Each futures contract for U.S. Treasury bonds has a face value of US$ 100,000, so his total purchase is equal in value to the amount that he plans to invest in July. He buys them at the current price of 68–10 (68.3125).

15.5.7. By July 2, suppose that interest rates have dropped as he expected, and, accordingly, the price of bonds has risen. He sells his 10 futures contracts at 80–07 (80.21875), for a profit of $11,906.25 on each contract, giving him a total profit of $119,062.50 for the 10 contracts. He has now received his US$ 1 million which he proceeds to invest in Treasury bonds. The price of cash Treasury bonds as distinct from futures has risen from 68–14 (68.4375), in April to 82–13 (82.40625) now.

15.5.8. If he had been able to invest in April, he would have made a profit of $139,687.50; this in effect is an opportunity loss for the portfolio, but this loss is offset by the gain in the futures market. In fact, while the manager pays $824,062.50 for $1 million face value 20-year 8¼% U.S. Treasury bonds with a yield of 10.14%, his effective cost is only $705,000 since he had a $119,062.50 gain in the futures market. In effect, by dealing in April in the futures markets, he had protected his July investment, and established, in advance, a yield higher than that available at the time of the deal in July.

15.5.9. In this example, the opportunity loss was $139,687.50 and the futures gain was $119,062.50. That is, the futures market was not a perfect hedge. The reason for this is that the futures market price and the "cash" market price do not move exactly in parallel: The cash price in April was 68–14 (68.4375), while the future price for September was 68–10 (68.3125). The cash price rose 13–13 (13.40625) between April and July, while the futures price rose only 11–29 (11.90625). In the futures market, this is referred to as a change in the basis (see Section 10).

SECTION 6.   CROSS HEDGING

15.6.1.   Our investor was able to trade in a contract which exactly matched the instrument which he wanted to buy. This would not always be the case. Instead of buying Treasury bonds, he might have been planning to buy corporate bonds. There is, at present, no futures market for corporate bonds. However, he might still have wished to protect his interest rate earnings, and might have decided that a hedge in the U.S. Treasury bond market was better than no hedge at all.

15.6.2.   This operation—hedging a risk in one instrument by a futures contract for a different, but related, instrument—is called a cross hedge. Let's look at a pension fund manager with a portfolio of corporate bonds with a face value of $10 million, an average maturity of 20 years, and a current market value of $7,346,875 on January 2. The pension fund manager wants to protect the value of the portfolio from a possible rise in interest rates. He sells 100 June Treasury bond futures at 81–20 in a U.S. Treasury bond futures market.

15.6.3.   By March 14, interest rates have risen and the manager decides to sell the corporate bonds. He sells the bonds at $6,440,625 for a $906,250 loss. He buys back 100 U.S. Treasury bond futures at 69–20 and gains $1,200,000. The extra profit here was because the price of the Treasury bond contracts fell over the period by 14.7%, compared with a fall of only 12.34% in the average price of his corporate bonds. The cross hedge was not "perfect." Equally, of course, he could have had a loss if the average price of the corporate bonds had fallen faster than the price of the Treasury bonds. The spread might have moved against him, rather than in his favor.

15.6.4.   In foreign exchange terms, the cross hedge operation is like hedging a position in a currency which cannot be dealt forward, because of exchange controls, by using a currency which is linked to it. For example, a receivable denominated in Trinidad and Tobago dollars might be hedged by selling U.S. dollars forward, since the Trinidad and Tobago dollar is linked to the U.S. dollar. This will remove some of the risk, but does not, of course, remove the risk that the relationship between the TT dollar and the U.S. dollar—the basis—might change.

SECTION 7. ADJUSTING FOR COUPON AND MATURITY: THE WEIGHTED HEDGE

15.7.1. So far we have looked at two types of operation: hedging a cash position in U.S. Treasury bonds with a futures position, and hedging a cash position in corporate bonds with a Treasury bond futures position. In the second case, we took the risk of a change in the relationship, or basis, between the two types of bonds. In the first case, we implicitly assumed that the U.S. Treasury bonds held were the same coupon and maturity as those traded in the futures contract. On average, this will not be true.

15.7.2. In this situation, a third type of hedge, the "weighted hedge," is needed to cope with two factors: differences in maturity, and differences in coupon. The simpler case is differences in maturity. The value of a one basis point yield change is $50 for a $1 million six-month discounted instrument and $25 for a $1 million three-month discounted instrument:

$$90 \text{ days: } \frac{0.01}{100} \times \$1,000,000 \times \frac{90}{360} = \$25$$

$$180 \text{ days: } \frac{0.01}{100} \times \$1,000,000 \times \frac{180}{360} = \$50$$

15.7.3. To see this in practice, let's assume that, for policy reasons, we need to invest $15 million in a six-month (180-day) CD on August 28, 1982. Today is July 31, 1982, and the rate today on a 180-day CD is 15%. To save complications about different coupons (which we look at in our next example), assume that the yield curve is completely flat; that is, a 90-day CD also yields 15% today. If today's rates prevailed on August 28, we would earn $1,125,000 in interest on our 180-day CD. To protect those earnings we buy 90-day CD futures. Suppose we did not weight our hedge to compensate for the fact that the futures maturity is half what we need. We would buy $15 million worth, that is, 15 contracts, at 85 (100–15%).

15.7.4. Suppose on August 28 the rate for a 180-day CD (and a 90-day CD) has fallen to 10%. Then when we buy our $15 million CD we will only earn $750,000 instead of the $1,125,000 we had hoped for, a loss of $375,000. But our futures contracts are now priced at 90 (100–10%). So we have picked up 500 basis points on 15 contracts. We know that on a 90-day CD contract one basis point in dollar terms is worth $25, so we have made a profit of $500 \times 15 \times \$25 = \$187,500$. But this is only half our interest loss on the CD. So in fact we need 30 contracts to be properly hedged.

15.7.5. Similarly we need to adjust for different coupons. In Treasury bonds, for example, a higher coupon bond's price changes more than a lower

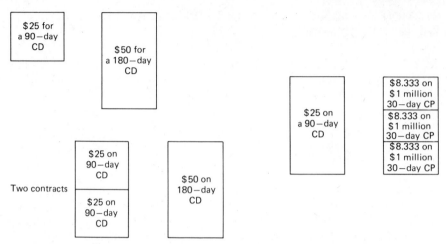

FIGURE 15.6. Effect of Maturity on Value of a Basis Point on Face Value $1 Million.

coupon bond's, for any given yield change. The higher coupon bond is more volatile. The T-bond futures contract is for an 8% coupon. If one is hedging against bonds with a different coupon, their cash price will move in a different way from the futures price.

15.7.6.   Suppose on May 30 I own $1 million 10⅜% Treasury bonds whose current price (in decimal form) is 100.31, so their current value is $1,003,100. I decide to hedge them by selling 10 December T-bond contracts, for which I get 79.72. On September 30 I decide to sell my bonds and cut out the hedge. Suppose interest rates have risen, so I receive only 87.50 for my bonds; and I buy December T-bond futures at 68.91. Then I have lost 12.81 points on my cash bonds (i.e., $128,100), but I have only earned 10.81 (i.e., $108,100) points on my futures, because the 8% futures T-bond is less volatile. So I have a net loss of 2.00 points, or $20,000.

15.7.7.   This problem can be solved by selling 12 contracts, in which case my futures profit is 1.2 times higher than before, that is, $108,100 × 1.2 = $129,720. This gives me a small net profit of $1,620. In fact, to work out how much one should weight a T-bond hedge to allow for coupon, we can use as a rough guide the factors that are used in converting different coupons to the standard basis for delivery (see 15.3.4). The conversion factor for the 10⅜% bond is 1.2505, so we could have sold 12 or possibly 13 contracts, since of course we cannot sell a fraction of a contract. To get exact weighting rates, rather than use the conversion factor, brokers use mathematical models or historical relationships.

SECTION 8.   TRADING FUTURES: THE LEVERAGE EFFECT

15.8.1.   The discussion so far has been in terms of hedging some existing commitment. Now suppose the trader deliberately takes a position, either as a straightforward speculation, or as an arbitrage. The simplest case is the trader who wants to back his judgment on the outlook for interest rates or currencies. The essential difference between doing this in the futures market and doing it in the "cash market" is that in the futures market, one can trade on margin. This gives a very high degree of leverage. This leverage, or gearing in U.K. terminology, lets the speculator make large profits compared with the amount of margin money committed.

15.8.2.   Suppose on December 1, 1981, a trader thinks interest rates will rise in the next few months, causing bond prices to fall. He deposits the required margin (say, $4,000 per contract) with his broker. He sells two Treasury bond futures contracts at 67–00. Two weeks later, interest rates have risen. Prices for Treasury bond futures contracts have dropped to 66–08. The trader closes his position by buying two bond futures contracts. He makes a profit of $750 on each contract. The $1,500 profit on the $8,000 margin is a return of over 18% during the two weeks, before deducting commission and exchange fees. Leverage has increased his return—as it could have increased his loss.

SECTION 9.   STRADDLES AND SPREADS

15.9.1.   The deal described above is a straight speculation on interest rate changes. The second type of speculation is on the change in relationship between two different instruments. The futures market calls this a straddle, or intercommodity hedge, but some people call it a spread. Earlier we saw a cross hedge between Treasury bonds and corporate bonds. A pension fund manager held corporate bonds and hedged his position in the Treasury bond futures market. But it would equally be possible for a trader to open up a cross position to profit from a change in relationship between two instruments. The operation might look like a cross hedge, but would in fact be a speculative position. Figure 15.7 shows the result of a position in the Treasury bill/CD spread.

Day 1	Buy 10 March CD contracts at 84.7.	Sell 10 March T-bill contracts at 86.6
	Spread = 190 basis points.	
Day 15	Sell 10 March CD contracts at 85.1.	Buy 10 March T-bill contracts at 86.8
	Spread = 170 basis points.	
Profit:	40 basis points × $25 × 10 contracts = $10,000	
Loss:	20 basis points × $25 × 10 contracts = $5,000	
Net profit = $5,000		

FIGURE 15.7.   Speculating on the Spread.

The trader expects this to narrow, so goes short of T-bills and long of CDs at a spread of 190. When the CD rate falls in relation to T-bills, so the spread narrows to 170, the position is closed at a profit.

15.9.2. A third operation of this type is to take a position in the same instrument but in different periods, one against the other. This is usually called a spread, but some people call it a straddle. Suppose interest rates are rising. On March 14, 1982, a trader sees that the December 1982 Treasury bond contract is trading at a discount to the March 1983 contract (i.e., December interest rates are above those for March). The trader thinks the yield curve will change shape. Interest rates will peak soon and begin to fall. When they do, the December contract will yield a lower interest rate compared with the March contract. That is, the spread between the two contracts will shift from negative to positive. The trader decides to gamble on this by buying a December 1982 T-bond contract at 69–26 and selling a March 1983 contract at 70–18. (The price spread between the two contracts is a negative one of 24/32.)

15.9.3. Three months later, on June 14, the yield curve has shifted from negative to positive. The spread between the two contracts has become more positive—it has strengthened. The December contract at 81–22 is now trading at a premium to the March 1983 contract at 81–15. This is a positive spread of 7/32 compared with the previous negative 24/32. Prices for both contracts moved up but at different rates. So the trader's losses on the short March position were more than offset by the gain on the long December position. The loss on the March contract was 10–29 (10.90625 points), while the gain on the December contract was 11–28 (11.875). The net gain was 31/32. Since each point or 1/32 is worth \$31.25 on the Treasury bond contract, the net gain was \$968.75.

15.9.4. Two typical spreads are the bear spread and the bull spread. The bear spread is based on the idea that, generally, during a falling market, the nearby month will fall faster than the further month. The trader will go short of the nearby month and go long of the further month. This is equivalent, in money market terms, to borrowing the nearby month and lending the further month because we expect short rates to rise faster than long rates. In futures market terms, the operation is called selling the spread. The bull spread is called buying the spread—buying (going long or lending) the nearby month and selling (shorting or borrowing) the further month. Again, the assumption is that the nearby month is likely to move faster than the further month.

SECTION 10. KEY CONCEPTS: BASIS, CHEAPNESS, AND THE STRIP YIELD CURVE

15.10.1. We met the concept of basis very briefly in 15.5.9; it's time to look at it in more depth. *Basis is defined as the arithmetic difference between the cash price and the futures price (basis = cash − futures).* If the futures contract and the cash contract are for the same instrument, we can say that it is like the margin in the forward foreign exchange market, which is the difference between the spot, or cash, price and the price for a date in the future. But if the futures contract and the cash contract are not the same, the basis risk also includes the risk of a change in relationship. Earlier we suggested that a cross hedge was like a forward sale of the US$ to protect a TT $ receivable, on the grounds that the TT$ and US$ are linked. If that link changes, there is a change in the basis. The basis would include both the US$ forward margin and the change in spot TT$/US$ rate. For simplicity we will look at the basis where the futures instrument and the cash instrument are the same.

15.10.2. As the delivery month on the futures contract approaches, the cash and futures prices tend to converge, so the basis approaches zero. This is because the influences on the price of both the cash commodity and the expiring futures contract are identical at the time of actual delivery. If there were a difference between the two prices, there would be an opportunity for arbitrage. If the Treasury bond futures contract sold at a higher price than cash Treasury bonds, traders could sell the futures contract, buy Treasury bonds in the cash market, and make delivery on the futures contract to cover their futures sale, realizing an arbitrage profit.

15.10.3. Once again, there is a similarity to the forward exchange margin. The forward margin also tends to get smaller as the period of the forward contract shortens. It reaches zero when the forward price is for spot. And just as the forward margin is influenced by the relative interest rates of the two currencies involved, so the basis is influenced by interest rates, although in a different way. Basis is positive or negative, depending on whether the cash price is higher or lower than the futures price.

15.10.4. If short-term interest rates are below long-term rates, dealers who hold bonds are earning coupon income which is more than the cost of financing them. They can afford to quote lower prices on deferred sales. That leads to discounts on distant contracts. In this situation, basis is positive (basis = cash − futures = +). Putting it in another way, the dealer is earning "positive carry"—coupon income exceeds financing costs. *Positive carry means a positive basis, and a positive yield curve* (see Chapter 11, Section 3). If the yield curve has a negative slope, so that long-term rates are below short-term rates, dealers face financing costs which are more than their coupon income. So they must charge higher prices on deferred sales to compensate for holding the bonds. They face negative carry, and the futures market will show a negative basis. *Negative yield curve, therefore, means negative carry and negative basis.*

15.10.5. A second concept, which takes on its full importance at the time of delivery, is "cheapness." The idea of cheapness comes originally from the bond market. It can be defined in a number of different ways.[2] An investor will look at coupon income, capital gain, principal amortization, and reinvestment of the respective cash flows. This will show that one bond is cheap relative to another. It is not always possible to take all of these factors into account. Often, the concept of cheapness is derived simply from a comparison of the relative price history of two bonds. One looks to see if the relative price at the present time is out of line. If so, one bond is cheap relative to its past relationship to the other bond.

15.10.6. Cheapness in the futures market shows up through the delivery mechanism. Specifically, the short side of the deal—the one who has the obligation to deliver the bond—will look for the cheapest bond. Let's take a long-term T-bond contract. Suppose the futures market is at a dollar price of 79–05. Suppose also that the cash market has just three issues available for delivery against that contract. These are the 8¾% 2008 at 85–28 (10.30%), the 9⅛% 2009 at 88–29 (10.34%), and the 10⅜% 2009 at 99–27 (10.39%). Comparing yields, the 10⅜% is the highest; while in terms of price, the 8¾% is the lowest. Intuitively, therefore, it would seem that one of these two bonds is the "cheapest" in the futures market.

15.10.7. However, if the T-bond futures conversion factors are 1.0790, 1.1194, and 1.254 respectively (these were the actual factors on the day in question), then the price of the 8¼% bond would have to be 85.41 (in decimal terms) while the 9⅛% would have to be 88.61 and the 10⅜% 99.26. (These prices are got by multiplying the futures dollar price of 79–05, or 79.15625 in decimal terms, by the relevant factor.)

15.10.8. We now compare these with the cash prices of the different bonds in the market. We can see that if the short is buying in the market, he will make a loss of 0.465 points on the 8¾%, and 0.58375 on the 10⅜%, while he will show a loss of only 0.29625 on the 9⅛%. Therefore, of these three issues, the 9⅛% is the "cheapest" for the short to buy. The 10⅜%, which in yield to maturity terms was "cheapest" or best value, represents the greatest loss in terms of delivery to the futures market.

15.10.9. Another important concept is the yield curve implied by futures prices. (The yield curve is defined in Chapter 11.) This implied or synthetic yield curve is referred to as the *strip yield curve*. It is a yield curve based on manufactured future instruments. A security of any given maturity can be manufactured by buying a short-term maturity of the instrument and a strip of consecutive futures contracts running on from the maturity of the physical instrument. For example, one could manufacture a 15-month Treasury bill by buying a three-month bill, and four successive 90-day T-bill futures contracts.

15.10.10. The formula for calculating the strip yield can be got from forward forward pricing. If we are looking at a strip yield curve for CDs, say, we argue like this. Suppose today is March 15. We know that if we have, say, a 90-day CD and a 180-day CD, we can work out what the break-even yield over 90 days from June 13 would be. But in the futures strip yield curve problem, we know this last rate, because it is the June 90-day contract, and we know the 90-day rate. We have to work out the 180-day rate from the 90-day rate plus the futures rate.[3]

15.10.11. The quickest way is to set this up as a formula. We have $y^\circ =$ break-even rate, which is the futures rate. We know y_S, the short rate; we need y_L, the longer rate. By switching the formula around we get:

$$y_L = \frac{360}{t_L}\left[\left(y^\circ\left[\frac{t_L - t_S}{360}\right] + 1\right)\left(1 + \frac{y_S\, t_S}{360}\right) - 1\right]$$

where

$\left.\begin{array}{l} y_L = \text{longer CD rate} \\ y^\circ = \text{futures CD rate} \\ y_S = \text{short CD rate} \end{array}\right\}$ all quoted as decimals: 15% = .15

$t_L = $ longer maturity in days
$t_S = $ shorter maturity in days

15.10.12. To get this clear, let's take an example. Today is March 15. We know what the 90-day CD rate is in the ordinary, or "cash," market. We know the 90-day CD prices on the IMM for June, September, and December. What we want to know is what, in the ordinary CD market, the rates for 180-day, 270-day, and 360-day CDs would have to be to match the prices implied by the futures market. Suppose we have:

90-day CD	14.40%
IMM June CD	84.88 = 15.12%
September	84.96 = 15.04%
December	85.16 = 14.84%

15.10.13. So we take the cash CD rate and the June futures CD rates for 90 and 180 days respectively. Plugging them into the formula, we get:

$$y_L = \frac{360}{180}\left[\left(0.1512\left[\frac{180-90}{360}\right] + 1\right)\left(1 + \frac{0.1440 \times 90}{360}\right) - 1\right]$$
$$= 2\left[(0.0378 + 1)(1 + 0.036) - 1\right]$$
$$= 0.1503216$$
$$= 15.03\%$$

15.10.14. So a 180-day CD should fetch 15.03% to match the combined 90-day CD plus June futures contract. The next step is to work out a 270-day CD, using the 180-day rate we have just calculated as the cash rate, y_S, in our formula. The result of combining the 15.03% "synthetic" 180-day CD with the 15.04% on the September futures contract comes out at 15.4%. We then take this "synthetic" 270-day rate and combine it with the December futures contract rate to produce a "synthetic" 360-day CD at 15.696%.

15.10.15. These successive steps have produced a strip yield curve that looks like this, compared with the actual (or cash market) yield curve:

	Strip Yield Curve	Cash Market Yield Curve
90-day "cash" CD	14.40%	14.40
Synthetic 180-day CD	15.03%	14.40
Synthetic 270-day CD	15.41	14.30
Synthetic 360-day CD	15.696	14.30

15.10.16. The strip yield curve calculated from these formulae differs from the implied forward rates in the "cash" markets. There are two reasons. First, the participants in the futures markets may not entirely share the view of participants in the cash markets. Second, the two markets may be imperfectly linked. Specifically, arbitrage between the cash and the futures markets depends on adequate collateral and financing. It is difficult anyway in the CD markets because of liquidity problems; but there are problems also in the bond markets. Suppose that the futures strip yield curve implies that in a year's time, interest rates will be lower than are expected in the cash market. Then, since bond prices will be higher according to the futures market, it would be worth buying a bond in the cash market and selling a futures contract forward one year. Then the bond can be delivered against the futures contract. For this arbitrage to work, the bond itself must be financed by finding one-year finance at a fixed rate today. Otherwise, the arbitrage will not be perfect, since the arbitrager does not know exactly what his financing costs will be over the period. But it is not always easy for some traders to get one-year money at a fixed rate in the domestic U.S. market. Hence the scope for arbitrage can be limited. Another reason for an imperfect link between the yield curve and the strip yield curve is that trading in the futures markets is not perfectly understood by all participants in the cash markets and vice versa. In particular the futures prices tend to be unaffected by considerations of interest on interest. So the scope for arbitrage is limited also by a limit on the number of potential participants.

SECTION 11.   OPEN INTEREST AND VOLUME

15.11.1.   Any trader in the futures markets needs to know the liquidity and depth of his markets. The two most general measurements of liquidity and depth for any futures market are trading volume and open interest. Trading volume is the number of contracts traded during a period of time; open interest is the number of open contract units at a point in time.

15.11.2.   Futures trading volume is reported as one side only. In other words, a daily volume of 12,000 means 12,000 contracts bought and 12,000 contracts sold. Buys and sells are not added together. The number of contracts bought always equals the number sold since there must be a buyer for every seller. A large volume of trading is a good indication of a liquid market. Liquidity can be gauged by the ability of market participants to execute commercial-size orders quickly at a price close to the price of the last transaction.

15.11.3.   Open interest is the number of contracts recorded with the exchange at the close of business each day as transactions that have not been offset by an opposite trade or settled by delivery. Open interest, like trading volume, counts one side only—an open interest of 5,000 is 5,000 bought positions and 5,000 sold positions. A relatively large open interest tends to indicate commercial hedging, because hedgers are more likely than speculators to hold positions as prices fluctuate.

15.11.4.   Both volume and open interest are frequently watched as technical indicators of the state of the market. For example, a gradual increase in volume during a downtrend often indicates a continuation and acceleration of the price decline. Gradually increasing volume during an uptrend suggests a further rise in prices. Equally, a rising price trend with a gradual increase in open interest means that new long hedgers or speculators are entering the market. They are paying higher prices to persuade new short hedgers or speculators to sell. If this process continues for several days, the new long speculators will be accumulating profits and additional buying power (because they have extra margin). The new speculative sellers will have losses and will be feeling financial pressure (because they have to put up extra margin). Such a market is technically strong, particularly if volume is increasing along with open interest.

SECTION 12.   REGULATIONS AND ACCOUNTING

15.12.1   We come to the question of regulation of trading in the financial futures markets. Both the U.S. Controller of the Currency and the Federal Home Loan Bank Board have issued regulations outlining the acceptable uses of interest rate futures by the banks that they supervise.[4] In November 1979 the Federal Reserve Board, Federal Deposit Insurance Corporation, and the

Comptroller of the Currency issued a joint policy statement on commercial banks engaging in futures, forward, and standby contracts for U.S. government and agency securities. The policy statement became effective January 1, 1980, but was revised in March 1980.[5]

15.12.2. A proposal for conducting such activities must be submitted to the Legal Advisory Services Division of the Comptroller of the Currency. It must include information concerning the type of trading objectives and controls. Banks must open an account with a firm that deals in interest rate futures contracts. The guidelines state that all open positions should be reviewed and market values determined at least monthly. Banks must use either a mark to market or lower of cost or market accounting method, solely for the hedge in the financial futures market of their cash assets or liabilities. This requirement applies no matter what accounting method is used on the cash asset or liability which is being hedged.[6] The policy statement also bans the issue of long-term standby contracts, that is, those for 150 days or more, which give the other party to the contract the option to deliver securities to the bank. Bank holding companies may not hedge their bank subsidiaries, who must trade for their own account.[7]

15.12.3. In essence these regulations represent an admission by the authorities that banks can and will trade in financial futures. The official attitude, initially one of discouragement, has now shifted to being one of careful regulation.

15.12.4. Until recently, accountants did not have standard accounting principles to apply to interest rate futures transactions. This has meant the development of a number of different accounting practices. These include: (1) mark to market, which reflects the change in the value of the futures contract in the income statement at the end of the period; (2) deferral, which adjusts the basis of the underlying asset/liability and amortizes the changing value of the contract as adjustment to interest income or expense over the life of the asset/liability; (3) lower of cost or market, which defers gains and amortizes them as in (2) above; and (4) hybrid method, a mark to market of the hedge contract and also of the hedged assets. This last is a symmetrical approach where the change in value of the futures contract and the change in value of the cash market asset/liability are both reflected in the income statement on a current basis.

15.12.5. The American Institute of Certified Practitioners of Accountancy forwarded in November 1980 a draft issues paper on the need for a uniform set of accounting principles governing transactions in interest rate futures to the Financial Accounting Standards Board. While not authoritative, the paper does give guidance on the current thinking of the accounting profession. In November 1981, the Financial Accounting Standards Board announced it would study this issue. Any statement eventually produced may differ from the AICPA view. The AICPA position paper generally supports mark to market accounting, with one important exception. That exception applies to transactions satisfying the narrowly defined criteria of a hedge, for which deferral accounting is recommended. According to the paper, a hedge must satisfy the following conditions:

1.   The asset/liability being hedged should be specifically identified and the purpose of the hedge documented in the accounting records.
2.   The hedging contract and the related cash asset or liability should be closely related, in the sense that a high degree of positive price correlation should exist between the hedging contract and the related asset or liability.
3.   A hedging contract taken out in anticipation of the need to hedge should have a reasonable expectation of being fulfilled.

15.12.6.   The AICPA position paper observes that failure to complete transactions as originally intended may be a clue that purported hedging activities are more akin to trading or speculative operations. So, if futures contracts used as anticipatory hedges are repeatedly closed out, mark to market accounting must be used for all later futures transactions, regardless of the stated intent to hedge.

NOTES

1.   R. H. Hobson, "Futures Trading in Financial Instruments," Commodity Futures Trading Commission, reproduced in International Commodities Clearing House Ltd., *Financial Futures in London,* November 1979.
2.   The classic discussion is: S. Homer and M. L. Leibowitz, *Inside the Yield Book,* Prentice-Hall Inc., 1972. See also for example, M. S. Dobbs-Higginson, *Investment Manual,* Credit Suisse First Boston, London 1980.
3.   The formula is derived from that on p. 82 of M. Stigum, *Money Market Calculations,* Homewood, Illinois: Dow-Jones, Irwin 1981.
4.   Part 545 of Rules & Regulations for Federal Savings & Loan Systems, para. 545.9 and para. 545.29.
5.   Press release 15.11.79.
6.   *Coopers & Lybrand Newsletter,* October 1981, p. 3.
7.   J. V. Baker, "A Beginner's Guide to Proper Use of Interest Rate Futures," *ABA Banking Journal,* February 1982.

16

THE GOLD MARKET

In this chapter we explain why gold matters to foreign exchange markets, and what part it has played in the international monetary system. Then we look at gold as a reserve asset: who holds it and why, what U.S. policy has been, and how central banks mobilize their holdings by using gold swaps and collateralization. Section 4 looks at demand and supply in the gold market: the political and psychological factors, and the role of Russia and South Africa. Then we look at gold trading in London, Zurich, Hong Kong, and New York, and at the gold futures markets.

SECTION 1. GOLD AND FOREIGN EXCHANGE MARKETS

16.1.1. From the relatively young financial futures markets, we come now to the gold market. Gold has been traded for thousands of years. It has a mystique all its own. But it is important to foreign exchange and money markets for several reasons. First, many countries and individuals buy gold as an investment alternative to foreign currencies, so movements in foreign currencies compared to gold can change what these investors do in the market. Second, moves in the gold price often reflect changes in confidence, either in an individual currency, in the world inflation outlook, or in political developments.

16.1.2. In many ways, gold's mystique offends common sense. "Nobody could ever have conceived of a more absurd waste of human resources than to dig gold in distant corners of the earth for the sole purpose of transporting it and reburying it immediately afterwards in other deep holes, especially excavated to receive it and heavily guarded to protect it."[1] But thousands the world over have known for generations that gold is the ultimate passport. Those who bought their way out of Southeast Asia in the late 1970s know that they owe their lives to gold. Gold is bedrock.

16.1.3. Even at the less life-and-death level of investing, gold has always stood for the ultimate hedge against political instability and inflation. George Bernard Shaw once put it like this: "You have to choose [as a voter] between trusting to the natural stability of gold and the honesty and intelligence of members of the government. And, with due respect for these gentlemen, I advise you, as long as the capitalist system lasts, to vote for gold."[2]

16.1.4. The natural stability of gold has not been much in evidence recently, since the price went from $35 per ounce in 1971 to $850 in 1980, and back down to below $300 per ounce in 1982. But as a long-term investment, gold is probably still high on most people's lists. And in the short term, which is our concern, movements in the gold price can signal nervousness about a particular currency, especially the dollar, and can also affect particular currencies. Most notably, falling gold prices can be expected to weaken the South African rand. And movements in gold prices will often affect the Hong Kong dollar, as local traders buy or sell the currency in order to switch into or out of gold. So it is important to get a good feel of developments in the market.

16.1.5. In some ways the gold market is more difficult to get a grip on than foreign exchange markets. We need to know about the role of gold as a reserve asset. But we must also take into account the physical distribution of gold holdings, and physical uses (and supply of) gold for electrical components, jewelry, and dentistry applications among others. To start with, we need to understand a little of the history of gold's relationship to the international monetary system.

SECTION 2.   GOLD AND THE INTERNATIONAL MONETARY SYSTEM

16.2.1.   The career of gold as a part of the international monetary system has been a checkered one. Under the Bretton Woods system, gold was used as the denominator against which the par value of a currency was fixed. Also, gold formed a large part of the international reserves (see Section 3). The weakness of the system was that, as we saw in Chapter 2, the move to convertibility in 1958 showed that existing exchange rates were out of line. And when investors expected a currency to devalue, they moved into gold. This happened first in the autumn of 1960. Then renewed demand for gold during 1961 led to the formation of a gold pool in the autumn of that year. This was a group of major central banks, including the Federal Reserve, which was managed by the Bank of England. The pool agreed to provide gold to support the dollar. For some years, the gold pool kept the market fairly stable.

16.2.2.   But in June 1967 France left the pool. And the Arab-Israeli Six Day War caused a new flight into gold. Total private purchases of gold more than doubled in that year. The main victim of the pressure was sterling, which was devalued in November. But this only switched the problem to the dollar. Demand for gold continued. In March 1968 the gold pool had to be suspended, and a two-tier gold market formed. This set up two prices for gold: an "official" price (which stayed at U.S. dollars $35 per ounce), and the "free market" price.

16.2.3.   But the pressure on the dollar continued. In August 1971 President Nixon was forced to take the historic step of breaking the gold-dollar link. Until then, the United States had been officially committed to selling gold at $35 per ounce to other central banks. With this move, the last official link between the gold price and the international monetary system was broken. The United States now began pressing to "demonetize" gold (see Section 3). But at the same time, a bill was passed in the United States legalizing private ownership of gold. Aiming to prevent its own citizens from undermining its policy of reducing gold's attractiveness, the U.S. government tried to insure that Americans would not start a stampede into gold. It announced that the U.S. Treasury would sell 2 million ounces of gold by public auction in January 1975. The sale brought bids for only 753,000 ounces, so they succeeded temporarily in dampening demand. But, as we shall see, in the long run they failed.

16.2.4.   In the following year, the United States was heavily involved in negotiating the Second Amendment to the Articles of Agreement of the IMF, which abolished the official gold price. Under U.S. pressure, the IMF went further, and laid down that gold will not be the denominator of any future par value system. It also set central banks free to buy and sell gold. Also, under the Second Amendment, the IMF sold gold for the less developed countries during

1976 to 1980. During that period, there were 44 IMF auctions and 778 tons of gold sold. Following the IMF example, in May 1978 the United States decided to resume selling some of its gold stock. The press statement at the time said that: "these sales serve three important U.S. objectives: (1) they help reduce the U.S. trade deficit, which has been a major factor in the weakness of the dollar; (2) they respond directly to conditions in the gold markets, which have contributed to the adverse psychological atmosphere in the foreign exchange market which is undermining international monetary stability; (3) they promote the internationally agreed effort to reduce gradually the monetary role of gold." During 1978 and 1979, the United States sold 491 tons of gold. Until October 1979 the gold was sold at regular monthly auction; the Treasury then announced that future sales would take place at irregular intervals.[3] This seems to have meant effective suspension of the auctions.

16.2.5.   In effect, the U.S. conceded defeat. Ever since the start of the 1960s each U.S. administration has tried to push ahead with the demonetization of gold (except for an eccentric element of the Reagan administration, which pushed briefly for a gold standard). The Carter Administration was no exception, and the auctions of 1978–1979 were designed to discourage people from buying gold. The language of the press statement quoted above hid the naked fact that the United States has never wanted a competitor for the dollar in the shape of gold. But sales of gold by the IMF and the United States did not dampen demand; on the contrary, the gold price was exploding even as the United States conceded defeat.

16.2.6.   The catalyst, as so often in the gold market, was instability in the Middle East. In November 1979, the U.S. Embassy in Iran was seized by militant students. The U.S. freeze on Iranian assets made governments with dollar reserves aware that if they quarreled with the United States, those reserves might not be available to them. Gold, a freely transferable and internationally acceptable asset, started to look more attractive. Then the attack on the Grand Mosque in Mecca made Middle Eastern investors nervous of the risk of instability in Saudi Arabia. At the end of December 1979, these fears were compounded by the Soviet invasion of Afghanistan. Investors who were concerned about their physical safety did not care about the interest rate on monetary assets. Once again, gold was bedrock. The gold price exploded upward, by $30 and $50 a day, reaching a peak of US$ 850. As events cooled down, the gold price subsided as fast as it had risen. It is estimated that as much as 150 tons of gold in jewelry and bar form was sold from private stocks between January and March 1980, equivalent to around a sixth of free world output.[4] The outbreak of the war between Iran and Iraq in September 1980 brought a sharp rise in gold prices.

16.2.7.   But from then on, the trend was one way. Difficulties in Poland meant that the market thought the Russians would be forced to sell gold to finance Polish repayments. At the same time, the Russians needed to sell gold to buy grain. And there was a severe deficit on the South African balance of payments. The South African Reserve Bank arranged gold swaps (see below) but these were not enough; South Africa had to keep selling gold into a weak market. Also, Iran became a distressed seller of gold to finance its spending for the Iran-Iraq war. On the other side, Iraq and various other OPEC countries were probably also net sellers of gold, as the falling price of oil drained their cash reserves. By March 1982 the gold price had tumbled down to $310.

16.2.8.   This brief outline shows that the gold price can be affected by many things: its role as a reserve asset, the balance of payments needs of producing countries, confidence in currencies, and political decisions taken by major gold holders. To get into these a little more deeply, we need to understand some of the issues surrounding gold as a reserve asset, and we turn now to these.

SECTION 3.   GOLD AS A RESERVE ASSET

16.3.1.   At the start of the Bretton Woods system, around 1950, gold holdings of all countries in the world totaled 952 million ounces. At the then official price of $35 per ounce, the value of world gold holdings was $33.3 billion. Holdings of foreign exchange totaled $13.3 billion. In other words, the ratio of gold holdings to foreign exchange was more than two to one. Twenty years later, in 1970, the value of foreign exchange holdings had overtaken the value of gold holdings. The physical volume of gold held had remained almost stable, but foreign exchange holdings had risen rapidly. Physical gold holdings even today remain about the same as they were in 1970, though of course their valuation has now risen sharply. At the end of November 1981, world official gold holdings were worth $393.1 billion at the then current gold price of $414 per ounce, compared with world holdings of foreign exchange of $329.5 billion.[5]

16.3.2.   As the figures show, holdings of gold as an official reserve asset are very important to many countries. For many years, though, the United States tried to encourage other countries to demonetize their gold. Essentially, the problem was that the United States did not want a competitor to the dollar. If there was to be a competitor, they would prefer that it was the SDR (see Chapter 14), which they developed during the late 1960s as an alternative to gold. The main resistance to the United States view came from France. We saw in 3.10.9 the classic statement of the French position by General de Gaulle: "We hold as necessary that international exchange be established . . . on an indisputable monetary base that does not carry the mark of any particular country." France, in effect, objected to the establishment of a world dollar standard. It preferred a world gold standard, which would place the United States under the discipline of the balance of payments like any other country.

16.3.3.   France's real objection was to the fact that the United States had profited immensely by breaking the link between the dollar and gold. During

1969 to 1979, total international monetary reserves exploded from US$ 78.7 billion to US$ 390 billion. Most of the growth in world foreign exchange holdings was invested in dollars, and particularly U.S. Treasury securities. The United States got cheap balance of payments financing from other central banks. Robert Triffin has pointed out that the total increase in U.S. foreign borrowing of $285 billion over 1970 to 1977 "is exactly equal to the total increase of U.S. federal debt over this period, from $279 billion at the end of 1969 to $564 billion at the end of 1977—a bizarre coincidence, but arguably not entirely accidental!"[6] The United States gains a great deal by being able to finance its balance of payments deficit by borrowing from overseas central banks. It is this cheap finance to which France was objecting.

16.3.4. After the dollar devaluation of 1971, France continued to press for a wider role for gold, and in December 1974 the Martinique Agreement between President Ford and President Giscard of France allowed central banks to value gold at market-related prices. In January 1975, France became the first major country to value its gold reserves at a market-related price. It has since been followed by most major countries, with the exception of the United States, Belgium, and Spain.[7]

16.3.5. The overall total for official gold holdings hides much movement between countries (shown in Table 16.1). If we allow for the effect of gold re-

TABLE 16.1. Gold Holdings (in Millions of Ounces).

Country	1950	1960	1970	1980
United States	650.00	508.69	316.34	264.32
Canada	16.57	25.29	22.59	20.98
Japan	0.2	7.06	15.20	24.23
Austria	0.2	8.38	20.39	21.11
Belgium	16.78	33.44	42.01	34.18[a] (42.72)
France	18.91	46.89	100.91	81.85[a] (102.31)
Germany	—	84.89	113.70	45.18[a] (118.97)
Italy	7.31	62.95	82.48	66.67[a] (83.34)
Netherlands	9.01	41.46	51.06	43.94[a] (54.92)
Spain	3.17	5.09	14.23	14.61
Switzerland	42.00	62.43	78.03	83.28
United Kingdom	81.76	80.00	38.54	18.84[a] (23.55)
Iran	3.97	3.71	3.74	—
Kuwait	—	—	2.46	2.54
Libya	—	—	2.44	3.08
Saudi Arabia	—	0.51	3.40	4.57
Venezuela	10.66	18.71	10.97	11.46
World Total	951.99	1,083.3	1,057.9	938.0[a] (1023.63)

[a] Excludes 20% of gold reserves swapped for ECUs. Adjusted figures in parentheses.

SOURCE: IMF, *International Financial Statistics Yearbook*, 1980 and 1981.

serves swapped for ECUs by members of the European Monetary System (see below), we can see that between 1950 and 1980 the total of gold holdings rose by 71.64 million ounces, only 7.5% in volume. Holdings by United States fell by 387.4 million ounces. These sales were taken up by Germany, rising from nil to 119 million ounces (adjusted for swaps), France, rising by a roughly similar amount to about 102 million ounces, and Italy, rising by 76 million ounces. The Netherlands and Switzerland also bought a good deal of gold. Along with the United States, the other large net loser of gold over the period was of course the United Kingdom. U.K. holdings fell from 81.8 million ounces to 23.5 million.

16.3.6. Despite the alleged preference of the newly rich Arab countries for gold, the official reported holdings of Iran remained virtually unaltered throughout the period. (They have almost certainly fallen sharply since.) Those of Saudi Arabia have risen by only four million ounces since 1957, when the first figures became available. According to the official figures, the main buyers of gold in the last year or two have been Indonesia, Libya, and Colombia.

16.3.7. A major problem with gold as a reserve asset, from the central bank's point of view, is that it is not always easy to mobilize. They have evolved two main techniques to try to avoid the problem of selling gold into a falling market: the gold swap, and the use of gold as a collateral. In fact, South Africa did use the gold swap technique during the early autumn of 1981 in an attempt to make sure that its need for foreign exchange did not depress the gold price. The technique of a gold swap is just like that of a currency swap: a spot sale, combined with a forward repurchase or vice versa. The forward price, of course, like a currency forward, includes an element of interest charge for the operation. South Africa first arranged swaps in 1976. The swaps were done when the price was well under $150, but were later unwound in 1979 and 1980 when the price had risen to around $600 plus. Even allowing for the interest which South Africa had to pay in the meantime, the swaps proved profitable. Another central bank which has used gold swaps was the Central Bank of Kuwait. It was obliged until 1978 to keep a 40% gold backing for its note issue. It was unwilling to buy gold on the free market as the note issue rose, since this might push up the price. Instead, Kuwait arranged a spot purchase combined with a forward sale of gold through the Bank for International Settlements.[8] In fact, the BIS has always been active in making gold deposits and swaps as part of its services to central banks. In its 1981 balance sheet, for example, it showed deposits in gold equivalent to $9.1 billion.[9]

16.3.8. Another important use of gold swaps is in the European Monetary System (see Chapter 4). This system created a new international reserve asset for the EEC member countries, the European Currency Unit (see Chapter 14). In order to create an initial stock of ECUs, each Community Central Bank involved contributed 20% of its gold and dollar reserves to the European Monetary Fund (see Chapter 3). The contributions took the form of three-month revolving swaps against ECUs. So the EMF is a large gold holder through the medium of these swaps. At the beginning of each quarter, adjustments are made to the revolving swaps. This ensures that each central bank's contribution to the EMCF is still 20% of its gold reserves. The valuation basis for the gold is the current market price or the average price for the last six months, whichever is the lower.

16.3.9. Apart from swaps, the other main method by which central banks have mobilized their holdings of gold is using it as collateral. The ministers of the Group of Ten approved such arrangements in June 1974.[10] The first country to take advantage of them was Italy, in August 1974. She borrowed $2 billion from Germany, using large holdings of gold as collateral. For the purpose of this loan, the value placed on the gold was 80% of the market price.[11] The same technique was later used also by Portugal.

SECTION 4. DEMAND AND SUPPLY IN THE GOLD MARKET

16.4.1. The main elements in demand and supply in the gold market are set out in Table 16.2. For reasons which will be explained later, non-Communist production has tended on balance to fall since 1970. Communist sales of gold to the market have varied in line with their balance of payments needs. Central banks have generally been net sellers of gold, except in 1970, 1972, and

TABLE 16.2. Supply and Demand in the Gold Market, 1950–1980.

Year	Non-Communist Production	Trade with Communist Sector	Net Official Sales (+)	Net Official Purchases (−)	Total Increase in Private Sector Holdings
Average—1950–1959	833	102	—	464	472
Average—1960–1969	1204	174	206	277	1308
1970	1273	− 3	—	236	1034
1971	1236	54	96	—	1386
1972	1182	213	—	151	1244
1973	1117	275	6	—	1398
1974	1006	220	20	—	1246
1975	954	149	9	—	1112
1976	970	412	58	—	1440
1977	972	401	269	—	1642
1978	979	410	362	—	1751
1979	961	199	544	—	1704
1980	943	90	—	230	803

SOURCE: Consolidated Gold Fields, *Gold 1981*, p. 16.

TABLE 16.3.   Changes in Private Sector Gold Holdings (in Metric Tons).

Year	Fabricated Gold	Bullion	Total Private Sector Demand
1970	1376	− 342	1034
1971	1387	− 1	1386
1972	1344	− 100	1244
1973	859	539	1398
1974	735	511	1246
1975	983	129	1112
1976	1363	57	1420
1977	1419	223	1642
1978	1596	155	1751
1979	1315	389	1704
1980	521	282	803

SOURCE: Consolidated Gold Fields, *Gold 1981.*

1980. All these supplies have been absorbed, on a net basis, by the private sector. The demand from the private sector can be split into two main components: for hoarding, and for physical use. Physical uses are mainly jewelry, electronics, dentistry, and medallions. Despite the glamor and attention which surround hoarding, demand for fabricated gold has outweighed the demand for bullion in every year of the 1970s. (Of course, some of the fabricated gold, especially jewelry and coins, is bought for hoarding purposes.) The figures are set out in Table 16.3. Most of this demand is very price sensitive, and is affected by substitutes (e.g., silver or platinum for jewelry, and silver-palladium for dentistry). For traders in the gold market, these complexities are important to understand; for foreign exchange dealers, though, it is bullion which is most relevant.

16.4.2.   The demand for bullion is linked, of course, to the demand for gold as a reserve asset. But it is also heavily influenced by the international political situation, the level of hoarding, and worldwide inflation rate and interest rate trends. In the longer run, there is a cyclical pattern. As the world economy grows faster, inflation tends to rise. Investors buy gold as an inflation hedge. Then governments become concerned about inflation. Fiscal and monetary policies are tightened. Interest rates rise. This makes it expensive to finance gold holdings. It also improves the investor's confidence that inflation will fall. Gold is sold. By the time interest rates have bottomed out, investors have become concerned about new inflation and begin to buy gold again.

16.4.3.   The spectacular 1979–1980 price movement was not just cyclical, but political as well. The attack on the Grand Mosque in Mecca, the Iranian crisis, and the freezing of Iranian assets increased the attractions of gold, a liquid asset out of the control of the United States. The Soviet invasion of Afghanistan redoubled investors' fears. Supply of physical gold dried up and the price rose sharply. Worldwide publicity for the price rise brought in a new wave of buyers when the price broke $600. Then, as the price moved toward its peak of $850, selling from stocks of jewelry and bars began in all parts of the world.

16.4.4. The supply side of the equation is what makes the politics of the world gold market so delicate. The major beneficiaries of any rise in the price of gold are the Soviet Union and South Africa. Neither are at the top of any international popularity poll. South African production for 1980 was 675 metric tons of gold. The best available estimate for current Soviet output is in the range of 280 to 350 tons per annum. A long way behind these two come Canada, with an annual output in 1980 of 45 tons, Brazil (35 tons), and the United States (28 tons). Between them South Africa and the Soviet Union account for almost 80% of world gold production. South Africa's dominant position is unlikely to be challenged for many years, provided the country remains stable. So we must understand the basic principles which govern South African output.

16.4.5. First we need to understand the "pay limit."[12] This has a very important role in setting South African production. The pay limit is the minimum amount of gold in a ton of rock which will produce enough revenue to cover costs. The higher the gold price, the lower the pay limit needs to be. As costs rise, so the pay limit has to rise; each ton of rock has to yield more gold to make it worth mining. The South African gold mines use these pay limits to calculate their reserves. The higher the pay limit, the more gold must be mined to earn a given amount of money. The lower the limit—that is, the higher the gold price—the smaller the amount of gold that has to be mined. So a higher gold price tends to mean lower South African production. Hence the decline of South African production in the 1970s; less gold had to be mined to pay for South Africa's needs.

16.4.6. When costs were rising and the sales price was fixed at $35 per ounce, the pay limit rose steadily. This cut back the amount of reserves it would be profitable to mine. That, in turn, made it hard to justify investment needed for a new mine. (Anglo-American's Elandsrand mine cost $220 million before a single bar of gold was poured, and $350 million to bring it to full production.) The sharp rise in the gold price during the 1970s let the gold mines exploit the lower grades of ore which in the past were uneconomic to mine. This lengthened the potential lives of many of the mines. It encouraged mines with marginal ore reserves to expand their operations. At the same time, the move to mining lower-grade ore cuts back the physical volume of output. Between 1970 and 1980 the average grade of ore milled by gold mines fell by nearly half to 7.3 grams per ton. And world production fell from over 1,000 tons of gold in 1970 to 943 tons in 1980.

16.4.7. The South African mining industry can afford to manage its production so as to maximize the life of the mines, for in many ways the structure of the industry is more like that of a state enterprise than that of a short-term private competitive business. The mines are privately owned, but they cooperate closely through the medium of the Chamber of Mines of South Africa. This handles recruitment of labor for the industry as a whole, and also coordinates research. Summing up, future predictions of South African output are uncertain, both because of the volatility of the gold price and because of the possibility of political instability in South Africa. But it seems likely in the immediate future that about 700 tons per annum will be produced, almost all of this to be sold in the world market.

16.4.8. Estimates of Soviet production are much more difficult. Early estimates suggested annual production of 600 tons per annum. But these have now been cut. A recent estimate by Consolidated Gold Fields based on a wide study of the Russian technical press and of satellite photographs yields an estimate of 280 to 350 tons.[13] The proportion of this which is sold to the West probably varies. No one, of course, knows exactly how the Soviet Union decides on its selling policy. It has been suggested that Russians have an annual foreign exchange target to be met by sales of gold. If this is so, then a high gold price means a smaller level of Russian sales. Conversely, a low gold price (as in the winter of 1981–1982) forces a higher volume of sales. If this is true, then clearly Soviet activity in the marketplace could be destabilizing. However, the Soviet Union has been selling gold to the West in a sophisticated way for many years, and is well aware of the problems of marketing its production. Most of it is channeled through the Bank for Foreign Trade's subsidiary, the Wozchod Handelsbank in Zurich. The Wozchod has become an active trader in the gold market, both as a buyer and as a seller. (For example, it is said that once in 1976, the gold price dropped from $148 to $128 in a single afternoon, because of heavy sales from a major European bank. Wozchod, supported by the Bank for Foreign Trade, bought several tons to stabilize the price.)[14]

SECTION 5. TRADING IN GOLD

16.5.1. We will look here at some of the major gold markets, concentrating on London, Zurich, New York, and Hong Kong. The traditional physical gold market was for many years the preserve of London. But in March 1968 the temporary closure of the London gold market during the two-tier market crisis (see Section 1) gave the Swiss banks the chance to step in and take over the handling of South Africa's physical sales of gold. They set up a cooperative trading pool in Zurich, and committed themselves to taking most of South Africa's 1969 output at prices well over $40 per ounce. Though the three banks lost heavily on this deal, they were repaid by up to 80% of South African production during the early 1970s.[15] Despite this blow, London fought back, and the "London fixing" is still the most important international barometer of the gold price. The fixing consists of five members: Mocatta and Goldsmid (a subsidiary of Standard Chartered Bank Ltd.); Sharps Pixley Ltd. (a subsidiary of Kleinwort Benson Ltd.); N. M. Rothschild and Sons; Johnson Matthey Bankers Ltd. (a subsidiary of Charter Consolidated Ltd., which in turn is associated with Anglo-American Corporation); and Samuel Montagu and Co. Ltd. (a subsidiary of Midland Bank Ltd.). By tradition the fixing is held twice daily at the offices of Rothschilds. Each of the people present is in touch with the gold dealing room of his own bank by telephone, and when the chairman of the fix announces an opening price, this is relayed back to the dealing rooms. They in turn relay the price to their customers, and on the basis of the orders received, tell their representative to declare as a buyer or seller. Members are then asked to state the number of bars in which they want to trade. If the size of the buying and selling orders do not balance, the same sequence is followed again at higher or lower prices until they do. At this moment the chairman announces that the price is "fixed." The process can take some time, particularly if the market is volatile. Also, by tradition, a member of the market can stop the price being fixed by raising a flag on his or her desk. This gives them time to communicate with their dealing room and act on any changed orders. As long as any flag is raised, the chairman may not declare the price fixed. A major benefit of dealing at the fixings is the very narrow spread between buying and selling prices, since commission is payable only by buyers. Sellers receive the fixing price without deduction.

16.5.2. Outside the fixings, the London market trades throughout the day. The unit of trading is usually a gold bar weighing about 400 troy ounces. Prices are quoted in U.S. dollars per ounce *loco* London (i.e., for delivery in London). Delivery is at the vault of the member of the market. But many customers don't want physical delivery of their gold. They open gold accounts. In such unallocated accounts the customer has a general entitlement to gold, rather than specific bars set aside for him. This is the usual method of holding gold as it is convenient and cheap. Allocated accounts are opened when a customer needs his gold to be physically segregated and needs a detailed list of weights and assays.

16.5.3. Dealers in the London market will also quote forward prices for gold, but this is not a very important part of their business. It accounts for perhaps 10% of total turnover. The forward gold market is not like the forward foreign exchange market, with prices widely available; each price has to be negotiated individually. But forward deals in gold can occasionally be important in connection with gold swaps with central banks or other traders. The vast bulk of forward trading takes place in the futures markets (see below). At the moment, futures business is done through the United States, and to a small extent Hong Kong and Sydney, but in April 1982 a London gold futures market opened. It is hoped that this will attract some of the gold futures trading to London.

16.5.4. The other major center for physical trading of gold is Zurich. The Swiss banks have been active in worldwide gold trading for many years, but Zurich's main coup was to secure the marketing of South African gold in 1968. This, combined with the Russian decision to market most of its gold through Zurich from 1972, gave the Swiss a very strong position in the physical gold market. In recent years, though, London has fought back to some degree, particularly after the Swiss imposition of a 5.6% tax on transactions in physical gold at the start of 1980. Protests by the Swiss banks that the tax was damaging their business led the Swiss finance ministry to exempt central bank transactions from the gold tax in December 1981.[16] It remains to be seen whether Zurich can keep its place as a physical gold center.

16.5.5. The Hong Kong gold market is a curious hybrid of physical and futures markets. The basic contract is a lot of 100 taels (1 tael equals 1.2 troy ounces). Its unique feature is that it imposes no time limit on settlement. It is in effect an undated futures contract. Buyers can delay payment as long as they like; sellers can delay delivery. The delay is charged at an interest factor, which is really a premium or storage charge. The interest factor is fixed daily at 11:30 A.M. If demand for physical gold exceeds supply, interest will be positive, because buyers who need gold will be paid interest by sellers unable to deliver. Conversely, if supply exceeds demand, buyers who do not take delivery will be charged. Because the volume of gold traded is quite large (it can reach two million ounces daily), it can happen that gyrations in the interest factor and the demand for gold can affect the Hong Kong dollar itself, since turnover in that currency is not enormous by international standards. The gold market in Hong Kong is an active physical market for the Southeast Asian region. Also, it is a key link in the time zone chain of gold markets around the world.

16.5.6. The New York gold market is a new phenomenon, having developed basically since 1975. Before then, of course, gold had been traded to meet the needs of manufacturers, jewelers, and so on, but the prohibition on private ownership of and trading in gold had limited the market. When this ban was removed at the end of 1974, the U.S. gold futures markets were able to start developing. After a great deal of initial ballyhoo in 1975, it became clear in 1976 that Americans were not about to lead a mad rush into gold, and the volume of trading dropped. But from 1977 onward, trading grew enormously. Annual volume on the New York Commodity Exchange (the leading gold futures exchange) increased more than tenfold in four years, from 980,000 in 1977 to 10,400,000 in 1981. The second main gold futures exchange is the IMM in Chicago, but its growth has not been anything like so spectacular: from 900,000 in 1977 to 2,500,000 in 1981. To put these two markets in per-

TABLE 16.4.   Open Interest in COMEX Gold Contracts, March 16, 1982.

Month	Number Outstanding
March	13
April	40,781
May	0
June	34,082
August	18,840
October	18,477
December	10,557
February 1983	17,355
April	9,658
June	2,008
August	689
October	564
December	62

SOURCE: *Wall Street Journal*, March 17, 1982.

spective, it is worth mentioning that the turnover on the Comex and IMM during 1981 was over 40,000 tons, more than 40 times total world production in that year. The turnover in these two markets dwarfs that of all other markets put together. Their attraction, of course, is that they are very cheap to deal in, very efficient, and, of course, very liquid indeed. The mechanics of futures trading are discussed in Chapter 15, so we shall only mention here that the Comex and IMM gold futures contracts are virtually identical, each specifying gold in units of 100 troy ounces with 0.995 minimum fineness. Comex trading is conducted for delivery during the current calendar month; the next two calendar months; and any February, April, June, August, and December falling within a 23-month period beginning with the current month. Inevitably, the bulk of activity is concentrated in the nearer end of the market, but the Comex is liquid out at least for a year, possibly 18 months. For example, Table 16.4 shows the open interest in Comex gold contracts in March 1982. The very nearby months, March, being very close to delivery, and May, for special reasons, were very low in volume; but April, June, and the other months through April 1983 all show substantial volume. The value of the April 1983 open interest, for example, was about $347 million at the April price of $359.60 per ounce.

16.5.7.   The success of the gold futures contracts in the United States have encouraged gold dealers and users worldwide to follow U.S. gold futures price movements continuously during the working hours of the exchanges. That, in turn, has encouraged other centers to move into the gold futures markets. Time differentials have also been important in the development of the Asian gold futures market and the market opening in London. Most of these exchanges have, on the whole, rather small volumes. The Gold Exchange of Singapore was organized in 1978; the 100-ounce contract recorded only modest trading volume during its first years of existence. The Sydney Futures Exchange also began trading a gold contract in 1978, which now operates along with its currency and interest rate futures market. Contract regulation and clearing delivery are handled by the International Commodities Clearing House, which is now a joint subsidiary of the major British clearing banks and Standard Chartered Bank Ltd. The ICCH also handles the Hong Kong Commodity Exchange gold futures market, which began operations in August 1980. The gold contract there is for 100 troy ounces. After its opening, HKCE's gold futures trading averaged 290 lots daily. So far, none of these exchanges has been able to match the growth and depth of the American futures market.

16.5.8. Before leaving the subject of gold trading, we should look at the links between the various markets. Arbitrage between physical markets and futures markets, and between markets in different locations, is a very specialized area. The first point, of course, is that gold is physically heavy and also very valuable. This makes transporting it both expensive and potentially dangerous. Consequently a number of firms make it their business to specialize in "location swaps." These work like this. Suppose a manufacturer of gold jewelry in California finds that demand for his goods is less than he expected, so that he has surplus gold in his factory. At the same time, demand for gold may be strong in Saudi Arabia. The specialist gold trader will buy gold from a California manufacturer and sell gold in Saudi Arabia. Usually, the gold involved will not be physically transported, but got to Saudi Arabia through a chain, if necessary, of swaps between other locations. Clearly, this kind of business requires first-class market contacts around the world, together with the ability to store and if need be transport gold around the world. It also requires the ability to handle other kinds of swaps, for example, quality or time swaps. A quality swap would be the swap of gold, say, 0.995 fine, against gold 0.999 fine. A time swap, of course, is between gold at one date and gold at another, usually carried out through the futures market. The gold trader might find himself swapping 0.999 fine gold, *loco* Geneva, deliverable today against 0.995 gold, *loco* Singapore, deliverable in three months.

SECTION 6.   THE GOLD PRICE

16.6.1. To sum up this chapter, the price of gold is dictated by many factors which have nothing whatever to do with the foreign exchange market. Demand for gold in dentistry and electronics, or the production rate of Russian mines, are affected by factors well beyond the knowledge of foreign exchange dealers. But as far as the markets are concerned, the gold price is an important signal and needs to be watched. Because gold is so liquid and internationally acceptable, it can be treated for practical purposes as another currency. It is another competitor for the dollar, the deutsche mark, and so on. Just as at times there can be a flight out of other currencies into the dollar, or into the yen, so there can be a flight from all currencies into gold. This usually happens at a time of major uncertainty over the political outlook, as in 1979 and 1980, or when investors worldwide are concerned about inflation. At that point, they start to think in terms of holding a physical asset rather than paper currency.

16.6.2.   Having said that, the gold price is determined also by physical demand and supply, and gold's relationship to other precious metals such as silver or palladium is important too. During the Nelson Bunker Hunt fiasco, the gold market was quite seriously affected by a slide in the silver price. Like currencies, gold is a very sensitive barometer reflecting many different pressures.

NOTES

1. Robert Triffin, *Gold and the Dollar Crisis,* Yale University Press, New Haven, 1961.

2. Quoted in Timothy Green's excellent survey, *The New World of Gold,* Walker & Co., New York, 1981. I have drawn heavily on this very readable account in several parts of this chapter, and also on Consolidated Gold Fields Ltd.'s annual series, *Gold 19—.* See also S. Strange, *International Monetary Relations 1959–71,* Royal Institute of International Affairs, London, 1976, for a thorough discussion of events of the early part of the period. Later events are covered, as far as the political background goes, in R. Hellmann, *Gold, the Dollar and the European Currency Systems: the Seven Year Monetary War,* Praeger, New York, 1979. See also the references to Chapter 2.

3. Consolidated Gold Fields Ltd., *Gold 1980* p. 17.

4. Ibid., p. 45.

5. IMF, *International Financial Statistics,* various issues.

6. R. Triffin, "Gold and the Dollar Crisis: Yesterday and Tomorrow," *Princeton Essays in International Finance* no. 132, December 1978, p. 8.

7. D. A. Brodsky and G. P. Sampson, "The Value of Gold as a Reserve Asset," *World Development* vol. 8, 175–192, Pergamon Press Ltd., United Kingdom, 1980.

8. Timothy Green, *The New World of Gold,* p. 191.

9. BIS's *51st Annual Report,* p. 155.

10. IMF's 1976 *Annual Report,* p. 39–40.

11. Brodsky and Sampson, "The Value of Gold."

12. For a general discussion of the pay limit, see *Gold 1981,* pp. 71–85.

13. There is a thorough discussion in *Gold 1980,* pp. 46–58.

14. Timothy Green, *The New World of Gold,* p. 68.

15. Ibid., p. 129.

16. *Financial Times,* December 30, 1981.

17

CONTROL OF FOREIGN EXCHANGE AND MONEY MARKET OPERATIONS

The Banking Perspective

In this chapter we look at how a bank controls its foreign exchange and money market operations. We start by looking at how it sets up an exchanges ladder; how exchanges positions are revalued; how money market maturity and interest mismatch ladders are set up. Then we look at the other credit risk and position limits. Next we look at the management of liquidity, balance sheet ratios, and compliance with local regulations. Finally, we look at some internal issues: internal pricing, loan pricing, and tax issues.

SECTION 1.   BANKING AND CORPORATE PROBLEMS

17.1.1.   Control of foreign exchange and money market operations in a
bank and control in a corporation are different in several ways. But the main
issues are the same: the measurement and control of exposure to foreign exchange and interest rate movements. Another issue which is much the same in
a bank or in a corporate treasury is that of centralization versus decentralization, and transfer pricing. This is the price at which the central treasury lends
to or borrows from the operating arms, or at which it takes them out of their
foreign exchange exposure. Another issue of concern to both is liquidity. (A
bank, by the nature of its business, is totally dependent not only on maintaining but also on being seen to maintain a good level of liquidity. So the issue is
of even more importance to a bank than to a corporation.)

17.1.2.   But other issues only crop up in banking. These include central
bank regulations and reporting requirements. Then there is the issue of the size
and structure of the bank's balance sheet in relation to its capital availability
and needs. Also, a bank has different tax problems.

SECTION 2.   EXCHANGE BOOK; EXCHANGE LADDER

17.2.1.   Let's start with some of the concepts used in the control of a bank
treasury. The first of these is the *exchange book*. It is the total of all outstanding
exchange contracts in any one currency at any one time. The size of the

TABLE 17.1.   Deutsche Mark Ladder.

Period	In (+)	Out (−)	Net	Cumulative
Spot	+ 100,000	—	+ 100,000	+ 100,000
One month	—	− 1,000,000	− 1,000,000	—
Two months	+ 2,000,000	—	+ 2,000,000	+ 1,000,000
Three months	—	− 2,000,000	− 2,000,000	− 1,000,000
Six months	+ 1,000,000	—	+ 1,000,000	+ 1,000,000
Twelve months	+ 500,000	—	+ 500,000	—
Twenty-four months	—	− 500,000	− 500,000	− 500,000
Total	+ 3,600,000	− 3,500,000	+ 100,000	

total book is found by adding up all the outstanding contracts in all currencies, in terms of a single common currency—usually the local currency or the U.S. dollar.

17.2.2.   The foreign *exchange ladder* registers every purchase and every sale of a currency in maturity date order. An example is set out in Table 17.1. This bank's book is long overall of DMK 100,000. It has sold DMK 1 million in the one-month period against a purchase in six months; bought DMK 2 million in the two-month period against a sale of DMK 2 million in three months; and bought DMK 500,000 in the one-year against DMK 500,000 sold in the two-year period. Because its positions do not balance exactly in every period, this bank has a mismatch or gap position. Therefore it is vulnerable to rate movements against it. If the deutsche mark spot price falls, it will lose on the spot position. And if the forward dollar discount/deutsche mark premium should rise in the two-year maturity compared with the one-year, it would lose money on the DMK 500,000 one-against-two-years position.

17.2.3.   Management will aim to control the risks by setting a mismatch limit for each period. Suppose that the two-year mismatch limit was only 250,-000, but that the spot limit was DMK 2,000,000. Then the dealers might have to cut down the two-year position and might do it by making a swap of DMK 250,000; they would sell spot and buy forward to bring the new two-year figure back to the limit. Or, if the spot limit were full but they had room in the six-month band, they might bring part of the position back to the six-month period.

SECTION 3.   REVALUATION

17.3.1.   The exchange position ladder is a key tool for management of the bank's position. But of itself, it is only a record of what deals were done. It gives us no information about their current profit. In order to know that, banks

TABLE 17.2. Deutsche Mark Position Equivalents.

Period	DMK Amount	Original Rate	Original US$ Equivalent
Spot	100,000	2.00	− 50,000.00
One month	− 1,000,000	2.01	497,512.43
Two months	2,000,000	1.95	− 1,025,641.03
Three months	− 2,000,000	1.95	1,025,641.03
Six months	1,000,000	1.93	− 518,134.72
Twelve months	500,000	1.89	− 264,550.26
Two years	− 500,000	1.76	284,090.91

will revalue their foreign currency "book" from time to time. The profit or loss is taken to the bank's profit and loss account. Let's look at a U.S. bank which is dealing U.S. dollars against deutsche marks. The way its deutsche mark exchange ladder might look is shown in Table 17.2. This, though, does not tell us if we are making money on the deals. Let's ask ourselves what would happen if the bank were required to go out of business tomorrow. That is, at what prices could we liquidate these contracts? Suppose that we take today's prices for the various periods involved and apply them to the current book. Table 17.3 (overleaf) shows how the position might look.

17.3.3. As we can see, the overall book now shows a loss. There is a small profit in the spot position, since the deutsche mark has strengthened to 1.99. But where the bank had paid a premium of DMK 0.09 for its six-month-against-one-month swap, it would now only earn a premium of 0.02 for reversing the deal. Where it had sold three-month DMK for a nil premium against two months, it would now have to pay a premium of 0.01 to reverse the swap. There is a small profit on the one-against-two-year deal, since the two-year was sold at a premium of 0.13 against the one-year. The bank would have to pay only 0.10 to reverse the swap.

17.3.4. The benefit of the revaluation is that it gives current information about which positions are profitable and which are turning into loss. Of course, the example we looked at was simple. It assumed that the various contracts outstanding were for the "standard" maturity dates. A bank will normally have nonstandard forward contracts as well. Assuming that the process is computerized, it will be possible to produce interpolated rates for every single date and to revalue every contract. For practical reasons, it might be easiest to consider contracts to be matched if they fall within the same calendar week, the same semimonthly period, or even the same month.

TABLE 17.3. Deutsche Mark Position Revalued.

Period	Currency Amount	Original Rate	Original US$ Equivalent	Current Rate	Current Value	Profit/ Loss
Spot	100,000.00	2.00	− 50,000.00	1.99	50,251.26	251.26
One month	− 1,000,000.00	2.01	497,512.43	1.98	− 505,050.51	− 7,538.08
Two months	2,000,000.00	1.95	− 1,025,641.03	1.97	1,015,228.40	− 10,412.62
Three months	− 2,000,000.00	1.95	1,025,641.03	1.96	− 1,020,406.16	5,232.87
Six months	1,000,000.00	1.93	− 518,134.72	1.96	510,204.08	− 7,930.64
Twelve months	500,000.00	1.89	− 264,550.26	1.91	261,780.10	− 2,770.16
Two years	− 500,000.00	1.76	284,090.91	1.81	− 276,243.09	7,847.82
Totals	100,000.00		− 51,081.64		35,762.19	− 15,319.45

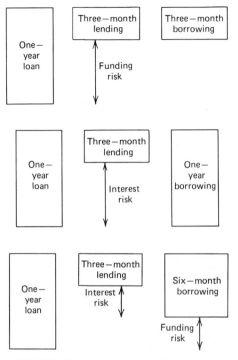

FIGURE 17.1. Interest versus Funding Risk.

SECTION 4.   MONEY MARKET MATURITY LADDER

17.4.1.   Different problems arise on the money market side. The bank will normally have two distinct risks. They have different consequences. The first risk is liquidity, or funding. Liquidity risks are caused by a mismatch in final maturity dates. A lending with a final maturity date of one year, funded by a one-month deposit, causes a liquidity risk for the remaining 11 months. The bank cannot be certain of laying its hands on the money for the next 11 months. In an extreme case, if a bank becomes so illiquid that it cannot fund itself from day to day, it must close down. A second risk is an exposure to interest rate changes if there is a mismatch in roll-over dates, as well as the final maturity (see Figure 17.1). Suppose a lending has a maturity of one year, but is based on a three-month roll-over. If it is funded by a three-month deposit, the funding risk remains for the last nine months. The interest rate risk is nil for the current three months. And it is cut out in future each time the bank funds the three-month roll-over with a three-month deposit. But if the three-month roll-over lending is financed by a six-month deposit, there is not only a liquidity risk but also an interest risk. The interest rate that the bank might earn for the last three months before the next roll-over date is uncertain (since the rate will only be set at maturity of the first three-month lending). These two different risks can only be measured on separate ladders, since the same item can put the bank at risk in two different periods. A five-year loan funded by a three-month borrowing would cause a five-year funding risk, but the interest risk will be covered every three months. If roll-over business is an important part of a bank's total book, it may need a separate interest rate ladder. Finally, problems can arise even when the bank's book is totally matched. Suppose a trader borrows one year funds at, say, 14% in the expectation that rates will rise, but instead they fall sharply, soon afterwards. He decides to minimize further loss by covering the position at 13%. As far as liquidity and interest mismatch are concerned, he is exactly matched: but there is a built-in loss in his position that needs to be detected.

17.4.2. In any event, a deposit maturity mismatch ladder will normally be essential. The methods used will depend on the business of the bank; an example might be as follows. Separate ladders are made up for local currency liabilities and assets, and foreign currency liabilities and assets, by currency. Maturities are split into time bands, on the basis of time left to maturity (not the original life of the deal, nor the next roll-over date). The time band used is (1) the first date at which call or notice deposits can be required to be repaid; (2) the due dates of bills of exchange, promissory notes, or CDs; (3) the last repayment date of a government stock or similar security; (4) the agreed repayment dates for time deposits; or (5) the agreed repayment date for each installment of a medium-term loan. Table 17.4 shows what the effect of this might be.

17.4.3. If we look at this we see that call assets in local currency exceed liabilities. The opposite situation occurs in the foreign currency book. So the net final mismatch is negative at 4,733 in accounting currency terms. In both local and foreign currency this mismatch is slightly increased by a net borrowing in the one-to-seven-day period, while in the eight-day-to-one-month period the position is dominated by a large overlent position in the foreign currency book. This brings the cumulative final mismatch to an overlent position. This runs up to the three-to-six-month period, from when on the bank is overborrowed up to the three-year period.

17.4.4. The maturity mismatch ladder will need to be supplemented by various items of other information. For example, the treatment of overdrafts (if any) will be influenced by the extent to which some of them are "hard core," that is, being used as a permanent borrowing. In setting up Table 17.4, we assumed that anyway, in practice, overdrafts are not repayable on demand, but need to be treated as 12-month assets. Hard-core overdrafts ought properly to be treated as even longer. It is also important to include information on other commitments. If we do, we can see the bank's exposure if customers were to use all existing facilities in a crisis. Undrawn money market lines or overdraft facilities can cause large potential extra exposure. Contingent liabilities under

TABLE 17.4 Deposit Mismatch Ladder.

Period	Local Currency				Foreign Currency				Final Mismatch	
	Liabilities (1)	Assets (2)	Mismatch −P (3)	Mismatch −C (4)	Liabilities (5)	Assets (6)	Mismatch −P (7)	Mismatch −C (8)	−P (9)	−C (10)
Call and Savings	(2,322)	6,460	4,138	4,093	(8,982)	111	(8,871)	(9,624)	(4,733)	(5,531)
One–seven days	(4,045)	4,000	(45)	4,112	(6,998)	6,245	753	(3,566)	(798)	546
Eight days–one month	(14,743)	14,762	19	4,332	(3,159)	9,217	6,058	1,024	6,077	5,356
One–two months		220	220	7,425		4,590	4,590	9,468	4,810	16,893
Two–three months		3,093	3,093	5,472		8,444	8,444	(8,198)	11,537	(2,726)
Three–six months	(22,281)	20,328	(1,953)	3,198	(36,314)	18,648	(17,666)	(13,897)	(19,619)	(10,699)
Six–nine months	(4,713)	2,439	(2,274)	4,293	(7,498)	1,799	(5,699)	(15,124)	(7,973)	(10,831)
Nine–twelve months	(2,345)	3,440	1,095	4,317	(6,119)	4,892	(1,227)	(13,399)	132	9,082
Overdraft[a]		24	24	6,707		1,725	1,725	(11,625)	1,749	4,918
One–two years	(5,005)	7,395	2,390	7,293	(3,847)	5,621	1,774	(11,457)	4,164	(4,164)
Two–three years	(654)	1,240	586	9,597	(320)	488	168	(9,429)	754	(4,164)
Three–four years	(3,760)	6,064	2,304	17,267	(92)	2,120	2,028	(9,429)	4,332	168
Four–five years	(698)	8,368	7,670	25,242				(9,429)	7,670	7,838
Longer		7,975	7,975					(9,429)	7,975	15,813
Capital and Infrastructure	(20,316)	4,503	(15,813)	9,429					(15,813)	nil
Totals	(80,882)	90,311	9,429		(73,329)	63,900	(9,429)		nil	nil

NOTE: P = this period, C = cumulative.
[a] Treated as 12-month loans.

TABLE 17.5.   Interest Mismatch Ladder.

Interest Rate Period	Euro		Local Currency		Net
	Liabilities	Assets	Liabilities	Assets	
Non-interest bearing	1,100	—	22,795	12,171	− 11,724
At variable rates (notice up to seven days)	4,255	300	2,000	24	− 5,931
Fixed rates up to three months	19,846	13,421	22,958	20,688	− 8,695
Three–twelve months	31,422	35,347	31,174	36,775	+ 9,526
One–two years	6,111	8,481	6,455	7,227	+ 3,142
Two–three years	3,980	5,054	640	1,625	+ 2,059
Three–four years	377	1,905	3,680	4,049	+ 1,897
Four–five years	849	1,150	680	2,520	+ 2,141
Five years plus	79	148	—	6,232	+ 6,301
	68,019	65,806	90,382	91,311	− 1,284

standby arrangements, documentary credits or acceptances also need to be measured.

17.4.5.   Also we cannot judge the bank's overall position without knowing what mismatch the local central bank will accept. And we need to know from the ordinary interest income and expense accounting procedure whether the book is currently profitable. We need also to know how much the book is vulnerable to sudden shifts in interest rates; the interest rate risk.

SECTION 5.   INTEREST MISMATCH LADDER

17.5.1.   For this purpose, as we said earlier, an interest rate mismatch ladder will be needed. This classifies balances by the time for which the interest rate is fixed rather than by their final maturity. So a loan repayable after five years and rolled over at a six-month rate would be shown in a five-year band in the deposit maturity mismatch ladder, and in the six-month band in the interest mismatch ladder. Table 17.5 shows an interest mismatch ladder in its simplest form.

17.5.2.   Table 17.5 serves to show where the bank is most at risk from sudden interest rate movements. In the case shown, for example, the bank is overlent in the Euromarket in all periods beyond three months. As a result, a sudden rise in certain interest rates would make much of the longer-term book unprofitable until the fixed rate assets had run off.

17.5.3.   If sophisticated computer facilities are available, it would be a help to produce a more refined interest rate mismatch ladder. This would take into account the interest rates at which the deals were originally done. We can find

TABLE 17.6. Weighted Average Rate per Block.

Contract	Amount		Days		Product 1		Rate		Product
1)	2	×	5	=	10	×	12	=	120
2)	3	×	10	=	30	×	11.5	=	345
3)	5	×	28	=	140	×	11	=	1540
					180				2005

NOTE: Weighted average rate for time block = 2005/180 = 11.14%.

the weighted averages for outstanding contracts on the ladders for placings (assets) and raisings (liabilities) by time blocks. We will take into account the amount, number of days from report date to maturity date, and the rate. For example, if the placings maturing in a one-month time block on a ladder at report date were US\$ 2 million maturing in 5 days at 12%, US\$ 3 million maturing in 10 days at 11½%, and US\$ 5 million maturing in 28 days at 11%, then the weighted average for the placings in that time block could be calculated as shown in Table 17.6. We can see from this example that the effect of the US\$ 5-million deal at the lower rate of 11% has tended to pull down the weighted average rate for the time block.

17.5.4. An example of this technique can be seen in Table 17.7 (overleaf). This is a simplified balance sheet of a domestic money market dealing room. Short-term operations are broken down into overnight, call and notice, one-week, and one-month. Thereafter monthly time blocks are used up to the one-year period, after which the division is into years. We can see that the overnight operations are running at a profit, but the call and notice and one-week periods are both generating a loss. Apart from these, though, and the seven-month, ten-month, and three-year operations, all the other time blocks are showing a profit. Notice that the row labeled "cumulative mismatch" is cumulated from the furthest date and not the nearest date on the ladder. The reason for this is to prevent long-term problems from being hidden by short-term cosmetics. Suppose the bank were heavily overlent in the longer periods, such as the two-, three-, or four-year, but were very much overborrowed in the shorter periods. Cumulating from the near end to the far end might give the idea that the bank is overfunded for most of the earlier part of its book, and that the overlending in the far periods was adequately financed. It is simply a matter of presentation, of course, and cumulating in another way may be better in other circumstances.

SECTION 6. OTHER CONTROLS

17.6.1. Having discussed some of the tools used by treasury management in analyzing its exchange and interest rate risks, we now turn to the question of how to make proper use of the tools. To belabor the obvious, sophisticated

TABLE 17.7.   Domestic Money Position.

	Overnight	Call and Notice	One Week	One Month	Two Months	Three Months	Four Months	Five Months	Six Months
Raisings									
Banks	87	31	66	222	102	37	6	8	24
Commercials	15	130	39	31	53	21	16	3	4
CDs	—	—	5	28	35	24	12	15	29
Branches and subsidiaries	18	16	17	28	36	7	3	2	4
Subtotal	120	177	127	309	226	89	37	28	61
Average cost	11.63	11.60	12.07	12.21	12.49	12.56	12.50	12.66	12.64
Lendings									
Reserves	110	—	—	—	—	—	—	—	—
CDs	—	—	—	—	17	18	14	6	11
Banks	34	4	40	51	51	55	86	26	26
Commercials	10	—	74	41	41	38	5	—	—
Branches and subsidiaries	4	—	16	57	57	11	7	5	16
Other lendings	—	—	10	—	—	9	—	—	—
Subtotal	158	4	140	149	166	131	112	37	53
Average yield	11.87	11.4	11.85	12.67	12.99	12.59	13.42	13.12	14.19
Period mismatch	38	− 173	13	− 160	− 60	42	75	9	− 8
Cumulative mismatch	24	− 14	159	146	306	366	324	249	240

tools are useless unless the basics are right. The golden rule is that rigid rules are no substitute for a good relationship with the dealing and backup teams. But there are obvious basics. The first is separation between the dealing room and the backup. This should prevent unauthorized dealing from being concealed by inadequate backup procedures. The risk is that (as in the Lugano affair) an unauthorized position loses money and is "doubled up" in the hope of turning around. In this context a truism which bears repeating is that the test of a dealer is not how much profit he or she makes but the ability to take losses early rather than hang on until too late. Certain banks set traders profit targets; they are then given incentives, or pressurized, to meet or exceed them. There is a risk that this policy can lead to overtrading. Another sensitive area is the question of requests to deal at rates which are "away from the market." This may sometimes be needed to help a broker. The broker is then expected to repay the "points" (away from the market price) he has "borrowed" later. But it can also be a sign that a dealer is beginning to try to conceal a position which is going sour. And it is also important to make sure that too much business is not directed toward one broker or bank.

17.6.2.   There are other controls needed to reduce exchange and interest rate risk. The first area is the setting of limits. These can be structured in many

Seven Months	Eight Months	Nine Months	Ten Months	Eleven Months	Twelve Months	Two Years	Three Years	Four Years	Five Years	Five Years +
1	8	1	20	1	1	1	4	—	—	—
3	13	—	1	—	—	3	—	—	—	—
2	2	12	11	1	2	—	5	—	—	—
13	2	3	2	1	1	—	5	24	—	—
19	25	16	34	3	4	4	14	24	—	—
13.64	12.40	13.50	12.24	12.01	12.50	13.35	13.33	12.04	—	—
—	—	—	—	—	—	—	—	—	—	—
14	19	26	15	7	11	20	1	5	1	2
9	14	15	27	6	16	—	9	28	—	2
—	—	11	—	—	—	4	—	2	—	—
4	10	1	3	1	—	—	—	1	—	—
—	7	—	—	—	14	28	37	14	7	—
27	50	53	45	14	41	52	47	50	8	4
13.55	13.12	13.57	11.98	12.85	13.17	13.41	13.11	13.71	14.07	13.30
8	25	37	11	11	37	48	33	26	8	4
248	240	215	178	167	156	119	71	38	12	4

different ways; the following is only an example. First, a limit on the total foreign exchange book is set. Clearly, it is necessary to have some control on the volume of activity to prevent overtrading and to keep total exposure under reasonable control. Normally the aggregate book would be defined as all outstanding foreign currency contracts (purchases plus sales, spots plus forwards) with customers, banks, branches, and subsidiaries. Interest arbitrage spot and forward contracts with counterparties should be included, but if interest arbitrage transactions are generated internally within a dealing room (say, between subsections of the room), these ought to be excluded. They do not put the bank at risk in the outside world. A similar limit would apply to the total outstanding volume of the Eurocurrency and domestic currency book.

17.6.3. The second set of limits will cover the bank's total uncovered open foreign exchange position. This would be defined as the aggregate uncovered position in all maturities, comprising overbought plus oversold positions in all foreign currencies, without offsetting between different currencies. It would be normal to set two separate open position limits, one being for normal trading hours, and the second for overnight positions (perhaps about half of the daylight limit—clearly a position left overnight is potentially subject to greater risk from unforeseen developments).

17.6.4.   The third set of overall limits will be the mismatch limits. As was seen above in the revaluation exercise, a swap deal can incur a potential loss if the forward margins moved between the time the swap was taken out and the time when it has to be reversed. Clearly, the problem increases over time. A five-year mismatch is likely to be subject to greater movements in rates during the life of the deal than a two-month mismatch. So a mismatch limit would probably be set for mismatches of up to six months, with a smaller limit for the six-month-to-one-year bracket, a yet smaller one for one- to two-years, and so forth. A similar mismatch limit would be applied to the Eurocurrency and domestic currency book. This latter limit, of course, is to control the funding and interest rate risk discussed earlier.

17.6.5.   As well as these limits, a bank will set credit limits. The more obvious limits are on the money market side. First, there may be limits on its total lendings to any single counterparty. These will be set just like any other lending limit. A refinement would be to set sublimits, smaller in size, for medium-term lending. A less obvious credit risk is incurred when taking deposits. First, when accepting an overnight deposit in a currency in a distant center (e.g., a London bank taking overnight Eurodollars), a bank can find itself repaying the deposit before it is sent the initial confirmation that the deposit was made. It may be repaying a nonexistent deposit. Second, a bank which takes a very large amount of deposits from a single customer may become vulnerable to sudden withdrawals. This latter risk is not so much a credit risk as a liquidity risk.

17.6.6.   Credit risks in foreign exchange occur in two areas. The first type of risk is on outstanding forward contracts. Suppose a customer went bankrupt after doing a forward sale of deutsche marks to a bank. The bank would have to buy forward deutsche marks to replace those it would have been receiving from the customer. It is at risk because the rates might have moved against it. The risk is marginal rather than total. The amount at risk is determined by the possible exchange rate movement. This type of risk is controlled by an aggregate limit on outstanding forwards. The second area of risk is often called the capital risk, or credit risk. It is best seen in the failure of Herstatt Bank. Herstatt was closed during trading hours. Banks which had delivered DMK to Herstatt against US$ found that they did not receive the US$ although they had paid DMK to Herstatt. So banks will normally set a limit on the total value they will allow at risk on any one day. A refinement would be to include in this amount a part of outstanding forwards, say over one year.

17.6.7.   Let's look at an example. Bank A might set a limit for a company in the following terms: capital (or credit) risk, US$ 15 million; aggregate risk, US$ 50 million; marginal risk on deals over one year, 30% to be treated as capital risk. Suppose we have the following deals between Bank A and Company X:

Spot	$ 5 million
One month	$10 million
Six months	$ 8 million
One year	$ 7 million
Two years	$ 5 million

The total outstanding is $35 million. Capital risk on one-month date is $10 million + $1.5 million (being 30% of the $5 million done beyond one year). So the bank can do another $3.5 million in the one-month date, another $10 million on the spot date.

SECTION 7.   LIQUIDITY

17.7.1.   In addition to the control of risks from exchange and interest rate movements, a second area of vital interest to the bank is control of its liquidity. In setting up liquidity policy, it needs to think first of the times when it might need cash, and its reliance on marketable assets and liquid claims on others. It will have to look at their safety if there is a general market crisis. Second, it has to make sure it can finance any immediate or expected need for cash.

17.7.2.   As far as concerns protection against crisis, the usual policy is for banks to buy government securities or prime certificates of deposit of first-class banks to give a "cushion" of assets which are readily marketable. They can then be sold for cash if the bank has an urgent need for them. This assumes that these are institutions whose credit standing will be untouched in a crisis. Therefore the bank will be able to sell the assets without incurring a great loss. This is, of course, only an assumption; but it is the only practical one which can be made. If Armageddon comes there will be little that even the most far-sighted treasurer could do to protect his bank.

17.7.3.   The second line of defense will be stand-by arrangements made between banks. If one of the parties to the stand-by arrangement falls into difficulties, the counterparty will provide funds to help. The third line of defense is the "lender of last resort:" the central bank of the country in which the headquarters of the bank are located. As we saw in Chapter 1, the Basle Concordat of 1975 among the major central banks of the world began to lay the foundations for supervision of international banking operations. At the same time, there was to some extent an implicit acceptance of a lender-of-last-resort function for international banks' operations. However, the Banco Ambrosiano affair showed that there are limits to certain central banks' willingness or ability to interpret the Concordat in a broad way.

SECTION 8.   BALANCE SHEET RATIOS; LOCAL REGULATIONS

17.8.1.   A third area of concern to the treasurer of a bank is the control of the size and structure of the bank's book. He has to match it to the volume of activity in various markets, and to the amount of capital available to support the total book. In a multicurrency bank, this can cause complications. The bank will probably want a certain ratio of capital to total balance sheet, and will in fact generally be required to do so by law or by custom. For example, in Germany the Bundesaufsichtsamt für das Kreditwesen (Federal Banking Supervisory Authority) and the Bundesbank have jointly laid down certain "Basic Principles" which essentially limit a bank's total lending and investments to 18 times capital. But in a multicurrency bank maintaining such a capital ratio can cause problems unless the capital itself is distributed in proportion with the different currencies of the balance sheet.

17.8.2.   Suppose a German bank, with a capital denominated purely in deutsche marks, wanted to maintain, say, a 5% capital ratio, but had half of its balance sheet in U.S. dollars because of Eurodollar operations. Then the fall in the deutsche mark exchange rate of about 13% in the year to December 1981 would have forced the bank to raise an extra 6½% of its existing capital (assuming that it had already been at its limits). But the alternative of selecting capital denominated in different currencies according to the proportions which they currently hold in the balance sheet is not entirely satisfactory. It makes it difficult for the bank to switch the composition of its balance sheet from currency to currency according to its business needs.

17.8.3.   The treasurer also needs to ensure that his bank complies with the local regulations of the central bank. Typically, these will cover foreign exchange positions, liquidity requirements, and exchange control compliance. In the United States, foreign exchange position limits are not formally set. The dealing activities of individual banks are, of course, closely supervised by the relevant authorities (see Chapter 1, Section 6). The system of visiting examiners substitutes for extensive rules. In Germany, following the Herstatt crisis of 1974, the extent of foreign exchange position taking by banks was tightly controlled. The so-called Basic Principle lays down that the net open position in foreign currencies (and gold, silver, or platinum), independent of maturity, should not exceed 30% of capital.[1] The net open position within any one month or half year should not exceed 40% of capital.

17.8.4.   In the United Kingdom, the Bank of England issued a paper called "Foreign Currency Exposure" in April 1981.[2] Unlike the German regulations, the total permitted open position was not rigidly fixed. In Paragraph 12 of the paper, the bank stated that "The Bank will not set any formal limits on the size of a bank's foreign currency positions, but will agree dealing position guidelines with each institution individually. These will take account of the institution's particular circumstances and expertise. As a general rule, for banks which are experienced in foreign exchange the Bank will expect to agree the following guidelines:

   "(1) net open dealing position in any one currency: not more than 10% of the adjusted capital base . . .

"(2) net short open dealing positions of all currencies taken together: not more than 15% of the adjusted capital base.

". . . these reporting requirements will not change the existing informal arrangements whereby the Gold and Foreign Exchange Office of the Bank may from time to time discuss dealing positions directly with dealers."

17.8.5.   A similar range from rigid to flexible controls can be seen in central banks' arrangements for liquidity control. In the United States, the only liquidity requirements at a national level are those imposed by the Federal Reserve in the form of its reserve requirements. Individual states also have provisions for liquidity and asset maintenance requirements. And the relevant supervisory authorities will look closely at the liquidity of a bank. The Bank of England's approach has recently become more formal. It has replaced its traditional reserve assets ratio approach. Cash and assets classed as "liquid" are still compared with sight and nearsight liabilities. But also other liabilities and assets are inserted in a maturity ladder. The net positions in each time period are accumulated. The key to this approach is that no distinctions are made among the different types of deposit on the liabilities side. The idea is that the volatility of a deposit is determined by its terms and by confidence in the deposit-taker, both of which do not depend on who holds the deposit. Commitments which are not due to be met on a particular date (for example, undrawn overdraft and standby facilities made available by the bank to others) are included as liabilities. Assets are measured on the basis of their maturity. Marketable assets are valued at current market value and discounted to reflect the possibility of loss on immediate sale.[3]

17.8.6.   A much tighter control system is exercised in France by the Commission de Controle des Banques. Banks must maintain liquid assets at 60% of short-term liabilities at all times. If the ratio is between 60% and 70%, the commission is entitled to "address recommendations" to the banks involved if it seems that their liquidity ratio is coming under pressure.[4] If the proportion of foreign currency assets and liabilities in a bank's balance sheet exceeds 10%, it must calculate two liquidity ratios, one for operations in French francs, and the other for currency operations. The 60% ratio is only applied to French franc operations, with currency operations then being separately scrutinized by the commission. A string of other ratios are also applied (see Chapter 3, Section 10), with 8 possible ratios and 21 subtotals.

17.8.7.   France also operates a very tight system of exchange controls. The regulations involved run to four fat volumes, so any summary is necessarily an oversimplification. Essentially, however, exchange controls on banks control a position against French francs. Currency against currency positions are—within prudential limits—uncontrolled. However, the very detailed reporting requirements laid down by the authorities and their close supervision of the market make it extremely unlikely that a bank would be able to deviate far from prudent exposure.

SECTION 9.   INTERNAL PRICING

17.9.1.   It should be clear that the treasurer of a bank will have to cope with widely varying regulations from country to country. In addition, he or she has many internal control problems to contend with. One of the most widespread of these is the so-called "transfer pricing" issue. The question here is intimately related to the whole question of centralization versus decentralization. Since, in general, most banks centralize their treasury functions, it is a fairly widespread problem. It comes up both in foreign exchange and in deposit business. The issue is most clearly seen in foreign exchange. In the event that a customer calls for a price, he will very often be routed either through a branch or through a "corporate desk." The branch or corporate desk will then get a market price from the professional market foreign exchange dealers. The issue is whether the customer desk or the branch should be given a "turn" or "loading" and so be able to show a profit for its efforts. Clearly, as it has done the work to produce the business, it is important that some recognition be given. At the same time, the problem is that by adding the extra loading, the overall quotation may be out of line with the competition.

17.9.2.   A similar but more complex problem arises in deposit business. For a lending which is linked to some clearly defined rate such as LIBOR (see Chapter 11), the question of transfer pricing is relatively straightforward. The dealers will lend the money to the office making the loan at LIBOR, and the loan-producing office will then add a margin which has previously been agreed upon with the customer in advance. It is then reasonably clear-cut to say whether the trading room has funded itself successfully or not, by comparing the average funding cost with the LIBOR rates used for on-lending. The issue here is relatively simple, because a rate like LIBOR is defined for set periods such as one month, two months, three months, and so on.

17.9.3.   The question becomes more complex when we look at loans which are linked to base or prime rate. In general, such loans are repayable on demand, theoretically at least, although on occasion they may be made available for a fixed period. For theoretically overnight lendings, it seems clear that the right cost-of-funds measure is an overnight interest rate. But these can move very sharply, while the prime or base rate of a bank is normally rather "sticky" in its movements. So the dealing room can experience unexpected profits or losses which have little to do with its own skill in funding the bank's book. They have much more to do with the desire of the bank's management to keep its base or prime rate stable. There is no clear-cut answer to this problem. All one can suggest is that one should consider the overall structure of a bank's book and select the interest rate which seems most appropriate for measuring cost of funds. Then one should stick with it consistently, making due allowances for short-term distortions which may arise as a result of market conditions.

SECTION 10.   LOAN PRICING

17.10.1   The issue of transfer pricing is closely connected with the overall issue of loan pricing. This is by no means purely a responsibility of the treasurer, since the lending and marketing personnel of a bank will also be concerned. However, since the aim is to ensure a viable overall balance sheet, the treasurer has to be concerned that loan pricing is appropriate. That is, pricing must not be so aggressive that it leads to a rapid expansion of lending and a "ballooning" of the balance sheet to the point where capital and other ratios are breached; equally, it cannot be so conservative that no business is ever done. At least three problems are relevant: average pricing versus marginal pricing, reserve asset costs, and required return on capital.

17.10.2.   The average versus marginal cost argument sometimes occurs when lending officers want to adjust the "cost of funds" formula used in loan pricing to reflect the fact that a bank has access to so-called free balances. These will be in the form of current accounts obtained through the branch network, travelers' check float, or other cheap sources of funds. The crucial point is that such free balances are inherently limited in supply. As the bank's balance sheet expands, so they must support a larger and larger volume of business. We represent the situation graphically in Figure 17.2.

17.10.3.   This chart is based on the assumption that there is a fixed pool of free balances available to a bank, and that additional funds have to be raised in the marketplace at the going interbank rate. This tends to rise against the bank as its bidding for funds increases, because other banks become increasingly less willing to lend to it. As the volume of business expands beyond the crossover point Z, we see that if the bank still prices its loans on the average cost of funds, it is starting to incur a loss. The average cost of funds to it is more than the average yield. For each new loan that it puts on the books it is increasing its losses, since the yield of the loan is below the cost of the funds.

17.10.4.   A second issue is the pricing of reserve asset costs. The issue doesn't really come up if a loan is linked to prime or base rate. These rates generally take into account the average cost of holding reserve assets against lendings. The problem occurs when a bank is making a lending linked to a money market rate, such as LIBOR. In the Euromarkets, reserve costs can be ignored. But in domestic markets, they need to be included when pricing a loan of this kind. It may be argued that reserve costs should be borne by the depositor, but this would be hard to justify to the depositor and would create problems in pricing, for the term of the deposit is quite likely to be shorter than that of the loan and possibly shorter than the term of the reserve asset, if this is a government security, for example. Also, and more important, banks compete with many institutions for funds; not all these institutions have reserve costs. The reason for charging the reserve asset cost to the lendings on

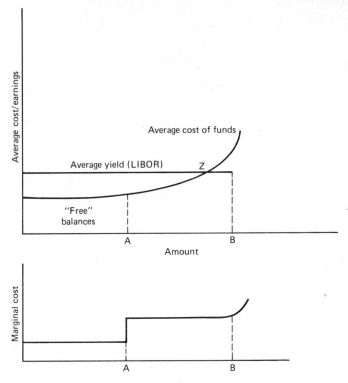

FIGURE 17.2. Average versus Marginal Cost of Funds.

the other hand is as follows. A bank's holding of reserves is usually based on eligible liabilities. Interbank lending in the money market is generally offset (in most countries) against interbank liabilities to work out the total of eligible liabilities. So, in general, interbank lending has no reserve cost while a customer lending creates a need for reserve assets. The exact formula for calculation of reserve asset costs is laid out in Chapter 13, Section 5.

17.10.5.   A related issue is the required return on bank capital. Clearly, if a bank makes a loss it should be suffered by its shareholders and not its depositors. Any bank which loses its depositors' money also loses the raw material of banking, depositors' confidence. It can no longer carry on business. Thus it must have a capital cushion—working capital. Assessing the capital adequacy of a bank depends first on the regulations set in the individual country concerned. In the United States, discussions have been underway for some time among the banking community, the Federal Reserve, and the Comptroller of the Currency about setting firm rules on capital adequacy and leverage. At present, specific ratios are negotiated by the banks with their supervising bodies. The Federal Financial Institutions Examination Council recently recommended a broader definition of bank capital, which has been adopted by the Federal Reserve.[5]

17.10.6.   In the United Kingdom, the Bank of England published a paper in 1980 called "The Measurement of Capital." This paper considered two methods for assessing the adequacy of a bank's capital. The first is the gearing or leverage ratio (as used in the United States or France). This is defined as deposits from the public in relation to free capital (the capital over and above that used in the premises, etc., of the bank). The main problem with the gearing ratio is that it ignores the risks that may be involved in using depositors' funds. The alternative is to look at the different risks in the assets of a bank. The Bank of England has decided to use the second approach for its discussions of adequacy with individual banks. (The Banque de France uses a similar approach—see 3.10.7.)

17.10.7.   Risk is measured by weighting all assets by a given series of coefficients. Holdings of cash are given a nil risk, lendings to the money market and local authorities (municipalities) a risk weighting of 0.2, customer advances and leasing a weighting of 1.0, and purchases of premises a weighting of 2.0. That is, the less liquid the investment, the higher the risk weighting. A risk asset ratio is then calculated which is defined as the ratio of the adjusted capital base to weighted risk assets. The Bank of England then sets an agreed risk asset ratio for each bank, depending on the type of its business and so on.

17.10.8.   Suppose that the ratio were 10%. Suppose that the capital base of the bank were 100 units. Then the capital available will support weighted assets of 1,000 units. An expansion of customer lendings (which are weighted at 1.0) of 100 will therefore increase risk weighted assets by 100. This will need an increase of 10 units in the capital base. According to the overall cost of capital, the loan pricing would need to be adjusted. If the cost of capital is 10%, then approximately 1% has to be charged into the price of the loan (less any assumed earnings on capital). An expansion of money market lendings, though, needs less capital to support it so the capital cost factor will be lower.[6]

SECTION 11.   TAX

17.11.1.   Another question in loan pricing which may concern the treasurer is the tax factor. This has two aspects. First, let us look at the straight problem of recovering the cost of taxes. An example of this is seen in Euromarket facilities, where loan agreements normally make provision for recovery of withholding tax if it should be imposed. If withholding taxes already apply, the bank will need to make some adjustment to the pricing, for it will normally be out of funds between the time that the withholding tax is deducted by the authorities and the time that the bank is able to reclaim the tax from them (see 13.5.2). Another important point, of course, is to structure loans for best use of the bank's available tax capacity. Since the use of foreign and other tax credits is an area of interest not only to the banks but also to the fiscal authorities, it is an area which is constantly developing. The comments made here can relate only to general principles.

17.11.2. The OECD Model Double Taxation Agreement was first published in 1963, and has helped the growth of a wide network of double taxation agreements between individual countries. They vary, so in each case the treasurer needs to know whether interest earnings are to be treated as business profits or interest. The effective rate of withholding tax also varies depending on the countries involved. And some double taxation agreements, particularly those between developed and developing countries, have "tax sparing" articles. The articles normally lay down that where interest payable on an approved investment incentive loan is exempt from withholding tax in the source country, the tax which has been "spared" can still be credited against income in the borrower's country. Spared tax is particularly useful to a bank. It is treated in the same way as withholding tax actually paid when it comes to working out credit relief. But the interest earned need not be grossed up by the spared tax in working out taxable income.

17.11.3. But there has been strong competition among banks in the spared tax market. In some cases this has produced negative margins on lendings. The reason is that by using the tax credit on spared tax loans, the bank can earn the same net after-tax profit as it would have made on an ordinary loan at a positive margin. The whole area of tax credits is of constant concern to the revenue authorities, however, and it is essential to keep track of developments. For example, in March 1982 the United Kingdom took steps to eliminate "tax sparing."[7] The U.S. Internal Revenue Service has been very active in developing Regulations 1.861-8 and the concept of "fungibility" to allocate and apportion expenses (including interest costs) between foreign and domestic income in order to set limits to the use of foreign tax credits.

17.11.4. These tax angles may be relevant to the treasurer's function insofar as they lead to a switching of the locations through which certain loans are booked. So, for example, it may be convenient for certain reasons to book Euro-deutsche mark loans through Brussels. This means that the Brussels operation's deutsche mark fundings must rise to match the deutsche mark lendings, with implications for its book.

NOTES

1. Reproduced (in the German edition) in Bundesbank's Annual Reports each year.
2. *Bank of England Quarterly Bulletin,* April 1981.

3. *Bank of England Quarterly Bulletin*, September 1982.

4. Commission de Controle des Banques, "Reglement: Dispositions applicables aux banques," Articles 141–154. See also J. F. Ferronniere and E. de Chillaz, *Les Operations de banque*, sixth edition, Dalloz, Paris 1980, pp. 321–324.

5. *Federal Reserve Bulletin*, December 1981, p. 901.

6. See for example, D. C. Child, "Setting the Price of the Corporate Loan," *The Treasurer*, United Kingdom, September 1981, pp. 5–10.

7. One source of information on this subject is *Foreign Tax Credits Available to Banks in Selected Countries*, Peat, Marwick, Mitchell & Co., London, 1981.

18

MEASUREMENT OF EXPOSURE IN THE CORPORATION

In this chapter we turn from the problems faced by a bank to those of the corporation. We begin with how its exposure is to be measured. Section 1 sets out basic concepts, touching on economic, transaction, and translation exposure especially. Section 2 explains the effect of taxation, and we then look at the U.S. Financial Accounting Standards Board's Statement 52 on accounting for foreign exchange rate changes. Section 4 returns to taxation and shows how the draft U.S. proposals mesh with FASB 52, while the last two sections take up some complications arising from the concepts discussed.

SECTION 1.   BASIC CONCEPTS

18.1.1.   We come now to the measurement of exposure in the corporation. In many ways this is intrinsically more complex than in a bank. In the banking case we are concerned with purely monetary assets and liabilities; in the corporation the asset to be hedged may consist of a trading receivable, or it may consist of a fixed asset such as property which forms part of the corporation's balance sheet. Equally, the bank's trading operations will usually be subject to a fairly uniform tax treatment because its profits and losses on foreign exchange will (normally) be part of its ordinary income.

18.1.2.   There are many different measures of exposure which have been applied to corporations. *Economic, transaction, translation,* and *operational exposure* are all terms which have been used at various times. The broadest, perhaps, is *economic exposure.* It has been defined as the impact of exchange rate changes on discounted cash flow of a company at a specified future date.[1]

18.1.3.   Two other widely used measures are transaction and translation exposure. They are used by the Financial Accounting Standards Board of the United States, which in 1975 published its Statement Number 8, now generally referred to as FASB 8 (see Section 3 below). In brief, *transaction exposure* concerns actual transactions in foreign currencies, whereas *translation exposure* deals with the valuation of overseas assets.

18.1.4.   Finally, another measure which is widely used is consolidated after-tax exposure. This, as the name suggests, looks at the translation component and the tax effect of the transaction component of the exposure from a consolidated after-tax viewpoint. This concept of after-tax exposure is often used by corporations with a centralized exposure management function.

18.1.5.   The choice of definition is controversial. FASB 8, the first definitive statement of its kind on this subject, ran to over 20,000 words, much of it devoted to justifying the Board's decision. But it was subjected to intensive international criticism. After six years of debate, some of the main principles of FASB 8 were abandoned, and a new statement, FASB 52, was published. In the United Kingdom, Exposure Draft 21 on foreign currency translations was published in 1977 but met with widespread criticism, leading to a new Exposure Draft 27, "Accounting for Foreign Currency Translations." As of the time

TABLE 18.1.   Transaction Loss by German Subsidiary.

	Period 1	Period 2
Exchange rate US$ 1	= US$ 1	1
	DMK 2	1.7778
	SFR 2	1.60
Subsidiary's account receivable		
in US$	100	100
in DMK	200	177.78
in SFR	200	160.00
Subsidiary's transaction loss		
in DMK	—	− 22.22
in SFR	—	− 20.00

of writing, ED27 had not yet been finally adopted.[2] Similar controversies took place in a number of other countries.

18.1.6.   As far as concerns FASB 8, there were a number of specific criticisms. But the most widespread concerned the problem of *translation losses* or profits. The problem was that these had to be reported in current quarterly or annual *income statements.* This could have very inconvenient and misleading reporting effects. FASB 52 now requires these profits and losses to be taken to an *equity account* in the balance sheet, rather than being shown in the income statement. FASB 52 also, in general, requires assets and liabilities to be translated at the current exchange rate (see Section 4).

18.1.7.   To see how these concepts work in practice, let's take some examples.[3] Let's look at a Swiss corporation with a German subsidiary. Assume that the Swiss corporation has no foreign exchange exposure of its own. The only foreign exchange exposure of the German subsidiary is an account receivable in U.S. dollars, for $100. At the start of the first period, the exchange rates are US$ 1 = DMK 2 = SFR 2. By period 2, the dollar has depreciated against both the DMK and SFR: US$ 1 = DMK 1.7778 = SFR 1.60. These rates mean the deutsche mark has depreciated also against the Swiss franc, from a relationship of parity, DMK 1 = SFR 1, to DMK 1 = SFR 0.90. Clearly the subsidiary has an exchange loss by being long of a dollar receivable when the dollar is falling. This transaction loss, measured in deutsche marks, totals DMK 22.22. The Swiss franc equivalent of this transaction loss is SFR 20.0. (See Table 18.1.)

18.1.8.   So far we've looked at this purely from the point of view of the subsidiary. It has a transaction loss. When it comes to collect the account, it will receive less in deutsche marks than it expected. This loss will have to be shown in the profit and loss statement. But look at it now from the point of view of the parent. The subsidiary's account receivable in dollars was an overseas asset

TABLE 18.2. Swiss Parent's Translation Loss.

	Period 1	Period 2
Exchange rate US$ 1	= US$ 1	1
	DMK 2	1.7778
	SFR 2	1.60
Subsidiary's account receivable		
in US$	100	100
in DMK	200	177.78
in SFR	200	160.00
Subsidiary's transaction loss		
in DMK	—	− 22.22
in SFR	—	− 20.00
Parent's translation loss		
in SFR	—	− 40.00

of the parent. So the parent will show a translation loss on the account receivable.

18.1.9. This loss is the difference between the original value in the parent company's currency, namely SFR 200, and the value now, namely SFR 160. That is, the parent company will show a translation loss in Swiss francs of SFR 40. As far as the subsidiary is concerned, the transaction loss will show up in cash terms when the account is collected. But from the point of view of the parent company, the loss shows up as a balance sheet adjustment. (See Table 18.2.)

SECTION 2. TAXATION

18.2.1. We must now look at the impact of taxation. In many countries, exchange transaction losses or profits in the ordinary course of business will be taxed just like other profits and losses. But translation profits or losses often are not taxed. Suppose now that the subsidiary pays tax at 60% on its transaction profits or losses. Then the transaction loss of DMK 22.22 will reduce taxable income and therefore taxes. The tax benefit, of course, is the 60% of DMK 22.22 which would otherwise have been payable in taxes, namely DMK 13.34. So the subsidiary's transaction loss, net of tax, is reduced to DMK 8.88, or SFR 8.00. The parent's overall translation loss (net of the subsidiary's tax credit in SFR terms of SFR 12.00) is reduced to SFR 28.00, as we can see from Table 18.3 (overleaf).

18.2.2. The different effects of transaction and translation losses become clear when we look at the local bookkeeping for intercompany exposures. The

TABLE 18.3.   Tax Effect on Transaction and Translation Loss.

	Period 1	Period 2
Exchange rate US$ 1	= US$ 1	1
	DMK 2	1.7778
	SFR 2	1.60
Tax rate: translation	0.00	0.00
transaction	0.60	0.60
Subsidiary's account receivable in US$	100	100
Value in DMK	200	177.78
Value in SFR	200	160
DMK gain/loss	0.00	− 22.22
SFR gain/loss	0.00	− 40.00
Subsidiary's transaction loss		
in DMK	0.00	− 22.22
in SFR	0.00	− 20.00
Subsidiary's tax credit/charge		
in DMK	0.00	− 13.34
in SFR		− 12.00
Subsidiary's transaction loss net of tax:		
DMK	0.00	− 8.88
SFR	0.00	−8.00
Parent's translation loss SFR	0.00	− 40
Parent's translation loss net of tax		
SFR	0.00	− 40
Parent's translation loss after subsidiary's tax credit/charge net of tax		
in SFR	0.00	− 28
Parent's transaction loss	0.00	0.00
Parent's transaction loss net of tax	0.00	0.00

translation of intercompany accounts doesn't normally give rise to gains or losses on the *consolidated* accounts. Intercompany exposure nets out. From a consolidated viewpoint, the two parties involved (the parent and the subsidiary) are long and short in the same currency.

18.2.3.   Let's suppose that the only foreign currency exposure of the subsidiary is now an account payable to its parent, denominated in dollars. Assume the same exchange rate changes as before. Then the subsidiary will benefit to the tune of SFR 40 from the depreciation of the dollar. This will show through in translating the subsidiary's accounts. The parent, on the other hand, has a loss of SFR 40 equivalent in the value of its account receivable from the subsidiary. Table 18.4 summarizes the situation.

18.2.4.   At the translation level, therefore, the effects of currency changes wash out. But the individual companies will usually keep their books in their own currencies. (In FASB 52 terminology, in their "functional currencies"—

TABLE 18.4. Intercompany Exposure.

	Period 1	Period 2
Exchange rate US$ 1	= US$ 1	1
	DMK 2	1.7778
	SFR 2	1.60
Subsidiary's account payable to parent		
in US$	100	100
in DMK	200	177.78
in SFR	200	160.00
Parent's account receivable from subsidiary		
in US$	100	100
in DMK	200	177.78
in SFR	200	160.00

see 18.3.2.) In our example, therefore, *transaction* gains and losses have to be reported at a subsidiary level and at the parent level. The overall effect will depend on the rates of taxation in the two countries. For example, suppose, as before, that the subsidiary is taxed at 60%. Suppose, though, that the parent is taxed at 45%. Then we have the situation shown in Table 18.5.

18.2.5.   Here the subsidiary has made a transaction profit, in DMK, of DMK 22.22, which is taxable at 60%. So the tax bill is DMK 13.34, and there is an after-tax profit of DMK 8.88, or SFR 8.00. The parent, on the other hand, has a transaction loss in Swiss francs of SFR 40.00. Its tax rate is 45%, so this loss yields a tax credit in Swiss francs of SFR 18.00, producing a net after-tax loss of SFR 22.00. In other words, the group as a whole has lost SFR 14.00, purely because the tax rate in the parent company's country has reduced the tax credit obtainable on its transaction loss, compared with the tax cost applied to the subsidiary's transaction profit.

SECTION 3.   FASB 52

18.3.1.   Enough has been said, perhaps, to show that this whole area can be very complex. The problem comes from the difficulty of applying standard monetary methods to corporations which may have different underlying situations. This problem was highlighted by the publication of FASB 8 and its successor FASB 52. As we mentioned earlier, FASB 8 was heavily criticized because the impact of exchange rate changes on the balance sheet was shown up on the income statement, with sometimes misleading results.

18.3.2.   As a result of these criticisms, the FASB undertook a review of FASB 8. The revised approach was published as FASB 52, "Foreign Currency Translation" in December 1981. Briefly, FASB 52 has switched away from the

TABLE 18.5.   Tax Impact on Intercompany Exposure.

	Period 1	Period 2
Exchange rate US$ 1	= US$ 1	1
	DMK 2	1.7778
	SFR 2	1.60
Subsidiary's account payable to parent		
in US$	100	100
in DMK	200	177.78
in SFR	200	160.00
Parent's account receivable from subsidiary		
in US$	100	100
in DMK	200	177.78
in SFR	200	160
Tax rate on parent	45%	45%
subsidiary	60%	60%
Subsidiary's transaction profit in DMK	—	22.22
Subsidiary's tax in DMK	—	13.34
Total in DMK	—	8.88
Total in SFR	—	8.00
Parent transaction loss in SFR	—	40.00
Parent tax credit in SFR	—	18.00
Parent loss net of tax in SFR	—	22.00
Overall effect: Parent's after-tax loss + subsidiary's after-tax profit		− 14.00

approach of FASB 8 toward the so-called "net investment approach." That is, each foreign branch, division, or subsidiary is looked upon as a net investment of the parent. So the parent's exchange risk is related to the business as a whole and not to individual assets and liabilities. FASB 52 lays down:

> The assets, liabilities, and operations of a foreign entity shall be measured using the functional currency of that entity. An entity's functional currency is the currency of the primary economic environment in which the entity operates; normally, that is the currency of the environment in which the entity primarily generates and expends cash. [FASB 52, para. 5]

18.3.3.   Once the functional currency for a foreign entity is determined, its accounts must be cast in terms of the functional currency. If its accounts are not maintained in the functional currency, remeasurement into the functional currency is required (paragraph 10). The accounts are then translated into the reporting currency of the parent, in the following manner:

All elements of financial statements shall be translated by using a current exchange rate. For assets and liabilities, the exchange rate at the balance sheet date shall be used. For revenues, expenses, gains and losses, the exchange rates at the dates at which those elements are recognized shall be used. . . .

13. If an entity's functional currency is a foreign currency, translation adjustments result from the process of translating that entity's financial statements into the reporting currency. Translation adjustments shall not be included in determining net income but shall be reported separately and accumulated in a separate component of equity. [FASB 52, paras. 12 and 13]

18.3.4. FASB 52 has transferred the impact of translation adjustments from the profit and loss account to the balance sheet. It removes erratic fluctuations in income, at the price of erratice fluctuations in the balance sheet. ITT, a corporation which had vehemently criticized FASB 8, switched to FASB 52 in 1982 and showed a swing in the equity adjustment of nearly $500 million between 1980 and 1981 (on a stockholder's equity of $6 billion). Clearly for companies with critical balance sheet ratios, for example, leverage ratios, the random fluctuations of the balance sheet may cause just as much of a problem as the random fluctuations in income experienced in FASB 8.

18.3.5. There are a good many grounds on which one can criticize FASB 52, but on the whole it seems a great deal more sensible than its predecessor. Indeed, other countries seem likely to follow the overall lead given by the FASB. In the United Kingdom, the Accounting Standards Committee produced an Exposure Draft, ED27, "Accounting for Foreign Currency Translations" in 1980. This followed the FASB 52 approach in adopting the "net investment" approach to overseas companies. It seems likely that the UK SSAP will, when in due course it is published, correspond reasonably closely with the revised FASB 52. It also seems probable that these two will be harmonized with the appropriate Canadian standard.

SECTION 4.   TAXATION: CURRENT U.S. PROPOSALS

18.4.1. We now return to a topic touched on earlier, taxation. The first point to make is that this is a constantly changing area, and one where the results of a given situation will depend entirely on the facts of a particular case. It is a vast subject. It varies from country to country, and depends on case law, tax statutes, and the court's interpretation of the facts in a particular case. It is absolutely essential to seek skilled professional advice before assessing any real-life situation. The following discussion only serves to bring out a few simple concepts. It focuses on the United States.

18.4.2. The first point to make is that the Internal Revenue Service has recently issued a proposal for a system for taxing foreign exchange gains and losses, which is discussed below; but it is necessary to begin by looking at the system being replaced. The issues that arise include: whether exchange gains are taxable as ordinary income or capital gains; whether exchange losses are deductible as ordinary or capital losses; and when is the gain or loss recognized, that is, must a transaction be concluded before recognition? Unfortunately, there is a mass of cases and rulings which produce substantially different results on slight differences of the underlying facts.

18.4.3. Oversimplifying, the basic rule which has emerged is that foreign currency is to be treated as property or as a commodity and that exchange gains or losses are calculated separately from the business giving rise to the foreign exchange deal. This is known as the "separate transactions" theory.[4] And, in general, whether the exchange gain or loss is treated as capital or ordinary depends on the basic nature of the underlying transaction. Therefore, ordinary gain or loss will result where the latter is an integral part of the taxpayer's business, or trade.

18.4.4. The taxation of foreign exchange gains or losses arising from forward contracts to hedge exposure depends on several points. Among them are the characterization of the gain or loss (capital or ordinary) and the source of the gain or loss (foreign or domestic).

18.4.5. Let's turn now to the IRS proposals.[5] Briefly, the proposed regulations are designed to fit the framework of FASB 52 (see Section 3). Under the proposals, the functional currency (see 18.3.2) plays a key role in working out income or loss for tax purposes. Suppose a firm's functional currency is the U.S. dollar but its accounts are kept in a different currency. Then net gain or loss would be computed under a "separate transactions" method (as, in general, under the old system). By contrast, if its functional currency is not the U.S. dollar, income or loss in the functional currency is translated directly into dollars at the appropriate exchange rate; that is, a "profit and loss" method is used.

18.4.6. Briefly: (1) a corporation's exchange gains or losses would be recognized for tax purposes at the time of the sale or exchange of a foreign currency asset (or on repayment in the case of a foreign currency loan); (2) gains or losses would be treated as if interest income received or paid with respect to that asset or loan had been increased or decreased by the amount of the gain or loss; (3) gain or loss on certain designated balances of foreign currency could be accrued by valuing such balances at the current exchange rates; (4) if a forward contract was hedging a specific item, gain or loss on the contract would be treated the same as gain or loss on the hedged item; (5) gain or loss on a forward exchange contract hedging an accounting exposure arising under generally accepted accounting principles (e.g., a U.S. parent's hedging of its translation exposure or hedging stock investments in a controlled foreign corporation) would be ordinary and domestic source.

18.4.7. These rules are the first step toward bringing some order to the chaotic U.S. tax rules on foreign currency gains and losses. The question of gains or losses from the hedging of accounting translation gains has been especially controversial. Depending on the taxpayer's particular circumstances, capital gain could be desirable or not. So could sourcing the gain or loss as U.S. or foreign. By saying that all such gain or loss is ordinary in nature and U.S. source, the Treasury has at least simplified the guidelines. And the proposal to adjust income/expense on the sale/repayment of foreign currency receivables/payables at least ties the foreign exchange gain/loss to the original transaction in a way which is much more clear cut than at present.[6]

SECTION 5. INVENTORY, FIXED ASSETS, AND LONG-TERM BORROWING

18.5.1. Up to now we have concentrated on transaction and translation exposures only from current assets and liabilities. We needed to simplify, to make the concepts clear. But in the process certain complications have been glossed over. The first of these is inventory. Under FASB 8, FASB 52's predecessor, the U.S. Financial Accounting Standards Board permitted corporations to value inventory in two ways. They could value at current exchange rates if inventory was valued at current cost or historic exchange rates if inventory was valued at historic cost. But the borrowings to finance the inventory were generally valued at current exchange rates. Clearly it was possible to get some odd results. If the currency of the country in which the inventory was held began to appreciate and the inventory were valued at historic cost, the exchange value of the inventory would be held at the old rate while the value of the borrowing rose. The company would appear to lose money.

18.5.2. A similar distortion arose in the case of fixed assets, and this case points up wider issues. Take the case of a U.S. company buying fixed assets in Brazil. Suppose that during that year inflation in Brazil runs at 100%, while there is no inflation in the United States. Suppose that in Year 1 US$ 1 = CR 100, and in Year 2 US$ 1 = CR 200. In Year 1, the U.S. company buys a machine in Brazil costing CR 10,000 that is, US$ 100. At the end of Year 2, the valuation in historic terms is CR 10,000 = US$ 100. In current terms the machine's value has fallen to US$ 50 owing to the fall in the exchange rate. But the Brazilian price of such a machine, owing to the 100% domestic inflation, has doubled from CR 10,000 to CR 20,000. So if the U.S. company were to replace the machine in Year 2, its cost in U.S. dollar terms would be US$ 100. In this case, measuring the value of the machine at the current exchange rate understates its value to the company. The domestic price level change has exactly offset the exchange rate movement.

18.5.3. In the converse case, take a Brazilian company investing in the United States. In Year 1 it buys a machine worth US$ 100 for CR 10,000. At the end of Year 2 the valuation of the machine is still US$ 100 as there has been no inflation in the United States. Valued at the historic exchange rate, this produces a value of CR 10,000. In current terms, though, the machine's value of US$ 100 translates to CR 20,000. The price arrived at in current terms is the same as that which would apply to the purchase of a new machine. A new machine will also cost US$ 100, there having been no inflation.

18.5.4. In the case of a U.S. company investing in Brazil—that is, an investment in a soft currency area—the historic rate is the more appropriate measure of the fixed asset. The apparent loss to the company from the exchange rate movement would be fully offset by the domestic price level change. In the reverse case (the Brazilian company investing in the U.S., a hard currency area) the exchange rate movement is not offset by any change in the domestic price level, so the current basis of translation gives the more sensible result.

18.5.5. These very simple examples, of course, oversimplify the position. If both countries are inflating at different speeds, neither the current nor the historical method will be completely accurate. It will in general tend to be true that the historic basis will give the more accurate result for investments in weak currencies, while the current basis is better for investments in strong currencies. (These problems are expecially acute in hyperinflationary countries, which FASB 52 essentially treats as if they were being accounted for under the old FASB 8 rules.)

18.5.6. But even this qualified conclusion is subject to further qualifications. Most important, the example above implicitly assumes that the "right" way of valuing the asset at the end of Year 2 was by comparing it with a replacement. For most purposes, what matters to the company is not the replacement cost, but how much local currency income the asset can produce. We may be right in assuming that a fall in the exchange rate of a country where the asset is held will later be offset by a rise in the domestic price level. This would help the asset to produce future income. Then it would be reasonable to assume that the value of the asset to the company will remain constant. In this case the historic measurement will be appropriate. The crucial assumption, though, is the ability of the asset to keep its income generating capacity in "real" terms. If the Brazilian devaluation were accompanied by price controls, the "real" value of the machine in our example would have fallen.

18.5.7. Another area of complication is the question of translation exposures on long-term borrowings. In the case of investment in fixed assets, the exchange risk is a bit unreal in that the corporation does not have to put up hard cash if exchange rates move. But in the case of foreign currency borrowings, which have to be repaid, the position is very different. "Cheap" Swiss francs borrowed for 10 years in 1965 at SFR 4.3730 per dollar would have cost around 80% more to repay in 1975 at SFR 2.6200. If these changes were not reflected in the balance sheet of the company, serious distortions would arise in assessing the company's ability to repay its debts.

18.5.8. But suppose the Swiss franc borrowing was to finance a Swiss franc fixed asset. Revaluing the borrowing at current exchange rates while leaving the Swiss franc asset at the historic exchange rate could produce significant distortions as well. Even though the fixed asset in Switzerland might not conveniently be saleable to repay the Swiss franc borrowing, it does exist and may provide security for a further Swiss franc borrowing with which to refinance the old borrowing, or it may generate a Swiss franc cash flow sufficient to service the borrowing.

SECTION 6.   CASH VERSUS INCOME VERSUS ACCOUNTING

18.6.1. Finally, we need to look at the conflicts among the various types of exposure management strategy.[7] A hedge in the foreign exchange market has an impact on cash flow, net after-tax income, and accounting gains or losses. The cash, income, and accounting impact will vary according to whether the company decides not to hedge, to hedge on a before-tax basis, or to hedge on an after-tax basis. Each of these strategies (if the hedge is properly done) will cut out the impact of exchange rate fluctuations on one of the three variables (cash, net income, or accounting gain/loss).

18.6.2. However, each strategy will at the same time add to the impact on the other two variables. If all other things are equal, we can say that the accounting gain or loss is likely to fluctuate most with no forward cover and least with cover arranged on a before-tax basis. Net after-tax income is most volatile with no cover, and least if the hedge is on an after-tax basis. In contrast, the cash flow effect of translation exposure is nil if it is left completely unhedged, greater if cover is taken on a before-tax basis, and greatest if hedged on an after-tax basis.

18.6.3. A further potential problem is where the hedging should be done. This is linked to the question of centralization discussed earlier, and also to the existence of exchange controls in the countries involved. For example, a U.S. corporation with a French subsidiary would not be able to instruct its French subsidiary to hedge against possible translation exposure because of French exchange controls. The U.S. company would have to do the hedging operations itself in the U.S. market and accept the consequent cash flow and income implications. Equally, a subsidiary in, say, Switzerland might be able to do the hedge, but might not be able to sustain the possible cash flow or income impact.

NOTES

1. R. M. Rodriguez, "Measuring and Controlling Multinationals' Exchange Risk," *Financial Analysts' Journal,* November/December 1979.
2. For background see, for example, P. McMonies and B. R. Rankin, "Accounting for Foreign Currency Translations," *The Accountant's Magazine,* November 1980.
3. These are adapted from B. Antl (ed.), "Currency Risk and the Corporation," *Euromoney Publications,* London, 1980.
4. *Ibid.,* pp. 107–134.
5. *Internal Revenue Bulletin* No. 1981–2, January 12, 1981. These are very much the first draft, and may change.
6. See *Coopers and Lybrand Newsletter,* New York, October 1981, pp. 7–8.
7. The discussion in this section draws on B. Antl, "Currency Risk and the Corporation," pp. 162–164 especially.

19

EXPOSURE MANAGEMENT IN THE CORPORATION

This chapter looks at some of the options open to the corporation in managing its exposure. It begins with some of the organizational questions: choice of trading philosophy and the question of whether or not to centralize. This leads to multinational netting systems. Then we look at other methods of exposure reduction. These fall into two broad areas: nonfinancial and financial. Nonfinancial steps include choices relating to production, pricing and marketing. Financial steps include choice of borrowing currency, back-to-back loans, currency swaps, and "simulated currency loans."

SECTION 1.   ORGANIZATION

19.1.1.   Having discussed how exposure is measured, we come now to the question of what to do about it. This raises a number of issues, but perhaps the most pervasive is the organizational effect of exposure management. The issue surfaces in two particular ways: corporate foreign exchange trading policy and the role of a central treasury. But these in themselves mesh in with many other aspects of a corporation's management style.

19.1.2.   Perhaps the most basic question is the corporation's trading aims. In some firms, a high level decision has been taken to lay down general guidelines for foreign exchange trading policies. In others, there is a general style which is clearly understood in the treasury area. In others again, the policy is just to respond to events.

19.1.3.   As exchange rates have become more volatile, the risk of large losses has greatly increased. So it would be sensible for a set of formal guidelines to be worked out if this has not yet been done. At least the exercise will help all concerned decide whether the present policies meet the firm's needs. Professional bank dealers deliberately take positions which open up foreign currency exposure, to make a profit from them. Some corporations do the same. At the opposite extreme are those companies who feel that "our business is making widgets, not trading in currency." For each company, the right answer will depend on its size and the scale of its international business.

19.1.4.   Following is a conservative view:

> The shareholders are entitled to expect the management of the company to put itself in a position to manage (its foreign exchange) problems but this does not authorise that management to behave like a bank. A reasonable compromise position is to argue that it is acceptable currency management to leave open a foreign exchange exposure that has arisen in the normal course of business. Opening up an exposure which is not necessary is, on the other hand, speculative and accordingly not acceptable[1]

19.1.5.   Many others take a more aggressive approach. The right answer for each company must lie in its own circumstances and skills. The crucial point is that clear guidelines should be laid down by senior management to those who carry out the company's transactions. To date, relatively few corporations have suffered serious losses from unwise foreign exchange dealings. But the experience of the commodity markets, and of certain banks in the foreign exchange markets, suggests that it might happen.

19.1.6.   A second issue which has to be looked at is how far foreign exchange trading should be centralized. The drawback to central control is that it can create a central bureaucracy which is removed from day-to-day problems. A central treasury function can also curb the freedom of the individual profit centers if they lose control over their cash. Also, if the operating divisions no longer have responsibility for their exposure, they may take more risks. (An obvious example is a salesperson pressured to invoice in an undesirable currency.) The group as a whole can suffer because the central treasury has drained foreign exchange skill from the operating units.

19.1.7.   But there are arguments in favour of centralization. It helps to justify better facilities. The most obvious is direct telephone lines to foreign exchange dealing rooms in the banks. A direct line gives a much faster response from the banks. It also makes it easier for the corporation to get simultaneous quotes from two or three banks, which is essential for a fair comparison. Secondly, a centralized treasury can ensure that the firm gets the best rates. It can put together "marketable" amounts. Centralization also makes it easier to match exposures. In general, it is a waste of money if one subsidiary is, say, buying yen while another is selling yen. By the same token, centralization can be a great help to cash management on an international basis. Finally, it helps to concentrate the foreign exchange skills which would otherwise be scattered. This gives scope for full use of the company's information sources and skills.

19.1.8.   If the firm decides to centralize, it has to decide how to set the exchange rates within the company. Again, this depends on the volume of foreign currency business done. In some companies, it may be simplest for the central treasury to issue a regular circular telling the units the rates applying for the month or quarter to come. Or it may be best for the central treasury to act like a bank to the rest of the company. When a division has made a commercial contract, the exposure is passed to the central treasury by a "deal" between the division and the center.

19.1.9.   Various rates may be used for this deal. First is the rate at which the center later covers in the market. This kills any suspicion by the division that it is being "robbed" by the center. But it will probably cause delay because the center may not cover the deal at once. And it may not be possible to match up the deals exactly.

19.1.10.   A second choice is the spot rate on the day that the deal is passed from the division to the center. But if the contract is for a future date, the division may ignore the forward premium or discount on the currency in its pricing. This will harm the group's overall pricing and exposure. A better rate is that for the date that the underlying cash flow will take place. Once the center has bought the currency from, or sold it to, the division, it is the center's job to turn the trade at a profit in the marketplace.

19.1.11.   For a multinational treasury, there is an obvious problem in centralizing exposures between countries. Legal, fiscal, and other factors may prevent this. But it is sometimes possible for a corporation's currency (and tax) exposure to be centralized in a reinvoicing vehicle (see Section 2).

19.1.12. Having looked briefly at some of the broader issues, we turn to some of the specifics. In the rest of this chapter we assume that the corporation is concerned to reduce its exposure, and we look at ways and means to do this. We can divide the major strategies into two broad areas: those which are mainly nonfinancial and organisational, such as decisions on netting, production, input sourcing, and marketing, and those which are more purely financial.

SECTION 2. MULTINATIONAL NETTING

19.2.1 A logical step forward from the process of considering exposure on a group basis is the reinvoicing vehicle. This is sometimes referred to as a netting vehicle, or an indirect invoicing approach. Under this system, every company in the group routes all its intragroup transactions and all its external transactions, other than those in its own domestic currency, through a single group company. The central company through which the transactions are routed and which nets out the exposures can be any group company. But often a new subsidiary is set up in a country which is suitable for tax purposes. The latter choice raises tricky considerations, as the tax authorities have to be convinced that no evasion is taking place.

19.2.2. The operation of a reinvoicing company can be complex, but a simple example will show the principles. The following case assumes a group consisting of three companies. Each has a certain number of intragroup payments to make. We assume payments and receipts are made at the same time of the month. For simplicity's sake we also assume that all the underlying invoices were booked at the same time. Payments are made at the spot rate on the day of settlement. So each company has a profit or loss according to the difference between the booking rate and the settlement rate. (See Table 19.1.)

19.2.3. We see, for example, that the U.S. company had a net sterling exposure. It was long of £150,000. Sterling rose from US$ 2.0 to US$ 2.20 between the time of booking and the time of settlement. So the U.S. company made a profit of US$ 30,000 on its sterling. The profits and losses in the group totalled US$ 9,333.33.

19.2.4. Suppose now that we set up a reinvoicing vehicle. It buys all exposures from group member companies at the booking rate. So it will buy the U.S. company's £150,000 at the booking rate of US$ 2.0 per pound. This gives it a receivable from the U.S. company under the sterling exposure heading. At the same time, it must pay the U.S. company the dollar equivalent, namely

TABLE 19.1. Intercompany Exposure: Direct Settlement.

Company Ownership	Payments	Receipts	Net	Exchange Rates Booking Rate	Exchange Rates Settlement Rate
U.S.	DMK 400,000	200,000	− 200,000	US$/DMK 2.0	US$/DMK 1.80
	£STG 100,000	250,000	+ 150,000	£STG/US$ 2.0	£STG/US$ 2.20
German	US$ 100,000	300,000	+ 200,000		
	£STG 300,000	200,000	− 100,000		
British	US$ 300,000	200,000	− 100,000		
	DMK 100,000	180,000	+ 80,000		

	Exposure	Booking Rate	Settlement Rate[a]	Profit/Loss
U.S.	− DMK 200,000	2.0	1.80	− US$ 11,111.11
	+ £STG 150,000	2.0	2.20	+ US$ 30,000
German	+ US$ 200,000	2.0	1.80	− DMK 40,000
	− £STG 100,000	4.0	3.96	+ DMK 4,000
U.K.	− US$ 100,000	2.0	2.2	+ £STG 4,545.46
	+ DMK 80,000	4.0	3.96	+ £STG 202.2
	Total profit/loss in US$ (using settlement rates)			US$ 9,333.33

[a] Settlement rate = rate against home currency.

TABLE 19.2.   Intercompany Exposure: Use of Reinvoicing Company.

	Payable	Receivable
DMK Exposure		
Vis-à-vis U.S. company	200,000	
Vis-à-vis British company		80,000
Vis-à-vis German company	400,000 (against US$)	
		400,000 (against £STG)
	600,000	480,000 Net: − DMK 120,000
£STG Exposure		
Vis-à-vis U.S. company		150,000
Vis-à-vis German company	100,000	
Vis-à-vis British company		50,000 (against US$)
(against DMK)	20,000	
	120,000	200,000 net: + £STG 80,000
US$ Exposure		
Vis-à-vis German company		200,000
Vis-à-vis British company	100,000	
Vis-à-vis U.S. company		100,000 (against DMK)
(against £STG)	300,000	
	400,000	300,000 net: − US$ 100,000

US$ 300,000, for this sterling receivable. This opens up a U.S. dollar payable exposure in favor of the U.S. company of US$ 300,000, which is entered under its U.S. dollar exposure position. Also the sale to the British company of US$ 100,000 to cover that company's short dollar position of US$ 100,000 is in the reinvoicing company's U.S. dollar exposure account. And it creates a sterling receivable of £50,000 from the British company under the sterling exposure heading. The overall result of these operations is shown in Table 19.2.

19.2.5.   We can see that when the payments are booked the reinvoicing vehicle acquires a short deutsche mark position of DMK 120,000, a long sterling position of £80,000, and a short U.S. dollar position of US$ 100,000. These positions balance out at the booking rates. The long sterling position is worth US$ 160,000; the short DMK position is worth US$ 60,000. But at the settlement date exchange rate movements mean that the short DMK position is equivalent to US$ 66,666.67 while the long sterling position is equivalent to US$ 176,000. The US$ 16,000 profit on the sterling position net of the US$ 6,666.67 loss on the DMK position produce a net profit of US$ 9,333.33.

19.2.6.   This, of course, is exactly the same profit as would have been made under the previous arrangements (see Table 19.1). All that has happened is that the profit has been put in the reinvoicing vehicle. But before, six foreign exchange deals would have been needed—two deals per subsidiary. Consolidation means that the reinvoicing vehicle only needs to sell sterling and buy deutsche marks to square its position. The inherent matching abilities of the reinvoicing vehicle have cut down the complexity of the foreign exchange position. Also, centralizing exposures in one company makes it easier to handle exposure and cash management. By leading or lagging a payment, funds can be switched inside the group, within the constraints of exchange control regulations.

19.2.7. Having considered the implications of organization of the foreign exchange function in the corporation, and the extension of centralization to a multinational netting system, we need now to look at other ways of structuring a company's operations to handle exposure. We start by looking at the implications of production, pricing, and marketing.

SECTION 3. PRODUCTION, PRICING, AND MARKETING STRATEGIES

19.3.1. The choice of production location implies an exchange exposure. It may not be obvious to a U.S. firm which is exporting, say, 10% of its output that by locating its production in the U.S. it has made an exchange rate decision. But, in a converse situation, Volkswagen during the 1970s came to realize that by exporting to the United States from Germany it was making itself vulnerable to DMK revaluations. No amount of hedging in the forward market could offset this basic economic exposure. As a result Volkswagen ultimately decided to locate some of its production in the United States.

19.3.2. It is possible to be exposed to the movement of a currency without producing in that currency's country or selling to that country. For example, sales of aeroengines by Rolls-Royce in Britain to India are affected by movements in the dollar. For in the world aeroengine market there are effectively only three major players, General Electric, Pratt & Whitney, and Rolls-Royce. Since the other two firms are American, the market prices are in dollars. Rolls' profit margins, therefore, are vulnerable to movements in sterling against the dollar, as the company found during the late 1970s.

19.3.3. Another important concern in the area of pricing and marketing is the question of invoicing currency. In the example just mentioned, Rolls-Royce's choice of invoicing currency was fixed by market conditions. In other cases, companies producing in a country with a weak currency have chosen to invoice in a strong currency, such as the deutsche mark or U.S. dollar, to protect the value of their receivables. There are a number of statistical surveys on this topic. Most of these were carried out in a European context. The first study was in 1973 by S. Grassman.[2] He found that by and large exports are invoiced in the exporter's currency. The exception was the reserve currency countries. Exports to (as well as imports from) the United States and the United Kingdom were mainly invoiced in the dollar or pound. This general pattern has been confirmed by a number of other surveys, which are summarized in a recent book on the subject.[3] This pattern is more common in large economies. (Germany, for example, invoices more than 80% of exports in deutsche marks, but the figure for Belgium is usually 40–50%.) In the United Kingdom's case, about 76% of exports were invoiced in sterling; only another 4% were covered forward in the exchange markets. About 5% were protected against foreign exchange risk by other methods. This left 15% of exports exposed.[4]

19.3.4. In general, therefore, exporters try to use their own currency as currency of invoice. This lets them protect themselves against exchange rate fluctuations. But there have been periods—notably, for example, in the United Kingdom during the prolonged weakness of sterling—when exporters switched their invoices into stronger currencies. That gave them flexibility. They could profit from the devaluation of the domestic currency. Or they could cover forward in the foreign exchange market or alternatively borrow foreign currency against the foreign currency receivable.

19.3.5. The choice of invoice currency is not only dictated by financial considerations. It also depends on what the salesperson can persuade the buyer to accept (or vice versa if the goods are being imported). At this point, exposure management touches the commercial thinking of the firm. The exposure management team needs to know the commercial pressures in the marketplace where the salespeople are working. It is equally important for those selling the company's goods to know the risks they may commit the company to if they accept a change in invoicing currency.

19.3.6. The greatest flexibility, of course, lies in the choice of invoicing currency in trade within a multinational group. If the exporting parent sells in its own domestic currency to its subsidiary, then the subsidiary has the exposure. Alternatively the parent can invoice in the subsidiary's currency and keep the exposure at home. The latter case generally gives more flexibility. Exceptions to this rule would make sense if the parent company's domestic currency were expected to be weak relative to the subsidiary's. Then, provided the subsidiary's profits were taxable at a lower rate than the parent's, invoicing in the parent's currency and shifting profits to the subsidiary might be desirable. A second exception is in the converse case, where the parent's currency is expected to be strong and the parent's tax rate is lower. In this case also parent currency invoicing might be desirable.

19.3.7. Of course the price of this flexibility is complexity at the center. In addition, flexibility could be hampered by exchange controls. Suppose we have a U.S. company with a low domestic tax rate, with a French subsidiary which is paying high taxes. The dollar is expected to appreciate against the French franc. The parent decides to invoice its sales to France in dollars. The exposure is passed to the French subsidiary. But French regulations forbid forward cover more than two months in advance of delivery of the goods. Suppose the goods are shipped on 180 days' credit. Then the French subsidiary is exposed to movements in the franc for four months until they can take cover. The uncertain impact on local profitability may be demoralizing. In this situation, it might be better to invoice in francs and to handle the exposure centrally.

SECTION 4.   CHOICE OF BORROWING CURRENCY

19.4.1.   A second obvious method of reducing exposure is to consider the choice of currency for borrowings. Suppose, for example, a U.S. corporation has a British subsidiary which has net assets. It can hedge these through forward sales of sterling in the foreign exchange markets or by borrowing sterling and selling it spot. Or it can instruct the U.K. subsidiary to build up its sterling borrowings and pay down its foreign currency borrowings, or remit the proceeds to the parent, to the point where the net currency asset position is eliminated. Or, if there were a net liability position in sterling (under FASB 8), the U.S. parent might have lent the British subsidiary dollars, letting it pay off some of its sterling borrowings to bring the net position back to zero.

19.4.2.   But these operations depend on freedom from exchange controls. And there may be other problems. Funds may not be available from local financial institutions for a sufficiently long maturity. Building up local borrowings, or paying them down, may not be convenient because of balance sheet limitations or loan covenants, as well as possible exchange control problems. Hence various other techniques have been developed to reduce exposure. These are the so-called back-to-back and parallel loans, currency swaps and "simulated currency loans."

SECTION 5.   BACK-TO-BACK LOANS

19.5.1.   Parallel and back-to-back loans tend to be words which are used interchangeably. Some people mean by back-to-back what others mean by parallel, and vice versa. I shall use "back-to-back" to refer to those loans which enjoy a right of set-off, and parallel to those which do not. These deals can involve two, three, or even four parties. Where more than two parties are involved, U.K. law at least (in the British Eagle case, decided by the House of Lords in 1975) seems not to support the right of set-off.[5]

19.5.2.   In the typical two-party deal, the U.S. company lends, say, U.S.$ 18 million to the U.K. company, and the U.K. company lends, say, £STG 10 million to the U.S. company at the same time (assuming the current exchange rate is £STG 1 = US$ 1.80). The loan does not provide a new source of borrowings because each party must have currency available. But it does provide a fixed interest rate foreign currency loan for a relatively long period, which might not otherwise be available. A U.S. company would have little chance of borrowing sterling on a long-term fixed rate basis because of local market conditions and, until recently, exchange control considerations.

19.5.3. The structure of the loan is that the dollar loan agreement and sterling loan agreement will be essentially identical. Both loans will mature on the same date, and interest will be payable periodically over the term of the loan on the same dates. Both loan agreements are typically subject to the law of the same jurisdiction. This is so that any dispute over interpretation can be resolved on a consistent basis. At maturity the loan is repaid in its respective currency. The amounts repaid are equal to the amounts originally borrowed, that is, £STG 10 million and $18 million in our example.

19.5.4. An important feature of most back-to-back loan transactions is the security. Normally, this security consists of right of set-off in a two-party transaction. In other words, if the U.K. company defaults on the repayments of its dollar loan, the U.S. company can set off the amount due to it under the dollar loan against its obligation to repay the sterling loan, and vice versa. This has two benefits: First it limits the credit risk to which the parties are exposed. Second, accountants in many countries, including the United States, will normally allow the parties to set the two loans against each other. So the deal is "off balance sheet." As we said, though, the issue of set-off is not entirely clear cut, particularly in the case of loans involving more than two companies.

19.5.5. It is important to know whether or not withholding or other taxes will be imposed on the payment of interest or principal; in a two-party back-to-back deal between a U.S. company and a U.K. company, the withholding tax position is covered by the U.S.–U.K. Income Tax Convention. Under Article 11 of the new Convention for the Avoidance of Double Taxation, no withholding tax will be imposed on payments of interest by either the U.K. or the U.S. company, provided certain conditions are met.

19.5.6. A number of other possible tax complications can arise. For example, when the U.S. company lends the proceeds of its foreign currency loan to a foreign subsidiary, the U.S. company may be required to charge an interest rate equal to its borrowing rate plus appropriate expenses, rather than relying on the "safe haven" rule which permits it to charge its foreign subsidiary a lower interest rate.

19.5.7. Further complications arise, as we have seen in the previous chapter, on the treatment of foreign exchange gains or losses. Briefly, it would seem that the U.S. tax position is that if repayment of a foreign currency loan is made when the exchange rate has moved against the borrower, the loss will be capital unless the taxpayer can show that the foreign currency borrowing was used in an integral part of its business. If the borrowed money is invested in the stock of an affiliate, the loss will normally be capital (unless the taxpayer is in the banking business).[6] However, as mentioned earlier (chapter 18), the Treasury is currently considering revisions to the rules which will affect this position. In the United Kingdom, a long-term gain or loss is generally ignored for tax purposes.

SECTION 6. CURRENCY SWAPS

19.6.1. A parallel or back-to-back loan and a currency swap are similar techniques for achieving the same objectives. But there are differences:

1. Some accountants differ on how parallel and back-to-back loans should be reported by the parent company on its balance sheet. They feel that both loans should appear on the balance sheet rather than being treated as off-balance-sheet items. A currency swap is definitely off balance sheet.
2. In a parallel loan transaction, each borrower has a tax deductible interest expense. In a currency swap (see below), the annual fee paid by one party may or may not be tax deductible.
3. Currency swaps generally give a right of offset, where there may be problems with back-to-back loans.

19.6.2. Since the currency swap is structured as a spot deal combined with a forward exchange contract, the arrangement falls under contract law both in the United States and the United Kingdom. Thus if the forward contract is not completed, the other party is entitled to sue for damages if there is a loss. As a result, the documentation is simpler than for a parallel loan. So the overall cost of the deal is less. Taxation effects of the deal should be the same as the taxation consequences of foreign exchange gains and losses generally (see above). (In the United Kingdom, as the deal is long term, gains or losses will normally be ignored for tax purposes.)

19.6.3. If the corporation involved did not want to take the credit risk on the other corporation, a bank would normally step in as intermediary between the two parties. It would charge a small fee for its services. This also provides the advantage of confidentiality, in that neither side's identity need be disclosed, and flexibility in that the bank can rearrange the swap more easily, for example, if one party later wants to unwind (see 19.6.9).

19.6.4. So a currency swap can at times be preferable to a parallel or back-to-back loan. The underlying effect of a currency swap is exactly the same as in a parallel loan, except that in a swap each party's domestic cash is sold rather

TABLE 19.3.   Currency Swap.

Sterling principal	£5,000,000
Spot exchange rate	$2.00
Dollar principal	$10,000,000
Sterling interest rate	14.625%
Dollar interest rate	15.375%
Difference (adjusted to 365 day basis)	0.9635%
Difference payable to dollar lender	$96,350 per annum

than lent to the other party. For example, suppose that the current exchange rate is approximately US$ 2 = £1. A U.K. pension fund might engage in a swap with a U.S. company in which it sells £5 million to the U.S. company, in exchange for $10 million. At the same time the two parties do a forward exchange deal that would exactly reverse the spot exchange at the end of the agreed term. Let us say for the sake of argument that it is five years. Then in Year 5 the U.S. company will receive back $10 million from the U.K. pension fund in exchange for £5 million.

19.6.5.   The forward exchange is done at par with the spot rate (i.e., at $2). But typically the interest rates on the two currencies will differ. So one party has lost the benefit of the forward premium which it might otherwise have received. Suppose that the five-year sterling rates are above five-year dollar rates. The dollar should be at a premium to sterling. Then it is the forward seller of dollars (the U.K. pension fund) which has lost the benefit of the forward premium. So the U.S. company will pay the pension fund annual fee approximating the interest differential between sterling and dollars. For tax (and in some countries exchange control) reasons, underlying nominal interest rates are agreed upon at the outset. And, although a floating rate basis can be adopted, the interest rates are commonly fixed for the term of the swap. However, as we said, interest is not paid gross as in a back-to-back loan. The difference between the two rates, known as the differential, is payable by one party or the other each year.

19.6.6.   Let us look at our example again. It is summarized in Table 19.3. We have a U.S. corporation providing five-year U.S. dollars to a U.K. pension fund which is providing sterling. Suppose the exchange rate is $2.00 again and the amounts are £5 million and $10 million. Suppose the rate for five-year U.S. dollars is 15⅜% and for five-year sterling, 14⅝%. Then the nominal U.S. dollar interest payable is $1,558,854.17 each year. The nominal sterling interest is £731,250.00 (bearing in mind that the U.K. rate is calculated on a 365-day basis against 360 for the United States). At the current spot of $2 the sterling interest is equal to $1,462,500.00.

19.6.7.   So the U.K. pension fund must pay the difference—U.S.$ 96,354.17. (Another way of looking at it is to put both rates on a comparable basis, say

365, so the U.S. rate is approximately 15.5885%. The net differential is thus 0.9635%. This differential is payable on $10 million, giving us the same net cash difference payable, roughly, at $96,350.)

19.6.8. The U.K. pension fund is therefore exposed to exchange rate movements insofar as it must find nearly $100,000 annually. It can cover these directly in the forward market. If, for any reason, the interest is payable gross, it has a larger exposure. Then it could negotiate a provision in the deal that movements in the exchange rate will be offset. To see how this would work, suppose at the interest date in Year 2 that the spot rate had fallen to $1.7700. Then the interest on the pension fund's sterling lending would be worth, in dollar terms, only $1,294,312.50. So the difference between its gross dollar interest cost and its sterling earnings in dollar terms is $264,541.67, which is $168,187.50 more than it bargained for. Conversely, the U.S. company is better off by that amount. To prevent this, the two parties could agree in advance that "windfall" profits or losses would be compensated for—in this case the U.S. company would hand back $168,187.50 to the U.K. fund.

19.6.9. Now let us look at an example of an unwinding of a swap. During 1978 a U.K. company did a swap with a U.S. company for 10 years. The amount was for £5 million, against U.S.$ 9.3 million. There was a differential payable to the U.K. company of 1⅜%, based on underlying interest rates at 9% on sterling and 7⅝% on dollars. By 1980 sterling had improved to U.S.$ 2.38, and the U.K. company decided to take its capital profit on the swap. It turned to its bankers and asked them to step into its shoes by raising in the market an eight-year fixed rate £5 million deposit and placing U.S.$ 9.3 million on the market also for eight years at a fixed rate. The £5 million would be paid to the U.K. company, who would pay $9.3 million to the bank. The bank would then assume, by way of assignment, the responsibilities of the U.K. company.

19.6.10. This would give rise to a funding loss for the bank for each year of the deal. For, at that time, the sterling deposit would cost the bank 14¼% compared to interest received under the swap of 9%, producing a funding loss of 5¼%. On the other side, the bank would pay only 7⅝% on the dollars and would receive from its lending to the market 10¾%, a profit of 3⅛%. But the dollar earnings were less than the sterling costs. Therefore the U.K. company would in addition pay to the bank at the outset the discounted value of those future funding losses. The bank would fix its dollar profits in each year at the outset in sterling terms by taking forward cover on these dollar profits and setting them against the annual sterling short-fall, giving a net total annual sterling short-fall. This latter item is then discounted to give the discounted funding cost. This is then paid out of the U.K. company's exchange profit.

SECTION 7.   SIMULATED CURRENCY LOAN

19.7.1.   Finally, it is worth mentioning another possible financing technique, the "simulated currency loan."[7] This is a loan in a given currency where the amount of repayment is expressed in terms of a second currency. The interest rate charged is based on the rate structure of the second currency. For example, a U.S. multinational company with a successful subsidiary in Spain may own blocked Spanish Pesetas, while a second U.S. multinational may be about to invest fresh dollar capital into its Spanish subsidiary. A simulated dollar loan from the first subsidiary to the second would be made in Pesetas but denominated in dollars. It would be repayable in Pesetas in an amount equal to the original dollar equivalent of the loan and carry a negotiated interest rate at or near the dollar Libor rate, payable in Pesetas or dollars.

19.7.2.   This arrangement has the attraction, for the lender, of effectively unblocking Peseta assets. For the borrower, the arrangement may give the chance to pick up cheaper medium-term funds than are available on the local market. The arrangement also avoids any possible risk of withholding taxes payable on the intercountry loans. However, there are drawbacks. First is the possibility of a credit risk. Secondly, the borrower takes an exchange risk. Third, the deal must be very carefully framed to insure that both the exchange control authorities and the tax authorities from the countries involved are satisfied on the underlying commercial rationale.

NOTES

1. J. A. Donaldson, *Corporate Currency Risk,* Financial Times, London 1980, p. 11. (Mr. Donaldson is the Deputy Treasurer of Imperial Chemical Industries.) This section and the next draw heavily on the discussion contained in that book.
2. S. Grassman, *Exchange Reserves and the Financial Structure of Foreign Trade,* Saxon House/Lexington Books, 1973.
3. S. Carse, J. Williamson, and G. E. Wood, *The Financing Procedures of British Foreign Trade,* Cambridge University Press, 1980.
4. *Ibid.,* Table 4.6, p. 67.
5. L. B. Samuels, "Federal Income Tax Consequences of Back-to-Back Loans and Currency Exchange," Tax Lawyer, Spring 1980.
6. *Ibid.,* p. 866.
7. See B. Antl, ed., *Currency Risk and the Corporation,* Euromoney Publications, Ltd., London, 1980, pp. 69–70; D. S. Kemp, "Hedging a Long-Term Financing," *Euromoney,* February 1981.

20

PAYMENTS SYSTEMS

This chapter explains what happens to a foreign exchange deal after it is done. It looks at the various international payments systems and the payments systems in different countries.

SECTION 1.   NOSTRO/VOSTRO ACCOUNTS

20.1.1.   The most brilliantly executed foreign exchange deal can turn out to be a disaster if the payments are wrongly made. So it is worth knowing something about the systems through which the funds end up being transferred. This chapter falls into two parts: domestic systems and international networks. The traditional nostro/vostro (due to/from) system and the SWIFT network comprise the latter. (We shall ignore such methods as money orders, mail payment orders, and the like since they are not typically used in settling FX or money market deals.)

20.1.2.   The outsider may not be aware that when a bank makes payments to other countries, very rarely are notes or other means of payment actually sent from one country to another. This only happens for very small amounts. For large payments, banks maintain an intricate network of accounts and counteraccounts among different banks all over the world. These accounts are referred to as due from (nostro) and due to (vostro) accounts. A due from or nostro account is the foreign currency account of a bank maintained with its foreign correspondents abroad. Thus Barclays Bank in New York will maintain a nostro account with Deutsche Bank in Frankfurt, in deutsche marks, from which it will make payments on behalf of its customers to German banks. Equally, the Bank of America will maintain a sterling account with National Westminster Bank, for example, in order to make and receive payments in the United Kingdom. Clearly, each account is the mirror of the other. Barclays Bank's account with Deutsche Bank is regarded by Barclays Bank as its due from or nostro account held with Deutsche, while Deutsche Bank regards it as its due to or vostro account held for Barclays. Equally, the Bank of America will regard its account with National Westminister as a due from account, while from National Westminister's point of view, it is a due to account.

20.1.3.   From the user's point of view, the real banking account is maintained in the books of the bank abroad. But in its own books it will keep a record of the transactions passed abroad. This gives a mirror image of the affairs of the nostro account abroad. A customer importing goods into the United States, for example, may ask his or her U.S. bank to arrange for payment in sterling to be made to the British supplier. The importer will be debited in dollars, and in order to maintain the system of double entry bookkeeping, the memorandum account in the U.S. bank's books will be credited with sterling. The bank in the U.K. would be instructed to pay sterling to the beneficiary in the United Kingdom, to the debit of the U.S. bank's account with them. Clearly, a major bank will find that a vast volume of payments flow through its nostro accounts overseas; much time is occupied switching funds into and out of the account, in order to minimize the working balances held there (which under normal circumstances would not be being credited with interest by the bank on whose books the account is held). The operational departments of major banks include a switches section whose sole function is to position funds correctly in nostro accounts.

SECTION 2. SWIFT

20.2.1. The vast growth in international payments has put increasing pressure on banks' communications network. In 1973, in an attempt to overcome this problem, the Society for Worldwide International Financial Transactions was founded. (The original impetus came from the pressure on European banks from the American banks who were seeking to get a foothold in Europe by offering very fast international transfer systems, and pressure in the domestic transfer systems from the national Giro systems.) SWIFT was founded as a cooperative nonprofit organization. Its headquarters are in Brussels. The original membership was 239 banks in 15 countries. During the first years, message text standards were finalized covering clean payments, confirmations of foreign exchange loans and deposits, and statements for nostro reconciliations. Operation started in May 1977 with 15 banks in Belgium, France, and Great Britain.

20.2.2. By September 1980, SWIFT had grown to serve 740 banks in 20 countries. From a daily average of 30,000 messages per day, the total had risen to 200,000. Message switching centers operate in Amsterdam, Brussels, and Culpepper, Virginia. The U.S. center was opened in November 1979. Much work has been done on connecting SWIFT to CHIPS. In many cases it is possible to provide a complete electronic conversion from SWIFT to CHIPS (see 20.3.1). For example, where the SWIFT remitter has used the SWIFT mnenonic address to identify the parties in a transfer, a bank can use computers to convert the data to identification numbers used by the CHIPS system. Chase Manhattan Bank estimates that 20% of incoming SWIFT volume can be processed without operator intervention.[1] A proportion of the messages in the opposite direction from CHIPS to SWIFT also require little or no manual intervention.

20.2.3. As well as passing payment messages, the SWIFT network can handle foreign exchange confirmation reconciliations. This has the particular advantage that spot deal confirmations will usually be received before the deal matures. Normally, confirmations sent internationally by mail will take at least five days to be received; that is, they will arrive three days after the transfer is made.

SECTION 3.   UNITED STATES

20.3.1. The U.S. payment system is something of a patchwork because of the unit banking system and the federal structure of the Federal Reserve System. Payments may be made by banks through correspondent banks, or by using an account at the regional Federal Reserve Bank. In addition, there is a network of local clearing houses and regional check processing centers operated by the Federal Reserve System, together with the New York Clearing House which is privately owned. As far as concerns foreign exchange deals, and the settlement of Eurodollar deals, it is the New York Clearing House which is most important internationally and in particular, the New York Clearing House CHIPS system (Clearing House Interbank Payments System). CHIPS was set up in 1970. Initially it serviced only international payments, and access to the system was restricted to banks belonging to the New York Clearing House Association. But within a short time domestic transfers were brought into the system and the association gave access to agencies and branches of foreign banks as well as other U.S. commercial banks and the like. By 1980, CHIPS served 100 financial institutions through a network of 250 sending and receiving devices linked to its central computer. It handled an average of 55,000 deals a day, worth $150 billion.

20.3.2. From the beginning, CHIPS settled tomorrow for deals done today. Given the huge flow, this created credit risks overnight; and it also caused complications in Eurodollar and foreign exchange markets (the "Thursday/ Friday" technicality). So in 1980 it was decided to change CHIPS to a same-day-settlement basis, and this was done on October 1, 1981. The new arrangement is that a special New York Clearing House account has been established at the Federal Reserve Bank of New York. Settling banks transfer funds into this account by Fed Wire (see 20.3.3) or are paid from it. Operationally same-day settlement is a great improvement in some ways but much more demanding in others: cutoff times had to be moved forward to cope. Currently the latest time at which a payment instruction can be entered into CHIPS is around 4 P.M. (there is a 4:30 cut-off) although for practical reasons many banks have a cut-off around mid-day or 1 p.m. Quite often—perhaps two or three times a month—the CHIPS system breaks down. In these circumstances, the Federal Reserve normally holds its system open as long as required to process payments when the CHIPS is restored.

20.3.3. The Federal Reserve is intimately involved in payments because of holding the CHIPS settlement account and also because of the Fed Wire. This has been running since 1918, and was computerized in the early 1970s. A bank's computer is linked to the Fed's central computer at its message switching center in Culpepper, Virginia. For example, suppose Bank of America in San Francisco must pay $10 million to Citibank in New York. It sends a message from its computer to that at the Federal Reserve Bank in San Francisco. The San Francisco Fed debits Bank of America's account with it. Then it relays the payment message via Culpepper to the Federal Reserve Bank of New York. The latter credits Citibank and notifies the payment to Citibank. The Fed Wire is used primarily for large transfers. Volume in 1979 was 35.1 million transfers, with a total value of $64,200 billion—making the average transfer amount $1.8 million. The Fed Wire's hours in 1972 were set up as 9:00 A.M. to 3:00 P.M. local time for interdistrict transfers, provided that the receiving office had not closed. Across the country, thererfore, there was a rolling cutoff time. During 1980 the system was switched to uniform, nationwide hours. These are 8:00 A.M. to 5:00 P.M. eastern standard time. There is a one-hour settlement period between 5:00 P.M. and 6:00 P.M. eastern standard time. Third-party payments for customers are not permitted during the settlement period, which is restricted to Federal funds transfers between banks holding reserve accounts at the Fed.[2] In August 1982 the Fed introduced a 12:00 p.m. presentment time for checks in New York City.

20.3.4. In addition to the Fed Wire, banks are also linked via the Bank Wire. This is a message system rather than a payments system. It is a telex system with computer switching. Its main function is to transmit advice of payments/debits. For example, if Exxon pays Citibank $5 million by debit to its account at Morgan, the latter would make payment by Fed Wire but would confirm by Bank Wire.

20.3.5. As well as the Fed Wire, the Federal Reserve System operates a network of automated clearing houses (ACHs). (The New York Clearing House is independent of this network, being privately owned.) The first ACH was set up in California in 1970; there are now 32 ACHs which cover the whole country. About 75% of all commercial banks and 10% of thrift institutions belong to ACHs, and over 15,000 companies use ACH services. Recently the National Automated Clearing House Association has begun studying direct corporation-to-corporation payments via ACHs. As to the nature of payments, they began by being mainly official: social security transfers, and so forth. But private sector volume rose by 90% in 1980 and again in 1981. By November 1981, ACHs were handling $7 billion in government payments compared with $26 billion in private sector transfers.[3]

20.3.6. It is worth mentioning that the Federal Reserve has embarked on a major program to modernize its communications network. The project is known as FRCS-80 (Federal Reserve Communications System for the Eighties). The current network, consisting of the Culpepper switching center, leased communication service, and 12 separate Federal Reserve district systems, will be replaced by a single standardized system. It will be a packet-switching system; that is, the data will be sent in packets, each addressed to a location in the system. Hence the system will be a distributed network rather than revolving around the hub at Culpepper. In other words, the Fed in Chicago could handle messages for the Fed in New York if the latter's computer went down.[4]

20.3.7. As well as the U.S. clearing system, dollar clearing systems exist abroad, notably in London,[5] and, it is planned, in Singapore.[6] The London dollar clearing system has its origins in the Insurance Companies Currency Scheme set up in the 1930s and used by the insurance business to settle dollar premiums and claims in London. The clearing is held each working day at the clearing house (see 20.4.1–2). It was originally set up by the clearing banks in 1975 at the request of the Stock Exchange Council, to ease settlement of stock exchange trades in U.S. dollars. It has since been extended to handle settlement of all types of United Kingdom–U.S. dollar "retail" customer business among some 50 banks in the United Kingdom. By mutual consent, "wholesale" interbank foreign exchange deals and Eurodollar settlements are at present excluded.

20.3.8. Settlement is on the basis of same-day value in New York funds (next working day if U.S. is closed on the day of a clearing). Mainly for reasons of credit control and to ease administrative problems, the interbank structure is set up to follow as closely as possible existing sterling clearing systems. In general, clearing banks act for the same banks for whom they clear sterling in London. Attendance at the clearing house each day is restricted to the six clearing banks who take turns on a two-month rotation basis to act as clearing agents. The advantage is that instead of every dollar check having to be cleared in New York, there is just one net balance for each clearing bank which is settled by one telegraphic transfer to New York, sent before 5:00 P.M. (London time) each day. Agency banks take part through a London–U.S. dollar settlement account with the clearing bank under arrangements negotiated individually. They settle net with their clearer in accordance with those arrangements. The system provides for the clearing of all U.S. dollar checks and drafts drawn on participant banks in the United Kingdom and for the issue of U.S. dollar bankers' payments. The monthly volume cleared is about 33,000 items with a value of $1.4 billion.

SECTION 4.   THE UNITED KINGDOM

20.4.1. The payment system in the United Kingdom is much simpler than that in the United States. Essentially, all payments are cleared through the Bankers' Clearing House, which is owned by the members of the Committee of London Clearing Bankers, or through the Bankers' Automated Clearing Service. The Bankers' Clearing House handles checks; BACS handles electronic transfers (mainly standardized credit transfers and automated direct debits). BACS can only handle preauthorized transfers allowing some time before execution; so foreign exchange and money market transfers are settled through the Bankers' Clearing House.[7]

20.4.2. The Bankers' Clearing House runs two clearings: the town clearing and the general clearing. The town clearing is almost invariably used for exchange and money market payments. Although it processes 0.3% of daily volume, the town clearing handles 90% of the value. To be eligible for the town clearing, a check must be for a minimum of £10,000. It must be drawn on, and paid into, a town branch of a clearing bank. (There are about 100 town branches, all in or near the City of London.) Town clearing checks are settled with same-day value. The clearing starts at 3:00 P.M. and settlement is made via the clearing banks' accounts at the central bank (in theory, up to 5:00 P.M.).

20.4.3. The general clearing handles smaller payments and those from outside the town clearing area. A check paid into a bank on Monday will normally go into the clearing on Tuesday; on Wednesday it will be presented to the branch on which it is drawn, and paid, provided all is in order. The general clearing is run in the morning; checks must be at the clearing house by about 11:15 A.M.

20.4.4. Automation plans are under way, with a Clearing House Automated Payments System (CHAPS) being developed. CHAPS will operate on a distributed structure using packet switching, like FRCS-80 (see 20.3.6). It will include settlement banks—the Bank of England, the London Clearing Banks, and possibly the Cooperative Bank, National Girobank, Central Trustee Savings Bank, and the Scottish clearing banks. Each settlement bank will offer its own customers (and nonsettlement banks) whatever services it thinks appropriate; but the CHAPS system itself will be connected to settlement banks by standard interfaces.

SECTION 5.   GERMANY

20.5.1. As in the United States, the German payment system is shared between the central bank and the banking industry. The Bundesbank, through its branch network, processes about 30% of checks, debit and credit transfers. It operates a computer center in each of the 11 German *Länder* which are heavily used for payments between cities.[8]

20.5.2. So far as concerns settlement of foreign exchange and money market deals, most transfers go through the Frankfurt clearing. There are three clearings, at 8:15, 11:00 and 1:30. The first clearing is that mostly used for foreign exchange and money market transfers; it consists mainly of large items of which the Bundesbank has been notified the previous evening. The second is the main domestic clearing. The third is for settlement of outstanding balances plus any small items that can be accommodated without upsetting banks' positions. It is possible to make same-day-value payments through the Bundesbank between 8:00 A.M. and 1:00 P.M., when the Bundesbank stops taking payment instructions. Transfers between provinces can be made through the *Landesbanks* in each province until around 11:30. Alternatively they can be made through the big deposit banks until 12:30 or 1:00 P.M. In the latter case, the balance will not necessarily be shown on the customer's account for several days, but good value will have been given.

SECTION 6.   FRANCE

20.6.1.   The Banque de France, like the Bundesbank and the Federal Reserve, is heavily involved in the French payment system. This revolves around a network of clearing houses (*chambres de compensation*).[9] The Banque de France runs these, except for the main Paris clearing house. This is run by an association of member banks, which includes the Banque de France. (It has 44 members and 295 submembers who clear through members.) Money market and foreign exchange settlements are made by bankers' payments (*avals de tresorerie*) which are settled with same-day value. The Chambre de Compensation de Paris runs three clearings, at 9:30, at 12:15, and at 3:15 P.M. The first clearing handles checks drawn on members, interbank transfers, and prepresented transfers. The second clearing is the main money market clearing as it handles bankers' payments as well as checks and interbank transfers. The third clearing is the final balancing session. When this is finished, balances are settled through the Banque de France. In an emergency, late payment can be made by transfers on the Banque de France's books until 5:00 P.M.

20.6.2.   Provincial clearing centers are run by the Banque de France. Formerly it ran a clearing in each town where it had a branch (over 200 of them). In October 1980 the system was streamlined. All banks were required to take part, directly or indirectly. All branches had to be linked to one of the principal clearing centers. These are located in Paris, Monaco, the capital of each department, and 10 other major provincial towns. The secondary clearing centers in each department are linked to the principal center.

SECTION 7.   JAPAN

20.7.1.   Japan has a network of over 150 clearing houses, the chief of which is in Tokyo. It is run by the Tokyo Bankers' Association, and handles nearly two-thirds of all payments in Japan.[10] Within the Tokyo Clearing House, a group of 18 heavy-volume banks agreed in 1967 to adopt a night clearing. That is, clearing begins at 9:00 P.M. the previous night for settlement through the next day's clearing. Daily clearings are at 1:00 P.M. (the main clearing) and 3:00 P.M. (final balancing). Settlement is made by check on the Bank of Japan for same-day value.

SECTION 8.   OTHER SYSTEMS

20.8.1.   Finally, in the general context of clearing and payment systems, it is worth mentioning that two international clearing systems handle Eurobond transactions. These are Cedel and Euroclear. Both of these operate a computerized system for safe custody, delivery, and settlement for Eurobonds and related securities. Cedel was founded in 1970 by a group of international financial institutions. By 1977 membership had grown to around 850 institutions and 2,400 issues were being cleared through the system. Euroclear is a similar system, operated by Morgan Guaranty on behalf of a group of international banks. In this context, it is worth mentioning that Morgan Guaranty also operates an SDR clearing system through its Brussels branch.

SECTION 9. GOOD VALUE CUTOFF TIMES

20.9.1. Because clearing systems change, cutoff times after which good value cannot be given will vary. However, cutoff times currently notified (all A.M. times except where noted) are:

Austria—8:30	Netherlands—12:00
Belgium—8:30	Norway—11:00
Denmark—8:00	Portugal—9:00
Finland—10:00	Spain—10:00
France—8:00	Sweden—8:00
Germany—8:00	Switzerland—8:00
Italy—8:00	United Kingdom—12:00
Luxembourg—10:30	United States—4:30 P.M.

It is important to mention that banks in France have adopted a later cutoff time, 8:30, with regard to inward SWIFT instructions. Also, although 9:00 is Portugal's official cutoff time, most banks in the country require instructions in their hands by 2:00 P.M the previous day. The British Bankers' Association has recommended a cutoff time of 12:00 for the execution of same-day-value sterling interbank payment instructions. The new cutoff time applies equally to SWIFT and non-SWIFT operations. It is possible, under certain circumstances, to effect large or urgent payment instructions after 12:00.

NOTES

1. A. Caccioli, "Our Solution—High Volume Users," SWIFT International Banking Operations Seminar, September 1980, Copenhagen; D. Bamber, "SWIFT Is Up and Running," *Euromoney*, London, November 1979.

2. There is a good description of the U.S. payments system (except that CHIPS is now on same-day settlement) in M. Stigum, *The Money Market—Myth, Reality and Practice*, Dow Jones Irwin, United States, 1978, pp. 280–283, 434–437.

3. B. Streeter et al., "Special Report—Automated Clearing Houses," *ABA Banking Journal*, New York, March 1982, pp. 128–137.

4. The "Federal Reserve and the Payments System," *Federal Reserve Bulletin*, Washington D.C., February 1981; "FRCS-80—What Is it?" *ABA Banking Journal*, New York, February 1982, pp. 82.

5. See P. Clarke, "The Quest for a Dollar Clearing Scheme," *Euromoney*, London, September 1978; M. Blanden, "New Moves on Clearing Systems," *The Banker*, London, April 1981.

6. P. B. La Porte and A. K. Young, "Clearing Asian Dollars through Singapore," *The Banker*, London, May 1981.

7. See M. Blanden, "New Moves on Clearing Systems."

8. "The Role of the Deutsche Bundesbank in Cashless Payments," Deutsche Bundesbank's *Monthly Report*, March 1982.

9. "L'évolution du système de paiement en France," *Banque*, Paris, December 1980; Chambre de compensation des banquiers de Paris, *Statuts et Règlement*, Paris, undated.

10. Federation of Bankers Associations of Japan, *Banking Systems in Japan*, Tokyo, 1976.

APPENDICES

INTERNATIONAL MONETARY CHRONOLOGY

1944

July	1	International Monetary and Financial Conference at Bretton Woods agrees to establish International Monetary Fund (IMF) and World Bank (IBRD).

1947

May	8	IMF extends its first loan: US$ 25 million to France.
June	5	U.S. Secretary of State Marshall proposes European Recovery Program (ERP).
July	15	United Kingdom restores convertibility of pound.
August	20	United Kingdom suspends convertibility of pound.

1949

September	18–29	Exchange rates of European countries devalued in amounts ranging from 30.5% for pound sterling to 12.3% for Belgian franc. Many non-European countries also devalue.

1950

July	1	European Payments Union, (EPU) established.
September	30	Canada adopts floating exchange rate (until 1962).

1957

August	12	France devalues the franc by 16.7%.

1958

January	1	European Economic Community (EEC) comes into existence.

December 27 Ten European countries restore the convertibility of their currencies for nonresidents. Five other European countries soon follow. EPU eliminated.

December 29 France devalues the franc by 14.8%.

1960

October Price in London gold market rises, touching $40 per ounce.

October 31 Presidential candidate Kennedy denies that he would devalue the dollar.

November United States and seven other countries begin to sell gold in London market through gold pool.

1961

March 6–7 Germany and the Netherlands revalue their currencies upward by 5%.

March U.S. Treasury starts operations in foreign exchange markets.

1962

January 5 Proposal for IMF to borrow from 10 industrial countries— General Arrangements to Borrow (GAB)—approved.

May 1 Canada reestablishes a par value for its currency.

1963

July 18 President Kennedy proposes interest equalization tax on American purchases of foreign securities.

1964

October 17 Newly elected Labour Government decides against devaluation of sterling.

November 20 First use of GAB as U.K. borrowing of $1 billion from IMF is announced.

November 23 Bank of England raises bank rate from 5% to 7%.

November 25 Credits of $3 billion extended to United Kingdom by United States and 10 other countries plus BIS.

1965

February 5 President de Gaulle calls for return to gold standard.

May 12 United Kingdom draws additional $1.4 billion from IMF.

June	15	French Finance Minister Giscard d'Estaing rejects a return to gold standard.
September	10	Federal Reserve and other central banks enter exchange markets to support sterling.
September	28	Group of Ten instructs deputies to undertake "contingency planning" to meet future reserve needs.

1966

February	25	President de Gaulle meets with his senior officials and adopts stand against "contingency planning" for a new reserve asset.
July	20	British government announces drastic stabilization program.
September	13	Increase in credit lines to Bank of England from Federal Reserve and other central banks.

1967

April	17–18	Finance ministers of EEC, meeting in Munich, agree on joint position on SDR.
May	2	Germany's agreement not to buy gold from the United States announced.
May	17	President de Gaulle rejects proposal that United Kingdom join EEC.
June	5	Arab-Israeli Six Day War begins.
July		United Kingdom draws on central bank swap lines again.
July	17–18	Ministers and governors of Group of Ten meet in London to iron out differences on SDR.
September		Outline of SDR facility approved at IMF annual meeting in Rio de Janiero.
November	16	British cabinet formally decides on devaluation.
November	17	Bank of England sells more than $1 billion in foreign exchange market to support sterling exchange rate.
November	18	Britain announces 14.3% devaluation of pound, from $2.80 to $2.40. President Johnson issues statement reaffirming intention of United States to maintain official price of gold at $35 per ounce.
November	23	France announces that in June it had ceased supplying gold to the gold pool.
November	26	Governors of central banks of active members of gold pool meet in Frankfurt and agree both to continue pool sales and to support existing pattern of exchange rates.

November 30 IMF provides standby credit of $1.4 billion to United Kingdom.

1968

March 9–10 Central bankers meet in Basle and are persuaded by Chairman Martin to continue gold pool.

March 12 U.S. Congress rescinds legal requirement for gold backing of domestic currency, mobilizing $10 billion worth of U.S. gold for international commitments.

March 14 FOMC agrees to increase Federal Reserve swap network by $2.8 billion.

March 15 London gold market closed for two weeks, during which Zurich gold market seeks to supplant London in marketing South African gold.

March 16–17 Meeting of active gold pool members in Washington establishes two-tier gold arrangement and abandons gold pool.

March 29–30 At Stockholm, Group of Ten, with France reserving its position, resolves final issues on establishment of SDR.

May Student and worker uprisings in France.

June 5 France draws $100 million on Federal Reserve swap.

June 18 France sells $400 million of gold to United States and three European countries.

September 9 Basle arrangements to guarantee sterling balances announced.

November 1–19 Speculation on exchange rate changes in Europe; Bundesbank takes in $2.8 billion.

November 24 President de Gaulle announces refusal to devalue franc.

1969

April 28 After losing referendum, President de Gaulle resigns and is succeeded in June by Georges Pompidou.

April 29 German Finance Minister Strauss suggests publicly that Germany might revalue mark as part of a multilateral realignment

April 30– Bundesbank takes in $4 billion in order to hold exchange
May 9 rate.

May 9 German cabinet rejects revaluation *immer und ewig* ("for eternity").

May 12 Germany introduces new controls on inflows of funds.

June		Federal Reserve introduces reserve requirements on U.S. banks' Eurodollar borrowings.
July	28	SDR amendment enters into force.
August	8	France devalues the franc by 11.1%.
September	28	Social Democrat/ FDP victory in German elections.
September	29	Germany lets the mark float.
October	24	Germany establishes new par value, up 9.3%.

1970

January	1	First allocation of SDRs, in the amount of $3.4 billion.
June	1	Canadian dollar floats.
June	9	EEC sets 1980 as target date for monetary and economic union.

1971

April		Germany acquires $3 billion of foreign exchange to hold exchange rate.
April	26	German Economics Minister Schiller proposes joint float of European currencies. French Minister Giscard d'Estaing proposes devaluation of dollar.
April	28	Bundesbank suspends purchases of dollars in forward market.
May	4	Bundesbank takes in $1 billion. Secretary Connally issues statement saying "no change in the structure of exchange parities is necessary or anticipated."
May	5	Bundesbank takes in $1 billion for first hour and then suspends official operations in foreign exchange market.
May	9	Austria revalues by 5% and Switzerland by 7.1%.
May	10	Germany and the Netherlands let their currencies float.
May	28	Secretary Connally declares, in a speech at Munich: "We are not going to devalue. We are not going to change the price of gold."
June		Central banks of Group of Ten agree to stop depositing funds in Euromarket.
August	15	President Nixon announces price wage freeze, 10% import surcharge, and suspension of convertibility of dollars into gold and other reserve assets.
August	16–20	Bank of Japan takes in $2 billion in attempt to hold exchange rate.

August   19 France rejects German proposal for joint float of European currencies and establishes two-tier foreign exchange market.

August   23–27 Bank of Japan takes in another $2 billion and then decides to let yen float.

December 13–14 Presidents Pompidou and Nixon meet in the Azores and announce agreement on a devaluation of the dollar and a revaluation "of some other currencies."

December 17–18 Group of Ten meets at Smithsonian Institution in Washington and agrees on a realignment of currencies, including devaluation of dollar.

1972

March   1 Germany imposes *Bardepot*—cash deposit on borrowing abroad by German businesses.

March   7 EEC decidees to narrow margins for their currencies to 2.25% to form EEC snake in the Smithsonian "Tunnel."

April   24 Snake begins.

May   1 United Kingdom decides to join EEC snake, with Denmark and Ireland.

May   23 Norway joins snake as an associate member.

June   23 United Kingdom leaves EEC snake (with Ireland) and floats, after losing $2.5 billion of reserves in six days.

June   26 After "closing" exchange markets, EEC finance ministers meet and decide to maintain snake, apart from Denmark's withdrawal, but to permit Italy to intervene and settle in dollars.

June   28– European central banks and Bank of Japan purchase $6 bil-
July   14 lion to hold exchange rates.

June   29 German government, over objection of Economics Minister Schiller, adopts an exchange control measure—prohibition of sale of German bonds to foreigners; *Bardepot* raised to 50%.

July   2 Schiller submits resignation and is later succeeded by Helmut Schmidt. Swiss introduce negative interest rates.

July   19 Federal Reserve undertakes operations in foreign exchange markets for first time since August 15, 1971 (to share burden of making Smithsonian work).

October   10 Denmark rejoins snake.

1973

January	1	United Kingdom, Ireland, and Denmark become EEC members.
January	20	Italy establishes two-tier foreign exchange market.
January	23	Swiss franc permitted to float.
February	4	Germany announces additional exchange controls.
February	5–9	Bundesbank purchases $5 billion in effort to hold exchange rate.
February	12	Foreign exchange markets "closed" in Europe and Japan; U.S. announces 10% devaluation of dollar, phase-out of IET, capital controls.
February	12	Japan adopts floating exchange rate, followed by Italy and Switzerland.
February	13	Italy leaves snake.
February	14	Exchange markets reopen.
March	1	European central banks purchase $3.6 billion and withdraw from foreign exchange markets.
March	11	EEC ministers announce joint float of snake currencies (while Britain, Italy, and Ireland float independently). Germany revalues mark by 3%. Sweden joins snake as an associate member.
March	13	Austria revalues its currency by 2.25%.
March	16	Group of Ten central banks agree to withdraw funds "gradually and prudently" from Euromarkets.
June	29	DMK revalued 5.5% against snake currencies.
July	10	Federal Reserve resumes intervention in foreign exchange markets and expands swap network.
October		Oil embargo imposed and oil price raised during Arab-Israeli War.
November	12	Central bank governors, meeting in Basle, terminate two-tier gold agreement. They are able to sell gold in the free market but not to buy (because of IMF regulations).
December	23	Oil price raised again, quadrupling from level of early October.

1974

January	19	French franc drops out of EEC snake.
January	29	United States terminates controls on outflows of capital.
January	30	Germany relaxes restrictions on inflows of capital.

April	22–23	EEC finance ministers, meeting at Zeist in the Netherlands, propose that central banks be given the freedom to buy gold from each other.
June	25	Herstatt Bank of Cologne (Germany) fails.
August		Bellagio agreement between Germany and Italy on $2 billion gold-backed loan.
December	31.	U.S. ban on private ownership of gold removed.

1975

January	6	U.S. Treasury gold auction attracts poor response.
January	7	French gold reserves revalued to market-related level.
February	1	Central bank governors of Germany, Switzerland, and United States meet in London and agree on more concerted intervention to maintain orderly markets.
July	10	French franc rejoins EEC snake.
August	31	Interim Committee of the IMF and Group of Ten, meeting in Washington, agree on treatment of gold. Central banks to be free to trade gold among themselves, but not to increase total holdings for two years.
November	17	Snake meeting on admission of Swiss as an associate member is canceled.

1976

January	7–8	Interim Committee, meeting in Kingston, Jamaica, completes interim reform, with agreement on IMF quota increases, exchange rate system, treatment of gold, trust fund.
January	21	Banca d'Italia withdraws from exchange markets (until March 1); FX reserves depleted to $594 million. Draws $250 million Federal Reserve swap.
March	1	Italy resumes FX intervention; draws another $250 million Fed swap.
March	4	Pound falls through $2.00.
March	15	France withdraws from snake; Benelux "worm" (1% band) dissolved.
May	6	Italy imposes 50% import deposit and tightens restrictions on holding foreign currency from exports and purchases of foreign currency for imports.
June		United Kingdom borrows $5.3 billion international standby facility ($2 billion from Federal Reserve) to expire December.

August		Italian situation improved: $500 million in German gold-backed loan repaid, but arrangement extended for another two years. Total reduced to $1.5 billion because of lower gold price.
September	29	United Kingdom applies for $3.9 billion from IMF to repay June standby.
October	1–15	Italy applies special 10% foreign exchange tax on residents' foreign exchange purchases; discount rate raised 3% to 15%. Heavy inflow into DMK; pressure on £STG.
October	15	Italy bans nonresident drawings on existing credit lines in Italy; foreign exchange tax extended for four months.
October	17	Snake realignment; DMK revalued 2–6% against other currencies.
October	24	*Sunday Times* says IMF wants £STG 1 = $1.50.
October	28	Pound falls to $1.5550.
November	19	United Kingdom bans third-country trade finance in sterling. Italy repays U.K. share of EEC loan and borrows $236 million under German gold-backed facility.

1977

January		IMF approves U.K. loan; BIS and 11 countries approve $3 billion standby facility, via BIS, for official sterling balances. United Kingdom to issue foreign currency securities. Sterling starts to recover.
April	1	Swedish krona devalued 6%; Nowegian and Danish krone 3%.
July	27	Bank of England allows sterling to rise over $1.72, links official intervention to effective exchange rate.
August	29	SKR withdrawn from snake, NKR and DKR devalue by 5%.
September		Italy repays $500 million of German gold-backed loan.
September	27	Switzerland bans forward sales of Swiss francs under one month to nonresidents.
October	17	Minimum Lending Rate cut to 5%.
October	31	United Kingdom abandons intervention.
November	17	Japan imposes 50% marginal reserve requirement on "free yen" balances.
December	16	Bundesbank increases marginal reserve requirements on nonresident deposits to 100%. Ban on nonresident purchase of German bonds extended.
December		President Carter announces plans to cut U.S. energy imports and a more active intervention policy.

1978

January		Bundesbank imposes 100% reserve requirement on increase in liabilities to non-residents.
January	4	Federal Reserve and Bundesbank announce new enlarged swap agreement. Fed intervenes in SFR (first time since 1975).
January	10–13	United States sells deutsche marks worth $500 million. French franc under pressure ahead of March elections; Swiss franc strong.
February	12	Norwegian krona devalued 8% against snake currencies.
February	27	Swiss National Bank extends negative interest to central deposits.
February		Central banks' agreement not to increase gold holdings expires (see August 31, 1975).
March	12	DMK strong against FFR: new record rate FFR/DMK 2.3873.
March	13	Federal Reserve/Bundesbank swap line doubled. U.S. Treasury announces readiness to sell Germany SDR 6 million and draws on IMF reserve to acquire currencies.
March		Italy repays SDR 300 million to IMF, $500 million of German gold-backed loan, and $350 million to EEC. Bank of Japan raises marginal reserve requirement on free yen to 100% and prohibits sales of short-term bonds to foreigners.
April		Canada makes issues of $700 million equivalent in DMK and announces it has arranged a $3 billion standby credit with United States and other foreign banks.
May		Second Amendment of IMF Articles comes into effect: floating is legalized. U.S. Treasury gold auctions begin.
June	1	Bundesbank ends 100% marginal reserve requirement for nonresidents.
July		SDR basket amended.
August	21	U.S. discount rate raised from 7¼ to 7¾%.
August	24	Fed eliminates reserve requirements on Eurodollar borrowings from banks.
September	22	U.S. discount rate raised to 8%.
October	15	Snake realignment: deutsche mark revalued 4% against Norwegian krona, Danish krona, 2% against Belgian franc, Dutch guilder.
October	16	U.S. discount rate raised to 8½%.

October	24	President Carter announces antiinflationary program but makes no reference to monetary policy. Heavy pressure develops on U.S. dollar.
November	1	U.S. Fed raises discount rate 1%, imposes new reserve requirements and announces mobilization of $30 billion of foreign exchange for intervention, including activation of swap agreement with Bank of Japan and issue of $10 billion worth of foreign currency-denominated securities.
December	17	OPEC announces 14.5% oil price rise; Shah of Iran's position crumbles.
December	18	Irish exchange controls imposed against sterling.

1979

January	16	Shah leaves Iran.
February	1	Khomeini arrives in Iran.
February	27	South African rand floated.
March	13	European Monetary System set up.
March	30	Irish punt splits from pound sterling.
April	6	President Carter announces phase-out of U.S. oil price controls.
May	3	Conservative party wins U.K. general election, pound hits $2.08.
June	27–29	OPEC raises oil prices 24%; summit of seven major industrial countries agrees to hold oil imports stable.
July	15–20	President Carter reshuffles cabinet. Mr. Paul Volcker appointed chairman of Fed.
July	20	Federal Reserve raises discount rate by ½% to 10%.
July	26	Pound hits $2.33.
August	30	French government announces FFR 30 billion reflation program.
September	18	U.S. discount rate raised to 11%.
September	23	EMS realignment: DMK revalued 5% against DKR, 2% against other EMS currencies.
September	30	Gold price hits $397.25 per ounce.
October	2	DMK hits 1.7250 against US$, near record peak.
October	6	Federal Reserve raises U.S. discount rate 1% to 12%, imposes 8% marginal reserve requirement; "New Monetary Policy" to focus henceforth on reserve levels rather than interest rates.

October	7	Japanese LDP party reelected with unexpectedly small majority.
October	9	Bank of Canada raises discount rate ¾% to 13%.
October	24	U.S. Treasury announces two issues of Carter bonds of up to DMK 2 billion each.
October	31	German Lombard and discount rates raised 1%.
November	2	Swiss National Bank cuts negative interest rate on bank deposits from 10% per quarter to 2½% per quarter, and raises discount rate 1%. Japanese discount rate raised 1%.
November	4	Iranian militants seize U.S. Embassy in Tehran.
November	6.	Bazargan government falls in Iran.
November	14	United States freezes Iranian assets.
November	15	United Kingdom raises MLR from 14% to 17%.
November	27	Japan announces yen support package.
November	29	Danish krona devalued by 5% in EMS.
December	1	Swiss National Bank eliminates negative interest charges.
December	6	Banca d'Italia raises discount rate 3%.
December	13	Canadian government loses vote of confidence.
December	17	OPEC raises oil price on average 30%; no unified pricing.
December	27	Soviet Union invades Afghanistan.
December	31	Gold price at $512 per ounce.

1980

January	1	IMF allocates SDR 4 billion to members.
January	2	Switzerland imposes 5.6% tax on gold transactions.
January	25	Gold at US$ 850 per ounce.
February	20	Switzerland allows payment of interest on nonresident deposits; ceiling on sales of SFR to nonresidents increased.
February	28	Bundesbank raises discount rate 1% and Lombard rate 1½%; Swiss National Bank raises discount and Lombard rates 1%.
March	2	Bank of Japan announces that the Federal Reserve, Bundesbank, and Swiss National Bank will cooperate to avoid excessive decline of yen; Japanese banks permitted to make foreign currency loans to their customers and to borrow Euroyen.
		Canadian general election.
March	14	U.S. President Carter announces tightening of 1981 fiscal policy, surcharge on imported oil, and special restraints on credit. Federal Reserve raises marginal reserve require-

ment to 10% and imposes 3% surcharge on excessive discount window borrowings. Short-term rates soar to 20%.

March	14	Banca d'Italia imposes penalties on excess credit growth.
March	19	Bank of Japan raises reserve requirements and interest rates; public expenditure cut and anti-inflation measures adopted.
March	27	Swiss National Bank announces it will defend the SFR "as forcefully as required."
March	31	Gold price at $494 per ounce.
April	8–10	Yen hits low of 264; deutsche mark and Swiss franc rise 5½% and 7¾% respectively against dollar.
April	15	Group of ten and Switzerland agree to monitor international banking developments via Standing Committee on Euromarkets.
April	25	Bank of Japan and Bundesbank agree on DMK 2.5 billion swap line. Saudi Arabia and Japan agree on Saudi purchases of Japanese bonds up to $2.5 billion per annum.
April	30	Bundesbank raises discount rate ½% and Lombard rate 1% but reduces reserve requirements.
May	7	Federal Reserve eliminates 3% surcharge.
May	20	Canadian referendum on Quebec defeats separatists.
May	22	Federal Reserve eases credit restrictions.
June	11	OPEC price rise of 5–6%.
June		United Kingdom reaches agreement with EEC on £750 million reduciton in U.K. contribution to EEC.
June	22	Japanese reelect LDP.
June	23	Venice meeting of heads of government of seven industrial countries.
July	3	Federal Reserve lifts remaining credit restrictions.
July	24	Pound reaches $2.3992. Central Bank of Greece announces establishment of a managed interbank market for the drachma.
August	1	UAE passes law providing for establishment of a central bank.
August	20	Bank of Japan lowers discount rate ¾% to 8¼%.
August	31	Switzerland lifts all restrictions on nonresidents' SFR deposits.
September	1	Deutsche Bundesbank cuts minimum reserve requirements for commercial banks' domestic and foreign liabilities by 10%.

September	5	Japanese government announces expansion package.
September	19	Bundesbank lowers Lombard rate from 9½% to 9% and supplies liquidity via repurchases.
September	22	Iran–Iraq war breaks out.
September	26	Federal Reserve raises discount rate 1%.
September	28	Italy tightens exchange controls and raises discount rate 1½% following fall of Cossiga government.
October	20	Bundesbank acts to expand liquidity. Sterling hits US$ 2.4565.
November	4	Germany allows nonresidents to buy bonds of over one year (reduced from two years).
November	7	Banque de France introduces 5% reserve requirement; money market intervention rate cut ¾% to 10¾%.
November	11	Greek drachma freed from dollar peg.
November	17	Federal reserve raises discount rate to 12% and imposes 2% surcharge.
November	24	U.K. MLR reduced 2% to 14%; measures announced to reduce public sector borrowing requirement.
December	1	New Japanese exchange regulations.
December	5	Federal Reserve raises discount rate to 13%.
December	19	Canadian Bank Rate raised 17.4%.

1981

January	1	New Simplified SDR comes into effect.
January	20	U.S. hostages released from Iran. President Reagan assumes power. Swedish discount rate raised 2% to 12%.
January	27	President Reagan announces decontrol of domestic oil prices.
January	31	Banca d'Italia tightens credit control.
February	3	Swiss National Bank raises discount and Lombard rates ½%.
February	19	Bundesbank announces suspension of Lombard facility; special Lombard facility to be made available at its discretion. DMK call money hits 20 to 30%.
February	20	Swiss National Bank announces discount and Lombard rates up ½.
March	10	U.K. budget raises indirect taxes and cuts MLR 2%.
March	17	Japanese expansion package announced. Bank of Japan cuts discount rate 1% and eases credit conditions.
March	21–22	Italian lira devalued 6% in EMS. Discount rate raised 2½% to 19%. Reserve requirements tightened.

March	26	Belgian discount rate raised to 13%.
March	30	Assassination attempt on President Reagan. Belgian government resigns. Belgian discount rate raised 3%.
April		United States announces exchange intervention will be minimal.
May	10	M. Mitterand wins French Presidential election.
May	11	Swiss National Bank raises discount and Lombard rates 1%.
May	14	Banque de France raises Treasury bill discount rate 4½% to 18%.
May	22	Banque de France raises Treasury bill discount rate to 22%. *Devises—titres* market for purchase of foreign securities set up.
June		United Kingdom cuts North Sea oil price by $4.25. Sterling weakens.
June	21	French Parliamentary elections.
June		South Africa raises bank rate 1% to 10½%.
July	19	Ottawa summit of seven major nations.
July	31	Sterling falls to $1.84.
August	4	Gold falls to $391.25.
August	20	Bank of England abolishes MLR, adopts unpublished interest rate band.
August	21	OPEC fails to agree on oil price.
September	2	Swiss Lombard and discount rates raised 1%.
September	14	Bank of England raises money market rates 1%. Swedish krona devalued 10%.
September	16	U.K. clearing bank base rates rise 2%.
September	22	Federal Reserve reduces discount rate surcharge from 4% to 2%.
October	1	U.K. clearing bank base rates raised to 16%. France announces 35% increase in budget deficit.
October	4	EMS realignment: DMK, HFL revalued by 5½%, FFR and LIT devalued 3%.
October	6	President Sadat murdered. Gold hits $469.
October	13–14	U.K. clearing bank base rates reduced to 15½%.
October		South Africa swaps gold worth estimated $1 billion for currency.
October	29	OPEC agrees on a unified price structure; Saudi market crude price raised $2 to $34.
October	30	Federal Reserve cuts discount rate 1% to 13%.

November	9	U.K. base rates cut to 15%. Sheikh Yamani announces Saudi Arabia will hold oil price one year.
November	24	Citibank cuts prime to 16%.
December	4	U.K. base rates cut to 14½%. Bundesbank cuts Special Lombard rate from 1 to 10½%.
December	14	Military takeover and martial law in Poland. Israel annexes Golan Heights.
December	18	Polish fleet seals Baltic coast. Seven Polish miners killed.
December	19	United States suspends strategic agreement with Israel.
December	21	Swiss National Bank announces 3% money supply target for 1982.
December	23	Banque de France relaxes loan ceilings in France.

APPENDIX **2**

GLOSSARY

This is a list of some of the terms used in the markets. More terms are defined in my *Dictionary of International Finance* (Greenwood Press, United States/ Macmillan, London).

Offered at
Comes at
I give at   Seller or lender of currency
I sell at
I offer at _____
I bid at
I pay at
I take at   Buyer or borrower of currency
I buy at

AROUND.   Used in forward quotes. Five-five around would mean five points on either side of par—that is, on either side of the present spot rate. Also can mean around the "big-figure"—for instance, 92/02.

ASSOCIATION CAMBISTE INTERNATIONALE.   The international society of foreign exchange dealers. National "Forex clubs" are affiliated on a worldwide basis. The ACI's headquarters is at 16 Boulevard Montmartre, Paris.

BID, WANTED, FIRM, STRONG.   The currency in question is appreciating, or in demand, and buyers of the currency predominate.

BIG FIGURE.   The first three digits of an exchange rate, for instance, $1.82 per pound, or DMK 2.02 per dollar. Dealers might quote the deutsche mark as "40–50," leaving the "big figure" understood; that is, DMK 2.0240/50.

BROKEN PERIOD.   A deal which is not for a standard maturity (normally one, two, three, or six months and sometimes twelve months) involves a broken period.

CABLE.   Slang for the dollar/sterling spot exchange rate (from cable transfer).

DETAILS.   Information a dealer requires following the completion of a transaction, that is, rate and dates, and so forth.

DISCOUNT.   (1) In foreign exchange, a currency at a discount can be bought more cheaply for a future date than for immediate delivery. For example, if $1 buys DMK 2.3100 for delivery now, while it buys DMK 2.2900 for

421

delivery 12 months hence, then the dollar is said to be at a discount against the deutsche mark. (2) In money markets, to discount means to buy paper for less than its face value. The difference between the price paid and the face value is the implied rate of interest.

EFFECTIVE EXCHANGE RATE.   An attempt to summarize the effects on a country's trade balance of its currency's changes against other currencies. For example the dollar may rise against the pound and fall against the deutsche mark. To find the effective exchange rate for the dollar, we try to measure the effect on U.S. trade arising from these changes. Then we work out what change in the value of the dollar (all other currencies being unchanged) would have been needed to have the same effect on U.S. trade. Similar rates are calculated for most major currencies. (See Chapter 14.)

END-END.   A foreign exchange/Eurocurrency term relating to value dates. If the spot date is the last possible spot date for the month, then the value date for standard forward dates is the last day in the month when both dealing centers are open. For example, in dealing forward dollar-yen, if the dealing date is Wednesday, April 24, spot date Friday, the 26th, Tokyo is on holiday Monday the 29th and New York on the 30th, so the 26th is the last spot date in April. The one-month value date will therefore be May 31.

EURODOLLAR.   A dollar deposit acquired by a person or bank not resident in the United States and held outside the United States.

EUROPEAN CURRENCY UNIT.   In the European Monetary System, the European Currency Unit is defined as DMK 0.828 + FFR 1.15 + LIT 109 + DFL 0.286 + FBC 3.66 + LuxFr 0.14 + £STG 0.0885 + IEP 0.00759 + DKR 0.217. That is, the ECU consists of the sum of quantities of each of the national currencies of the members of the EEC, so the value of the ECU changes in terms of third currencies, such as the dollar, as the values of the national currencies change. The ECU is used by the European Monetary System to define a parity grid. The second role of the ECU is in the calculation of a "divergence indicator." This shows which currency is diverging from its central rates and putting pressure on other member currencies (see Chapter 14).

EUROPEAN MONETARY SYSTEM.   Set up in March 1979, the EMS succeeded the former EEC snake. The EMS includes France, Germany, Italy, Belgium, the Netherlands, Denmark, Luxembourg, and Ireland, but not the United Kingdom (see Chapter 4).

FED.   Abbreviation for Federal Reserve System of the United States. In the domestic context "Fed" usually refers to its board of governors or to the Federal Reserve Bank of New York; in the foreign exchange context it usually refers to the latter.

FEDERAL OPEN MARKET COMMITTEE.   Key decision-making committee of the Federal Reserve System. The minutes of its meetings are published about a month later and show the current stance of U.S. monetary policy.

FED FUNDS (FEDERAL FUNDS).   Cash balances held by banks with their local Federal Reserve Bank. They are immediately available—that is, not subject to clearing delays.

FED FUNDS RATE.   The rate of interest payable on Fed funds. It is probably the key short-term interest rate in the United States, because it signals current policy. Usually after a rise in the money supply figures the Fed will drain money from the market which will induce a rise in the Fed funds rate.

FIGURE.   Dealers' slang meaning "00" and denoting an exchange rate level. If the deutsche mark is quoted at 2.0300/2.0310 per dollar the rate may be quoted "figure/ten" (leaving 2.03 understood).

FIRM.   A dealer making an offer or bid on a "firm" basis commits the bank, but he would be advised to put some restriction on at the same time (e.g., "firm for one minute" or "firm for one million only"). The word "firm" can also be used in the context of strength (see Bid, etc.).

FIX, FIXING.   A daily meeting in certain European countries at which rates are "fixed" officially. These rates can then be used for nonbank purposes, for instance, tourist business. The meeting usually takes place around lunchtime and includes a representative of the central bank.

FOR INDICATION (ONLY)—FOR INFORMATION (ONLY).   Quotations which are not firm, and intended as an indication of unwillingness or inability to deal.

FORWARD FORWARD.   This refers to a deal for a future date in an instrument which matures on a further forward date. The aim is usually to even out a mismatch without upsetting the bank's total book, or else to take a position on future rate movements.

INTEREST PARITY.   The interest parity theory is that if there are two financial instruments in different currencies but identical in risk and maturity (eg., U.K. and U.S. three-month Treasury bills), then a difference in the interest rate on the instruments will be reflected in the premium or discount for the forward exchange rate (see Chapter 5).

LOMBARD RATE (ALSO LOMBARDSATZ, LOMBARDZINFUSS).   German term for the rate of interest charged for a loan against the security of pledged paper. Particularly used by the Bundebank, which normally maintains its Lombard rate at about ½% above its discount rate (q.v.).

LONDON INTERBANK OFFERED RATE (LIBOR).   The interest rate at which banks in London are prepared to lend funds to first-class banks. LIBOR is used to define the interest rate payable on most Eurocredits and is also used in the sterling market. A typical Eurocredit LIBOR clause might define LIBOR as "the arithmetic mean of the respective rates notified to the agent by the 'reference banks' as the rate at which deposits of the relevant amount for a period equal to the relevant interest period and in the relevant currency were offered to prime banks by the reference banks in the London InterBank Eurocurrency Market as at 11:00 A.M. (London time) two business days prior to the date of draw-down or renewal for value on such date."

MATURITY GAP EXPOSURE.   The risk arising from having an asset and liability of the same size and in the same currency but of different maturity. If a bank buys DMK 5 million spot and sells DMK 5 million three months forward, this leaves it long of DMK now, and short in the future; the risk is that it may be forced to "close out" the swap before it matures at an unfavorable rate.

MINE.   The dealer takes the spot, forward, or deposit, whichever has been quoted, from his counterparty. (Note: This is a very dangerous term unless amounts have been qualified first.)

MISMATCH.   A situation where assets and liabilities in a currency do not balance either in size or maturity.

NEGATIVELY SLOPING YIELD CURVE.   A yield curve where interest rates in the shorter dates are above those in the longer. For example, if one week dollars cost 16%, one month, 15½%, and six months, 15%, the slope is negative. This happens when interest rates are expected to fall.

OUTRIGHT.   A purchase/sale in the forward market without a corresponding spot contract. If I contract to buy dollars three months forward I make out an outright forward purchase (see Chapter 9).

PARITY (OR "SAME").   No proposition on the rate(s) quoted by the other party. It does not imply that the party using this expression is ready to deal at the rates quoted. The expression "nothing to propose/suggest" is clearer.

PARITY GRID.   A term used in the European Monetary System. The gird consists of the upper, central, and lower intervention points of the system.

POINT.   0.0001 of a unit; for instance, if the £/$ rate is 1.8495, then 1.8494 is one point lower.

POSITIVELY SLOPING YIELD CURVE.   A yield curve where interest rates in the shorter periods are below those in the longer. If one week sterling costs 15%, one month, 15½%, and six months, 16%, the yield curve is said to slope positively. This is the normal form (see Negative Yield Curve).

PREMIUM.   A forward exchange rate, at a premium over today's rate means that the currency is more expensive in the forward market than now (see Chapter 9).

REPURCHASE AGREEMENT.   Agreement by a borrower to sell securities with a commitment to repurchase them. These agreements (often called repos or RPs) may have a specific period or may be open-ended. They are used by the Federal Reserve as a means of temporarily supplying funds to the market (see Chapter 1 and Chapter 11).

SHORT DATES.   Usually means periods up to one week, but sometimes the term is used to refer to periods up to a month (see Chapter 12).

SNAKE.   The European system of narrower exchange rate margins which was set up in April 1972 and superseded in 1979 by the European Monetary System.

SPECIAL DRAWING RIGHT. Introduced in 1970, the SDR was an attempt by the IMF to expand international liquidity. A country holding SDRs may use them to acquire foreign, currency by transferring them (via the IMF Special Drawing Account) to another country in exchange for foreign currency supplied by that country. SDRs are treated as part of a country's international reserves (see Chapter 14).

SPOT. "Spot" deals are settled in two working days' time. For example, a purchase of dollars against sterling made on Tuesday will be settled on Thursday. It is possible to deal for settlement the following working day or even the same day in certain circumstances (see Chapter 8 and Chapter 12).

SPOT/NEXT. A purchase of currency on Monday for settlement on Thursday will be done at the exchange rate for spot delivery *plus* an adjustment for the extra day; the adjustment is called spot/next (see Chapter 12).

SQUARE. Purchases and sales, or foreign currency assets and liabilities, are equal; that is, no position, or no further interest in dealing.

SWAP. (1) The purchase/sale of a currency in the spot market combined with a simultaneous sale/purchase in the forward market (see Chapter 10). (2) In central banking terms "swap" refers to the bilateral standby credit agreements ("swap lines") which have been made among a number of central banks under which temporary payments imbalances may be financed by swaps of currencies—that is, purchases with a commitment to reverse within three months (see Chapter 3).

TOM/NEXT. From tomorrow to the next business day. Spot deals are for value two days hence. A company may require value tomorrow. In this case the tom/next rate will have to be used to adjust the spot rate. Suppose the selling US$/£STG rate is 1.8072 for spot delivery and the tom/next is 10 points sterling discount/dollar premium; then the US$/£STG rate for value tomorrow is 1.8082 (see Chapter 12).

ULTIMO. Continental (especially Swiss, German) term for the end of a month or of a year.

UNDER REFERENCE. A deal cannot be finalized without reference to the bank which placed the order, whose name should not be mentioned until reference has been made to that bank.

VALUE DATE. The date on which payment is made to settle a deal. A spot deal on Wednesday will be settled on Friday; the deal is "value Friday."

YARD. Slang for 1,000 million (from "milliard").

YOURS. Reversal of "mine," the dealer giving the spot, forward, or deposit. (Note: This is a very dangerous term unless amounts have been qualified first.)

EMS AND CURRENCY BASKETS

A3.1. The parity grid (see Chapter 4) is simple in bilateral terms. If currency A is at its limit against B, the two central banks must intervene. But the presence of other currencies in the grid means that the apparent 2½% fluctuation margins are actually less than they seem. Suppose we have three currencies in our system. They declare the following central rates against the ECU: ECU 1 = DMK 2.5 = FFR 6 = FBC 40.

A3.2. This implies the following parity grid:

	FBC	DMK	FFR
		15.6440	6.5184
FBC	1	16	6.6667
		16.3640	6.8184
	0.06111		0.4074
DMK	0.0625	1	0.41667
	0.06392		0.4261
	0.1467	2.3466	
FFR	0.15	2.4	1
	0.1534	2.4546	

(Note that the upper and lower limits calculated here are not exactly 2¼% above or below the parity. The factors are +2.2753% and −2.2247% or, to put it another way, the central parity is multiplied not by 1.0225 and 0.9775 but by 1.022753 and 0.977753. The latter number is the reciprocal of the first, and 0.045 less (i.e., the total difference is twice 2¼%, as it would be if 1.0225 and 0.9775 were used). Hence the DMK/FBC lower limit of 16.3640 multiplied by the FBC/DMK upper limit of 0.06111 produces 1, just as the central rates do when multiplied).

A3.3. Given this grid, the only way that the deutsche mark can move its full theoretical 4½% range from the bottom of the EMS to the top is if both other currencies were exactly at their central rate, that is, FFR/ FBC 6.6667. In that case the DMK/FBC rate can move freely between 15.6440 and 16.3640. But suppose the French franc is at its lower limit against the Belgian franc, that is, FFR/FBC 6.5184. Then the DMK/FBC range is cut in half since long before the deutsche mark has got to its upper limit against the Belgian franc it has reached its upper limit against the French franc. To be exact, the DMK/FBC range is 4½% less the spread between the French franc and Belgian franc; if that spread is at its limit of 2¼%, then the most that DMK/FBC can move is 2¼%.

A3.4. As a practical point we should add that if the deutsche mark rose to its upper limit against the French franc, invervention would probably start to pull the French franc up with the deutsche mark, so that it could move more against the Belgian franc. But this applies less is the case of thinly traded currencies. For example, if instead of the deutsche mark, the Danish krona was moving, the volume of DKR/FFR business would be smaller and less likely to pull the French franc up against the Belgian franc.

A3.5. Another factor which could give greater freedom to "heavy" or important currencies such as the deutsche mark compared with the Danish krona is the technical construction of the ECU. A currency which is pegged against a basket containing the currency has more freedom than if the basket does not contain the currency. To see why, let's look first at a currency which is pegged against a basket not containing itself, the Saudi riyal, for instance. The Saudis peg the riyal against the SDR, say, at SDR 1 = SAR 4. The SDR consists of US$ 0.54 + DMK 0.46 + £STG 0.071 + FFR 0.74 + ¥34. Suppose we have US$/ DMK = 2.30, £STG/US$ = 1.80, US$/FFR = 6.0, US$/¥ = 220. Then SDR 1 = US$ 1.1456 (see Chapter 15) and the Saudi riyal rate will be US$ 1 = SAR 3.4916. Now suppose that the deutsche mark strengthens by 10% to US$/DMK = 2.07. If all other rates are unchanged, SDR 1 = US$ 1.1679 and US$ 1 = SAR 3.4249. In other words, the deutsche mark's strength against the U.S. dollar pulls up the SDR against the U.S. dollar. This in turn pulls up the riyal against the dollar. The percentage change in the riyal against the dollar is the same as the change in the SDR, that is, 2% (which is the 10% deutsche mark change weighted by the share of the deutsche mark in the SDR, which is about 20%).

A3.6. Now let's look at what happens when a currency is pegged against a basket which includes itself. In this case, if the currency moved 10% as before, and the currency's weight were 20% as before, its movement against the basket would be *less than* 10%, because it would pull the basket up with it. Let's look at the deutsche mark in the EMS. Currently the ECU/DMK parity is ECU 1 = DMK 2.41815. The ECU is defined as DMK 0.828 + FFR 1.15 + £STG 0.0885

+ HFL 0.286 + LIT 109 + FBC 3.66 + DKR 0.217 + IEP 0.00759 + LuxFr 0.14. Suppose we have the following rates against the U.S. dollar: US$/DMK = 2.30, £STG/US$ = 1.80, US$/FFR = 6.0, US$/HFL = 2.5550, US$/LIT = 1250, US$/FBC = 42.50 (also for LuxFr which is at parity with FBC), US$/DKR = 7.7750, and US$/IEP = 1.5200. These rates give us ECU 1 = US$ 1.0389 which implies ECU 1 = DMK 2.3895. Suppose as before the deutsche mark rises by 10% to 2.07 per U.S. dollar. This pulls the ECU up to ECU 1 = US$ 1.0789 which implies ECU 1 = DMK 2.2333 − a movement of 6½% compared with the 10% US$/DMK move.

A3.7. This technical factor is relevant to the divergence indicator. The divergence indicator is the movement of a currency from its ECU central rate. The EMS allows a 2¼% movement; within this, there is a "threshold of divergence" at 75% of the permitted movement. As we have seen, a rise in the deutsche mark of 10% against the U.S. dollar would be a rise of only 6½% against the ECU, for the rising value of its deutsche mark component is pulling the ECU up against the U.S. dollar. But if we assume the same initial rates, and look at a 10% rise of the Danish krona, to DKR 6.9975 per US$, we find that the ECU rises only to $1.0421 from $1.0389, instead of rising to $1.0789 as it did when the deutsche mark rose 10%. The reason of course is that the DKR's weight in the ECU is less − only about 3% compared with more than 30% for the deutsche mark. It follows that a 2¼% move of the deutsche mark against the ECU will allow the deutsche mark to move further against the dollar than would be allowed for the Danish krona, because the deutsche mark would pull the ECU further up than the Danish krona would. To compensate for this, the EEC calculates an "adjusted divergence" indicator, which is given by ADI = DI × (1 − w) where ADI = adjusted divergence indicator, DI = divergence indicator, and w is the official weight for the currency. In the case of the deutsche mark, w = 0.33 (i.e., 33%), whereas for the Danish krona w = 0.031. Hence for the deutsche mark ADI = 0.67 × DI whereas for the Danish krona, ADI = 0.969 × DI.

A3.8. Unfortunately there is one more calculation to be made before we have the finally adjusted divergence indicator. This is to take account of currencies (like the lira) which have a wider band than 2¼%, and of currencies (like sterling) that have no band at all. The problem is that if, say, sterling rises by 10% against the U.S. dollar, pulling the ECU up with it, other currencies would be forced to move up against the dollar to keep their divergence indicator within the threshold. The EEC solution is to pretend that sterling and the lira stay within a 2¼% band. That is, the divergence indicator is adjusted to strip out the effects of movements in sterling and the lira that exceed 2¼%.

A3.9. To do this, we start by finding the weakest currency in the EMS. Then we see if it has moved more than 2¼% against sterling. If it has, we calculate an adjustment. This is the percentage change in the currency against sterling from the base date, less 2¼%, multiplied by sterling's weight in the ECU. A parallel factor is calculated for the lira. The two factors are added together to produce a combined adjustment. This is then deducted from the divergence to get the fully adjusted divergence indicator (see A3.11). The results of these calculations are published daily in the *Financial Times* of London and elsewhere. A sample (from the *Financial Times*) follows:

EMS European Currency Unit Rates

Currency	ECU Central Rates	Currency Amounts against ECU— May 19	Percent of Change from Central Rate	Percent of Change Adjusted for Divergence	Divergence Limit (Percent)
Belgian franc	44.6963	45.0216	+ 0.73	+ 1.05	± 1.5440
Danish krona	8.18382	8.09319	− 1.11	− 0.79	± 1.6428
German deutsche mark	2.41815	2.38250	− 1.47	− 1.15	± 1.1097
French franc	6.19564	6.21283	+ 0.28	+ 0.60	± 1.3743
Dutch guilder	2.67296	2.64957	− 0.88	− 0.56	± 1.5039
Irish punt	0.686799	0.687866	+ 0.16	+ 0.48	± 1.6689
Italian lira	1305.13	1322.21	+ 1.31	+ 1.31	± 4.1242

Changes are for ECU; therefore positive change denotes a weak currency.

SOURCE: Financial Times, May 20, 1982.

A3.10. A final technicality arises in the calculation of new central rates. In the snake, parities were declared against the European Monetary Unit of Account. This was fixed in terms of gold. Its value did not change as exchange rates changed. So if it was agreed to revalue the deutsche mark by 10%, all that was needed was to change the DMK/EMUA rate by 10%. But a deutsche mark revaluation against the ECU pulls up the ECU. Suppose the deutsche mark revalues 10%; it will pull the ECU up by about 3⅓% (as its weight is about one-third of the ECU). So the net deutsche mark movement against the ECU is only 6⅔%, and the deutsche mark and all other currencies will be below their ECU parities, so all EMS currencies would look weak at once. To prevent this, the deutsche mark revaluation has to be combined with devaluations by other countries. A 10% deutsche mark revaluation needs to be achieved by combining a 3⅓% devaluation of all other currencies with a 6⅔% deutsche mark revaluation.

A3.11 For those who prefer symbols, the following is a brief summary of the above. We define $W(i)$ as the fixed currency amounts in the ECU; for instance, if the deutsche mark is currency number one, we have $W(1) = 0.828$. We define $A(i)$ as the current central rates of each currency against the ECU (e.g., $A(1) = 2.41815$ for the deutsche mark, $C(i)$ as the present market exchange rate against the U.S. dollar for each currency. Note that sterling and the Irish pound have to be inverted to make them consistent. We define $G(i)$ as the current percentage weight of each currency in the basket. Then the value of the ECU is give by:

$$\text{ECU} = \sum_{i=1}^{9} \frac{W(i)}{C(i)} = E$$

Clearly

$$G(i) = \frac{W(i)}{A(i)} = \frac{0.828}{3.41815} \simeq 34\% \text{ for the deutsche mark}$$

To calculate the divergence indicator $D(i)$ we first find the current exchange rate for each currency against the ECU, $E \times C(i)$. Then we define:

$$D(i) = 100 - \frac{100 \times E \times C(i)}{A(i)}$$

To allow for the effects of sterling and the lira we find the weakest currency, K, and calculate (assume sterling is currency two and the lira currency three):

$$Q(2) = \left[\left(\frac{C(K)}{C(2)} \times \frac{A(2)}{A(K)} \times 100\right) - 2.25 - 100\right] \times G(2)$$
$$Q(3) = \left[\left(\frac{C(K)}{C(3)} \times \frac{A(3)}{A(K)} \times 100\right) - 2.25 - 100\right] \times G(3)$$

The final adjustment $Q = Q(2) + Q(3)$. We then compare $D(I) + Q$ with the permitted threshold.

FURTHER READING

"Intervention Arrangements in the European Monetary System," *Bank of England Quarterly Bulletin,* June 1979.

R. S. Masera, "The Operation of the EMS: A European View," *Economia Internazionale,* Genoa, November 1979.

R. Shone, "Recent Developments in Exchange Rate Links," *Department of Economics Working Paper,* University of Stirling, United Kingdom, November 1980.

R. Shone, "Some Technical Aspects of the European Monetary System," *University of Stirling Discussion Paper no. 73,* July 1979.

EUROPEAN COUNCIL RESOLUTION ON THE EMS

RESOLUTION OF THE EUROPEAN COUNCIL

on the establishment of the European Monetary System (EMS)
and related matters

(Brussels, 5 December 1978)

A

THE EUROPEAN MONETARY SYSTEM

1. *Introduction*

1.1. In Bremen we discussed a 'scheme for the creation of closer monetary co-operation leading to a zone of monetary stability in Europe'. We regarded such a zone 'as a highly desirable objective' and envisaged 'a durable and effective scheme'.

1.2. Today, after careful examination of the preparatory work done by the Council and other Community bodies, we are agreed as follows:
A EUROPEAN MONETARY SYSTEM (EMS) WILL BE SET UP ON 1 JANUARY 1979.

1.3. We are firmly resolved to ensure the lasting success of the EMS by policies conducive to greater stability at home and abroad for both deficit and surplus countries.

1.4. The following chapters deal primarily with the initial phase of the EMS. We remain firmly resolved to consolidate, not later than two years after the start of the scheme, into a final system the provisions and procedures thus created. This system will entail the creation of the European Monetary Fund as announced in the conclusions of the European Council meeting at Bremen on 6 and 7 July 1978, as well as the full utilization of

431

the ECU as a reserve asset and a means of settlement. It will be based on adequate legislation at the Community as well as the national level.

2.   *The ECU and its functions*

2.1. A European Currency Unit (ECU) will be at the centre of the EMS. The value and the composition of the ECU will be identical with the value of the EUA at the outset of the system.

2.2. The ECU will be used:
   (a) as the denominator (numéraire) for the exchange rate mechanism;
   (b) as the basis for a divergence indicator;
   (c) as the denominator for operations in both the intervention and the credit mechanism;
   (d) as a means of settlement between monetary authorities of the European Community.

2.3. The weights of the currencies in the ECU will be re-examined and if necessary revised within six months of the entry into force of the system and thereafter every five years or, on request, if the weight of any currency has changed by 25%.
   Revisions have to be mutually accepted; they will, by themselves, not modify the external value of the ECU. They will be made in line with underlying economic criteria.

3.   *The exchange rate and intervention mechanism*

3.1. Each currency will have an ECU-related central rate. These central rates will be used to establish a grid of bilateral exchange rates.
   Around these exchange rates fluctuation margins of ± 2.25% will be established. EC countries with presently floating currencies may opt for wider margins up to ± 6% at the outset of EMS; these margins should be gradually reduced as soon as economic conditions permit to do so.
   A Member State which does not participate in the exchange rate mechanism at the outset may participate at a later date.

3.2. Adjustments of central rates will be subject to mutual agreement by a common procedure which will comprise all countries participating in the exchange rate mechanism and the Commission. There will be reciprocal consultation in the Community framework about important decisions concerning exchange rate policy between countries participating and any country not participating in the system.

3.3. In principle, interventions will be made in participating currencies.

3.4. Intervention in participating currencies is compulsory when the intervention points defined by the fluctuation margins are reached.

3.5. An ECU basket formula will be used as an indicator to detect divergences between Community currencies. A 'threshold of divergence' will be fixed at 75% of the maximum spread of divergence for each currency. It will be calculated in such a way as to eliminate the influence of weight on the probability of reaching the threshold.

3.6. When a currency crosses its 'threshold of divergence', this results in a presumption that the authorities concerned will correct this situation by adequate measures, namely:
(a) diversified intervention;
(b) measures of domestic monetary policy;
(c) changes in central rates;
(d) other measures of economic policy.
In case such measures, on account of special circumstances, are not taken, the reasons for this shall be given to the other authorities, especially in the 'concertation between central banks'.
Consultations will, if necessary, then take place in the appropriate Community bodies, including the Council of Ministers.
After six months these provisions shall be reviewed in the light of experience. At that date the questions regarding imbalances accumulated by divergent creditor or debtor countries will be studied as well.

3.7. A very short-term facility of an unlimited amount will be established. Settlements will be made 45 days after the end of the month of intervention with the possibility of prolongation for another three months for amounts limited to the size of debtor quotas in the short-term monetary support.

3.8. To serve as a means of settlement, an initial supply of ECU will be provided by the EMCF against the deposit of 20% of gold and 20% of dollar reserves currently held by central banks.
This operation will take the form of specified, revolving swap arrangements. By periodical review and by an appropriate procedure it will be ensured that each central bank will maintain a deposit of at least 20% of these reserves with the EMCF. A Member State not participating in the exchange rate mechanism may participate in this initial operation on the basis described above.

4. *The credit mechanisms*

4.1. The existing credit mechanisms with their present rules of application will be maintained for the initial phase of the EMS. They will be consolidated into a single fund in the final phase of the EMS.

4.2. The credit mechanisms will be extended to an amount of 25 000 million ECU of effectively available credit. The distribution of this amount will be as follows:
Short-term monetary support = 14 000 million ECU
Medium-term financial assistance = 11 000 million ECU

4.3. The duration of the short-term monetary support will be extended for another three months on the same conditions as the first extension.

4.4. The increase of the medium-term financial assistance will be completed by 30 June 1979. In the meantime, countries which still need national legislation are expected to make their extended medium-term quotas available by an interim financing agreement of the central banks concerned.

5. *Third countries and international organizations*

5.1. The durability of EMS and its international implications require coordination of exchange rate policies *vis-à-vis* third countries and, as far as possible, a concertation with the monetary authorities of those countries.

5.2. European countries with particularly close economic and financial ties with the European Communities may participate in the exchange rate and intervention mechanism.

Participation will be based upon agreements between central banks; these agreements will be communicated to the Council and the Commission of the European Communities.

5.3. EMS is and will remain fully compatible with the relevant articles of the IMF agreement.

6. *Further procedure*

6.1. To implement the decisions taken under A., the European Council requests the Council to consider and to take a decision on 18 December 1978 on the following proposals of the Commission:

(a) Council Regulation modifying the unit of account used by the European Fund of Monetary Cooperation, which introduces the ECU in the operations of the EMCF and defines its composition;

(b) Council Regulation permitting the EMCF to receive monetary reserves and to issue ECUs to the monetary authorities of the Member States which may use them as a means of settlement;

(c) Council Regulation on the impact of the European Monetary System on the common agricultural policy. The European Council considers that the introduction of the EMS should not of itself result in any change in the situation obtaining prior to 1 Janaury 1979 regarding the expression in national currencies of agricultural prices, monetary compensatory amounts and all other amounts fixed for the purposes of the common agricultural policy.

The European Council stresses the importance of henceforth avoiding the creation of permanent MCAs and progressively reducing present MCAs in order to re-establish the unity of prices of the common agricultural policy, giving also due consideration to price policy.

6.2. It requests the Commission to submit in good time a proposal to amend the Council Decision of 22 March 1971 on setting up machinery for medium-term financial assistance to enable the Council (Economics and Finance Ministers) to take a decision on such a proposal at their session of 18 December 1978.

6.3. It requests the central banks of Member States to modify their Agreement of 10 April 1972 on the narrowing of margins of fluctuation between the currencies of Member States in accordance with the rules set forth above (see paragraph 3).

6.4. It requests the central banks of Member States to modify as follows the rules on short-term monetary support by 1 January 1979 at the latest:

(a) the total of debtor quotas available for drawings by the central banks of Member States shall be increased to an aggregate amount of 7 900 million ECU;

(b) the total of creditor quotas made available by the central banks of Member States for financing the debtor quotas shall be increased to an aggregate amount of 15 800 million ECU;

(c) the total of the additional creditor amount as well as the total of the additional debtor amount may not exceed 8 800 million ECU;

(d) the duration of credit under the extended short-term monetary support may be prolonged *twice* for a period of three months.

B

MEASURES DESIGNED TO STRENGTHEN THE ECONOMIES
OF THE LESS PROSPEROUS MEMBER STATES OF THE
EUROPEAN MONETARY SYSTEM

1.   We stress that, within the context of a broadly-based strategy aimed at improving the prospects of economic development and based on symmetrical rights and obligations of all participants, the most important concern should be to enhance the convergence of economic policies towards greater stability. We request the Council (Economic and Finance Ministers) to strengthen its procedures for coordination in order to improve that convergence.

2.   We are aware that the convergence of economic policies and of economic performance will not be easy to achieve. Therefore, steps must be taken to strengthen the economic potential of the less prosperous countries of the Community. This is primarily the responsibility of the Member States concerned. Community measures can and should serve a supporting role.

3.   The European Council agrees that in the context of the European Monetary System, the following measures in favour of the less prosperous Member States effectively and fully participating in the exchange rate and intervention mechanism will be taken.

3.1. The European Council requests the Community Institutions by the utilization of the new financial instrument and the European Investment Bank to make available for a period of five years loans of up to 1 000 million EUA per year to these countries on special conditions.

3.2. The European Council requests the Commission to submit a proposal to provide interest rate subsidies of 3% for these loans, with the following elements: The total cost of this measure, divided into annual tranches of 200 million EUA each over a period of five years shall not exceed 1 000 million EUA.

3.3. Any less prosperous member county which subsequently effectively and fully participates in the mechanisms would have the right of access to this facility within the financial limits mentioned above. Member States not participating effectively and fully in the mechanisms will not contribute to the financing of the scheme.

3.4. The funds thus provided are to be concentrated on the financing of selected infrastructure projects and programmes, with the understanding that any direct or indirect distortion of the competitive position of specific industries within Member States will have to be avoided.

3.5. The European Council requests the Council (Economics and Finance Ministers) to take a decision on the abovementioned proposals in time so that the relevant measures can become effective on 1 April 1979 at the latest. There should be a review at the end of the initial phase of the EMS.

4. The European Council requests the Commission to study the relationship between greater convergence in economic performance of the Member States and the utilization of Community instruments, in particular the funds which aim at reducing structural imbalances. The results of these studies will be discussed at the next European Council.

ISLAMIC
VALUE DATES

A5.1. There are a number of complications in value dates for Islamic currencies. They are caused by the different working week and also by Ramadan.

A5.2. Friday is a holiday in Islam. By contrast, Saturday and Sunday are normal working days. So a dealing room in a Moslem country dealing a currency such as the Saudi riyal deals the following dates:

Dealing Date	Spot Value
Monday	Wednesday
Tuesday	Thursday
Wednesday	Dollars Friday/Riyals Saturday
Thursday	Monday
Saturday	Wednesday
Sunday	Wednesday

Wednesday deals have split value dates as no Gulf payments can be made on a Friday. The Thursday value date moves to a Monday to enable people to deal against the dollar without making weekend adjustments. Saturday and Sunday deals move the value date to Wednesday to be in line with the rest of world markets when they open on Monday. As regards money market deals, people try to avoid having maturities on a Sunday or a Tuesday as spot deals are not usually done for these value dates.

A5.3. Ramadan is another factor. Ramadan is the traditional month of fasting in Moslem countries. As a general rule, economic activity slows somewhat during this period; the problem for dealers is that the holiday at the end of Ramadan (Eid) is determined by the sighting of the moon at the start of Ramadan. Hence it is difficult to determine in advance. Also, the official holiday is three days, but some banks may close for up to 10 days. The accepted market practice with deals maturing during a holiday is to extend the deal at the existing rate until the first accepted clearing day after the holiday.

A5.4. The following general remarks may be of help in understanding the Arab calendar. The Arab calendar is a lunar calendar, rather than the solar or Gregorian calendar used in the West. It starts from July 15 or 16 of 622 A.D., the year of the Hijra (Mohammed's flight to Medina). It is a 354-day year with 12 months. The odd months have 30 days and the even months 29 days. To keep the calculated lunar calendar in line with the new moon, leap years have to be included. There are 11 leap years in every 30 years: the 2nd, 5th, 7th, 10th, 13th, 16th, 18th, 21st, 24th, 26th and 29th. So, to find out if a particular year is a leap year, one has to divide it by 30, take the remainder and see whether it matches one of these years. For instance, 1982 A.D. is equivalent to 1403 A.H. We divide 1403/30 = 46.76: 46 × 30 = 1380, so the remainder is 23, which is not one of the leap years in the cycle. So 1403 is not a leap year, although 1404 will be since 24 is one of the cyclical leap years.

A5.5. To convert a Hijra year into its A.D. equivalent we proceed as follows:
1. Find out how far the Hijra calendar is ahead of our calendar by dividing the Hijra year number by 33, since 33 Hijra years are quivalent to 32 years in our calendar.
2. Subtract the quotient (ignoring the remainder) from the Hijra year number. The answer will give the number of solar years since the Hijra.
3. Add 621 to the answer (since 621 is the number of whole years between the base dates of the two calendars). For example, take the Hijra year 1399. 1399/33 = 42.39; so in 1399 lunar years the Hijra calendar gained 42 years on ours. We subtract 42 from 1399 to find that 1357 solar years have elapsed from the Hijra. Then we add 621 to find that 1399 A.H. = 1978 A.D.

A5.6. The conversion formulas to get from Hijra years to Gregorian years and vice versa therefore are:

$$G = H - \frac{H}{33} + 621 \quad H = G - 621 + \frac{G - 621}{32}$$

bearing in mind that 33 Hijra years = 32 Gregorian years. These formulas give the Gregorian year in which the Hijra year begins. if we want the year in which it ends, we adjust by 622 rather than 621.

A5.7. Because the two years do not match, Ramadan is continually starting earlier in the Gregorian year. As a matter of fact, Ramadan starts and ends on the following dates:

Hijra	A.D.	1 Ramadan	30 Ramadan
1403	1982	June 12	July 11
1404	1983	May 31	June 29
1405	1984	May 21	June 19
1406	1985	May 10	June 8
1407	1986	April 30	May 29
1408	1987	April 18	May 17
1409	1988	April 7	May 6
1410	1989	March 28	April 26
1411	1990	March 17	April 15
1412	1991	March 5	April 3
1413	1992	February 23	March 24
1414	1993	February 12	March 13
1415	1994	February 1	March 2

Note that there may be slight variations from country to country. In particular, the Iranian calendar is different. And there may be a difference of a day or two between eastern and western Islamic countries as the visible new moon there differed from the astronomic new moon calculations based on Mecca. There is an interesting general discussion in V. V. Tsybulsky, *Calendars of Middle East Countries*, U.S.S.R. Academy of Sciences Institute of Oriental Studies, Moscow, 1979.

SWIFT AND ISO CURRENCY CODES

**ALPHABETICAL LIST OF CODES FOR THE
REPRESENTATION OF CURRENCIES AND FUNDS
BASED ON INTERNATIONAL STANDARD ISO 4217**

Code	Currency	Country
AED	UAE Dirham	United Arab Emirates
AFA	Afghaṇi	Afghanistan
ALL	Lek	Albania
ANG	Netherlands Antillian Guilder	Netherlands Antilles
AOK	Kwanza Angola	Angola
ARP	Argentina Peso	Argentina
ATS	Schilling	Austria
AUD	Australian Dollar	Australia
		Christmas Island
		Cocos (Keeling) Islands
		Gilbert Islands
		Heard and Mcdonald Islands
		Nauru
		Norfolk Island
		Tuvalu
BBD	Barbados Dollar	Barbados
BDT	Taka	Bangladesh
BEF	Common Belgian Franc	⎱ Belgium
BEC	Convertible Belgian Franc	⎰ Luxembourg
BEL	Financial Belgian Franc	
BEB	Bilateral Burundi Belgian Franc	⎱ Belgium
BER	Bilateral Rwanda Belgian Franc	⎰ Luxembourg
BEZ	Bilateral Zaïre Belgian Franc	

Code	Currency	Country
BGL	Lev	Bulgaria
BHD	Bahraini dinar	Bahrain
BIF	Burundi Franc	Burundi
BMD	Bermudan Dollar	Bermuda
BND	Brunei Dollar	Brunei
BOP	Bolivian Peso	Bolivia
BRC	Cruzeiro	Brazil
BSD	Bahamian Dollar	Bahamas
BUK	Kyat	Burma
BWP	Pula	Botswana
BZD	Belize Dollar	Belize
CAD	Canadian Dollar	Canada
CHF	Swiss Franc	Liechtenstein Switzerland
CLP	Chilean Peso	Chile
CNY	Yuan Renminbi	China
COP	Colombian Peso	Colombia
CRC	Costa Rican Colon	Costa Rica
CSK	Koruna	Czechoslovakia
CIP	Cuban Peso	Cuba
CVE	Cape Verde Escudo	Cape Verde
CYP	Cyrpus Pound	Cyprus
DDM	Mark der DDR	German Democratic Republic
DEM	Deutsche Mark	Germany, Federal Republic of
DJF	Djibouti Franc	Djibouti
DKK	Danish Kroner	Denmark Faeroe Islands Greenland
DOP	Dominican Peso	Dominican Republic
DZD	Algerian Dinar	Algeria
ECS	Sucre	Ecuador
EGP	Egyptian Pound	Egypt
ESA	Spanish Peseta Account 'A'	Spain
ESB	Spanish Peseta Account 'B'	Spain
ESP	Spanish Peseta	Andorra Spain Western Sahara
ETB	Ethiopian Birr	Ethiopia

Code	Currency	Country
FIM	Markka	Finland
FJD	Fiji Dollar	Fiji
FKP	Falkland Islands Pound	Falkland Islands
FRF	French Franc	Andorra France French Guiana French Southern and Antarctic Territories Guadeloupe Martinique Monaco Reunion St. Pierre and Miquelon
GBP	Pound Sterling	British Antarctic Territory Canton and Enderbury Islands United Kingdom
GHC	Cedi	Ghana
GIP	Gibraltar Pound	Gibraltar
GMD	Dalasi	Gambia
GNS	Syli	Guinea
GQE	Ekwele	Equatorial Guinea
GRD	Drachma	Greece
GTQ	Quetzal	Guatemala
GWP	Guinea-Bissau Peso	Guinea-Bissau
GYD	Guyan Dollar	Guyana
HKD	Hong Kong Dollar	Hong Kong
HNL	Lempira	Honduras
HTG	Gourde	Haiti
HUF	Forint	Hungary
IDR	Rupiah	Indonesia
IEP	Irish Pound	Ireland
ILP	Israeli Pound	Israel
INR	Indian Rupee	Bhutan India
IQD	Iraqi Dinar	Iraq Neutral Zone (between Saudi Arabia and Iraq)
IRR	Iranian Rial	Iran
ISK	Iceland Krona	Iceland

Code	Currency	Country
ITL	Lira	Italy San Marino Vatican City State (Holy See)
JMD	Jamaican Dollar	Jamaica
JOD	Jordanian Dinar	Jordan
JPY	Yen	Japan
KES	Kenyan Shilling	Kenya
KHR	Riel	Kampuchea, Democratic
KMF	Comoros Franc	Comoros
KPW	North Korean Won	Korea, Democratic People's Republic of
KRW	Won	Korea, Republic of
KWD	Kuwaiti Dinar	Kuwait Neutral Zone (between Saudi Arabia and Iraq)
KYD	Cayman Islands Dollar	Cayman Islands
LAK	Kip	Lao People's Democratic Republic
LBP	Lebanese Pound	Lebanon
LKR	Sri Lanka Rupee	Sri Lanka
LRD	Liberian Dollar	Liberia
LYD	Libyan Dinar	Libyan Arab Jamahiriya
MAD	Moroccan Dirham	Morocco Western Sahara
MGF	Malagasy Franc	Madagascar
MLF	Mali Franc	Mali
MNT	Tugrik	Mongolia
MOP	Pataca	Macau
MRO	Ouguiya	Mauritania Western Sahara
MTP	Maltese Pound	Malta
MUR	Mauritius Rupee	British Indian Ocean Territory Mauritius
MVR	Maldive Rupee	Maldives
MWK	Malawi Kwacha	Malawi
MXP	Mexican Peso	Mexico
MYR	Malaysian Ringgit	Malaysia
MZE	Mozambique Escudo	Mozambique

Code	Currency	Country
NGN	Naira	Nigeria
NHF	New Hebrides Franc	New Herbrides
NIC	Cordoba	Nicaragua
NLG	Netherlands Guilder	Netherlands
NOK	Norwegian Krone	Antarctica
		Bouvet Island
		Dronning Maud Land
		Norway
		Svalbard and Jan Mayen Islands
NPR	Nepalese Rupee	Nepal
NZD	New Zealand Dollar	Cook Islands
		Niue Islands
		New Zealand
		Pitcairn Islands
		Tokelau
OMR	Rial Omani	Oman
PAB	Balboa	Panama
PES	Sol	Peru
PGK	Kina	Papua New Guinea
PHP	Philippine Peso	Philippines
PKR	Pakistan Rupee	Pakistan
PLZ	Zloty	Poland
PTE	Portuguese Escudo	Portugal
PYG	Guarani	Paraguay
QAR	Qatari Rial	Qatar
ROL	Leu	Romania
RWF	Rwanda Franc	Rwanda
SAR	Saudi Riyal	Neutral Zone (between Saudi Arabia and Iraq)
		Saudi Arabia
SBD	Solomon Islands Dollar	Solomon Islands
SCR	Seychelles Rupee	British Indian Ocean Territory
		Seychelles
SDP	Sudanese Pound	Sudan
SEK	Swedish Krona	Sweden
SGD	Singapore Dollar	Singapore
SHP	St. Helena Pound	St. Helena
SLL	Leone	Sierra Leone

Code	Currency	Country
SOS	Somali Shilling	Somalia
SRG	Surinam Guilder	Surinam
STD	Dobra	Sâo Tomé and Principe
SUR	Rouble	Byelorussian SSR
		Ukrainian SSR
		Union of Soviet Socialist Republics
SVC	El Salvador Colon	El Salvador
SYP	Syrian Pound	Syrian Arab Republic
SZL	Lilangeni	Swaziland
THB	Baht	Thailand
TND	Tunisian Dinar	Tunisia
TOP	Pa'anga	Tonga
TPE	Timor Escudo	East Timor
TRL	Turkish Lira	Turkey
TTD	Trinidad and Tobago Dollar	Trinidad and Tobago
TWD	New Taiwan Dollar	Taiwan, Province of
TZS	Tanzanian Shilling	Tanzania, United Republic of
UGS	Uganda Shilling	Uganda
USD	US Dollar Common	
USN	US Dollar next day funds	United States
USS	US Dollar same day funds	American Samoa
USD	US Dollar	British Virgin Islands
		Canton and Enderbury Islands
		Guam
		Haiti
		Johnston Island
		Midway Islands
		Pacific Islands (Trust Territory)
		Panama
		Panama Canal Zone
		Puerto Rico
		Turks and Caicos Islands
		United States Miscellaneous Pacific Islands
		United States Virgin Islands
		Wake Island
UYP	Uruguayan Peso	Uruguay
VEB	Bolivar	Venezuela

Code	Currency	Country
VND	Dong	Viet-Nam
WST	Tala	Samoa
XAF	CFA Franc	Central African Empire Chad Congo Gabon United Republic of Cameroon
XCD	East Caribbean Dollar	Antigua Dominica Grenada Montserrat St. Kitts–Nevis–Anguilla St. Lucia St. Vincent
XEU	European Currency Unit (E.C.U.)	European Monetary Cooperation Fund (E.M.C.F.)
XOF	CFA Franc	Benin Ivory Coast Niger Senegal Togo Upper Volta
XPF	CFP Franc	French Polynesia New Caledonia Wallis and Futuna Islands
YDD	Yemeni Dinar	Yemen, Democratic
YER	Yemeni Rial	Yemen
YUD	New Yugoslavian Dinar	Yugoslavia
ZAR	Rand	Lesotho Namibia South Africa
ZMK	Zambian Kwacha	Zambia
ZRZ	Zaire	Zaire
ZWD	Zimbabwe Dollar	Zimbabwe

ACI CODE
OF BEHAVIOR
IN DEALING

The following code of behavior is reproduced with the permission of the ACI:

The Charter of the Association Cambiste Internationale emphasises that high professional standards should be maintained, and this is embodied in particular, in Article 5.

"The Forex National Organisations and their members will do all in their power to give to their profession the importance and high reputation to which it is entitled by constantly setting an example of propriety in business and of dignity in all circumstances."

Article 5 of the Charter is reprinted on the inside of the front cover of each edition of Forex Inter, as a reminder of the behaviour that is expected of each member of the profession and the Council of A.C.I. has requested that a code of conduct, practice and standard terminology be drawn up, setting minimum standards for dealers and brokers, which all members would be expected to observe, both in the letter and in the spirit.

The following minimum standards are fully endorsed by the Council of A.C.I. and it is strongly recommended that they are accepted by and incorporated into the rules of, each National Forex Organisation.

CONFIDENTIALITY

Confidentiality is vital to the preservation of that anonymity which is so important to the operation and function of a reputable and efficient market in both foreign exchange and currency deposits and it cannot be stressed too strongly that banks and brokers are equally responsible for the maintenance of confidentiality and have a common interest in preserving the anonymity of the market. Attempts to induce breaches of confidence are strongly condemned, as they only damage the mutual trust on which the market depends, as also does the general dissemination and discussion in the market of business being done by others.

In order to facilitate the smooth operation of markets and to minimise frustration on all sides, dealers should wherever practicable give brokers prior indication of those with whom they would be unwilling to do business and in any case should not put brokers under pressure to disclose information which it would be improper for them to pass.

Some banks' and brokers' offices in some financial centres have been in the habit of using loudspeaker equipment, through which all conversations taking place can be heard not only in that office, but also by anyone having a line to that office. This practice is inconsistent with the fundamental concept of confidentiality and anonymity in the market and should be avoided.

Also in the interests of preserving confidentiality, visitors to dealing rooms should be carefully supervised and approved and no dealing by a visitor should be allowed whilst on a brokers' premises.

PRACTICE AND ETHICS

Much of the dealing which takes place is done by word of mouth and unless very high standards are maintained the market cannot operate properly. This applies both to dealer-to-dealer and to deal-to-broker contacts and a very high degree of ethical conduct is required at all times from all participants in the market.

Firm prices given should always be honoured, provided responses are made reasonably quickly. Time limits on prices and quotations should be respected. The language used should be as clear and as unambiguous as possible (please also see appendix for recommended standard terminology). Prices which are not firm should always be qualified by the use of a phrase, such as "for indication only" or "for information only."

In case amounts involved are not reflecting normal practice, prior indication should be given when quoting. When concluding a deal the name of the counterparty should be given and approved immediately and this name may not be changed without good reason. Further details of business transacted should be passed as soon as possible. Differences arising from dealings should not be settled by adjustment in prices of later deals. Advantage should never be deliberately taken of an obviously incorrect quotation (e.g. a wrong "big" figure).

In the interest of maintaining good market practice and ethics, market participants should be aware of possible difficulties that may arise if certain practices are not carefully monitored and the following guidelines may be helpful in determining policy.

Dealers should never write out their own outgoing confirmation or receive incoming confirmations. All deals should be limited to transactions between personnel operating from the bank's premises and should be confirmed at once, including forward deals.

With the growing number of international financial centres spanning the world's time zones transactions will often be entered into where one of the parties is working outside his normal dealing day. It must necessarily follow that other market participants have to assume that a dealer calling outside normal hours transactions should be conducted (or immediately confirmed) by telex unless there are prior arrangements between the banks involved.

In this relationship with all participants in the market a dealer should act with the appropriate sense of responsibility, always bearing in mind that his first responsibility is towards his employers.

Where there is suspicion of improper conduct on the part of another participant in the market, the dealer should refer to his management before undertaking further business with that participant. Spreading of rumours in the market about participants however would be contrary to the above ethics.

In accepting the foregoing recommendations the basis of their interpretation should be that good faith, moral honesty, the spirit of co-operation and professionalism are, above all, fundamental to the continued wellbeing of the Association Cambiste Internationale and its members.

SOME WARNINGS

The purpose of this document is to provide market participants with a useful guide to help determine whether irregularities in dealing might be taking place.

A bank dealing in foreign exchange faces the following two risks:

a) the effect of unfavourable movements in exchange or interest rates on open currency positions, and

b) the failure of counterparties before their commitments, either spot, forward, or deposits are settled.

Examination of the losses suffered by several major banks reveals that these could be classified under two broad headings:-

a) operations carried out with the full knowledge and authority of the general management or a general manager of the bank concerned, and

b) operations carried out by the Foreign Exchange dealers of a bank without, or beyond, the authority of the general management.

Furthermore, in those cases where large speculative positions were opened, a substantial increase in the volume of business was also apparent.

As the total volume of business which a bank can place in the international market depends upon its reputation, standing and consequently its credit worthiness, it is practically impossible for other members of the market to ascertain the basis of the operations of a bank of undoubted standing.

Similarly, in view of the case with which large speculative positions could be built up within a comparatively short period of time without arousing suspicion, it would be impracticable to rely on the size of individual transactions as an indication that unusual dealings were taking place.

Those facets of dealing, which could indicate to a counterparty or correspondent bank that unauthorised dealings might be taking place, can be indentified as:-

a) A sudden increase in trading volume in relation to the size of the bank or branch concerned; it being appreciated, however, that in the case of major banks, as outlined above, this might be a questionable warning;

b) an unusual increase in the turnover in a bank's clearing accounts with correspondent banks, particularly if overdrafts were to occur frequently. As the turnover on clearing accounts aggregate the countervalue of any number of deals, which by themselves might not arouse the suspicion of the counterparties to those deals, this could be a useful warning:

c) a change in the "normal" pattern of dealing.

Open positions need not be taken only for forward delivery, but can be taken by buying or selling spot currency which is then swapped from day to day or for short periods. Such operations will lead to an increased presence in the market and normally, a consequent increase in turnover on clearing accounts.

Risk of losses also occurs when a bank runs a "forward book". Although there is no net open position as total purchases match total sales, there is a risk on the unmatched forward maturities;

d) failure to receive confirmations of deals, particularly of forward transactions;

e) no satisfactory response to requests for verification of outstanding contracts ("bien trouvés").

f) a willingness to deal at a price which is deliberately pitched outside the market level.

To avoid dealing with some banks a dealer may quote a rate with a wide spread between the buying and selling prices. If the other bank deals, particularly in a swap, it is probably due to that other bank having difficulties in carrying through its business;

g) a request to apply false spot rates on swap transactions. When a forward contract matures, it is normal for a bank, when extending the maturity, to have to apply the current market spot rate to liquidate the maturing contract and to base the new forward rate on that spot rate.

If the new spot rate is unfavourable compared with the rate on the maturing contract, a difference will have to be paid. If a dealer wishes to conceal from his management losses on maturing forward positions, he will try to avoid paying such difference by requesting that the rate on the new spot deal be the same as the rate on the maturing contract.

It is clear that if any dealer wishes to deceive or defraud his bank by unauthorised exchange transactions, he can only do so for a limited period except where there is substantial collusion or where close internal independent supervision of exchange transactions is not maintained.

The foregoing remarks apply in large measure also to operations in the deposit markets.

GENERAL RATES OF WITHHOLDING TAX ON INTEREST IN SELECTED COUNTRIES

Country	Rate (%)	Country	Rate (%)
Argentina	15	Luxembourg	NIL
Australia	10	Malaysia	15
Austria	20	Mexico	21 (3)
Belgium	20	Netherlands	NIL
Bolivia	30	Netherlands Antilles	NIL
Brazil	25	New Zealand	15
Canada	25	Norway	NIL
Denmark	NIL	Pakistan	55
Finland	30	Portugal	30 (4)
France	38 (5)	Singapore	40
Germany	NIL	South Africa	10
Guernsey	20	Spain	24
Ireland	35	Sweden	NIL
Italy	15	Switzerland	35
Japan	20	UK	30
Jersey	20	USA	30
		Venezuela	15

Notes
1. Rates quoted above apply to interest payable to nonresident banks, subject to any reduction in the rate provided in a relevant double taxation agreement. They are subject to change at any time and should be checked for recent changes.

2. The rates quoted do not necessarily apply to all classes of interest and in considering specific cases reference should always be made (i) to the domestic law of the country and (ii) to a relevant double taxation agreement.
3. Reduced to 15% in the case of payments to registered foreign banks.
4. The rate may be reduced to 15% in the case of qualifying deposits.
5. No withholding tax on interest arising on short term interbank deposits and foreign currency deposits.

SOURCE: Peat, Marwick, Mitchell & Co., *Foreign Tax Credits Available to Banks in Certain Countries*, London, September 1981.

VALUE OF A POINT IN A SPOT FOREIGN EXCHANGE DEAL

This table sets out the value of a point on a deal of $1 million. In the case of a normal currency, FC 10,000,000 is bought at 10 and sold at 9.9999 for $1,000,-010—a profit of $10. A reciprocal currency is bought at 9.9999, making FC 100,001 which is sold at 10 for $1,000,010. (FC = foreign currency.)

Exchange Rate	Profit in Dollars
10	10.00
9.75	10.26
9.5	10.53
9.25	10.81
9	11.11
8.75	11.43
8.5	11.76
8.25	12.12
8	12.50
7.75	12.90
7.5	13.33
7.25	13.79
7	14.29
6.75	14.81
6.5	15.38
6.25	16.00
6	16.67
5.75	17.39
5.5	18.18
5.25	19.05
5	20.00
4.75	21.05

Exchange Rate	Profit in Dollars
4.5	22.22
4.25	23.53
4	25.00
3.75	26.67
3.5	28.57
3.25	30.77
3	33.33
2.75	36.36
2.5	40.00
2.25	44.44
2	50.00
1.75	57.14
1.5	66.67
1.25	80.00
1	100.00
0.75	133.33
0.5	200.00
0.25	400.00

VALUE OF A
BASIS POINT PER
$1 MILLION

Days to Maturity	Value	Days to Maturity	Value	Days to Maturity	Value	Days to Maturity	Value	Days to Maturity	Value	Days to Maturity	Value
1	$0.28	31	$8.61	61	$16.94	91	$25.28	121	$33.61	151	$41.94
2	0.56	32	8.89	62	17.22	92	25.56	122	33.89	152	42.22
3	0.83	33	9.17	63	17.50	93	25.83	123	34.17	153	42.50
4	1.11	34	9.44	64	17.78	94	26.11	124	34.44	154	42.78
5	1.39	35	9.72	65	18.06	95	26.39	125	34.72	155	43.06
6	1.67	36	10.00	66	18.33	96	26.67	126	35.00	156	43.33
7	1.94	37	10.28	67	18.61	97	26.94	127	35.28	157	43.61
8	2.22	38	10.56	68	18.89	98	27.22	128	35.56	158	43.89
9	2.50	39	10.83	69	19.17	99	27.50	129	35.83	159	44.17
10	2.78	40	11.11	70	19.44	100	27.78	130	36.11	160	44.44
11	3.06	41	11.39	71	19.72	101	28.06	131	36.39	161	44.72
12	3.33	42	11.67	72	20.00	102	28.33	132	36.67	162	45.00
13	3.61	43	11.94	73	20.28	103	28.61	133	36.94	163	45.28

14	3.89	44	12.22	74	20.56	104	28.89	134	37.22	164	45.56
15	4.17	45	12.50	75	20.83	105	29.17	135	37.50	165	45.83
16	4.44	46	12.78	76	21.11	106	29.44	136	37.78	166	46.11
17	4.72	47	13.06	77	21.39	107	29.72	137	38.06	167	46.39
18	5.00	48	13.33	78	21.67	108	30.00	138	38.33	168	46.67
19	5.28	49	13.61	79	21.94	109	30.28	139	38.61	169	46.94
20	5.56	50	13.89	80	22.22	110	30.56	140	38.89	170	47.22
21	5.83	51	14.17	81	22.50	111	30.83	141	39.17	171	47.50
22	6.11	52	14.44	82	22.78	112	31.11	142	39.44	172	47.78
23	6.39	53	14.72	83	23.06	113	31.39	143	39.72	173	48.06
24	6.67	54	15.00	84	23.33	114	31.67	144	40.00	174	48.33
25	6.94	55	15.28	85	23.61	115	31.94	145	40.28	175	48.61
26	7.22	56	15.56	86	23.89	116	32.22	146	40.56	176	48.89
27	7.50	57	15.83	87	24.17	117	32.50	147	40.83	177	49.17
28	7.78	58	16.11	88	24.44	118	32.78	148	41.11	178	49.44
29	8.06	59	16.39	89	24.72	119	33.06	149	41.39	179	49.72
30	8.33	60	16.67	90	25.00	120	33.33	150	41.67	180	50.00

Days to Maturity	Value	Days to Maturity	Value	Days to Maturity	Value	Days to Maturity	Value	Days to Maturity	Value	Days to Maturity	Value
181	$50.28	212	$58.89	243	$67.50	274	$76.11	305	$84.72	336	$93.33
182	50.56	213	59.17	244	67.78	275	76.39	306	85.00	337	93.61
183	50.83	214	59.44	245	68.06	276	76.67	307	85.28	338	93.89
184	51.11	215	59.72	246	68.33	277	76.94	308	85.56	339	94.17
185	51.39	216	60.00	247	68.61	278	77.22	309	85.83	340	94.44
186	51.67	217	60.28	248	68.89	279	77.50	310	86.11	341	94.72
187	51.94	218	60.56	249	69.17	280	77.78	311	86.39	342	95.00
188	52.22	219	60.83	250	69.44	281	78.06	312	86.67	343	95.28
189	52.50	220	61.11	251	69.72	282	78.33	313	86.94	344	95.56
190	52.78	221	61.39	252	70.00	283	78.61	314	87.22	345	95.83
191	53.06	222	61.67	253	70.28	284	78.89	315	87.50	346	96.11
192	53.33	223	61.94	254	70.56	285	79.17	316	87.78	347	96.39
193	53.61	224	62.22	255	70.83	286	79.44	317	88.06	348	96.67
194	53.89	225	62.50	256	71.11	287	79.72	318	88.33	349	96.94
195	54.17	226	62.78	257	71.39	288	80.00	319	88.61	350	97.22

196	54.44	227	63.06	258	71.67	289	80.28	320	88.89	351	97.50
197	54.72	228	63.33	259	71.94	290	80.56	321	89.17	352	97.78
198	55.00	229	63.61	260	72.22	291	80.83	322	89.44	353	98.06
199	55.28	230	63.89	261	72.50	292	81.11	323	89.72	354	98.33
200	55.56	231	64.17	262	72.78	293	81.39	324	90.00	355	98.61
201	55.83	232	64.44	263	73.06	294	81.67	325	90.28	356	98.89
202	56.11	233	64.72	264	73.33	295	81.94	326	90.56	357	99.17
203	56.39	234	65.00	265	73.61	296	82.22	327	90.83	358	99.44
204	56.67	235	65.28	266	73.89	297	82.50	328	91.11	359	99.72
205	56.94	236	65.56	267	74.17	298	82.78	329	91.39	360	100.00
206	57.22	237	65.83	268	74.44	299	83.06	330	91.67	361	100.28
207	57.50	238	66.11	269	74.72	300	83.33	331	91.94	362	100.56
208	57.78	239	66.39	270	75.00	301	83.61	332	92.22	363	100.83
209	58.06	240	66.67	271	75.28	302	83.89	333	92.50	364	101.11
210	58.33	241	66.94	272	75.56	303	84.17	334	92.78	365	101.39
211	58.61	242	67.22	273	75.83	304	84.44	335	93.06	366	101.67

NOTE: Value of a basis point = $1,000,000 \times 0.01\% \times$ days to maturity/360.

FORWARD FORWARD DEPOSIT RATES

A11.1. This appendix works out some sample forward forward rates from the formula of Chapter 11, Section 6. It shows certain pairs of rates for certain dates. To interpret them we should proceed as follows. Suppose the near rate (say, 10%) is taken as the offered rate, and the far rate (say, 15%) is taken as the bid rate, for 60 days and 90 days respectively. That is, we borrow from the market for 60 days at 10%, and lend into the market's 15% bid for 90 days. Then the table says that the crude forward forward is 25%, with an interest-on-interest adjustment of 0.41%; we can bid up to 24.59% for the uncovered 30 days and still break even.

A11.2. Note that the interest-on-interest adjustment always reduces the forward forward rate from the crude rate if interest rates are not negative. To see why, we consider our formula again:

$$\text{Adjusted forward} - \text{forward rate} = \frac{R_2 \times N_2 - R_1 \times N_1}{(N_2 - N_1)\left(\dfrac{R_1 \times N_1}{360 \times 100} + 1\right)}$$

If we realize that the crude forward forward rate is given by

$$\frac{R_2 \times N_2 - R_1 \times N_1}{(N_2 - N_1)}$$

and we realize that

$$\left(\frac{R_1 \times N_1}{360 \times 100} + 1\right)$$

is always greater than 1 (unless R_1 is itself negative), it is clear that the adjusted rate must always be less than the crude rate.

A11.3.   The interpretation of this is that if we lend the near date and borrow the far date, the interest earned in the first period means we can lower our lending rate in the second period and still break even. Equally, if we take the near date and lend the far date, the fact that we have to pay away interest early means that we cannot afford to bid quite as much for the second period.

A11.4.   At certain points in the table the crude and true forward forward rates both equal zero. This is a very special case: $R_1 / R_2 = N_2 / N_1$. When this happens, $R_1 \times N_1 = R_2 \times N_2$ and the top line of the formula is always zero. Another special case is when the two interest rates are equal: $R_2 = R_1$. Then the crude forward forward rate equals the other two rates; and the size of the adjustment only depends on the number of days in the near period. So, if the near and far rates are 15%, for instance, the adjustment is 0.185% as long as the near period is 30 days, no matter what the length of the far period is.

Table of Forward — Forward Rates.[a]

Near /Far Rate/ Rate	30 days against 60 days	30 days against 90 days	30 days against 180 days
5%/5%	$5 - .021 = 4.979$	$5 \ - .021 = 4.979$	$5 - .021 = 4.979$
5/10	$15 - .062 = 14.938$	$12.5 - .052 = 12.448$	$11 - .046 = 10.954$
5/15	$25 - .104 = 24.896$	$20 - .083 = 19.917$	$17 - .071 = 16.929$
5/20	$35 - .145 = 34.855$	$27.5 - .114 = 27.386$	$23 - .095 = 22.905$
10/5	0	$2.5 - .021 = 2.479$	$4 - .033 = 3.967$
10/10	$10 - .083 = 9.917$	$10 - .083 = 9.917$	$10 - .083 = 9.917$
10/15	$20 - .165 = 19.835$	$17.5 - .145 = 17.355$	$16 - .132 = 15.868$
10/20	$30 - .248 = 29.752$	$25 - .207 = 24.793$	$22 - .182 = 21.818$
15/5	$- 5 + .062 = - 4.938$	0	$3 - .037 = 2.963$
15/10	$5 - .062 = 4.938$	$7.5 - .093 = 7.407$	$9 - .111 = 8.889$
15/15	$15 - .185 = 14.815$	$15 - .185 = 14.815$	$15 - .185 = 14.815$
15/20	$25 - .309 = 24.691$	$22.5 - .278 = 22.222$	$21 - .259 = 20.741$
20/5	$- 10 + .164 = - 9.836$	$- 2.5 + .041 = - 2.459$	$2 - .033 = 1.967$
20/10	0	$5 - .082 = 4.918$	$8 - .131 = 7.869$
20/15	$10 - .164 = 9.836$	$12.5 - .205 = 12.295$	$14 - .230 = 13.77$
20/20	$20 - .328 = 19.672$	$20 - .328 = 19.672$	$20 - .328 = 19.672$

[a] This table shows the crude forward — forward rate, less the interest-on-interest adjustment, and the true rate is 15%, the adjustment is 0.542% and the adjusted forward — forward rate is 14.458%.

60 days against 90 days	60 days against 180 days	90 days against 180 days	90 days against 360 days
$5 - .041 = 4.959$	$5 - .041 = 4.959$	$5 - .062 = 4.938$	$5 - .062 = 4.938$
$20 - .165 = 19.835$	$12.5 - .103 = 12.397$	$15 - .185 = 14.815$	$11.667 - .144 = 11.523$
$35 - .289 = 34.711$	$20 - .165 = 19.835$	$25 - .309 = 24.691$	$18.333 - .226 = 18.107$
$50 - .413 = 49.587$	$27.5 - .227 = 27.273$	$35 - .432 = 34.568$	$25 - .309 = 24.691$
$-5 + .082 = 4.918$	$2.5 - .041 = 2.459$	0	$3.333 - .081 = 3.252$
$10 - .164 = 9.836$	$10 - .164 = 9.836$	$10 - .244 = 9.756$	$10 - .244 = 9.756$
$25 - .410 = 24.59$	$17.5 - .287 = 17.213$	$20 - .488 = 19.512$	$16.667 - .407 = 16.260$
$40 - .656 = 39.344$	$25 - .410 = 24.59$	$30 - .732 = 29.268$	$23.333 - .569 = 22.764$
$-15 + .366 = -14.634$	0	$-5 + .181 = -4.819$	$1.667 - .060 = 1.607$
0	$7.5 - .183 = 7.317$	$5 - .181 = 4.819$	$8.333 - .301 = 8.032$
$15 - .366 = 14.634$	$15 - .366 = 14.634$	$15 - .542 = 14.458$	$15 - .542 = 14.458$
$30 - .732 = 29.268$	$22.5 - .549 = 21.951$	$25 - .904 = 24.096$	$21.667 - .783 = 20.884$
$-25 + .806 = -24.194$	$-2.5 + .081 = -2.419$	$-10 + .476 = -9.524$	0
$-10 + .323 = -9.677$	$5 - .161 = 4.839$	0	$6.667 - .317 = 6.349$
$5 - .161 = 4.839$	$12.5 - .403 = 12.097$	$10 - .476 = 9.524$	$13.333 - .635 = 12.698$
$20 - .645 = 19.355$	$20 - .645 = 19.355$	$20 - .952 = 19.048$	$20 - .952 = 19.048$

forward − forward. So, for example, if the 90-day rate is 15% and the 180-day rate is also 15% the crude

READING LIST

In addition to the individual references in the notes to each chapter, the following books and periodicals may be helpful.

GENERAL

H. Riehl and R. Rodriguez. *Foreign Exchange Markets.* New York: McGraw-Hill, 1977.

J. Heywood. *Foreign Exchange and the Corporate Treasurer.* London: Adam & Charles Black, 1980.

P. Coulbois. *Le change.* Paris: Editions Cujas, 1979.

G. Dufey and I. H. Giddy. *The International Money Market.* Englewood Cliffs, N.J.: Prentice-Hall, 1978.

M. Stigum. *The Money Market: Myth, Reality and Practice.* Homewood, Ill.: Dow-Jones Irwin, 1978.

T. Walker. *A Guide for Using the Foreign Exchange Markets.* New York: John Wiley & Sons, 1981.

J. B. Giannoni and R. W. Smith. *Treasury Management.* New York: John Wiley & Sons, 1981.

R. Rodriguez and E. Carter. *International Financial Management.* Englewood Cliffs, N.J.: Prentice-Hall, 1979.

J. K. Walmsley. *Dictionary of International Finance.* London: Macmillan/United States: Greenwood Press, 1979.

CURRENT INFORMATION

Many banks and brokers produce current bulletins; aside from the financial press and business weeklies, the following are worth seeing:
Euromoney, London (monthly).
IMF Survey (fortnightly).
Federal Reserve Bulletin (monthly).
Federal Reserve Bank of New York Quarterly Review.
Bank of England Quarterly Bulletin.
Bulletin Trimestriel de la Banque de France.
Monthly Report of the Deutsche Bundesbank.
Bank of Canada Review (monthly).

SPECIAL TOPICS

D. Marteau and E. De La Chaise. *Le marché monétaire et la gestion de trésorerie des banques.* Paris: Dunod, 1981.

A. Coutière. *Le système monétaire français.* Paris: Editions Economica, 1981.
S. F. Frowen, A. Courakis and M. H. Miller (eds.). *Monetary Policy and Economic Activity in West Germany.* New York: John Wiley & Sons, 1977.
H. Lipfert. *Devisenhandel.* Frankfurt: F. Knapp Verlag, 1968.
A. Prindl. *Japanese Finance.* New York: John Wiley & Sons, 1981.
L. S. Pressnell (ed.). *Money and Banking in Japan.* London: Macmillan, 1973.
Bank of Japan. *The Japanese Financial System.* Tokyo, 1978.

HISTORY

F. Hirsch. *Money International.* London: Penguin Books. 1967.
R. Solomon. *The International Monetary System 1949–81.* 2nd edition, New York: Harper & Row, 1982.
S. Strange. *International Economic Relations of the Western World 1959–71:* Vol. II: *International Monetary Relations.* United Kingdom: Oxford University Press for the Royal Institute for International Affairs, 1976.
R. Hellman. *Gold, the Dollar and the European Currency Systems: The Seven Year Monetary War.* New York: Praeger, 1979.
L. Tsoukalis. *The Politics and Economics of European Monetary Integration.* London: George Allen & Unwin, 1977.

ECONOMICS

R. Heilbroner and L. C. Thurow. *Understanding Macroeconomics*, 7th edition, Englewood Cliffs, N.J.: Prentice-Hall, 1981.
P. A. Samuelson. *Principles of Economics.* New York: McGraw-Hill, 1980.
J. Fleming. *Inflation.* United Kingdom: Oxford University Press, 1976.
B. Griffiths and G. E. Wood (eds.). *Monetary Targets.* London: Macmillan, 1981.
H. G. Johnson and J. A. Frenkel (eds.). *The Monetary Approach to the Balance of Payments.* London: Allen and Unwin, 1976.

DEALING CALCULATIONS

M. Stigum. *Money Market Calculations.* Homewood, Ill.: Dow-Jones Irwin, 1981.
Swiss Bank Corporation. *Foreign Exchange and Money Market Operations.* Zurich: 1979.
J. Heywood. *Foreign Exchange and the Corporate Treasurer.* London: Adam & Charles Black, 1980.
See also S. Homer and M. L. Leibowitz. *Inside the Yield Book.* Englewood Cliffs, N.J.: Prentice-Hall Inc., 1972.

FINANCIAL FUTURES

E. W. Schwarz. *How to Use Interest Rate Futures Contracts.* Homewood, Ill.: Dow-Jones Irwin, 1979.

Chicago Board of Trade. *An Introduction to Financial Futures.* Chicago, n.d.
Chicago Board of Trade. *Financial Instrument Markets: Cash-Futures Relationships.* Chicago, 1980.

GOLD

T. Green. *The New World of Gold.* New York: Walker & Co., 1981.
R. Jastram. *The Golden Constant.* New York: John Wiley & Sons, 1977.
See also references under "History."

EXPOSURE MANAGEMENT

D. R. Mandich (ed.). *Foreign Exchange Trading Techniques and Controls.* Washington, D.C.: American Bankers' Association, 1976.
B. Antl (ed.). *Currency Risk and the Corporation.* London: Euromoney Publications, 1980.
J. A. Donaldson. *Corporate Currency Risk.* London: Financial Times, 1980.
See also the books listed under "General."

INDEX